(we were alike in every detail.) Then we
parted our hair in the middle and slicked
it into two Undertakers scallops. (See picture)
Then we had handle bar mustachios and
little imperial beards, parted by protuberant
false teeth. Wing collars, bow ties, morning
coats, white flannel trousers rolled to look
just too short, plaid socks and black shoes.
Oh yes, and glasses and hats.

Lefty would have
appreciated our appearance
but I think you would
probably have wept to see
us. I must confess that
we did look pretty dramatic
I don't know what we were
meant to be but we were
quite funny and almost
unrecognisable.
Arthur was his usual
extraordinary Pantomime-ish
dame. Rose was a
washerwoman. Blyth took
a prize as a baby! And
Bert Jeffries had another
as an ingenious two-way
facing woman. I can't
explain it more than that

*Books by Joyce Grenfell*

Autobiography

JOYCE GRENFELL REQUESTS THE PLEASURE
IN PLEASANT PLACES

Monologues and Songs

GEORGE – DON'T DO THAT . . .

STATELY AS A GALLEON

TURN BACK THE CLOCK

Also

AN INVISIBLE FRIENDSHIP
(with Katharine Moore)

and

JOYCE
BY HERSELF AND HER FRIENDS
Edited by Reginald Grenfell and Richard Garnett

# JOYCE GRENFELL

*Darling Ma*

## Letters to her Mother, 1932~1944

### Edited and Introduced by James Roose-Evans

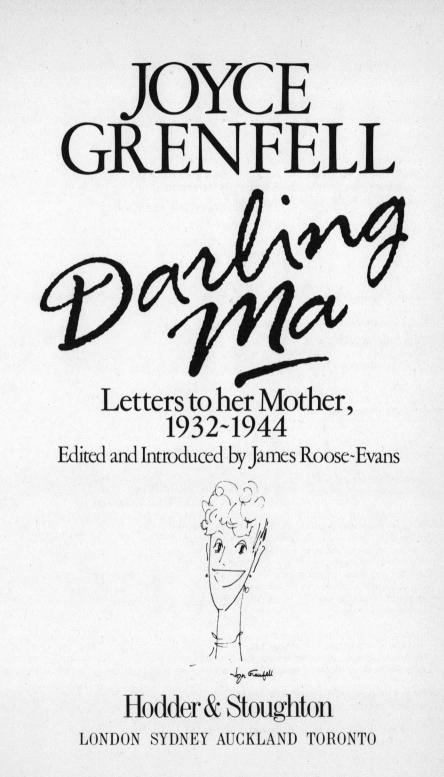

## Hodder & Stoughton

LONDON SYDNEY AUCKLAND TORONTO

The Publishers would like to thank The Literary Trustees
of Walter de la Mare and The Society of Authors as their
representative for permission to reproduce the extract from
'Fare Well' by Walter de la Mare on page 124.

British Library Cataloguing in Publication Data

Grenfell, Joyce, *1910–1979*
    Darling Ma: letters to her mother 1932–44.
    1. Entertainments. Grenfell, Joyce –
Correspondence, diaries, etc.
    I. Title     II. Roose-Evans, James
    791'.092'4

    ISBN 0-340-42368-4

First printed 1988
Second impression 1988

Published by Hodder and Stoughton,
a division of Hodder and Stoughton Ltd,
Mill Road, Dunton Green, Sevenoaks, Kent TN13 2YW
Editorial Office: 47 Bedford Square, London WC1B 3DP

Photoset by Rowland Phototypesetting Ltd,
Bury St Edmunds, Suffolk

Printed in Great Britain by St Edmundsbury Press Ltd,
Bury St Edmunds, Suffolk

For
REGGIE GRENFELL
and
FRANCES CAMPBELL-PRESTON
in gratitude for their
generous friendship

# Contents

# Illustrations

Reginald Grenfell kindly allowed the Editor and the Publishers to select many pictures for this book from Joyce's albums. Most of the photographs are family 'snaps', but if copyright has been inadvertently infringed the Publishers will be happy to include an acknowledgement in future editions.

Photographs appear between pages 104 and 105, and 232 and 233.

Reproductions of Joyce's letters appear on pages 65, 71, 181, 204, 215 and 270.

# THE GRENFELL, PHIPPS AND LANGHORNE FAMILIES

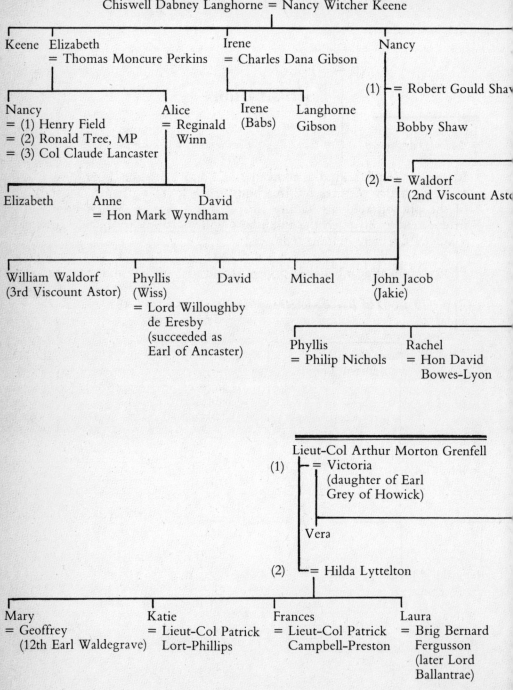

Chiswell Dabney Langhorne = Nancy Witcher Keene

Keene

Elizabeth
= Thomas Moncure Perkins

Irene
= Charles Dana Gibson

Nancy

(1) = Robert Gould Shaw

Nancy
= (1) Henry Field
= (2) Ronald Tree, MP
= (3) Col Claude Lancaster

Alice
= Reginald Winn

Irene (Babs)

Langhorne Gibson

Bobby Shaw

(2) = Waldorf (2nd Viscount Astor)

Elizabeth

Anne

David
= Hon Mark Wyndham

William Waldorf (3rd Viscount Astor)

Phyllis (Wiss)
= Lord Willoughby de Eresby (succeeded as Earl of Ancaster)

David

Michael

John Jacob (Jakie)

Phyllis
= Philip Nichols

Rachel
= Hon David Bowes-Lyon

Lieut-Col Arthur Morton Grenfell

(1) = Victoria (daughter of Earl Grey of Howick)

Vera

(2) = Hilda Lyttelton

Mary
= Geoffrey (12th Earl Waldegrave)

Katie
= Lieut-Col Patrick Lort-Phillips

Frances
= Lieut-Col Patrick Campbell-Preston

Laura
= Brig Bernard Fergusson (later Lord Ballantrae)

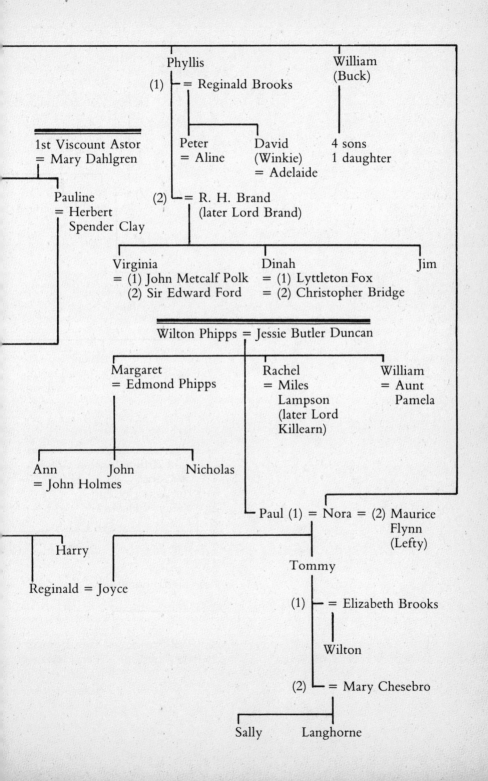

# Joyce's family and friends

Usually indicated by an asterisk * when first mentioned in the letters.
The nicknames and abbreviations given in brackets are those
most often used by Joyce in the letters that follow.

Addinsell, Richard (Dick, D.): Composer of incidental music in the theatre
and musical scores for many films including the Warsaw Concerto for the
film *Dangerous Moonlight*.

Astor, David: Second son of Waldorf and Nancy Astor. Became editor of
*The Observer*.

Astor, John Jacob (Jakie): Fourth son of Waldorf and Nancy Astor. Followed
his mother as MP for Plymouth (Sutton).

Astor, Michael: Third son of Waldorf and Nancy Astor. MP for Surrey
(Eastern), 1945–51; author of *Tribal Feeling*, a book about the Astors.

Astor, Nancy (Aunt Nancy, Aunt N.; 1879–1964): Elder sister of Joyce's
mother and married to Viscount (Waldorf) Astor, whom she succeeded as
MP for Plymouth (Sutton), thus becoming the first woman to take her seat
in the House of Commons.

Astor, Phyllis (Wiss or Wissie): Only daughter of the 2nd Viscount Astor and
his wife Nancy. In 1933 she married James, Lord Willoughby de Eresby,
who succeeded his father, the 2nd Earl of Ancaster in 1951.

Astor, Waldorf: 2nd Viscount (1879–1952). MP for Plymouth (Sutton) until
elevated to the Lords on the death of his father in 1919. He inherited wealth
based on investments and property in the United States.

Astor, William Waldorf (Billy, Bill): Eldest son of Waldorf and Nancy
Astor. Succeeded his father, as 3rd Viscount, in 1952; died 1966.

Bevan, Barbara: Aunt Pauline Spender Clay's niece, married to John Bevan.

Brand, Dinah: Joyce's cousin, daughter of Aunt Phyllis and R. H. Brand. She
later married Lyttleton Fox, and her second husband was Christopher
Bridge.

Brand, Jim: Joyce's cousin, son of Aunt Phyllis and R. H. Brand. Killed in
action in 1945.

Brand, Phyllis (Aunt Phyllis): One of the Langhorne girls, sister of Nora
Phipps and Nancy Astor. Her first husband was Reginald Brooks and they
had two sons, Peter and David (Winkie). She later married R. H. Brand
(later 1st Lord Brand) and they had three children, Jim, Virginia and
Dinah. She died of pneumonia in January 1937.

Brand, R. H. (Uncle Bob) (later 1st Lord Brand) Aunt Phyllis's second husband. They had three children, Virginia, Dinah and Jim, and lived at Eydon Hall, Rugby.

Brand, Virginia: Joyce's cousin, daughter of Aunt Phyllis and R. H. Brand. She later married John Polk; her second husband was Sir Edward Ford.

Brassey, Mary (Maria): Old friend of Joyce's and a fellow Christian Scientist.

Brooks, David (Wink or Winkie): Younger son of Aunt Phyllis Brand by her first marriage to Reginald Brooks. He died in 1936 after falling from a window in New York. He and his wife Adelaide had been married only five months.

Brooks, Peter: Elder son of Aunt Phyllis Brand by her first marriage to Reginald Brooks. His wife was called Aline.

Dane, Clemence (Winifred Ashton): Novelist and dramatist. In 1929, with Helen Simpson, she wrote *Enter Sir John*, and in 1932 a sequel. Her best-known plays are *Will Shakespeare* and *A Bill of Divorcement*.

Easden, Rene: A local girl, Joyce and Reggie's 'staff' at Parr's.

Farjeon, Herbert (Bertie): An expert drama critic, known best as the librettist of the wittiest intimate revues of their period, especially those at the Little Theatre, *Nine Sharp* and *The Little Revue*. He was also a dedicated Shakespearian scholar and critic. The brother of Eleanor and J. Jefferson Farjeon, he was married to Joan (née Thorneycroft) and they lived in Loudon Road, St John's Wood. He died in 1945 aged fifty-eight.

Flynn, Maurice (Lefty): Ma's second husband, an Irish-American former Yale football hero, nicknamed because of his left-footed kicking skills.

Graham, Harry: Part-author and lyricist of many operettas and musical plays, including *Sybil*, *A Southern Maid*, *Madame Pompadour*, *The Lady of the Rose* and *The Maid of the Mountains*. He and his wife, Dorothy, were friends of Joyce's parents and their daughter, Virginia, was Joyce's best friend. He died in 1936.

Graham, Virginia (Gin or Ginny): Joyce's best friend, later married to Tony Thesiger. As a writer she contributed to newspapers and magazines. She also wrote songs which Joyce performed.

Grenfell, Col. Arthur Morton: Reggie's father, whose first wife, Victoria, daughter of Earl Grey of Howick, died, leaving three children, Vera, Reggie and Harry. He married Hilda Lyttelton and they had four daughters, Mary, Katie, Frances and Laura.

Grenfell, Frances: The third of Reggie's half-sisters. She married Patrick Campbell-Preston in 1938.

Grenfell, Harry: Reggie's younger brother, a bachelor.

Grenfell, Hilda: Reggie's stepmother, daughter of General the Right Hon. Sir N. G. Lyttelton. She and Col. Grenfell lived at Chesham Place.

Grenfell, Katie: Reggie's second half-sister, married to Lt Col. Patrick Lort-Phillips.

Grenfell, Laura: Reggie's youngest half-sister. She later married Brig. Bernard Fergusson, who became Lord Ballantrae.

Grenfell, Mary: Reggie's eldest half-sister, married to Geoffrey Waldegrave, who succeeded his father as 12th Earl in 1936. They lived in Chewton Priory, Bath.

Grenfell, Reginald (Reggie): Joyce's husband since 1929. He was the elder son of Arthur Morton Grenfell and his first wife, Victoria, eldest child of the 4th Earl Grey of Howick. She died when Reggie was five. He trained as a chartered accountant. Became a director of Messina (Transvaal), a South African copper company.

Grenfell, Vera: Reggie's elder sister.

Grey, Countess of Howick: Reggie Grenfell's grandmother.

Jones, Dr Thomas, CH (T.J.): Formerly Deputy Secretary to the Cabinet, and from 1930 Secretary to the Pilgrim Trust. Of him Joyce wrote: 'He was a very dear friend.'

Nichols, Phyllis: Cousin to the Astor children, Joyce's contemporary, daughter of Aunt Pauline and Herbert Spender Clay, married to Philip Nichols.

Phipps, Elizabeth (Betty): Tommy Phipps' first wife (née Brooks) from Philadelphia. Her second husband was Edward Reeve.

Phipps, Nicholas: Joyce's cousin, son of Pa's sister, Margaret and Edmund Phipps (who was no relation, despite having the same name). A popular actor on stage and radio, he also wrote for the cinema. His brother was John Phipps and his sister, Ann, was married to John Holmes.

Phipps, Nora (Ma): The youngest of eleven children born to Nancy and Dabney Langhorne of Richmond, Virginia. One of the original Gibson Girls, made famous by Charles Dana Gibson in his black and white drawings, she married Paul Phipps, Joyce's father in 1909. They were divorced in 1930. She returned to America and married Maurice (Lefty) Flynn in 1931.

Phipps, Paul (Pa): Architect, studied under Lutyens; active Christian Scientist. His mother was American and his father English. Designed the extensions to Parr's where Joyce and Reggie lived on the Cliveden estate.

Phipps, Tommy (Tom): Joyce's only brother, four years her junior and born in America. As a freelance journalist, he spent some time in London. In America he wrote filmscripts very successfully. Joyce's feelings about him in her letters often appear harsh – she spoke her mind to Ma – but in later years they grew closer.

Potter, Stephen: Writer, critic, broadcaster. Joyce appeared in his *How* radio programmes. Later best known for his *Lifemanship* and *Gamesmanship* books. Married at this time to Mary (née Attenborough) a landscape artist known as Att. His second wife was Heather Jenner.

Rawson, Mrs Mildred: Joyce's Christian Science practitioner.

Shaw, Bobby (Bobbie): Nancy Astor's son by her first marriage, to Robert Gould Shaw.

Skimming, Sylvia (Sylvie): Joyce's childhood friend. Her parents and sister, Annette, lived in Taplow and Sylvia often spent the night at Parr's to keep Joyce company.

Smith, Hubert and Diana: Hubert Smith was the estate manager at Cliveden. He and his wife Diana lived at the White Place.

Spender Clay, Pauline (Aunt Pauline): Waldorf Astor's sister, married to Herbert Spender Clay.

Spender Clay, Rachel: Cousin to the Astor children, Joyce's contemporary, daughter of Aunt Pauline and Herbert Spender Clay, married to David Bowes-Lyon, brother of Queen Elizabeth the Queen Mother. They lived at St Paul's Waldenbury, Herts.

Tree, Nancy: Joyce's cousin, daughter of Thomas Perkins and Elizabeth (née Langhorne). At this time married to Ronald Tree, MP, her first husband had been Henry Field and she subsequently married Col Claude Lancaster. She was generous in sharing her beautiful clothes with Joyce and her mother. The Trees lived at Ditchley.

Winn, Alice (Al): second daughter of Elizabeth Perkins (née Langhorne). Her sister was Nancy Tree.

Winn, Reginald (Reggie): Husband of Joyce's cousin, Alice (née Perkins). They lived not far from Cliveden, at Taplow Lodge, and had three children, Elizabeth, Anne and David.

## The houses Joyce lived in or visited

Cliveden: The principal home of the Astors, overlooking the Thames above Windsor and Maidenhead. Designed by Charles Barry in the Italianate style, it was built in 1850 for the Duke of Sutherland.

Ditchley: Home of Ronald Tree, MP, and his wife Nancy. Winston Churchill frequently stayed at Ditchley during the Second World War.

Flat 8, 70 Ennismore Gardens (The Flat): The London home of Aunt Pauline and Bertie Spender Clay. Joyce and Reggie stayed there after they had moved out of Parr's during the war.

4 St James's Square (St Jas Sq.): The Astors' London home.

Little Orchard, Tryon, North Carolina ('Try'): Ma's house, given to her by Nancy Astor, visited by Joyce in October 1935 and in 1946.

St Leonard's Terrace, Nos. 21 and 28: 28 St Leonard's Terrace was Joyce's family home in London. She and Reggie moved to 21 St Leonard's Terrace on their marriage. It was their home till they moved to Parr's.

Parr's: A cottage on the Cliveden estate, lent to Joyce and Reggie by the Astors. It was named after the Astor family butler, who lived there until he emigrated to America. Nancy Astor engaged Joyce's father to modernise it.

# Introduction

In 1987 I was researching into the background of Joyce Grenfell and from the start Reggie Grenfell, Joyce's husband, gave me the freedom of Joyce's attic study. Here I discovered all her notes for broadcast talks and newspaper articles, sketches, songs; albums of newspaper cuttings and photographs, many of them including her own water-colour caricatures of friends; her paintings (she was a talented amateur painter); her wartime journals when she was touring for ENSA. Then, one afternoon, opening a drawer, I came across a series of folders containing thousands of handwritten letters, each of which bore the opening inscription, *Darling Ma*.

Joyce was very much the archetypal Englishwoman and yet she was more American than English, being the daughter of an American mother, Nora Langhorne, who was born and brought up in Virginia, and an architect Paul Phipps ('When I went on the stage I decided to change my name. Joyce Phipps – you could have trouble with that!'), whose mother was American and father English. As a child Joyce and her younger brother Tommy lived in Chelsea, which was to be her part of London throughout her life. The years at 28 St Leonard's Terrace were 'cosy', a favourite condition as her letters demonstrate. She went to various schools, notably Clear View in South Norwood, and then on to the Royal Academy of Dramatic Art, which she left after a single term because, as she would say, 'I met Reggie and he quite took my mind off theatre.' Her cousin, Alice Winn, remembers that, when young, Joyce was the least talented of a family given to amateur theatricals. Her mother was a born story-teller and loved making up characters, and from a very early age Joyce also played at being other people. She would have long made-up dialogues with her mother who would feed her as a stooge feeds a comic. 'My mother was two hundred times more talented than I was,' Joyce once wrote. 'The only difference was that I grew up to turn it into a job.'

Nora Langhorne's sister Nancy had married Waldorf Astor and so became Lady Astor. As a result Joyce and her parents were a part of the social scene at Cliveden. In 1929, when Joyce married Reginald Grenfell, the Astors paid half the cost of their first home, 21 St Leonard's Terrace, just down the road from Number 28. Later they were loaned Parr's, a cottage on the estate at Cliveden. Yet although Joyce was always grateful to Aunt Nancy and Uncle Waldorf for all their support and kindness, she did not altogether approve of the way her rich relations lived. In 1937, commenting on the lavish Christmas entertainments at Cliveden presided over by Aunt Nancy, she wrote to her mother: 'The whole unreality of the atmosphere flowed over me to suffocation point. I wonder what it is? Money? Not really. Complacency? – yes, and a sort of stark cynicism that turns all beauty to sawdust.' And later, during the war, she records, 'Cliveden was never quite my cup of tea, was it? The more I see of people brought up in the easy way, the more I lean towards socialism. Things will never, can never, mustn't ever, be the same as they were before the war.'

Of course there were highlights to the Cliveden connection: a ball at Buckingham Palace for one. She and Reggie were in Aunt Nancy's party and she wore a tiara (lent by Aunt Nancy). 'I've got a schoolgirlish sensation about the whole thing,' she told her mother when it was all over. 'I've never enjoyed anything more.' Her description of that ball is one of the many set pieces of these letters, revealing the emergence of her powers as an observer and a writer.

Joyce's parents' marriage broke up and Nora married Maurice Flynn, an Irish-American known as 'Lefty' for his ability to kick with the left foot in Yale football games. Hence these weekly letters to North Carolina – letters written often in period slang, with abbreviations, and punctuated idiosyncratically and in Joyce's eccentric spelling, but always with zest and love. For Nora they must have been lifelines, particularly during the war when in remote Tryon (or as Joyce called it 'Try') – in a house built for her by her sister Nancy – she would have found much that went on in Europe puzzling indeed.

As a performer Joyce was often asked if she had particular targets which she mocked or sent up. Pomposity and false values she always saw through, and folly – her own as much as anyone else's; yet she never set out to destroy her victims; that would have been too easy. But in her monologues, as in real life, she saw people in the round. Watching people, she once said, was like bird-watching, a hobby which she and Reggie loved. Even as a child she loved watching people, and at Cliveden there was always plenty to watch. Sparks flew, there was often brilliant talk, and a good many shouting matches. At parties she never missed a trick. She always knew exactly what everyone had worn, what they had eaten, whom they had sat next to, who had been bored. She knew what music had been played, who had flirted with whom, what jewellery the hostess had worn, and afterwards she used to mimic the voices of the people she had seen. And so she saw Aunt Nancy's faults but insisted also on her charm and wit; similarly she adored her mother and remembered the fun they had had together, but recognised also that she could be careless and muddle-headed; indeed, Nora's debts and her flirtatiousness were the main source of tension between her parents. Like a running gag, or sore, we see in these letters Joyce's continuing rebuke to her mother for not having paid a particular dress bill. Joyce gets furiouser and furiouser until PAY YOUR BILLS! leaps out in capital letters.

When, in the last war, Cliveden became a hospital for Canadian troops, Joyce was roped in to help. A naturally caring person, her feeling of responsibility towards the men in 'her' wards almost prevented her from returning to the theatre in which she had made such an unexpected and immediate success shortly before the outbreak of war. Shopping, writing letters, caring for the sick and invalided men, singing to them, and getting them to sing, was good preparation for what was to come when, in 1944, she was to tour the Middle East entertaining the troops.

After her marriage Joyce settled down at Parr's, eventually earning her living as a radio critic for *The Observer*, while Reggie travelled up to London daily on business. She conducted the Women's Institute choir (in one letter she describes a rehearsal in which they sang a song called 'The Wild Brown Bee is My Lover', an experience which we can see provided the basis for the sketch, 'Committee'). It was a quiet life and she wanted no other. London was only twenty-six miles away but they didn't have much money so they only went up to London on Special Occasions. One such special occasion was Friday, January 13th, 1939, a day that was to change her life. It was the day she was to meet Herbert Farjeon.

How Joyce Grenfell entered the theatre is told in these letters with all the breathlessness of a cliff-hanger. Joyce's way of writing these letters was in journal form, often a day-by-day account of her doings. And what makes these letters describing this unexpected development in her life so exciting is that she is writing to her mother who, herself, was an amateur performer, and eager (even perhaps a little jealous?) to know all the details from moment to moment.

If Joyce inherited her talent from her mother, it is probably from Ruth Draper, the famous *diseuse*, and an old family friend and distant relation, that she got the idea of doing monologues. Ruth Draper often used to perform some of her sketches to Joyce and Tommy when they were young, and would also perform at house parties at Cliveden. After Joyce's London debut in 1939 the *Daily Mail* carried the headline, 'LONDON HAS A RUTH DRAPER!' Curiously, Ruth Draper only once went to see Joyce perform and she never referred to her performance or the sketches. The last time Joyce saw Ruth Draper perform, at the St James's Theatre, shortly before Ruth Draper's death, she found herself moved more than ever by her performance. Giving her a hug she said, 'I don't know how anyone dares to mention my name with yours!' – to which Ruth Draper dryly replied, 'They *don't!*'

During the war Joyce not only looked after the troops at Cliveden, and entertained in various camps and hospitals; she also worked in the canteen at the National Gallery concerts in London, making sandwiches and serving coffee. One day, she records, they made a record 1700 sandwiches and would have made more if the butter had not run out. Again this experience was to provide material for future sketches such as 'Canteen' and 'Artists' Room'. She became a great friend of Myra Hess who organised these concerts and the experience deepened her natural love of music which had been implanted in her by her father: 'It was my Pa who introduced me to music. It was with him, as a girl, that I heard the three great B's: Bach, Brahms, Beethoven.' At the end of her life, in the highly successful television programme, *Face the Music*, she was to draw upon this love and knowledge of music.

Always her friends were very important to her and compensated for the fact that she and Reggie were unable to have children. When she entered the theatre the circle of friends widened to include Richard Addinsell, the composer, who wrote most of the music for her songs; the dramatist Clemence Dane; Edith Evans and Dorothy Dickson (who were in *Diversion* with her), Noël Coward (although she was always to have ambivalent feelings towards him) and many more. Yet as her career developed it became clear that success in the theatre was not the sole object of her life. Central to her life was her faith as a Christian Scientist in which faith she had been brought up by both parents and which she was to rediscover on a deeper level as an adult. Although she rarely spoke about this in public, some understanding of the beliefs and practices of Christian Science is necessary if the reader is to appreciate many references in these letters. Essentially Christian Science teaches that we are, as the Bible says, made in the image and likeness of God, therefore spiritual; and in God's universe there can be no sin, disease, or death; they simply do not exist. People's bodies die, of course, but the body is only the outward form, it is not the essence of that person. 'No matter what happens to the body,' Joyce wrote to a friend, 'it does not, cannot, touch the spiritual identity that is our eternal body.'

Christian Science believes that each individual must become 'Unselfed': to become unselfed is to become more spirit, more God. Buddhists speak in similar fashion of becoming ego-less, while the essence of Christianity is contained in the words of St John the Baptist, referring to Christ, 'I must become less that He may become more.' As Joyce herself once said, 'I think what I am doing is *losing* Joyce Grenfell, and finding out the person God made. The older you get the more you realise that happiness is losing your false sense of what you are, your *false self*. What was that lovely quotation from Goethe? "Become what you are!" Well, that interpreted, means become what your true potential is, your spiritual wholeness.'

Each day, as a reader of these letters will discover, a practising Christian Scientist will 'do the lesson'. The lessons are daily readings from the Bible, plus extracts from Mrs Mary Baker Eddy's major work, *Science and Health, Key to the Scriptures*. These lessons are published in the *Christian Science Quarterly*.

At one point in the letters, writing about her progress in theatre, Joyce writes:

'There are low moments when one feels one couldn't *possibly* be funny. But when I smell the scenery and see the lights I get a sort of circus horse instinct and all is well. From a C.S. point of view, it is particularly interesting. You see, the others seem to regard the audience as their potential enemy. Now Mrs Rawson said to me that the audience was part of me, and I'm sure she is right. We are both there for joy. This has helped me quite enormously; also the truth that everything *is now* and not to be got through or discovered. It's all complete.'

Mrs Rawson was Joyce's Christian Science practitioner at the time. A practitioner is like a spiritual guide, counsellor and friend, who may be rung up or visited at any time for help or spiritual healing.

In 1973 Joyce was due to leave for her fifth tour of Australia where she was, and is still, much loved. It was to be for two and a half months, and consisted of sixty-eight concerts in all. At the last moment she developed an eye infection which, in spite of Christian Science, would not heal. Under pressure from Reggie she agreed to see a doctor who said, 'Whoa! Stop! Cancel Australia!' So, with ten days to go before she was due in Perth, she had to cancel the trip. For the first time in her life she took pills and hated it. She lost the sight of one eye and had to retire from the stage. Six years later she was admitted to Moorfields Hospital to have the bad eye removed. It was in fact cancer, although cancer is not a word which Joyce would have used. In her very last letter to her closest friend, Virginia Graham, written from hospital the day before the operation, she wrote: 'I'm not interested in the pursuit of happiness, but only in the discovery of joy. The one thing I am truly grateful for is the sense of God's love I find everywhere. Indeed, "the lines are fallen unto me in pleasant places".' A month later on November 30th, 1979, she died at home. On February 7th, 1980, a Thanksgiving Service was held at Westminster Abbey. In a congregation of 2,000, with 1,500 reserved seats snapped up as soon as they were offered, there were queues around the Abbey well over an hour before the service was due to begin. People travelled from all over the country to be present, many of whom had never met her, but who, like one man remarked, 'I never knew her but whenever I heard her on the radio, or saw her on TV, I always thought that she knew me – and loved me.'

Lesley Blanch, reviewing Joyce Grenfell in Noël Coward's revue, *Sigh No More* (The *Leader*, September 15th, 1945) wrote: 'I don't think she'll ever belong wholly to the theatre. While enjoying her work and the profits and plaudits enormously, part of her seems to remain aloof.'

The enduring quality of Joyce Grenfell shines through these letters. Her life spanned dramatic changes, as dramatic as those of the Countess of Cotely, about whom Oscar Hammerstein thought she should write an entire musical:

'Though the distances she'll travel are incredible to tell,
And the quandaries she'll cope with will be absolutely hell,
She'll emerge in Forty-seven having done it rather well!'

JAMES ROOSE-EVANS

# *Editor's note*

Joyce often wrote her letters in diary form, giving minute details of shopping, cooking, journeys and daily life. In editing these letters I have tried to let Joyce's own story, during these crucial years, unfold in one flowing narrative. Having read through some millions of words several times before editing these letters I realised that to take an academic approach would have been tedious for the reader. I have not, therefore, indicated by the traditional dots where sentences or paragraphs have been removed. I have also tried to preserve Joyce's idiosyncratic style.

As the opening and signature of each letter was usually the same, I have retained only those for the first letter of each year. Letter heading addresses have been abbreviated after the first mention.

# 1932—1933

In 1932 Joyce and Reggie Grenfell were living at 21 St Leonard's Terrace. Joyce was twenty-two and had been married for three years. Reggie 'worked for mining companies his father managed, but they were precarious' and the Grenfells lived from crisis to crisis, assisted by their families, especially Nancy Astor. Joyce tried to augment the family finances by occasional writing for magazines and, having trained for two terms as a commercial artist at the Westminster Polytechnic, designing posters and selling a set of Christmas card designs to W. H. Smith.

In May 1932, Joyce and Reggie visited Ma in America, and a year later Joyce went to see her again. Ma, who had a beautiful voice and played the guitar, flirted with the idea of turning her talents to professional use in the entertainment world, in order to ease her own financial problems.

# 1932–33

☎ Sloane 7042
*November 19th, 1932*

21 St Leonard's Terrace,*
Chelsea,
London, SW3

Darling Ma

Two letters from you since I last wrote. First of all I must say how thrilled we are over your contract. If they decide to publish any of the records we must have them. Don't forget.

I lunched with Pa at 30 Royal Ave. We had a good laugh over what we asked of life and I'm ashamed to say that my ideal existence is summed up in the following: *A lovely padded rut with a salary at one end and a pension at the other.* No worries and no adventures. Yes, there's a lot to be said for sticking in a rut. Pa says it's unscientific but it's mighty cosy. He's in tearing form, really for the first time in about three years.

> Much love,
> Joyce

———◆———

*July 4th, 1933*

21 St Leonard's Terrace

The fourth of July and much too hot. I'm sitting, legs apart, stayless, stockingless and floppy, in front of the window – It's boiling. Personally I don't mind it as long as I don't have to move – Here there is a through breeze at the moment and it's just bearable. Out in the street it's red hot and very glaring. R. [Reggie] went off to the office in as little as possible and still pouring sweat at every step.

* Asterisks in the text indicate a biographical or residential note, pp. xiii–xvi.

Of course the big news is Wissie [Astor].*

On Thursday evening Bungs[1] came careering round, jammed on the brakes and was yelling all over the garden that she had some news.

It happened this way. She just called round to Wiss before dressing time in an ordinary way and they were just talking ordinarily when in blew Aunt Nancy [Astor]* back from playing a golf match with the Prince of Wales. She was beaten and she said to Wiss, 'It's all your fault. Every time I was about to hit a ball I thought of you and lifted my head and the shot was lost.'

So immediately Bungs thought Wiss was in a row about something and Aunt Phyllis [Brand],* who had just come in, asked what it was all about. And Aunt N. said, 'Tell them', and Wiss said, 'Well, the old girl's off at last. I'm engaged to James Willoughby.'[2] At which Bungs and Aunt P. nearly died and then Bungs rushed round to tell me.

It's been going on vaguely ever since last summer but it came to a head in Ascot week. He was staying at Cliveden* and on the Saturday he proposed and she didn't answer him for two weeks, not until June 28th in fact. They told Aunt N. – or rather Wiss did, on Thursday 29th – on Friday it was told to all the family and friends and on Saturday announced. I sent you a cable on Thursday as soon as Bungs had told me. Did you get it?

James is awfully nice – really really nice. Quiet, shy, calm, kind, good manners and cosy. The perfect person for Wiss as he has already calmed her down.

Of course the picture of Uncle Waldorf [Astor]* arming Eloise[3] down the aisle will be fairly funny. But apart from that it's OK everywhere.

When I last saw her she had no ring but wanted an emerald and probably has one by now. She is awfully in love and very happy. Aunt Nancy is a new woman and wreathed in maternal smiles. Wiss says that now she and Aunt N. are inseparable. Peas in a pod. They do nothing but discuss trousseaux, dressing gowns, a few simple little frocks, dozens of sets of lingerie and a coat or two.

Literally everybody is pleased. It's one of the most perfect engagements possible. They hope to be married in the last week of July, probably the 27th I think and down at Cliveden – Taplow church,

[1] Catherine (Bungs) Fordham, one of Joyce's oldest friends. In 1942 she married Major-General Sir John Kennedy, who was appointed Governor-General of Southern Rhodesia in 1946.
[2] James, Lord Willoughby de Eresby; succeeded his father, 2nd Earl of Ancaster, in 1951.
[3] James's mother, the Countess of Ancaster, elder daughter of W. L. Breese of New York.

that is – and reception at Cliveden. Aunt N. wants her to have gold in her wedding dress. She may be right as Wiss is very dark. But I think cream satin, don't you?

All child bridesmaids, and what they are wearing I don't yet know.

Honeymoon in Biarritz is the plan at present.

So now you know all the details. It's all very exciting and couldn't possibly have made more people happier. Bill [Astor]* is all brotherly and offers jewels, furniture or cheque as choice of present!

*1936*

In 1934 Joyce visited Ma in North Carolina. She and Reggie also travelled to Yugoslavia to see a mine, the Allatini, for which Reggie was responsible. No letters from this period survive.

1936 began with the death of George V and saw the brief reign of Edward VIII.

In April Joyce and Reggie moved to Parr's Cottage on the Cliveden estate, lent to them 'until such time as they were better off', Aunt Nancy commissioned Joyce's father, Paul Phipps, to modernise and extend it, even giving the Grenfells £100 to help in the furnishing. Joyce enjoyed living in the country, continuing with her freelance writing by contributing occasional verses to *Punch*, drawing whenever possible, sewing, listening to the radio and doing the crossword, as well as joining the local Women's Institute, and an Infant Welfare Centre in Slough Trading Estate. She played a great deal of tennis and tried to repay some of Aunt Nancy's generosity by helping with weekend parties at Cliveden and doing general odd jobs for her.

Reggie travelled up to the City every day and took a keen interest in the garden, which flourished under his care. To help with the housework Joyce employed Rene Easden, a local girl, who stayed with the Grenfells for many years.

# *1936*

Darling Ma

The King is very ill. In fact I think he's dying which is a very depressing thought, for that silly little P. of W. is in no shape to take over the monarch's position. Though of course if he knows he has to he probably will pull himself together, but he's made himself so cheap with Mrs Simpson and he's lost a good deal of his popularity, I should think. We listened in to the wireless bulletins all during yesterday and it looks as though he was just giving up and slowly going out. Poor old man. I'm glad he survived to enjoy the Jubilee and that he's had proof of the real and loyal devotion which, it's said, he didn't know the country felt for him. He realised that his sons were loved and were popular but he had no such ideas about himself.

We went to Buckingham Palace to see if there was a later bulletin. I was wearing my black velvet trousers and those red shoes with no toes and oh, it was cold. There were large crowds, very silent and bewildered and occasionally the flash from a photographer's light lit up their faces. It was all very dramatic. Top hats and evening clothes, soldiers, down and outs, and hundreds of old ladies. There were young men in plus-fours and taxi-drivers. We stood, almost in silence, while the police kept the long line of cars in motion and soon they changed the sentries and we heard Big Ben strike twelve. Nothing happened and no further bulletin appeared. (The King died just before midnight but we had left before it was announced and when we got home I turned on the radio and we heard the end of what we thought would be a health bulletin. We went to bed and were called at eight by Mary who said 'He's gone'; so what we heard on the radio was really the announcement of his death.)[1]

[1] King George V died on January 10th, 1936. The Silver Jubilee took place the previous year. The King was succeeded by the Prince of Wales, Edward VIII, who abdicated on December 10th, 1936 to marry Mrs Simpson and became the Duke of Windsor.

The *Daily Sketch* (which you'll see later) has the headline 'Our King is dead', which I find very moving.

Poor Queen. You know she doted on him in an inarticulate way and I believe they were very attached.

I don't yet know whether we'll all wear mourning. Vera [Grenfell]* says we will and she and Katie [Grenfell]* are draped in black. I'm wearing my only black frock and I can go on wearing it for a while but I don't think it will be such a serious mourning as there was pre-war.

All the theatres are shut today and R.'s just telephoned to say that they are closing the office so he'll be back here in a little while and we'll go off for a walk in the sunshine. (Yes, sunshine! Of a weak sort but definitely sun.)

Much love,
Joyce

*March 16th, 1936*                    21 St Leonard's Terrace

Pa and both Reggies [Grenfell and Winn]* dined here, but Alice [Winn]* and I 'obliged' Aunt N. and went to St James's Square* where she had hurriedly assembled all the League of Nations delegates and various ambassadors! She is a remarkable woman! But it's Uncle Waldorf who makes her give that sort of party. He has a sort of self-bestowed sense of Host of England that makes him collect celebrities and it isn't snobbish really, he thinks it's his duty. Quite beyond me.

I sat between Sir Roderick Jones[1] who is head of Reuters (world news agency) and a Spaniard called de Azcarate[2] who is an important official of the League and who lives in Geneva. We spoke French and had a very pleasant time.

Anne Islington[3] refused to shake hands with the Soviet Ambassador[4] and merely drew back her grey gloved hand with a shudder! I must say he isn't very attractive – like a small very fat musk-rat. And as yellow as a Chinese. Titulescu, the Roumanian is exactly like a

---

[1] Principal Proprietor of Reuters news agency. Knighted in 1918. Married to Enid Bagnold, dramatist (*The Chalk Garden*) and novelist (*National Velvet*).
[2] Pablo de Azcarate y Florez, Spanish Ambassador in London, 1936-9.
[3] Wife of the 1st Baron Islington, a former Governor-General of New Zealand. A great friend of Nancy's: when the cabaret for one of her London dances was held up in Paris by bad weather, Nancy and Anne Islington filled the breach, doing an impromptu caricature pas de deux in masks – to hilarious success. (Christopher Sykes's biography of Nancy Astor.)
[4] Ivan Maisky (1884-1975), Soviet Ambassador in London, 1932-43.

melting candle. Very uncanny; but said to be amusing and easy to talk to. The Belgian Minister is young and full of charm and so is their Ambassador, dear old Cartier.[1] Aunt N. sat between him and the German Ambassador.[2] She had Belgium on her right. The Salisburys and Bobbety Cranborne,[3] the Godfrey Thomases,[4] Norman Davis's,[5] the Roosevelts (don't know which; he governed the Philippines once)[6] and Baffy Dugdale,[7] etc, etc. Irene Ravensdale,[8] etc. We were making history I suppose. And *what* do you suppose Aunt N. did after dinner? Made us all play musical chairs! She really is a remarkable woman, for who else could think of such a thing? Some of the older ones stood by thinking, no doubt, that the English are mad, quite mad. But they smiled benignly and were amused. After this group conversations took place. My Spaniard and I took intelligent interest in Aunt N.'s china collection and admired the glorious flowers. (Whole cherry trees, great orchids and bowls of camellias.)

---

☎ Burnham 460                                    Parr's,*
*June 15th, 1936*                                 Cliveden,
                                                  Taplow,
                                                  Bucks.

We went to Lady Hillingdon's[9] dance on Monday evening and it was very chic and great fun to look at, but as the other guests were all debs or middle-aged we found few friends and didn't stay terribly

[1] Baron Cartier de Marchienne, Belgian Ambassador since 1927.
[2] Leopold von Hoesch, who died a month later, on April 10th. He was succeeded by Joachim von Ribbentrop, later Hitler's Foreign Minister.
[3] The 4th Marquess of Salisbury, formerly Leader of the House of Lords, and his son Viscount Cranborne, Robert Arthur James Cecil ('Bobbety'), at this point Parliamentary Under Secretary at the Foreign Office. He would resign with Anthony Eden in 1938.
[4] Sir Godfrey Thomas, 10th Bart., Private Secretary to the Prince of Wales, 1921-36, and now an Assistant Private Secretary to him as King.
[5] Norman Davis, American Ambassador, who preceded Joseph Kennedy.
[6] Theodore Roosevelt Jr, eldest son of the 26th President of the United States, Theodore ('Teddy') Roosevelt. After being a successful Governor of Puerto Rico, he was despatched to the Philippines as Governor-General.
[7] Blanche ('Baffy'), wife of Edgar Dugdale, daughter of A. J. Balfour's brother, Eustace.
[8] Baroness in her own right. Eldest daughter of Marquess Curzon of Kedleston (Viceroy of India and later Foreign Secretary, who with A. J. Balfour was a political patron of Waldorf Astor).
[9] Wife of the 3rd Baron Hillingdon, banker and at one time Unionist MP. She was the Hon Edith Mary Winifred Cadogan, daughter of Viscount Chelsea.

late. Besides we wanted to save ourselves for Aunt N.'s dance the
next night. This was a real ball and I've never enjoyed a party so
much before in my life. It was fun from the word go.

It was indeed a Ball. Over a thousand people and all in their best
dresses. Aunt N. in pale blue satin with her crown tiara on. Wiss in
a dinner dress of black and pink chiffon. She hasn't much idea of
what to wear to a ball, for, although she's just returned from Paris
with a trunk full of clothes, she had to wear a dinner dress to the
ball. She was looking pretty but dowdy and I think she is beginning
to get a little thinner. Alice wore white. Everyone was there, the
whole caboodle.

Huge laburnums were banked at each end of the ballroom and I
must say I find it a lovely room – the golden effect is becoming.

I was never off the dance floor from 10.30 till 4, almost literally!
We polka'd, waltzed and, trust Aunt N., Paul Jonesed. This was a
great success and the buds forgot to look bored and joined in,
starry-eyed. Harmon Vanderhoef's nephew, Maury Hecksher and
Rupert Allan and Henry Page were all there and what a treat it is to
dance with American men. I almost wore my shoes through.

Reggie was in tearing form. I've never seen him enjoy a party so
much before. He waltzed and waltzed and danced with all the debs
and said he could happily go on all night. Which we very nearly did
for it wasn't till 4 a.m. that Aunt N. made us stop. She was quite
right for it's always wiser to stop at the peak of a party. We had eggs
and bacon after the music had stopped and we all agreed it was the
world's best party. And on champagne cup and lemonade!

When we were undressing – R. whirling around in waltz time as
he undid his tie, shirt and trouser buttons – we decided that it was
the best house we knew for a ball. R. said he thought he'd 'come
out' again! He said he found the debs delightful and he'd had a grand
evening.

Next morning I lunched with Ruth[1] and a party of three other
ladies to meet her sister Dorothea Blagden. Jelli d'Aranyi,[2] Lady
Buxton and Lady Howard. Such food. Exquisite soufflé or egg and
salmon. Roast chicken and finally velvety strawberry whip and
sponge cake. Ruth had a matinée and after the car had taken her to
the Haymarket Theatre she sent me on in it to the New where I went
alone to see *The Seagull* of Chekhov,[3] it is quite lovely, gloomy but
thrilling.

[1] Ruth Draper, American diseuse. Friend of Joyce's family for many years. When
she wrote and performed her own monologues she was following in Ruth's footsteps.
[2] Hungarian violinist. From the age of fourteen lived in England.
[3] The New is now the Albery Theatre. Edith Evans as Arkadina; John Gielgud as
Trigorin; Stephen Haggard as Constantine; Peggy Ashcroft as Nina.

That evening R. and I dined at the Hungaria and went to see *The Ex-Mrs Bradford* with William Powell. From there we went to Lady Dunn's dance. At the head of the stairs we were received by Lady Dunn,[1] her daughter Patty Douglas aged seventeen and her former husband, Lord Queensberry! How's that?

It was a complete *Vogue, Tatler* and *Sketch* evening. We saw people in sculptured curls and with bits of corn in their hair, just as we see them in *Vogue*. All the professional lovelies were there and it was depressingly second rate and beautifully produced. One could have safely said, 'Faces by Molyneux, hairs by Antoine, ideas by *Vogue*, and men from Heaven alone knows where.' I'm sure it's the sort of crowd that Elsa Maxwell[2] has in New York. Completely without standard.

But the supper was wonderful. (This letter is a little menu-y, I'm afraid.) Black cherries and cream and hot lobster – Yum.

We didn't stay late and were in bed by 1.

---

*August 11th, 1936*                                        Parr's

The office news is not very bright. In fact it could hardly be blacker. R. is quite well on top of it, which is a good thing but it's being rather hellish and I don't know what the outcome will be. It's all a question of raising money to get the mine a going concern. But no one will put any into a business in Tanganyika at this point (it *might* go German again) and there doesn't seem a single source that hasn't been pumped dry.

So you see why I can't come this autumn. You do know tho' I want to so badly that as October grows near I tingle all over and *ache* to come. But I'm afraid I know that my place is with R. during this difficult time.

I'm still hoping for Xmas though. But *don't* count on it, please, because we may by then both be wage earners and not have the wherewithal to buy tickets. I'm seriously contemplating a job this autumn. What? I dunno. But I think I'll have to. We gotter eat!

Tom's job[3] with the *Daily Express* continues and he's now hot after a movie – one which looks rather good. Betty looks

---

[1] Marcia Anastasia, now married to Sir James (Hamet) Dunn, banker. Later became the second wife of Lord Beaverbrook.
[2] Influential American gossip writer and party-hostess.
[3] Tom (Tommy) Phipps,* Joyce's only brother, was a freelance journalist. The *Daily Express* job was temporary. His wife Betty (née Brooks)* was American.

well and thinks that her continued dosings of quinine have done the trick. She's not being sick any more; but of course that means nothing. She's terribly attractive I think. I don't know what she's thinking about but I know she's thinking. She's very well educated; shows T. P. [Tom] up sometimes, quite unintentionally. It's a pity he isn't more educated because he's certainly got ability but he's read *nothing*. They are well and look happy and I've a sneaking feeling that they won't be able to be away from the US for ever and ever. I should give them a year here. Perhaps two. After that I'd like to bet on their return. I think Betty gets a little homesick for the place, not the people. Everyone likes her.

Do seriously try and think of a job for R.

---

*September 29th, 1936*                                          Pan's

I'm afraid we can't just take three months off to come to America. You see R. is still in the office – things look a bit better there – and he's got to set about finding something else in the meantime. So far we've done no looking. He feels that having been through what he rightly calls a 'hard school' (worry, seeing the City from all its strange angles) he now is of real value to someone. He's full of confidence and talked about himself last night in a really frank way. He said he knew he had enormous capabilities but that he lacked push, go-getting. If he had a Jewish partner, he said, they'd be a knock-out! Anyway the main thing is that he's got confidence and he really has got a good business training, apart from his chartered accountant's degree. Lefty* said jokingly, that he was writing to Jim Perkins[1] about him. I wish he would, quite seriously. Or could you? Or should I? You see *he* wouldn't like to live permanently or all-time in America. That's very understandable. But at the same time if we could get a job which meant, say, three or four months of the year in America, *that* would be perfect.

I've not seen T. [Tommy] or Betty since I got back. They've taken a room in Half Moon Street and Pa has seen 'em and they played golf on Sunday with R. and Harry [Grenfell].* R. says Betty looks well and is very attractive. (He dotes on her.) T. still has no job but there is still that aroma of possible jobs floating around him. I rang them up yesterday but they were both out. I've asked 'em down for the weekend after this one. Gin [Virginia Graham]* is coming down

[1] An American banker.

this one, her first release since July. She's been an absolute saint with her family and Pa [Harry Graham].* She drives him around, is cheerful and gay; and underneath she's about all-in, materially speaking. But her C.S. [Christian Science] is better and better and she writes such good letters and is learning so much that I feel she'll emerge about a hundred per cent better, if that were possible. I'm having her here for a week. We'll walk and read and write and sing and go to a movie perhaps and perhaps play some tennis. You know – be girlish together.

You know, I don't often get *real* homesickness but at this moment the air is dry and sunny like it was at Try* last October and my whole being aches to swallow up the silly space between here and there. Ooh I'd like to be on the Spartanberg train, slowing down into the station . . .!

---

*November 23rd, 1936*      Parr's

What can I tell you about us? We are both really well and very happy. Reggie is in very good form these days and business looks better. Harry goes to E. Africa tomorrow for two months and possibly the Grenfells, *père et mère*, may go to South Africa after Christmas in search of money for the mine. So you see it doesn't look as if R. can leave and find a new job just yet. He's busy and feeling happier about things and is of course, as a result, much better in himself. We are loving being down here this winter. So far the journeying hasn't been too cold and trying for him. We had our first fog last night and this morning he went up by train instead of by car so as not to risk getting stuck on the Great West Road.

I'm not having a baby but R. is going to see a specialist in that line this week and I shall probably go too. I am *very* happy these days and feel a very wise and lucky person.

Maria Brassey* has been here all last week and we've done the lesson each day and had a good old C.S. bee; discussing and clearing up each other's muddles, if any.

You said in your last letter but one that you thought you might come over to England in March. I'm absolutely *longing* to see you but I don't believe you should spend any money on travel until you are really finally out of debt. I've given this a lot of thought and I didn't say anything in my last letter because I wanted to see it quite clearly before I said anything and now I'm quite sure it would be wrong for you to come until you are clear of debt.

It's all a question of principle, I feel, and I'm sure that you'll agree when you see it like that. It's taken me a long time to see it but now I know I'm right. Say you think so too.

————◆————

*December 29th, 1936*                                                      Parr's

Tom and Betty Phipps arrived here two days before Christmas. The house was looking lovely with holly everywhere and candles lit and the tree sparkling between the windows. We didn't go up to Cliveden that night but dined quietly here and played rummy. Next morning T. had to work so he drove off in his £12 car and R. went shooting at Cliveden. Betty sat in and read and I took a fairly final rehearsal of the children[1] in the recreation room. Betty went up to Cliveden for lunch but I refused because I had so much to do and a hairdressing appointment in Maidenhead at 2.30. I did some last shoppings and got back about 4.30. Then up to Cliveden for tea. About 5 Aunt P. [Phyllis] arrived with Peter and Aline [Brooks],* Adelaide,[2] Virginia [Graham], Dinah, Jim, and Uncle Bob [all Brand].* Then David* and Bill [both Astor] came, and Bobbie [Shaw]* and Reggie Winn* (from Melton where he'd been hunting) and Lionel and Pat Curtis[3] (nice) and Judy Judge[4] and two forlorn American girls Anne Paul from Philadelphia and Maud Tucker from Richmond who's pa is a bishop. Alice and the children were already there. I played carols after tea and we all roared them for about half an hour. We came down here to dress and Tom got in with an armful of shopping. He did up the funniest parcels you ever saw. Tiny, with rough twists of tissue paper and some gummed tape. We giggled a good deal and got up to the house just in time for dinner.

After dinner on Xmas Eve there was no organised amusing. We sat about and Aunt N. kept diving into her boudoir and the room next door and we were all yelled at if we approached the sacred precincts. Very exciting and Christmassy. We came back here about 10.30 and felt very festive so we opened our parcels that had come by mail, there and then, up in our bedroom before a roaring fire.

Finally we went to bed. Next morning we awoke to brilliant sunshine and spring!

[1] For an annual Christmas children's entertainment at Cliveden.
[2] Adelaide, widow of Peter's younger brother David (Winkie) Brooks.*
[3] Lionel Curtis, close friend of Nancy Astor. In Colonial Service; lectured on colonial history at Oxford. Fellow of All Souls. Pat: his wife.
[4] Journalist and social worker, he was an Astor friend from Plymouth.

R. and I were called at 8.15 and after we'd had our presents we bathed and went up to Cliveden for breakfast, followed soon afterwards by T.[Tommy] and B.[Betty] in their car. The hall was traditional. Piles of presents on every available chair, stool or sofa and the tree lit up at the foot of the stairs. R. and I distributed our packages to their various piles and then everyone came down and we went into breakfast. The Winn girls[1] were soon bouncing about the room longing to get out into the hall and at their presents and soon – about 9.40 – we all began undoing red ribbon and tissue paper and there was a series of exclamations, thank-you's, and excited squeaks.

About 10.40 Bill, A.[Alice Winn], R. and I piled into our car and drove over to Hitcham church. This is a lovely little church; white-washed and rather simple. Holly hung, stuck and tied to every possible place and high over head a sprig or two among the candles. Very cosy. At the back of the church four coatless men were pulling the bells and a benevolent verger ushered us into knife-board pews.

Thoroughly orthodox and English. Betty and Tommy came and Alice and Reg [Winn] and the girls and Peter and Aline and Adelaide. The rest of the party went to Taplow church but it's so High that all thoughts of God are passed from your mind by the incense and one is so fascinated by the vestments and the way the Reverend Phillips changes hats that one forgets the point of Christmas, Christianity and Deity!

Our service was good and straightforward and the address was from the shoulder and made us all wince a little. The vicar deplored our cynicism and our enjoyment of gossip, our readiness to see faults and comment on them. You know, the old stuff but all true. We came out chastened and determined to be a bit more Christian.

After church we went back to Cliveden and collected our presents. Then to the cottage with them and then over to Burnham to call on Granny Grey* who was in bed with a cold. She looked like Red Ridinghood's grandmother, for the cap on her head and the several shawls all looked like a disguise. She was mounted on at least half a dozen pillows in a room filled with flowers, knicknacks, a Christmas tree, a wireless, a table covered in bottles and countless photographs and copies of Italian masterpieces.

We couldn't stay long because it was getting near lunchtime, so we came back here and changed into country clothes and were looking over our presents when the telephone rang and Lee[2] said that Aunt N. had put through a call to you which was coming

[1] Winn girls: Anne and Elizabeth, daughters of Alice and Reggie Winn. Anne married the Hon. Mark Wyndham. Elizabeth did not marry.
[2] Lee was the Astors' butler.

through at any moment. So we tore up to Cliveden and hung around
the telephone room and it wasn't till nearly two o'clock that you
came through. Much better connection than last year, wasn't it? Aunt
N. was very sweet and let David, Bobbie, Bill, Jakie [Astor],* Reg,
Tom, Betty and I have the telephone so I felt as if I'd really heard you
this year instead of last year's garbled agony. We were just leaving the
telephone room when the operator came through to say we had a
little more time; the others were all in the dining room but I got to
the telephone in time for that extra bit. That's why Tommy didn't
come on again. Gosh, I wish I could have jumped down the mouth-
piece.

I was remembering last year and how miserable I'd been at Christmas. Everything has worked out so well since then – T.'s married
Betty, Aunt N. likes Lefty [Flynn],* etc, etc. All of which gives one
cause to rejoice – I'd sat in the telephone room waiting for that call and
only got a plate of cold meat and some salad for lunch! Which was just
as well really because usually one overeats on Christmas Day.

We played French and English[1] on the lawn below the terrace in
the traditional way and Aunt N. was magnificent, running like a
rabbit and looking incredibly young.

Then tea in the dining room and afterwards 'hide and seek' all over
the house for Anne and Eliz. [Winn]. Reg, Eliz. and Jakie were the
he's and it was an endless game.

We were to dress up for dinner so the chest on the French landing
was unlocked and we turned everything upside down and came upon
those same old velvet cloaks, Aunt N.'s old hats, a pierrot costume
and any number of mismatched shoes.

Dinner was at 7.30 for the children and we were rather lazy and
only wore masks. Aunt N. wore false teeth and her hair in a frizz on
top and was any very rich old woman in the Ritz in any country.
Quite uncanny and terribly funny.

I need hardly tell you that Bill was a Chinaman! It wouldn't have
been a real Christmas if he hadn't been. Alice was a crazy woman
with too many scarves, jewels and beads and who giggled. She was
really very funny. Most of the others were lazy like us and cheated
by wearing masks. We sat women on one side and men on the other
of the table and Aunt N. made that awful face of the woman who
has had a stroke. I thought we'd be sick we laughed so and when
you think of a room full of people roaring at something that in real
life is a terrible tragedy one wonders what humour is!

After dinner we played games with the children and later on Reg
Winn, Jakie, David and Jim Brand did a sort of sketch about English

---

[1] A game, sometimes called Flags, played with two teams, the French and English.

soldiers on the North West Frontier of India. Jim couldn't be funnier and he has all the Langhorne imitative powers.

Jakie and David did their famous ventriloquist act and Adelaide crooned. She's got a really low radio voice oozing with S.A. [Sex Appeal] and she sang songs like 'How deep is the ocean' without turning a hair, while Aunt P. [Phyllis] wept and Alice and Bobbie fidgetted with embarrassment. Most extraordinary. But she's quite un-hypocritical about it and I don't doubt she misses Wink awfully at times, but between whiles she's quite natural and normal and just exists.

Next day we slept till 11 and as we were going into the dining room for our coffee Aunt P. and Pat Curtis arrived and said they'd like some coffee too, so we all sat down and then Reg Winn and Eliz came along and joined us too. Quite a breakfast party. Alice, Peter, Aline, Michael [Astor]* and J. J. Judge arrived later and presently we all walked up to Cliveden through a mizzling fog for lunch.

After lunch I sneaked back here where I lay on the sofa and read till the others came down to dress for dinner. Bliss. I was a new woman as a result.

We dined at Cliveden and afterwards the boys all played billiards and the girls sat around and tried to keep awake after two days' gaiety. Next day Betty and I went to church with Aunt N. while T. and R. played golf with Reg Winn. My R. won!

Lunch at Cliveden and very energetic mixed hockey afterwards. That evening we dined down here and played cards and I wore my new tea gown and we went to bed at 10.

T. went off early Monday morning and R. and Betty lay around here by the fire while I rehearsed the brats for the afternoon's entertainment. It went quite well and I had fair hopes for the evening.

We lunched at Cliveden and Wiss was there looking pretty and well. Virginia [Graham] had arrived at 12 to help me with the concert and we all went up to Cliveden for lunch. Aunt N. gave her a cheque for £20, wasn't it lovely! Gin is still in a whirl about it.

We had the usual tea party at the tennis court first and the tree and presents and I was busily dressing my children and rouging their faces and pinning up their dresses. They looked enchanting in their different coloured flowered cotton Kate Greenaway dresses with ribbons in the hair. The boys wore white pants and shirts and gay ties. They behaved beautifully. We began with an opening chorus (by Virginia) and then Tim Irving (Ted from the stud's son) recited. Eliz Winn played a solo next, then a short sketch called 'Helping hands' in which some children decide to be helpful and sweep the chimney and get tea ready. Of course it's quite disastrous and they get sooty and break all the tea things. Very fatuous but they did it with great enthusiasm and got an ovation.

Then Anne Winn played a solo followed by Eliz singing a song. We did 'The King's Breakfast' next by A. A. Milne and all of us took part and sang like mad. After which Eliz recited in a resounding voice and we ended with two carols and the final chorus. In between items I had two tiny children carry on placards with the next item written on it in large letters. It was really a great success and Uncle Waldorf in his little speech at the end said lots of nice things about me and how nice it was to have me as a resident instead of merely a visitor. I got clapped and was very touched. Wasn't it nice?

We came back here for supper and then, very unwillingly went back to the recreation room for the dance.[1]

The fancy dresses were typical. Gladys Guy was 'Coronation 1937' in a number of union jacks and a sort of Britannia cap! Old Jeffries was 'Old Mother Slipper Slopper' in his grandmother's night gown, over ninety years old! Arthur[2] was a pantomime fairy in the racing colours and he called himself 'The Star of Bethlehem'! He was pretty funny, I can tell you! A housemaid came as a gramophone record and another was a cracker! You know the sort of thing. We didn't stay late.

---

[1] Annual Christmas fancy-dress party for the staff at Cliveden.
[2] Arthur was Arthur Bushell, Lord Astor's valet; Gladys Guy was the wife of an estate worker. Old Jeffries and his family worked for the Astors for many years; Old Jeffries's son, Bert, was Lord Astor's second chauffeur.

*1937*

Still finding it difficult to make ends meet. Joyce investigated the possibility of earning money as a professional singer with a band. This came to nothing, but in March 1937 she began a six-week apprenticeship as radio critic of *The Observer*. J. L. Garvin, editor of the paper, cut short the apprenticeship and Joyce's first piece appeared on April 11th, reviewing a Robert Mayer children's concert and a production of *The Cherry Orchard*. She was paid £10 a week for her articles: 'This was real money and we needed it,' she says in her autobiography and adds, 'My professional life had begun.'

Ma and Lefty paid a visit to England in the summer, and Joyce continued her activities with the Women's Institute, the Infant Welfare Centre and the church, though her daily routine was increasingly centred around the radio programmes she was reviewing.

# 1937

Darling Ma

Friday, [I] drove up to the back of beyond in the Tottenham Court
Rd district to a place called Billy Higgs Studio where I made a
gramophone record with Carroll Gibbons[1] at the piano!!!

He did it entirely out of kindness and to get me started. Wasn't it
nice of him? He took endless trouble, rehearsed me and coached me
and then we made a record of 'Easy to Love' and though it's full of
faults it *is* rather good. Quite unlike me though. A deep rich velvety
sound!

He is going to do a lot for me in the way of introductions and
there's a *faint* possibility that I might perhaps sing with the orchestra
at the Hotel de Paris at Bray! Just over weekends. He says there's
nothing like that for practice and giving one confidence. Now don't
mention this if you write to England because it's such a faint
possibility. But it would be a marvellous way of beginning for it
wouldn't interfere with my private life and would mean some extra
cash.

It's amazing to hear oneself. My vowel sounds are much too open
and I'm apt to hit the note instead of letting it flow. However Carroll
Gibbons says I'm pretty good and that's what I build on.

I was thrilled to hear of your New York offer. I think you were
quite right not to take it because night club life *must* be hell. But I
think the Hotel de Paris will be fun, *if* it comes off. You see I shan't
be the cabaret or anything. Just sing the choruses *with* the orchestra
for dancing. I can't think of anything I'd rather do. A microphone
goes to my head like drink and I could happily sing to one for hours.
To be paid for it sounds *quite* intoxicating.

There is also a possibility that I may join a jazz choir that one of

---

[1] Carroll Gibbons, well known pianist and band leader, was born in America. He
played at the Savoy Hotel and also wrote music for films.

the members of Carroll Gibbons's orchestra has inaugurated. It does sound fun, don't you think. It's to use for radio and records.

I do hope all this doesn't just fade – I don't think I'll let it.

Wouldn't it be fun if I did make a success of this singing business!

Much love
Joyce

---

*August 2nd, 1937*                                                    Parr's

Since you went the sun hasn't ceased shining; it's been hot enough for swimming and lolling around and we keep saying – if only you and Lefty were here to know what England is like when it's hot. It's quite perfect. I'm so glad because it's the Bank Holiday weekend, you know. We miss you a *lot* – but I'm not a bit sad. Let's see, what has happened since you sailed?

Well, on Saturday morning Reg went into Maidenhead and did our shopping for us and then we had some tennis before lunch. Gin is in good form, so is Harry so we are a most pleasant quartet. She, G., was very sweet to me in case I should be missing you. On Saturday afternoon there was a cricket match and we went and watched Reggie W. [Winn] and Jakie and Mike [Astor]* doing their bit. That evening, after a lot of energetic tennis and a swim, we dined early and went into Slough to see *Three Smart Girls*[1] which is a grand movie. Sunday was another lovely day.

After church we all lunched up at Cliveden. Aunt N. rather quiet and a little low, I gather. We were really just a family party except that Michael had brought a young Austrian movie actress called Lily Palmer[2] down with him. Did you see the picture about the making of the C.P. [Canadian Pacific] railway? Called *The Great Barrier*. She was the lead in it. A pretty little thing with reddish blonde hair, large eyes and rather a big mouth. The idea was to prevent Aunt N. knowing she was in the movies. Needless to say that was quite impossible. At lunch she bore up bravely under a torrent of questions. Poor Michael writhed but all was well for the girl was perfectly able to take care of herself and Aunt N. liked her spirit. The afternoon was spent in strenuous tennis. It was a perfect day and we enjoyed it

[1] The first Deanna Durbin film, with Alice Brady and Mischa Auer; Joyce became a Durbin fan.
[2] Lily (actually Lilli) Palmer, stage and film actress, born in Austria. She later married Rex Harrison with whom she played in *Bell, Book and Candle*.

to the full. That evening V. [Virginia], Harry, R. and I dined here and did a little listening – very little for the play was about Hereward the Wake in the tenth century.[1] Imagine that after a hot sunny day!

Yesterday – Monday was again fine.

Oh, I almost forgot to tell you what happened on Sunday evening. We were very late going to bed and when finally R. went to open the curtains in our room it was about 11.30. As he stood there we heard the most terrifying shriek of brakes followed by the sound of a long skid, then a crash, then complete silence. It came from the hill half way between our back entrance and Waugh's cottage. Harry and R. ran down to get our car out and drove around while V. and I – in our dressing gowns – ran blindly through the darkest night I've ever seen to the back gate. Negotiating our vast property in the dark took us as long as it did R. and H. to get there by car and we all arrived together. We found one of the new model Fords (V8 I think) lying on its side with the wheels just not still going round. The occupants – two girls, a man and a whippet dog were standing on the bank unscratched. There wasn't a crack in any glass in the car. All that had happened was explained to us. Not knowing the twists of the hill and going too fast the man had braked too swiftly twice – first left then right – and finally the car turned over facing the way it came! The girls were white and shaken and one of them was rather bruised I think and possibly concussed. V. and I urged them to come into the house, but they were all so vague and shocked that we couldn't persuade them. Human interest note was provided by the fairer of the girls who quite obviously oughtn't to be out with the man in question. She kept murmuring 'What will they say' and 'I ought to get home quickly' etc, and crying all the time. Harry took the two girls back to Beaconsfield followed by the man *driving* his own car. R., H. and a couple of strange men, conjured out of space, had righted the car and found all was well with it except of course for the side on which it had skidded. That was scratched and battered to bits. It says a lot for these all-steel bodies, you know.

After all the excitement we made ourselves tea in the kitchen and got to bed about 1.30!

———◆———

[1] In her autobiography Joyce says: 'There was a distinction between radio plays and radio dramas. It was the dramas I didn't fancy. I thought they were conceived on a scale too grand for the medium . . . They were "costume plays" for the most part, sometimes written in verse.' Clearly *Hereward the Wake* was one of these.

The house is empty once more and I've spent a hectic but happy morning trying the furniture another way round. Fruitless I'm afraid, and all the stuff is as it was. For economy I thought we'd dispense with a dining room fire during the week and eat cosily in the drawing room. The broadcasts I must hear always seem to happen just when we are eating so this new move will deal with that problem. I tried to inveigle the big table, now standing between the windows, into doing double duty as paper-flower-and-dining table. But I've had to abandon that project as impractical. I had it under the long window with the sofa facing the fire. But it was too congested and not very pretty either. So now I've evolved a plan by which we shall eat off a very small folding table that is neatly stowed away against the wall between meals. So we are as we were except for this little addition.

We had Tommy and Betty and Harry here for the weekend. Very pleasant it was too, but you know the size of this room. And in wintertime we all want the fire so it's sort of frenzied. Tommy and R. take up all the space by sprawling over a backgammon board. Harry is rather a neat relaxer but even so, armed with *The Times*, he's quite formidable. Betty needed a stool for her games of patience and I had to be near the radio and all my sewing tackle. Yes, it was snug all right and the ashtrays got full and the air thick and my tidying instincts had to be controlled except *just* before meals. Then I emptied the room and flung wide the windows.

In two days Betty has blown up like a balloon. When I saw her in London a week ago she was really very small and tidy. But then I met her at Taplow station on Saturday she sort of rolled out of the train. It seems to have shot up. It's huge and very prominent; boy or girl? She looks very well and is quite calm about it. I think she will want to be a little quieter now that it's increased in size. Up till now she has led her ordinary life and been out late at night as usual. Tommy is very sweet with her, considerate too. I must say she is v. good with him and I give her marks for being so understanding. He seems to have grown up a lot and is much less prickly and can actually stand being laughed at! He was very funny this weekend. About nothing in particular. Just funny.

He played golf on Saturday with some movie man; Betty came down by train from London in time for lunch. Harry had a cold and didn't do anything and R. worked like a beaver over the garden: all the autumn planting and some dividing of last year's plants. He continues as keen as ever and it gives him an increasing interest. I leave it entirely to him.

I lunched with Betty last Monday. The apartment really looks charming. The living room curtains are a great success. Sort of periwinkle chalky blue with white musical instruments rather faintly patterned on them. They are linen. So far the chairs are still in the covers they had at Swan Court. And my sofa and two chairs are in their old covers. Betty wants to find some red-coral stuff for two of them. It's not easy to get the right colours.

I got your letter today. Yes, hasn't it been a lovely summer. I couldn't be happier or more cheerful. Of course I miss you but not a bit sadly. Give my love to Lefty and write soon and often.

*P.S.* Virginia sends you her love. She's cutting lavender for me. H. [Harry Grenfell] and R. have gone to London. It's still misty but there's a boiling day ahead.

---

*November 9th, 1937*      Parr's

I was in London on Friday and I took Betty some delphiniums from the garden. (Nature note: delphiniums in flower in November!) She was having her bath when I got there – 10 a.m. – and I sat in her minute bathroom peering through thick red-hot steam while she used more lather than I'd thought possible. She rubbed Pears soap on to the wash cloth and then frothed it up all over herself. A fine sight. She's not as big as I'd thought. In fact she's really very neat. It's prominent and extremely round. What are your conclusions? Girl? Boy?

She was X-rayed about ten days ago and all is in order. The doctor told her it would be here in two weeks but she doesn't believe him. If he's right it should arrive about the 15th – before you get this letter. But I'm inclined to agree with Betty, for no *good* reason at all. She looks extremely well and happy. The apartment is charming and her maid is staying on as B. has engaged a helper for half the time. It seems ridiculous that one woman can't do a seven-roomed apartment. Maybe it's not 'can't' but 'won't'.

---

*December 13th, 1937*      Parr's

This is my Christmas letter – if it doesn't arrive after the actual day. So Happy X to you both.

Let's see. What's happened? Betty is home again.[1] Alice lent them

---

[1] Betty's baby was a boy, Wilton, born on November 24th.

her car and chauffeur to effect the trip. B. was *so* glad to be out of
the home. Her nanny is very nice, she says, and all goes well there.
I haven't seen her for a week but we've telephoned every other day.
She is still in bed but will get up this week.

As you probably know Aunt N. and Uncle W. sail for Florida at
the end of this week. (At least it is either the 19th or 20th or 21st.
They weren't quite sure when I last heard.) Uncle W. hasn't been
well as you know. It's something called inflamed bronchial tubes I
think. Anyway he craves the sun and what *is* the good of being that
rich if you can't do those sort of things occasionally? Aunt N. didn't
want to go a bit, at first; now she's resigned to it and anyway she
knows it's the right thing for her to do. I have only spoken to her
on the telephone so I know no details. She is coming here tomorrow
morning for a few hours to see about the garden, etc, in her absence.
I'm going up to the house to see her but I don't know if there'll be
time to write to you after I've seen her.

<hr />

Ditchley,*
Enstone,
Oxon.

*Christmas Day, 1937*

I'm crazy about my patchwork dressing gown. You can't think how
it has caught my fancy. I love it. And the tablecloth and mats are
perfect for the cottage. And the white mats. The hair combs with
the star sapphires in them exactly match a brooch and earrings Aunt
Nancy gave me! So now I'm completely equipped in star sapphires
– my real ring & your lovely paste combs and the matching brooch
and earrings. Then there is the manicure set! Being me I've hardly
used up the contents of the little hat-box set you gave me two years
ago! But having a new one is marvellous and I love the colour of
both varnishes.

I'm writing this with Lefty's new pen which I shall thank him for
in another letter. It is perfect and I shall use it from now on. We came
here to find your box awaiting us on Thursday. You'd addressed
them wrong! Ours went to Betty and Tommy and vice versa!
However we worked it out in time so it doesn't matter.

Thank you for all my simply lovely presents. I want every one –
they are not merely nice extras but perfect presents. So thank you
again.

I spent a busy week leading up to this great day. On Monday when
I went to the Infant Welfare I was told that there were some families

in such bad circumstances that they would have nothing in the house for Christmas. So together with several other helpers I adopted a family! (I didn't share the family – I mean we each took one.) Mine were called Mr and Mrs Stark and they have four children: a boy of thirteen, girl, eleven, boy, six, baby girl, six months. I went to the house first to see what they looked like and then on Tuesday I spent the day in London getting things for them at Marks and Spencer and Woolworths. You can't imagine what wonders I achieved with £2-0-0. A sweater for Pa, silk stockings for Ma, sweater and socks for girl, sweater for little boy, and pale blue wool outfit for the baby. Then I got a toy each for the children, found a perfectly good coat of mine for Mrs, an old overcoat for Mr – both in fine condition – and with a joint of beef, a Christmas pudding, jelly, chutney, cheeses, a fruit cake and nuts and dates, I took the whole lot along the next day. I had great fun tying up the packages in gay Christmas ribbons – all different. So that the children wouldn't see them I put them in a suitcase which Mrs Stark unpacked in the bedroom, hiding the presents, and I took it home empty.

You can't think what a good time I had doing it. Of all the forms of self-indulgence giving is the pleasantest.

On Wednesday there was a small shoot at Cliveden and R. took part in it. That evening we had twelve local friends in for sherry. As we were going away for Christmas it wasn't worth decorating the house with holly just for that evening. But to make it all look Christmassy I bought some red candles and lit them in the hall window without drawing the curtains. It looked so cosy from outside. I know because I went out to see before anyone came. We had very good 'snacks' for the sherry. Saltine biscuits spread with fresh cream cheese and powdered with finely chopped bacon. Delicious.

Next day R. left at dawn in the car to come over here for a shoot. I followed in the afternoon, driven over by Bert [Jeffries] in a car loaded with presents.

(You know the lavishness of our Christmas makes me feel terrible when I think of the dozens of families without *anything*. It is all so wrong and so difficult to combat. I'm feeling quite bolshy but hopeless, for I've had such lovely presents.)

I am listening to a concert from Hastings. Doesn't it surprise you that anyone would go to a concert on Christmas Day? There is a huge audience judging by the applause.

Jakie misses Michael awfully I think. He was rather low last night, but much better today. He talks very openly to R. and R. says he is rather worried about his future. What is a very rich young man to do?

The *world's* cosiest housemaid has just appeared with some coal.

She's obviously a very under underling suffering acutely from suppressed conversation. She told me all about the Christmas dinner they had in the servants' hall. '*Two* great turkeys, crackers, we were twenty-five – ooh it was *lovely*! The table looked ever so pretty. It's fun being so many together.'

It speaks well for Nancy's housekeeper that they all had such fun.

Damn – it's nearly teatime and I am having such a cosy time. But I suppose I'll have to go down.

So Happy New Year to you and thank you for *all* my lovely presents.

*P.S.* Nancy [Tree]* has taken *such* trouble over everything and it really is being lots of fun and beautifully effortless.

I'm afraid Aunt N. might be jealous if she knew what fun we were all having! But that doesn't mean we aren't missing the old tradition of a Cliveden Christmas because we all are.

1938

At the beginning of 1938 Joyce took over as president of her local Women's Institute. She continued listening-in to the radio and reviewing the programmes for *The Observer*. In March the paper presented her with a new Murphy radio set, a superior model, which, according to Joyce's autobiography, 'caused me to sit up into the early hours of the morning, twiddling knobs in the short-wave band, finding snatches of far-away conversations . . . Once I got a famous American programme called the Major Bowes Amateur Hour, and this made me feel close to my mother, for she always listened to that programme down in North Carolina.'

Relations with Ma were, however, strained throughout the year by the fact that Nora, generous but permanently short of money, neglected to pay for a dress she had given to Joyce during her visit the year before. Demands for payment were addressed to Joyce and the matter rumbled on for many months.

During this year the political situation in Europe deteriorated. In March 1938, with little opposition, Hitler moved against Austria and the Czechoslovak frontier now lay exposed to German advance. Anthony Eden resigned as Foreign Secretary in protest at Chamberlain's 'appeasement' policies in Europe and was replaced by Lord Halifax, who was known to agree with the Prime Minister's approach to the European situation.

# 1938

Darling Ma,

I don't believe I told you about our dress-up dinner on Christmas Day did I? The Brands came over and brought Ruth [Draper] with them. Dinah was dressed as a little girl in a smock with ankle socks and red shoes. She looked very pretty. Virginia wore Jim's clothes and looked very attractive and rakish. Ruth simply piled her hair up and wore a picture dress. Jim was an old man and Uncle Bob was undisguised. Peter Brooks was in bed with a cold. I haven't seen him yet.

Of our party Nancy was the best as Mrs Rittenhouse.[1] She wore a black velvet dress and padded her bosom and behind. Of course she looked lovely with her hair pulled up off her face. She was very funny and a little outrageous. Billy [Astor], Reggie Winn and Jakie were the Marx Bros. I was rather dreary as a 1900 lady with holly in my hair and the green velvet dress you sent me. Alice made an incredibly mad Sur-realiste picture. I helped her dress and we had fun putting inconsequential oddments about her. She wore a snowboot on her head tied under the chin by its laces. Then we painted a smiling mouth on one cheek and corked an eye on her chin. A glove on her bottom, a toothbrush dangled from a safety pin on her back, braces hung round her neck like a lei. (A garland of flowers, Hawaian.) I can't remember what else.

Bobbie [Shaw] was his same old curate and he made a little speech that was quite funny and, I'm glad to say, clean. After dinner Ruth did two monologues for us. 'The Debutante' and 'The Children's Party'. She was at her very best and the audience was thrilled. It was very good of her. Then we danced a little and played some games and so to bed.

After lunch on Sunday there was a hockey game and we all ran

---

[1] A Marx Brothers creation.

about a good deal and I personally avoided danger wherever possible by just not tackling the opposite side. Lack of the old team spirit, I'm afraid. I had to start work again that evening. There was rather a good little play from Dorsetshire.

On Monday there was a shoot and Jakie and David and Jeremy[1] went hunting. I went over to the meet with the Winn girls and Kenneth Pender.[2] It reminded me so much of the Cottesbrook days when you all thought I was walking out with Henry Tiarks![3] Those dreary, muddy mornings, the hounds arriving, the ladies emerging from their cars, cigarette dangling from a well-rouged mouth. Rather chic, very hard and frightening.

After lunch I wrote some letters and helped arrange some games for the party that evening. Nineteen people – of all ages – were coming over from Blenheim and the Brands and Margessons[4] from the other side of the county. We were about fifty in all. Dinner at little tables decorated with Christmas trees. I sat next to Gerry Koch de Gooreynd and Uncle Bob. V. pleasant. There were lots of children and they ate in the little breakfast room.

Afterwards we danced and played musical bumps – me at the piano. Then there was a good whistling relay race in teams.

During the whole weekend we played that good drawing game, clumps. Do you remember writing to me about it ages ago? I'd never played till now; Nancy knew it and we all got the craze. To vary it we also played it by acting the phrase which is quite as amusing. Of course your teams have to be in separate rooms.

One of the things we had to do was 'Sunny Side Up' and Peter Beatty[5] started a wrestling match with Alice in an effort to get her bottom 'Sunny Side Up'. It really was a sight to see. Al got such giggles and Peter B. is so leggy and hasn't a mite of strength.

We had the estate Tree and fancy-dress dance on Friday. It was very queer without Aunt N. and Uncle W. and they were missed by everyone. All the point of the party was gone. No fire to the thing. Bill did very well; but he can never hope to take their place. He just isn't the thing at all. But it was quite successful. A big tea as usual, then the presents, then a Punch and Judy show and ventriloquist. In the evening I returned for the dance. R. had slight collywobbles inside so he stayed here. Wiss was there, and David, Bill and Jakie

[1] Jeremy Tree, Ronald and Nancy Tree's son.
[2] Kenneth Pender was an American friend of the family.
[3] Cottesbrook was a house taken by Nancy and Ronald Tree in the Pytchley country; Ronald Tree had been Joint-Master of the Pytchley Hunt. Henry Tiarks was a businessman and banker. His daughter Henrietta married the Marquess of Tavistock.
[4] David Margesson, MP, Government Chief Whip.
[5] Son and heir of 2nd Earl Beatty.

and Bobbie. I was very conscious of not seeing old Jeffries. Oh dear, it was all very queer.

However there was a good deal of gaiety and a parade and the prize giving. And a Boston two-step, the Valeeta (?) Valita (?) and the polka. I didn't stay there to see in the New Year but came home to see it in with R. up in our room with the radio on.

He was fully recovered next morning and went over to Nettlebed to shoot with Peter Fleming.[1]

---

Joyce Grove,[2]<br>
Nettlebed,<br>
Oxon.

*January 8th, 1938*

We are spending the day here and since lunch it is pouring with rain so while Reggie trudges the woods with Peter in search of pigeons to shoot, the rest of us are enjoying an idle afternoon. The gramophone is playing, Celia[3] is playing bridge with Rupert Hart-Davis[4] and his wife Comfort, and a sister in-law of Peter's called Tish. Two other girls – blonde, *Bystander*ish and dumb – are knitting in the opposite corner.[5] I am happily employed writing to you.

We've been up at Cliveden all this week and it has been very pleasant. Alice and Reggie and the girls came down on Tuesday and Bobbie arrived last night. Of course Alice has got the anti-Bobbie complex to a far gone degree.[6] But I do sympathise with her. He has been at his nicest. Even that isn't good enough. His conversation is so tinged with bitterness and his cynicism is so poisonous that it pervades and fouls the atmosphere. He can't resist bullying the

---

[1] Author, then best-known for his travel books, *Brazilian Adventure* and *News from Tartary*. As a journalist he worked for *The Times*, the *Spectator* and had just helped launch a new glossy periodical, *Night and Day*. The brother of Ian Fleming, he was married to the actress Celia Johnson.

[2] A hideous Edwardian pile built for Peter Fleming's grandparents.

[3] Celia Johnson. Her first West End success was in *Debonair* (the Lyric, 1930) when only twenty-one. She made her first New York appearance the following year, playing Ophelia.

[4] Rupert Hart-Davis, publisher (with Jonathan Cape, would later run an eponymous imprint) and author (biographer of Hugh Walpole and editor of the collected letters of Oscar Wilde).

[5] The *Bystander* was a weekly illustrated magazine which later amalgamated with the *Tatler*.

[6] Bobbie Shaw had been imprisoned for a homosexual offence in 1931. Although his family stood by him throughout, the incident ruined him socially and he became embittered and drank heavily.

children and uses the most low methods of attack. This past twelve hours has proved to Alice, for always, that she cannot risk having her children exposed to his evil influence and she will never bring them to Cliveden again when he is there. (For me it is quite different. I have no children and I do know a little about right thinking. Nevertheless I wouldn't go out of my way to see him for there is no reason why I should. Aunt N. is to blame for the whole thing – in the main. Had she never allowed him to see her children in the beginning he would have been less assured and less destructive.)

Yesterday Alice and I took the children into Slough to see Freddie Bartholomew in *Captains Courageous*. Reg Winn was hunting up at Melton but my Reggie came down in time to go with us. I made the initial mistake of telling the girls I was sure to cry if it was at all sad. And it was *very* sad! So they never took their eyes off my face to see *if* I did cry. The strain of trying not to cry resulted in a scarlet and very swollen nose and I quite failed not to get wet through! Alice and Reggie were able to indulge in tears without interference for all attention was focussed on me. Have you seen *Capt. Cour.*? It *is* good.

It's so nice to see Rupert again. He is so happy nowadays. Two lovely fat, blonde babies, a house at Highgate and a fine job in a successful publishers. He is so gay and amusing and makes one feel warm when one sees him. He sends you his love. You can't imagine how *fat* he's got! It seems impossible doesn't it. Long, thin Rupert.

I've no more news.

I had my first Women's Institute meeting as president last week. It went quite well and I was relieved when it was over.

———◦◈◦———

Eydon Hall,[1]<br>Eydon,<br>Rugby.

*January [undated] 1938*

I haven't seen Tommy for weeks but B. says he's OK and had a good week in Paris. I must say he really is the luckiest person in the world to have found such a wife as Betty. Having been brought up as he was by you to expect attention, flattery and all the best of everything – (make you mad to have me tell you?!) – few women could bear his egoism. But by some God-given strength and understanding Betty really does seem to cope and not mind. More power to her. They have a housemaid now as well as Catharine and a nanny. Quite a

---

[1] The home of R. H. Brand (Uncle Bob) and his family.

household. Betty keeps the place looking so attractive and has a cosiness that I had not suspected originally, but which makes the flat a pleasure to visit. She seems to have a very full life and entertains her girlfriends quite often for lunch and bridge. She is looking very well and has quite regained her figure. She weaned the baby over Christmas, you know.

You are always telling me I should see more of Tommy but you must realise how very far apart our tastes and lives lie. We really have very little in common, you know, except family love. And then there is the difference in ages between B. and me and R. and T. You are always telling me how much T. loves us and admires, etc, etc. But *never* does he take the slightest trouble to keep in touch with us. He doesn't even write and say thank you for his Christmas presents; or for coming to stay, etc. He may feel all the things you say but I do think he's got to show a practical proof of his feelings before I entirely believe in them. I know you think special standards and exceptions should be made for him. I'm afraid that is why he is so unsuited to everyday treatment.

***

*February 14th, 1938*  Parr's

Tommy and Betty have just left here after spending the weekend. You will be glad to hear that they seem to be much less 'difficult' – I can't think of a better word – and much happier.

As far as I can make out they don't plan to go to America immediately, at any rate. Tommy wants to live here ultimately and he feels, rightly I think, that he must make every effort to see what can be done here before he abandons hope and tries America. He's very busy about a possible, isolated, story job. Not under contract, just a casual chance. And then he knows a Frenchman who *may* want a story. So you see there are several irons in the not very hot fire. Enough to keep them hopeful and he seems to be adequately monied, at any rate for the time being.

He was very sweet to Betty and they seemed to be getting on nicely. He is still apt to correct her all the time in public – her hair is wrong, her powder wrong or some small detail. But on the whole they were congenial and seemed happy.

I simply love my red velvet birthday dress. You really mustn't send me any more presents for years to come. The red is quite heavenly and I'm delighted with it.

I had rather a boring birthday because it fell on a very busy day. I went up to London in the morning and saw Aunt N. who'd arrived the night before. At once the family was humming again. Uncle Bob was there and Virginia came in and Bobbie Shaw, and then Billy and David, Wiss and Jakie all arrived for lunch. You know how it is. Awful! (But don't say I said so!) Everyone was very nice and the whole unreality of the atmosphere flowed over me to suffocation point and I was glad to get out into the air again. I wonder what it is? Money? Not really; complacency? – yes, and a sort of stark cynicism that turns all beauty to sawdust. After lunch I rehearsed with Virginia for the concert at the American Women's Club in aid of the swimming pool at Claremont.[1] We were really rather funny and we got those Scientifically hatted holy women – nearly all 1st Churchers[2] – into a pliable state of giggles.

I almost forgot to tell you that I had a very encouraging letter from Mr Garvin this morning. He is v. pleased with me, you'll be glad to hear, and is giving me a new radio set in March. Isn't it lovely!

———◆———

*February 20th, 1938*                                        Parr's

Well, by now you have had two letters and my cables dealing with the Phipps's situation. I've no more news this weekend on the subject. They left here last Monday, since when I've not heard a word from them. But I went to London on Friday and had a half hour session with the baby. B. and T. have gone to Wissie's for the weekend. The baby was very sweet and lively; he still looks faintly Japanese! But all the same it's an alluring orientalisation. His hair rises straight off his head and gives him the appearance of being continually in a high wind. He chats away about a great deal and rolls his eyes in delight when he laughs. So far I've no news of work from T. In fact I literally know no more than I did when I last wrote. But, as I said in my cable, I don't believe they will go to America – at any rate not yet awhile. T. doesn't want to live in America and any trip over would only be makeshift. No, I don't agree with you that America is the place for them. T. has made some roots here and likes it. So does B.,

[1] Joyce went to Clear View School in South Norwood where she had weekly elocution lessons – her only training, she says, for the stage. The school outgrew its premises and moved to Claremont at Esher.
[2] In each place where there are Christian Scientists the first church to be built is called First Church, and the next Second Church, etc. The First Church of Christ Scientist in London is at Sloane Terrace, which Joyce regularly attended.

I think. All the English in T. seems to have come to light in recent years and he feels at home here now.

------◈------

Aunt N.'s children's party was terrific. I got to St James's Square at 3 o'clock to find four of the nurses from Lady Carnarvon's home[1] – where Dinah [Brand] is for her appendix – whom Aunt N. had asked to see the rooms arranged. You really can't conceive of anything better done. Of course, on principle I'm *all* against it. But aside from that it was a pleasure to behold. The upstairs dining room was transformed into a market green, with artificial grass on the floor, stalls all around – fruit & flower, sweets, toys, fancy balloons – and draped in scarlet and white canvas. At one end there was a floodlit Punch and Judy theatre! In the ballroom was a three-piece orchestra. A wandering musician with an accordion wandered around in gipsy costume! Then there was a tea of major proportions. All the usuals plus angel cake, meringues fashioned into birds, ice cream of two sorts and dozens of little cakes, etc.

The invitations said 'Country or Peasant Costume'. This was fairly widely adhered to. Princess Elizabeth was a Dutch Peasant. What a charming child she is. She has lengthened out a lot and has now got quite a lovely little face, really graceful arms and generally is very attractive. She has a quiet poise that makes her remarkable among the other children. My word, she and Princess Margaret are well brought up. They have such unobtrusive manners and are natural – surely an achievement in their position – always being watched and concentrated on.[2]

The little Princess was hardly country or peasant. But she looked pretty nice in a Kate Greenaway costume. Elizabeth and Anne [Winn] were a Gipsy and a Cow Girl respectively.

After the tea and presents there was dancing and games in the ballroom. Bill is surprisingly good with children and had them all Follow-My-Leading all around the room and through the two drawing rooms and back again. Somehow a photographer got in, much to Alice's very slight indignation. It really was rather tacky,

[1] Fashionable nursing home of the period.
[2] Princess Elizabeth would be twelve the following month; Princess Margaret was seven. Queen Mary judged the fancy-dress competition, and a third Queen, Marie of Yugoslavia, was also present.

like a charity ball or Cecil Beaton party. Awful. But N.'s excuse was
that the Queen gave her permission.

Both Queens were there. Mary in regal grey and Elizabeth in old
rose. How nice *she* is. One couldn't help being a royalist with her
and George on the throne. They are so simple and honest.

I went to London yesterday to hear Myra Hess[1] give her concert
at the Queen's Hall. Virginia and Maria [Brassey] went too. It was
beyond words wonderful. I could listen to her for ever. She is so
impersonal and one feels her wisdom through her playing. Daddy
was there with a party of C.S. friends and sat right behind us which
was clever of him. Or us.

P.S. Have you sent me that cheque for £12-0-0 for Maria Koskill?
(Chez Beth)[2].

———◄◉►———

*April 11th, 1938*                                            Parr's

It's 6.30, Monday evening, and I usually have all my letters for
America written and mailed by mid-day. But this week everything
got out of hand – I had a committee for the Blind in Maidenhead this
morning and Infant Welfare all the afternoon and lunch at Cliveden
in between. So now there is about half an hour before I must take
my bath and start my listening.

On Thursday Maria [Brassey] came over from Lake End to have
high tea with us before attending our first Air Raid Precautions
lecture in the Institute. The lecturer was a Red Cross officer (in
uniform) who was most anxious that no one should be alarmed
and assured us that ARP are really to eliminate panic. She showed us
how to make a room proof against gas and what such a room
should contain – tinned foods, pencils and paper, cards, toys for the
children, books, etc, etc. Then she produced three different types of
gas masks and put them on in turn. Very gruesome. I'd rather
run out into a wood and get caught there than be cooped up in a
small room with the constant danger of incendiary bombs falling
on one.

The object of these talks is to instil into everyone the importance

[1] Pianist, best remembered for her wartime concerts in the National Gallery.
[2] Ma had given Joyce a ball gown – the white net crinoline – which she was to wear
to the royal ball of June 5th, to the Astor dance in May 1939, and again, a few weeks
later (July 1939) to a Court ball. The dress, which was to be Joyce's 'best' for many
years, came from a shop called Chez Beth, run by Maria Koskill.

of co-operation and order in a time of emergency, to give everyone something to do should the raids ever come – which I, for one, heartily doubt.

———◆———

Nannau,[1]
Dolgelly,

*April 17th, 1938*                              N. Wales.

Wales is looking its very best. It's very sunny and clear though rather cold on the corners. Ginnie and I had a heavenly drive through the orchard lands and kept exclaiming at the sudden new views dotted with fuzzy white cherry trees and the clashing greens of spring. We had our sausage rolls on exactly the same spot as you, Lefty, R. and I did last June. On top of that hill by a gate. There were no signs of our former visit.

Only the Col. and Mrs, Vera, Laura, Harry and us here. Very cosy. We have walked a great deal and played a lot of tennis. I'm quite stiff from so much exercise. I do love this place. It has got a very special loveliness about it that gives me great pleasure. Oh, and more than that.

R. saw Tommy at Cliveden on Thursday and said he looked well and was busy with his play. R. read a few pages of it and thought it quite good. T. has also written a golfing article for *Harper's Bazaar* – T. was at Cliveden for Easter. It is a young party; mostly Jakie's friends but I expect he'll enjoy it and there ought to be plenty of tennis anyway.

It's Easter Sunday today and we drove down to breakfast to find that the butler, Cripps, had decorated the table with an array of A HAPPY EASTER in flowers around a silver egg dish filled with dyed eggs! Mrs Grenfell has just gone off to church for the second time this morning. The rest of us are still digesting our breakfast and are going to play tennis at 11. I'm writing this with the sun pouring down my spine at the desk in the window. It is very pleasant.

———◆———

---

[1] Colonel Arthur Grenfell, Reggie's father, and Hilda, his stepmother, regularly took Nannau for their holidays. On this occasion they were accompanied by Reggie's sister Vera, brother Harry and half-sister Laura,* as well as Joyce and Reggie.

*April 24th, 1938* Parr's

About that Chez Beth bill. Can't you raise the money somehow and let me have it right away? It's been outstanding for over eight months and you really *MUST* do something about it or Maria [Koskill] must pay it herself. You know you haven't made much effort about it. I first wrote you at least two months ago and this last week's letter was the first time you even mentioned it. I'm sorry to harp on the subject but you must get orderly about debts.

———◆———

*May 1st, 1938*

Ford Manor,[1]
Lingfield,
Surrey.

The reason I didn't tell you about R. wanting a job was that I hoped he'd get one before long. Dinah [Brand] is exaggerating the situation. Col. G. [Grenfell]* hasn't lost all his money; R. is going to the office every day because there are still things to be done. What has happened is this: there was no more money to put into the gold mine and therefore work had to be stopped out there. This meant putting the company in the hands of receivers – whatever that may mean. Anyway R. has got a lot to do for the next few weeks in the office tidying up the Allatini Mine Company which is still in existence.[2] Meanwhile Uncle Bob is very sweetly looking out for something. But jobs are *very* scarce just now and I don't quite know what we'll have – maybe caretakers! We are not in the least low about it. It's been going on for so long now. Ever since Christmas. So you see there really was no point in putting it in letters to you because without a chance to talk about it you would probably think we were worse off than we are. But until things get settled I cannot make a definite plan about America this autumn. The point is that I must stick to the job until R. gets a job because we depend largely on my money just now.

Anyway you need not worry about us. We will always be alright.

Have you paid CHEZ BETH, because you've GOT TO AT ONCE. Maria has again written to me.

———◆———

[1] The home of the Spender Clays. Joyce spent happy holidays there when young, and it was at Ford, in 1927, that Joyce met Reggie, when she was seventeen.
[2] The Allatini Mine was in Yugoslavia. In December 1934 Joyce and Reggie had travelled to Yugoslavia for the official opening of this mine.

Rupert Hart-Davis and his wife Comfort are staying here this week-end. And John Phipps.[1] Rupert has grown rather fat, looks very well and is so happy. They live in a small house out at Highgate and have two small children – Bridget, three and Duff, one and a half. She is very intelligent, quiet, cosy and the perfect wife for Rupert. He is doing very well these days as a partner in Jonathan Cape's, the publishers. It's a pleasant party. No fuss. I wonder why some people evoke agitation and slight strain in the house while others simply fall into one's own line of living and it's relaxed fun to have them. The H.D.s are the latter sort. We seem to think alike about the essentials and there's an intellectual sympathy that I find very refreshing. Reg and Rupert talk endless cricket. We had to plan our day, yesterday, in order to listen in to the broadcasts from Lord's where the Australians were batting against the MCC.

We played some tennis in the morning, after I'd done the weekend shopping. It rained at intervals all day so two sets had to be played on the indoor court.

Uncle Waldorf isn't very well. He's in bed at St Jas. Squ. and won't be able to come to the party. It's supposed to be gallstones which is, I believe about *the* most painful thing you can have. Poor man. I've just spoken to Aunt N. for literally half a moment. She said it was awful seeing anyone in pain but that he had had a better day today. She said that I'm to wear her blue tiara tomorrow! I don't know why I feel so excited about this party. I suppose it's the King and Queen. I've got a schoolgirlish sensation about the whole thing. It should be lovely to look at, don't you think?

And that's about all I know. It is dusk – 9.30 p.m. – but R. is still in the garden!

*P.S.* Have you actually mailed that money? If not, you shouldn't be able to sleep at nights.

---

Summer is here at last. Simply lovely it is too. We've spent the whole day out of doors and are now pleasantly worn out with much tennis and sun. Of course the rain is still badly needed. But it's better to have sunny

---

[1] Joyce's cousin, son of Pa's sister Margaret, who married Edmund Phipps (no relation, in spite of having the same name).

rainless days than the boring grey days which do no one any good.

Tomorrow is Aunt N.'s royal party. My dress is a *dream*. We aren't dining; I've got to work first. But we are sleeping at St Jas. Square and so we'll go there after dinner and change. If I have a moment on Tuesday morning I'll write you a note after the party and tell you about it.

---

*June 6th, 1938*          Parr's

Well, the royal ball is over. Oh how heavenly it was! I have never enjoyed anything so much before. We spent the night at No 4 [St James's Square] and changed there before dining with Barbara Bevan.* Reg looked very handsome in his knee-breeches and white gloves. It's such a becoming costume; I wish we saw it more often. I wore my white dress again and Aunt N. lent me her turquoise tiara and ear-rings and brooch and Barbara lent me a pair of long white suede gloves. Virginia sent me a spray of white gardenias and lilies of the valley to wear on my coat – that long black taffeta one Nancy Tree gave me, with the white collar and cuffs. Before dinner we went down to say goodnight to Uncle Waldorf – who is *much* better. (Quite a remarkable healing it was.) Aunt N. was lying on the sofa in her dressing room while a girl from Eliz. Arden made her up. She looked lovely: very little colour, just enough rouge. Her dress, from Victor Stiebel,[1] sounds hideous but is really very lovely. White satin picture dress – very stiff slippersatin – with an over dress of very fine black lace. Red roses at the waist. Can you imagine it? It was good.

Aunt N. was dining with Nancy Tree. We found Maggie and Alex Alexander,[2] Pat and Kaitlin Bingham,[3] the Tom Veseys[4] and John[5] at our dinner. I sat between John and Pat. Barbara wore a pale green tulle dress and her mother's tiara – leaves in diamonds, rather high, very pretty. Maggie had on a lime green satin and her ma's second tiara – not so spectacular but very becoming. After a delicious

[1] Dress designer. He came into Joyce's professional life in the summer of 1942. From 1946 till 1951, when he retired, he made all her stage dresses.

[2] Major General, later Field Marshal and 1st Earl Alexander of Tunis. His wife, whom he married in 1931, was Lady Margaret Bingham, younger daughter of the 5th Earl of Lucan.

[3] George Charles Patrick (Pat), Lord Bingham; Major, Coldstream Guards, and his wife Kaitlin. He later became 6th Earl of Lucan. John Bingham was Lord Lucan's brother.

[4] Lieut. Col. Hon. Thomas Vesey, later Irish Guards, and his wife.

[5] John (Johnnie), husband of Barbara Bevan.

dinner – during which I risked nothing and tied my napkin around my neck – we went up to Barbara's room and did the final touches. I enjoyed wearing gloves – one feels so fresh and clean in them. Ordinarily my hands get so sticky. Then, down in the drawing-room again – we were all photographed by John Bingham. I haven't heard about the results but if they are good I'll certainly send you a copy.

We drove to the Palace in a car hired by Barbara and Johnnie. When we got to Hyde Park Corner poor Johnnie suddenly remembered he'd left his gloves behind so he had to get out and take a taxi while we went on not to lose our place in the queue. Actually there was no queue at all. We drove up, through the gates and into the inner courtyard without pause. Footmen with whitened heads and scarlet uniforms stood all over the hall. There were two special ones in high hats at the door and several elderly ones in black with long black sticks. We walked what seemed like miles to the cloakroom. There the housemaids all wore black silk dresses and white lace caps and each had her own coronation medal – one very old one had two if not three.

The ball was held in the big room where we were presented. Do you remember – it has three rows of red brocade-covered seats at different levels around it. At one end is the musicians' gallery, high up like a dress-circle. At the other are the two thrones on a dais. We got into the room in time to see the royal procession enter. Ambrose's Orchestra played soft incidental 'till-ready' music and then, down a distant corridor one could see something was happening. Away down the passage we saw them approach. The orchestra stopped its meanderings, struck a chord and played the National Anthem. Everyone stood up. In they came. The emotion was terrific. The King and Queen looked so *right*, so good, so lovely. She was wearing a white satin crinoline – a complete Victorian but with a pretty face. The blue Order of the Garter across was a gay touch. She had on a circular, rather high tiara. No one else could have gotten away with what was really complete fancy dress but she looked enchanting. There were no little kiss curls, just a plain hairdressing and that attractive intelligent face. He looked perfect too. It is astounding how much honesty and goodness do show in people's faces. One felt those two were there representing all that Edward could never have feigned to do. I was never so moved to fierce loyalty. Behind them came Queen Mary, magnificently upholstered in silver with immense jewels. Then the Kents, she looking lovely but, as usual, disagreeable. Then the Gloucesters – she charming in a cream-coloured satin picture dress he, at least, ordinary and nice if pretty ugly – if you can see what I mean!

They stood on the dais for the Anthem and then the band began playing 'Love walked in' and the King took the Queen on to the floor and began dancing with all eyes on them. As they passed near us the Queen signalled that we should begin to dance – Kents and Gloucesters were already at it. So couple by couple we started – 900 of us. So immense is the room that there was never the faintest sign of a squash. R. and I soon saw Daddy sitting with Aunt Pamela and Uncle Bill.[1] He came down to the floor and I danced with him while R. stood in an archway and watched. The vast proportions of the room made the company look tiny. Where an ordinary door arch is about ten feet high these were eighteen. And the ceiling was at least forty feet, I should think.

After dancing around once or twice we moved off the floor and connected with Reg once again. Then we three went in search of the picture gallery. We walked for miles – each long room giving into another. Great ornate rooms with little furniture but rather an amusing Victorianism about them all. The picture gallery is long and green walled. The pictures, mostly Dutch, are a wonderful collection. Lots of little interiors and a magnificent Rembrandt or two. Apart from there being a lot to see it was a wonderful party. All one's friends, dressed in their best – owned or borrowed – and the surroundings went to make it a grand evening. I can't remember who I danced with. David Lyon – Uncle Bill, Johnnie Bevan, Jimmie Smith[2] – I didn't know who. I had two suppers – one with Jimmie and one with Johnnie.

Nancy Tree was in completely Austrian fancy dress. A dirndl made of white silk organdie with a red velvet bodice and bands of red velvet around the skirt. Not quite right for her jewellery and the occasion, but a very gay dress.

Moggie Gage[3] was looking her best. A purple dress and diamond clips in her rather wiry curls. She's a changeable creature and that sort of looks always fascinates me. Good one minute plain the next. Patricia looked noble but rather dry. Lady Haddington[4] was attractive in a bright buttercup yellow satin picture dress with her heavy circular crown worn very forward in the Victorian manner. You've no idea how Victorian it all was. *The* dress of the year is that

---

[1] Pa's younger brother, W. D. (Bill) Phipps, was in the Navy. Pamela was his wife.
[2] The Hon James ('Jimmie') Smith, descendant of the founder of W. H. Smith and Son Ltd, and a Director.
[3] Wife of Viscount Gage; daughter of Lord Desborough (family name: Grenfell). The Desboroughs lived at Taplow Court and so were neighbours. She was called Imogen – hence 'Moggie'.
[4] Wife of Scottish peer.

satin one – and my pleated net one. Lady Diana Cooper,[1] Lady Titchfield,[2] the Duchess of Glos – all had it in different shades of yellow and Caroline Paget wore it in pillar-box red. I was the only one to wear the net dress that night but there had been several others at Aunt Nancy's party. We stayed till 3 a.m. – swept out in fact. So were Their Majesties! Quite unusual for them – but then this was a private party and *not* a State Ball.

The last hour was taken up with Viennese waltzes. Heavenly. R. and I spun round endlessly – it was perfect. A sort of marital exhibition – the King with the Queen, Reg with Alice, Patricia with Billy[3] – us, etc, etc.

The eggs and bacon supper felt good after that. I can truly say I've never enjoyed a party more in my life. It was all just right. Except for one false move – Ambrose had a female crooner in his band. One, Evelyn Dall, with a tough Bowery voice like a fog-horn. She hotted things up in a way that rather turned one's stomach. That was a bad touch and I don't know how it happened.

Aunt N. stayed till 3 too. So did the Lindberghs.[4] They are so charming. She is very friendly and gentle and he has all the quiet attraction one reads about. We met them here last year, remember.

It's lunchtime and I've been writing this for ages. Tommy and R. have just come in from playing billiards up at Cliveden. It's going to rain, I'm afraid.

I *love* my tea gown (the Palace party put it out of my head for the moment). It is so gay and just the perfect garment to wear on a hot night. Thank you *so* much for it. And for the Chez Beth dress – *Where is that money?*

How *could* you go North without sending it to me. That just isn't honest. The money you spent on fares *would easily have covered it.*

### PLEASE SEND IT

---

[1] The beautiful Lady Diana Manners who married Duff Cooper, Tory MP, later Viscount Norwich.
[2] Wife of the Marquess of Titchfield, elder son of the Duke of Portland. Formerly Maid of Honour to Queen Alexandra.
[3] William Henry Smith, 3rd Viscount Hambleden (a member of the W. H. Smith dynasty) and his wife, Lady Patricia (née Herbert), daughter of the 15th Earl of Pembroke.
[4] Col. Charles Lindbergh and his wife Anne. He flew alone from New York to Paris in 1927.

You said you had sent the money to Chez Beth so I wrote to Maria [Koskill] to find out if it had arrived and it hasn't. Where did you send it to? I think you'd better stop the cheque at your bank if it has actually left because otherwise it will be lost and you'll still be liable to pay that account. *Please do something about this will you? It's gone on so long.*

Last week was nothing but Outings. On Tuesday we had the Infant Welfare Mother's outing to an orchard in Farnham Royal. 250 of them *and* babies. It *just* didn't rain. I've never realised how heavy trays with cups of tea can be. Whew! On Thursday sixty mothers and sixty-five children from the Slough Nursery School came over to Cliveden for their outing. Once again it *just* didn't rain. They had games on the polo field, ice creams and candy, and were sent home with a fistful of flowers each. I was alone in charge of this affair but Eliz and Anne [Winn] came and helped and were very useful.

On Saturday we had our Buckinghamshire Women's Institute Rally and it *did* rain. And blow. Enid Lawson[1] lent Hall Barn, and 1600 of us turned up with macintoshes and umbrellas over our summer dresses. But it went off very well and we all worked like Blacks at rousing the placid Bucks women into enjoying themselves. The rally began with a procession of Banners – each WI has one and it was a great honour to be allowed to carry it. Three members from each WI formed a banner-party.

This was very gay and the rain kept off while it took place. Lady Desborough[2] opened the Rally. Then there were side-shows, a swimming display, an RAF drill display on the cricket pitch, a cricket match, an entertainment, teas, competitions, etc, etc. It was all to raise money for our county federation. We had a microphone for announcements and Enid and I couldn't be kept away from it for it was *such* fun to use! I was in charge of selling tickets for the entertainments and we had twelve performances and made £12-0-0 out of fourpences! Even your mathematical knowledge must realise how astonishing that is!

---

[1] Wife of Col. the Hon. Edward Frederick Lawson, son of Lord Burnham. He was general manager of the *Daily Telegraph*. They lived at Hall Farm, Beaconsfield.
[2] Lord and Lady Desborough lived at Taplow Court, near Cliveden.

We came here on Friday. It's the Holland–Martins' house. You know
that tall thin Ruby H.-M.[1] with a monocle, don't you? We used to
see him at Kelmarsh[2] in the old days. His mother is very attractive.
About seventy. Very energetic, intelligent, amusing and gay and the
father[3] is a character. Wears shirts with detachable sleeves and coats
without sleeves altogether and has a patent string contraption to hang
his hat from his lapel on a hot day in the city! There are five sons.
One was killed in the war. Only three of them are here this weekend
but the house is chock full of young things so that one finds three
sons-of-the-house enough. They are all very different; very good
manners, energy and humour.

We drove over from Taplow on Friday afternoon. It's the most
*lovely* trip across the Cotswolds with views over Oxfordshire vales
for miles on all sides. It's a good moment in the year with poppies,
purple mallow, yellow Stinking Willy and striped pink and white
convolvulus all garlanding the hedges.

This is a creamy yellow William and Mary house on the side of
Bredon Hill. Grass tennis courts just outside the dining room windows, a lovely open lawned garden to the south of the house and
beyond the wide swimming pool the vale of Evesham rolling in to
Gloucester. Just the sort of situation you'd love. Very cheerful, quiet
and open.

Yesterday morning we walked to the top of Bredon Hill and then
sat in the garden in the sun. (Summer is here, by way of a change.)
In the afternoon there was a great deal of very good tennis on the
grass courts. The noise of the balls pinging off grass is one of the
summeryest – and rarest – sounds I know. Afterwards we bathed
and the water was balmily warm.

When we'd had dinner we sat with all the windows wide to the
garden, so you can gather it really is hot for England. When the gents
joined us we had some community singing. It was rather fun. The
terrace was a good place for hymns so we moved out and rendered
some snappy harmonisings of all the well-known ones.

This morning it is warm and still hazy. Some of the party have
gone to church. There's a sound of humming coming across the

[1] Edward ('Ruby') Holland-Martin, banker.
[2] House belonging to Claude Lancaster, taken by Nancy and Ronald Tree for the
Pytchley Hunt season.
[3] R. M. Holland-Martin, CB, a banker and company director. He added the name
Martin to Holland by royal licence and inherited Overbury Court from his mother's
family, who were called Martin.

garden from the church which is practically next to the house. And the butler, in the dining room below my bedroom, is singing the 'Indian Love Call' and singing it rather well, for he is a Welshman. We are allowed to play tennis at twelve but not before, because the sound of the balls is said to distract the worshippers in the church! So I'm up in my room writing to you till it is time to change my shoes.

Thursday was a very busy and very hot day. I typed out my article before 10, then went over to High Wycombe for a WI committee meeting. Enid Lawson, Miss Serocold,[1] Alice and Maria [Brassey] came for lunch. In the afternoon we had a song practice of our WI for the autumn group festival. It was incredibly hot in the recreation room and we got flatter and flatter. One of our songs is called 'The Wild Brown Bee's my Lover'! I'm the conductor and Miss Serocold plays. Maria booms an octave lower than everyone else and none of them has any idea how to sing quietly.[2] They yell boldly and sound like cracked horns! After this hard work I went to tea at the Skimmings'[3] and ate a lot of very good Viennese cake made by the Viennese cook.

And on Friday we came down here.

Between the Committee on Thurs. and lunch I went back to Hall Barn with Enid to see the London Films take some shots in the garden. It seems that Geoffrey Toye[4] was talking to the director of Ruth Chatterton's[5] new picture about the Empress Josephine and he said that they must all go over to Malmaison to take some garden scenes. The London Film Co's studios are at Denham as you probably know; that is only about seven miles from Beaconsfield so Geoffrey Toye suggested that the director ask Enid's permission to use the garden at Hall Barn as they were designed by the same man that did the ones at Malmaison. 'Just a few shots of Miss Chatterton,' they said, so Enid agreed.

On Thursday at 8 a.m. when Enid and Fred were emerging from their swimming pool before breakfast *nineteen* cars drove up to the house! About ninety men got out and began preparing for Miss Chatterton's arrival. They had an enormous lorry with an electric plant in it and that was soon chugging away to make the necessary electricity. They put up a plaster pavilion and several statues about the lawns and fixed sound machines, cameras and chairs for the director and his aides.

[1] Miss Serocold lived in the village.
[2] The origin of Joyce's sketch, 'Committee'.
[3] The family of Joyce's childhood friend, Sylvia Skimming.*
[4] Conductor, and managing director of Covent Garden Opera from 1934–6.
[5] American stage and film actress; she appeared at the Globe Theatre, London, in *The Constant Wife* by Somerset Maugham, in 1937. The film was *A Royal Divorce*.

When Enid and I got back to Hall Barn the side of the bank looked like a mad dream of an inventor's. Wires, cables, lights, pulleys, arc lamps, etc all over the place, and in the cardboard pavilion, dressed in a pale Empire gown and coral pink shawl, sat Miss Chatterton, hideous in an all orange make-up. Enid and I sat silently on the grass and waited. And waited. It was then 12.30 and the company had been lined up since 9. But the sun had not obliged so they'd had to sit still. Suddenly it came out. Chaos. 'Bert, BERT! Sound!' 'Ready, Ed?' 'OK, this side!' etc, etc. And then Miss C., looking sullenly animated, said to an actor disguised as some Napoleonic aristocrat: 'And when do you leave for Dresden?' To which he answered, 'Tomorrow, Madame.' With that enormous scene done, all work was stopped. Miss C. drove away in a Daimler, make-up and all. The extras and electricians, etc, were fed with box lunches and ginger beer and Enid and I came away.

My God, I'm glad I'm not in the movies! Of all the soul-destroying industries that is the worst. The waiting, the extreme squalor of all the underlings engaged in it, the worn-out familiarities and the naked nastiness of one to the other. I do blame America and the Jews for degrading what might be a good thing. There's no control – or attempt at control – over tempers. It's the dominant yellers who win.

It's nearly 12 and there's a sound of activity below so I'm going to stop.

I hope you've having fun on your trip. *Have you paid Chez Beth yet?*

———◆———

Sandy Park House,
Chagford,
*August 21st, 1938*　　　　　　　　　　　Devon.[1]

I went to see the New York Theatre Guild Company in *Golden Boy*[2] last week at a matinée. It's a lovely play. And then all the Grenfells and us went to see Nicholas [Phipps's]* play *Spring Meeting*[3] which

---

[1] A hotel run by an Irishwoman, Miss Green: 'lovely small garden, and comfy beds, hot water and good plain food.'
[2] By Clifford Odets. At the St James's Theatre.
[3] Nicholas Phipps (Joyce's cousin) played Tony Fox-Collier in *Spring Meeting* by M. J. Farrell and John Perry. (M. J. Farrell was the pseudonym used by the Irish novelist, Molly Keane.) Produced at the Ambassadors; Margaret Rutherford played Aunt Bijou.

is incredibly funny. I don't remember ever seeing a funnier play. It's all very Irish; about a squire who raises race horses and neglects his motherless daughters, etc, etc. There's an elderly aunt in it – called Bijou – that you'd adore. A *little* mad, a little sad and wholly delightful to laugh at.

And now it's supper time and I'm *famished*.

---

*September [undated] 1938*                                                                    Parr's

We still don't know what is happening. The radio has been on almost continually and bulletins about Mr Chamberlain's movements come over at frequent intervals.[1] He got back from his second trip yesterday morning. We heard his aeroplane land at Heston and his few unrevealing words before driving straight to Downing St with Lord Halifax. Poor man, he must be worn out. From being a rather insignificant, gloomy-looking figure he has suddenly been transformed into a sort of Glamour Boy! The thing I admire about him is his courage – physical as well as moral. To put yourself into an aeroplane for the first time at seventy and get hurled across Europe is pretty good. His knowledge of music endears him to me; and he knows all about birds, too. Such men have integrity I feel, and I put my trust in 'em.

We talk of nothing but the 'situation' and the feeling of uncertainty is so potent that we can't settle to do anything. Even buying a hat is impossible. We just sit about waiting for news and I try to do a little constructive thinking and don't always succeed.

I cannot make up my mind whether it is better to have peace at any price or peace, through fighting, with honour. I don't believe in the latter; on the other hand it's damned silly to let Hitler get away with it yet again.

We hear very little about preparations in London but there are actually 900 anti-aircraft guns ready for action. All the tenants in Virginia's block of flats have been equipped with gas masks. Uncle Waldorf has sent all his pictures from St James's Square to Cliveden!

---

[1] On September 15th Chamberlain flew to Berchtesgaden to make a personal appeal to Hitler, in order to try to defuse the European situation. However, on September 24th, both Czechoslovakia and France mobilised and on the 28th the British Navy was mobilised. On September 29th Chamberlain, with Lord Halifax, the Foreign Secretary, flew to Munich, returning on October 1st to Heston airport, announcing that he had an agreement which meant 'Peace in our time'. Presumably Joyce wrote this letter on September 30th.

But you know what an alarmist he is. I absolutely refuse to do anything about Air Raid Precautions – I'd rather be blown up in a field than cower, masked, in a gas-filled house – wouldn't you?

━━◄●►━━

*October 1st, 1938*　　　　　　　　　　　　　　　　　　　　Parr's

Whew! What a week it's been. When I wrote to you on Monday things were just beginning to be really serious. When I lunched with Aunt Nancy at Cliveden that day word came through from London that evacuation was advisable. Several quite intelligent, unexcitable people thought that we might be attacked by air that night! By the Germans, one supposes. I left the lunch party to come back here in order to listen to a radio programme called 'Farewell Summer'. It was a particularly charming little programme, very peaceful and very English – about cricket and children having their final bathes of the holiday. Suddenly, the weight of fear and depression that hung over us all became too much for me and I burst into tears! The happy contrast of this radio programme seemed so very remote from the hideous present. I didn't have much of a cry, for Reggie's black labrador,[1] in a frenzy of perturbed affection, leapt at me and tried to be a lap dog. After tea I went up to Cliveden again to play tennis with Aunt Nancy. It rained a little and the news, at 6, was very bad. I telephoned to Betty to send the baby down to me. Tommy said they'd wait till the morning to see what Hitler had announced in Berlin. He – T. – was very funny, for, all of a sudden, the very seriousness of the situation had illumined reality for him and he was fully confident that the whole thing was simply evil screaming shrilly in the face of truth. He said, quite rightly, that good was bound to have the victory. All this from Tommy! It's funny how even the most sophisticated 'get' religion in times of stress! Even if it didn't last I should think he'd remember having once come almost in touch with reality.

　　It was impossible for me to work that evening. Fortunately there was nothing of importance to hear so, about 9, R. and I went up to Cliveden to hear what they all thought, and to get the literal translation of Hitler's speech from Carl Schintzler who was dining there. We found quite a big party. T. J. [Dr Thomas Jones]* and his sister, Mrs

[1] Reggie's labrador, 'with a tail like a windscreen-wiper', was called Nan, after Nannau, the house in North Wales where the Grenfells often took their holidays. Joyce had a spaniel, Gary (named after Gary Cooper), which was Ma's Christmas present to her in 1932.

Mackenzie, husband and daughter, another sister, Miss Jones, and
Alice and Reg and Bill, and the Lindberghs. We sat for hours listening
to the BBC's translation. Things felt horrid. One's feet were cold
and the uncertainty of everything made one yawny but not sleepy.
Colonel Lindbergh was pretty depressing, telling us how wonderful
the German air force is. He didn't think much of the Russian one; a
pity, for we were relying on them to make up our own rather small,
if efficient, air force. We left for home about 11, silent and not very
happy.

On Tuesday morning I tried to write. I tried to read. I tried to
order the food. I tried to concentrate, to think. It was quite impossible.
Virginia rang up to say that the maids were scared of living so high
up and if war came were going to leave. Could she come here? I said
of course. T. and B. decided to keep the baby a day longer. Maria
[Brassey] came to see me in the morning. All London had their gas
masks. It was a very cold looking day but actually, when you moved,
it was rather hot. There were radio bulletins all the time and one
couldn't resist them although one knew the news would be discom-
forting.

I lunched up at Cliveden with Aunt N., Jakie and Anne Lindbergh.
After lunch we listened to the Queen launching the new Cunarder,
*Queen Mary*.

*Sunday* (I've just sent you a cable for your birthday. It's a
pouring wet day here and we're huddling around the fire before
church.)

I daresay you will have seen the film of the launching. The broadcast
was particularly touching. The Queen sounded so alone somehow.
It was the first real speech she had made in public and her voice was
a pleasant surprise. After hearing this, Aunt N. sent Mrs Lindbergh
and me over to see Eric Kennington's memorial tomb for Lawrence
of Arabia. Mr Kennington[1] lives on the Chiltern Hills in a lovely
remote farm. We had tea with him and he showed us the statue. It
is perfectly beautiful. He's an extraordinary little man with a round
boyish face and a not always successful shave. He seems to leave out
certain bits. Under the chin for instance. The effect is very rustic. He
and Mrs Kennington were busily arranging accommodation for fifty
London children who were to have been evacuated. I enjoyed my
afternoon a lot. Mrs Lindbergh is a very remarkable person. To start
with she has a calm and the peace about her that is healing in itself.

[1] Official war artist in both wars. His recumbent effigy of T. E. Lawrence lies
in St Martin's Church, Wareham. Kennington lived at Homer House, Ipsden,
Oxfordshire.

She's enchanting to look at and although there are traces of suffering on her face it is quite unlined and she might be eighteen years old. We talked of poetry and music and of goodness. Somehow that last topic has been evident very strongly all these dark days.

Maria came to supper on Tuesday evening. Afterwards Reg went up to Cliveden to hear what they knew and thought of the PM's speech. On first hearing it we thought it a bit weak. But on reflection it was obviously just what needed saying. Some of the militant minded don't seem to realise that war cannot bring about peace. Ronnie Tree is one of these. To hear him yelling you'd think he was voicing a world opinion that the Germans must be taught a lesson. But they won't learn through violence. I'm sorry Hitler has had this bloodless victory. (Not that the bloodless part isn't a blessing; it's just that he's won again that is so bad.) But ANYTHING is better than bloodshed. I'd no idea how awful the feeling of war could be. One looked up at the sky and into the trees and thought – it *can't* ever come. But in one's heart there was a leaden certainty that the future was to be horrible. Even I felt this. It's a sort of mass hypnotism of course. But how seemingly powerful.

We didn't sleep very well that night! Reg began talking about joining the 9th Lancers and for the first time in my life I would have quite liked to die.

On Wednesday morning there was a rumour that the Germans would march at 2 p.m. More as a gesture of defiance than because I felt like it I decided to go up to London and a matinée with Virginia. Maria drove me up and we talked C. S. all the way. Do you remember the last section in the lesson on 'Unreality'? Look up *S & H*,[1] p. 263 – I *think*. The bit where it says about 'objects of creation which before were invisible will become visible'. Suddenly that illumined the whole situation. We'd been afraid of losing present beauties – flowers, peace, music, etc – and then we realised that the future couldn't take away anything. That the more we knew the more 'objects of creation' would become visible. That, at a time where one simply didn't see any future at all, was a big help. As we approached London the posters cried out that Roosevelt had sent another cable to Hitler. We bought a paper in Hammersmith High St and I read it out to Maria. The news that the 2 p.m. ultimatum had been false was encouraging. We felt a *lot* better by the time Maria dropped me at Daddy's office. Daddy said he supposed that as a good citizen he ought to gas-proof a room. The ARP [Air Raid Precautions] handbook said that one must remember that the raid would last perhaps for four hours and that preparations for sanitary arrangements

---

[1] Mary Baker Eddy's *Science and Health* (1875), the seminal Christian Science text.

should be made in a screened-off corner of the room. Nothing, said Daddy, would induce him to share a room for that purpose with Alice, his midget housekeeper! He'd rather take a chance, he said. He was in cheerful form and didn't believe that war would come.

I lunched with Virginia, her ma, and Antoinette Esher.[1] We swapped stories on the situation. V. and I went off to our matinée. It's a new play called *The Corn is Green*[2], all about Wales, and we *loved* it. We quite forgot about the outside world until just at the end of the last act. I must say I didn't much look forward to the evening press. The PM had made his speech to Parliament that afternoon while we sat in our pit, and we feared that the militant group might have forced us into war. But of course we found the happy news screaming on the posters – 'Hitler invites Powers to Munich Conference' – (not that that was the actual truth; of course the PM made the suggestion and Hitler fell for it. Thank God). Gin and I boarded our bus, armed with all three evening papers. Everyone looked happy; the sun was out for the first time in some days. We felt that the horrors were over. The enormous crowds in the Strand seemed gilded with happiness. The newspapers must have made mints. *Everyone* had a copy.

On Thursday the PM flew to Munich. That day I had to go up to the BBC to hear a recorded programme to lure young men into the air force. (Quite good too.) I lunched with Virginia, Elsie Suddaby and Jean Allen[3] at Swan & Edgar, and then we went to see Danielle Darrieux in *Rage of Paris*. That *is* a charming movie. Coming home on the train I began to wonder how the conference would end. For no reason I was more depressed that night than I'd been during the whole trouble. Reg went to see *Jezebel* in Slough with the Astors. I had my article to finish and type out so I stayed home. The radio announced that news of the conference hadn't come in but might do so at half past midnight. Still ridiculously fearful, I wouldn't wait up for it and we went to bed. Just as well, for the glad news didn't come through till about 3 a.m. And of course it *was* glad news.

When it was all settled our fears seemed remote. You can't imagine how curious it was to have felt, as I did from Mon – to Weds, that there was literally *no future*. Not merely – or Scientifically – that the present is the only reality, but that everything must stop, had stopped.

[1] Wife of 3rd Viscount Esher who was known for his interest in the theatre. He was Chairman of the Governors of the Old Vic.
[2] Emlyn Williams's autobiographical comedy in which Sybil Thorndike played Miss Moffat, a character based on his own teacher who got him to Oxford. It had opened at the Duchess on September 20th.
[3] Shared a house with Elsie Suddaby, a well-known soprano.

Seeing into the distance again was the nicest sensation I've ever felt.

I did nothing quite happily all Friday morning. My gas mask, sitting on the piano, looked only comic and not sinister. Lunch at Alice's was a gay affair. We laughed at our fears. Alice has entirely ruined her orchard by digging a large dug-out! My sole concession to preparation was the ordering of six dozen candles in case the lights failed. As they were not delivered by the time the peace was signed I cancelled the order and hadn't spent a sou on defence! In the late afternoon I went up to London to attend a prom-concert. R. was going to the Palladium with Jakie and a party, but I felt that Beethoven's Choral Symphony was a better peace celebration than a vaudeville programme. I had to queue up for half an hour in the rain and then stand throughout the concert. Three hours on me feet! But it was well worth it. What a joyful noise it was! Elsie was among the soloists and afterwards she, Jean and I went for supper to an aunt and uncle of Jean's in High Holborn. The uncle is very Scotch, about fifty-five, retired from rubber planting out East and is now in some City job. They warned me that he was Bohemian; that he might not be wearing socks! The flat was high in an old-fashioned block. The uncle wore a black velvet smoking jacket, open-necked silk shirt, and *no* socks! The aunt was attractive, about forty, and she gave us delicious home-made scones and very welcome hot tea. I enjoyed sitting down again as much as anything else! I caught the 11 o'clock train home and I must confess that with the crisis and my three-hour stand I was about all in. Ginny came down yesterday in time for lunch. R. spent the day shooting with Jakie.

Today it poured with rain. After church, which was packed with thanksgivers, we went to lunch with Sir Walford and Lady Davies. V. pleasant it was, too. He's Master of the King's Musick, you know. And a darling man. Margaret is nice too. After lunch we had a hotch-potch of music including 'Margaret Rose' (me and Gin), a new march for the London Fire Brigade (by Sir W.) and some Brahms and Handel.

We tea'd at Cliveden. Aunt N. says that Duff Cooper's[1] resignation is the hand of God; he hasn't drawn a sober breath for three months! That scandalous little libel may or may not be true.

By the way, Myra Hess, the pianist, is going to America in October till March. If she comes to Asheville or Spartanberg you *must* hear her. I told her that if she wanted a few days' quiet you'd love to have

---

[1] First Lord of the Admiralty when he resigned in protest at the Munich agreement; but by 1940 he was back in office, as Minister of Information (for a year only). From 1944–47 he was Ambassador to France. Created Viscount Norwich, he died in 1954, aged sixty-three.

her at 'Little Orchard'. She is the world's darling and such an artist. Jewish –

Well, thank God for the outcome of the nastiest week I've ever known – or want to know.

We are well and very pleased. Just tell any critics who murmur that we've 'let down' Czechoslovakia that they are a whole nation instead of an annihilated memory. Peace at Any Price is the answer. Chamberlain, bless him, is a great man –

---

*October 9th, 1938*          Parr's

First of all, in desperation, I have paid your account at Chez Beth. Maria wrote to me yet again and said that she was so short of funds could I possibly send the bill to you once more. I was so ashamed that I sent her a cheque by return of post. And now, please will you let me have the amount – £12-6-6 or 60 dollars – as soon as you can for I'm afraid I can't do without it.

Don't you feel badly now?

Well, never mind, only do please pay your debts, I don't want presents, really I don't, but it would be a lovely present to know that you didn't owe a penny anywhere. Now until that is the case will you *swear* not to send me anything for Christmas or birthdays? I don't *want* presents, knowing that you owe the money elsewhere. Please do that for me.

Nothing much has happened this week. We've slowly returned to normal and very nice too. One hears dissentient voices among the relieved but they are to be discounted for no one in his senses could fail to appreciate the situation in its true light.

What have we done lately?

I wrote to you last Monday. That afternoon I went to the Infant Welfare in Slough and worked very hard, for it was a busy afternoon. One mother took offence at being asked not to bring her whooping-coughing baby among the other children – thought we were insulting her. The more I see of these people the more certain I am that education – not revolution – is the *only* hope for their future. Their narrow stupidity is alarming. By education I don't mean only book-learning. But a wider, freer sense of citizenship and fellowship and *why* it's better to love your neighbour – and saner.

On Wednesday I lunched at Cliveden with Aunt N. She left afterwards for Plymouth via London. She's to be down there for two weeks. On Thursday we had Women's Institute and the demonstration was on Suitable Gifts for Christmas or the Bazaar Stall![1] Ye gods, if you could have seen the stuff! Birds made from pine cones, candlesticks made from old cotton reels, button holes from beech-nut husks (painted mauve and silver!) and then empty fish paste jars filled with bunches of daisies made by painting linen buttons and threading them on pipe cleaners! The women lapped it up, I'm sorry to say. Alice got the giggles and I nearly strangled *not* laughing.

Yesterday, Saturday, I spent the morning at the BBC, hearing a Priestley play that Celia was acting in. *Very* good. I dashed off a paragraph and sent it to the *Observer*.

AND PAY YOUR BILLS

---

*October 30th, 1938*     Parr's

I went up to London on Tuesday of last week to see Tommy before he went the next day. He and B. seemed quite congenial, I'm glad to say. Your grandson improves in looks and his charm increases. He has a new and very disarming parlour trick. You ask him if he wishes to go 'bye-byes'? And wherever he is he flops down and lays his head on whatever is to do for a pillow and there he remains with closed eyes for a time! His bottom does not always lie down. Its attitude of alertness rather adds to the turn.

I went to a concert at Londonderry House[2] with Tom Jones in aid of the Distressed Areas in S. Wales. When he asked me I did not think I'd be able to go. There was sure to be something I should hear [on the radio]. But no, there was nothing. So I asked Aunt N. if I could sleep the night at St Jas. Square because the fog was too thick to risk a late return down here. The concert was lovely. It had a lot of Gregynog[3] atmosphere and several Gregynog artists. Afterwards T. J. and Eirene[4] drove me back to St Jas. Square on their way to Westminster. How I dote on that man! He has opened

[1] Joyce's description of the WI demonstration obviously bore fruit. Certainly, it was the origin of her first professional sketch, 'Useful and Acceptable Gifts', gifts 'which were not only easy to *make*, but ever so easy to dispose of'.
[2] The London home of the Marquess of Londonderry. His wife was one of the most fashionable hostesses of her time.
[3] Gregynog Hall, Montgomeryshire, home of Miss Gwen and Miss Margaret Davies. They published limited editions and Gregynog was known for its summer music festivals. With Tom Jones and the Walford Daviesses, Joyce stayed at Gregynog which she found 'a mixed blessing. The music was unalloyed pleasure but the atmosphere of the house was cool, correct and daunting.'
[4] Jones (daughter of Tom Jones). In 1950, as Eirene White, Labour MP for East Flint.

up so much for me; in fact I owe him more than any other human being on earth. Through him I've met and made a whole new world of friends. Gregynog is the big thing in my year. And then there is now the Three Choirs Fest. Both mine through him. Tho' of course Gregynog is never a certainty and I've been incredibly lucky to have had three years of it. Maybe I shan't get asked next year. There's no reason on earth why I should be and the house holds a limited number. Anyway I *have been* three times and for those I'm grateful.

I left St Jas. Sq at 8 a.m. on Wednesday to catch an early train down to Taplow as I was going over to Aylesbury at 10 to the Half Yearly Council of the Women's Institute. Alice drove Miss Serocold, Diana Smith,* Mary [Brassey] and me over in her Bentley. After the business part of the day was concluded I ran a Spelling and Tongue Twisting Bee. It went quite well and there was a good deal of girlish giggling as the participants got tied up.

On Thursday morning I played three sets of singles with Aunt N. and she won them all! It really was a disgrace! She's jolly nearly sixty and is quite tireless. I did my very best – very inaccurately, I admit – and I managed to get two games in one set and three in the second and *none* in the third! I lunched up at Cliveden with Uncle Waldorf, Bobbie and Alice. Aunt N. was in London by that time, being godmother to Angela Laycock's[1] child.

---

Chewton Priory,[2]<br>Bath,<br>Somerset.

*December 4th, 1938*

Yes, all you say about my conception of Tommy is true. I've no excuses; you're quite right. I suppose it is his whole attitude that irritates me strongly. No good can come of this feeling, I agree. But from a maternal point of view you must admit that he is pretty trying. I can't make up my mind whether he and B. are through or not? He hasn't been in touch during the past few weeks, except to send Wilton a cable from Hollywood on his [first] birthday. No address given. Betty is now in Paris for a week with one of the Ward

[1] Angela Laycock (née Dudley Ward). Daughter of William Dudley Ward, Liberal MP, and his wife Freda, mistress of the Prince of Wales, and sister of Penelope Dudley Ward, the actress.
[2] Seat of the Waldegrave family. Geoffrey (Geoff) Waldegrave, who had succeeded his father as 12th Earl in 1936, was married to Reggie's eldest half-sister, Mary.

twins and his sister. I don't know what it all means. Their mode of living, their horizons, don't come anywhere near mine and we're completely out of touch – I telephone B. and she's always wonderfully cheerful, and about as expansive as an oyster. I've no idea what she thinks or does. The baby continues to thrive under the capable and affectionate hands of Nanny; but it's not a very good atmosphere for growing up. So abnormal and without those nice dull routines of family life. B. stays in bed all morning and doesn't see the baby. I don't know *when* she does see him actually. He seems fond of her when I've seen them together and she makes all the right noises at him but it's not as I think maternity should be! However he's their child, poor little thing.

Betty is going to America in January as you know and now she is trying to decide what to do about Nanny. She feels she can't afford to pay her passage and then, on top of that, American wages. She talks of looking after Wilton herself on the voyage and then getting an American nanny when she lands. I think that is probably the best plan. What happens about their apartment, I don't know. They have eighteen months lease to run and a big rent to pay. Their whole financial situation is a mystery – Daddy gave Betty some money last week because she was low and then her father cabled her some allowance I believe. But what a wretched hand-to-mouth existence! It's all wrong that they should ever have had Wilton – if Betty turns hard and goes her own way, as I think she will, or is doing, there's only one person to blame and that person is T.W.P. I suppose they'll both have to learn through suffering as they certainly don't through Science – Ah me, what an ugly mess – And in the middle of it that precious baby, pink and curly with square Phippsy hands and a solemn individual face.

Well, we had a very successful family wedding on Friday.[1] It was a perfect day, all blue sky and sun and Frances* looked a darling in her gold and white moiré gown with lace on her head and a red leather prayer book in her hand. I did the bridesmaids' dresses and they really were enchanting. Chalk white *velveteen*, which is dull and stiffer than velvet, with heart shaped necks, long sleeves and full skirts. On their heads wreaths of the brightest possible green leaves, real viridian green, mounted on scarlet ribbon with long streamers down their backs. The tinies had puffed sleeves and three red bows on the back of their bodices. The wedding was at St John's, Smith Square, in Westminster in the morning at 12.15. Mrs Grenfell had the hymn papers printed in red lettering on white and the whole effect was very gay and Christmassy. As a family they do have

---

[1] Frances Grenfell's wedding to Patrick Campbell-Preston.

cosy weddings! Afterwards there was a small luncheon reception at Chesham Place[1] and then the happy pair drove down to Heston to fly to Paris for a week or so.

I wore a new hat that I'd made myself. It's alright I swear – even Aunt N. thought it very pretty. It's made from a piece of red velveteen left over from my one evening dress and is simply a cap surrounded by my old black fur to match my old black fur coat. I also wore a new dress from John Lewis that was very cheap but extremely pretty, and will, I hope, be useful. It's black too.

What else did I do last week? I know it was a very full one. Let's see . . . Well, it began with Infant Welfare on Monday, as usual, and on Tuesday I went up to London for the day to look at the stuff we've had stored at the Pantechnicon since we moved from 21 and 28. Such junk – why we kept it I can't imagine. Odd pieces of china, half broken kitchenware, old brooms, kettles, a sack full of pillows! and of course those inevitable old trunks one of which has Granny's [Granny Phipps's] initials on it and which contains some of my baby clothes. We're selling the junk, giving Frances the furniture we shall never want – like the old kitchen table and chairs – a wedding present desk of incredible hideosity and some other odd pieces, and the trunks are coming down to Parr's next week for investigation. Of course I'm keeping the furniture Granny left me and anything else that is nice but it really is silly to hoard the rest of the stuff for it's extremely expensive and going to ruin in those vaults.

After that I went to see such a good movie called *Free to Live* with [Katharine] Hepburn and Cary Grant in it – I missed lunch and took a bun and a doughnut in with me wrapped in the most ear-splitting paper bag that exploded every time I foraged within for another mouthful! I got some dirty looks, I can tell you. Then for a bit of Christmas shopping and finally tea at Ginny's.

---

*December 18th, 1938*                                                Parr's

We're in the middle of a sensational nip. It's absolutely *freezing*; windy too. I took the dogs for a thirty-minute walk and it really hurt one's face to walk into the wind.

I'm alone this weekend as R. has again gone down to Chewton to shoot with Geoff [Waldegrave]. He is doing some business for Geoff in connection with reorganising his estates.

[1] Where Col. and Mrs Grenfell lived at this point.

Let's see what I did earlier in the week. I wrote to you on Sunday when Virginia was here. Next morning she and I drove up to London.

I did some shopping before lunching at 12.45 at Swan & Edgar by myself. I had it so early because I was going to sing with the choir at the memorial service for Lascelles Abercrombie[1] at St Martin-in-the-Fields and the rehearsal was at 2. I can never sing if I'm full and so I made do on a welsh rarebit and a cup of coffee. The service was at 3.30, after the rehearsal. It was all done by Walford Davies and the Misses Davies from Gregynog. They brought up about four members of the Gregynog choir and several friends supplemented them and the ensemble was really extraordinarily good. We were about sixteen. The whole service was beautifully free from gloom. The music quite *lovely*. Elsie Suddaby and Keith Falkner were the soloists and Elsie sang a bit out of Brahms's Requiem, with the choir doing an accompaniment. Professor Abercrombie's son read some of his father's poems.

After it was over, Elsie and I had a nice-cupper-tea at Lyons Corner House near Charing X. Then to the train, which R. missed! So I had to, too. I was furious, particularly as it was our wedding day. I don't know why that made me madder, but somehow it did.

However, he was very funny about it all and soon made me giggle in spite of myself, so I had to stop feeling furious. Nine years! Can you imagine it. Whew! I must say I can't ever remember *not* being married; all the same nine years is one hell of a long time (pardon!) and I must say it's been a very nice nine years. I've learned a lot and realise what a ninny I was nine years ago when I thought I knew *so* much.

On Wednesday morning I wrote some of my article and got it typed out before lunch.

On Thursday morning I went up to London with R. on the early train. We were spending the night with Aunt N. at St Jas. Square in order to go to a party with Virginia that evening.

Aunt M. [Margaret Phipps] had heard from Ruth who had a *terrific* success in Australia. Ruth didn't expect it and apparently rather dreaded going there but in the end had a lovely time and found very intelligent, appreciative audiences. Nicholas [Phipps] gets a week's holiday from his play [*Spring Meeting*] before Xmas. It's *the* big success in London and is booked for ages ahead so, anticipating the heavy work ahead, the management are very sensibly giving this pre-rush rest.

After lunch I bussed up to the Berkeley to meet Betty P. She has

[1] Georgian poet (1881–1938)

had a cable from Tommy, saying he's got a temporary job with Metro-Goldwyn and asking what her plans were and whether she needed money. She cabled him that she couldn't make plans till he told her more details and to please do so at once and, yes, she did need money. As you know her father is expecting her to go out to him in January. Whether to take Wilton or not is exercising her at the moment. She feels it may be only for two months and that seems so short to drag him all that way. I never advise her but in this case I did. I said that I thought she ought to have her child on the same side of the ocean as herself. If it was impossible to take him down to Palm Beach with her father – which I quite see – then I said I was sure you'd love to have him with you. Was I right? Wilton is well and behaved beautifully at Aunt N.'s party for Wissie's children a week or so ago. Wasn't there but B. says he didn't turn a hair even when Aunt N. focused all her somewhat concentrated attention on him.

I haven't heard any more from B. since Thursday so I don't know if she has made any further plans. I don't know what is to happen to the flat if she can't let it when she wants to go away. I'm sure she can't pay that big rent. Her whole finances are rather a mystery to me. She looks like a millionairess and seems to live like one. Sheer stockings, taxis, Antoine's, shopping at Fortnum & Mason! I dread to hear her debts – but maybe she hasn't got any. I know her father sends her something.

The dance on Thursday was quite something to look at. Lots of our young married friends there, piled up hair, a few crinolines, a good band and enough room to dance. It was in a house that is always rented for parties in Charles Street. We were six. Virginia, Barbara [Bevan] and I, Reggie, Francis Baring and Tony Thesiger, V.'s beau. She's obviously fallen for him and I pray he has for her. He's attracted, you can see that; but whether he means business or not I don't know. Gin has become very gentle and much slimmer and looks *so* attractive. *He's* an attractive young man. Tall and thin, with fairish brown curly hair and a small moustache. He's got humour and charm, and the right sort of shyness. He and R. got on like anything. Oh I *do* hope something comes of it. She sees a lot of him and I know she feels something she's never known before. It would hurt her terribly to love and not be loved. But perhaps he does love her. He's something of a bachelor though. Seems to have money. A lovely car and a flat in Arlington St near the Ritz.

I did my hair a new way that night. I'll see if I can draw it. [Reproduced opposite.]

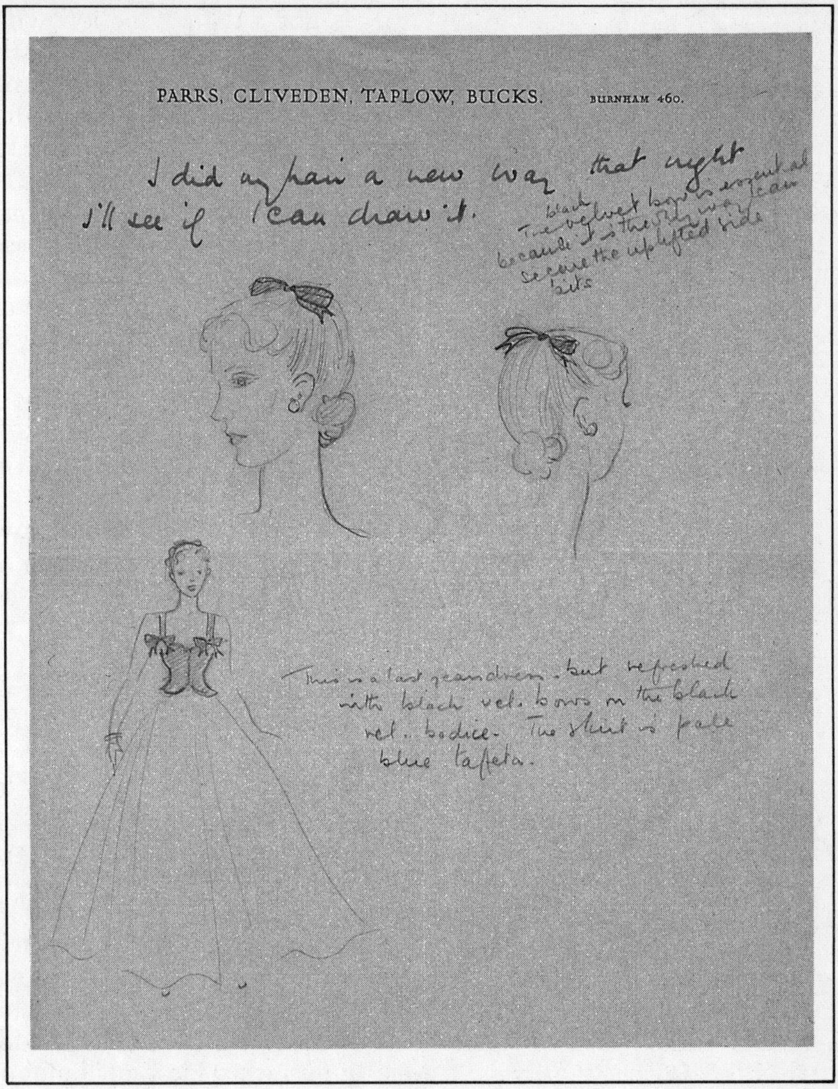


*December 18th, 1938*

*1939*

In 1939 Joyce turned her talents from being a popular guest ready to do a 'party turn' by singing a song or telling an amusing anecdote to becoming a professional entertainer. On Friday, January 13th, she met Herbert Farjeon and, as she says, 'the direction of my life was changed'.

At the beginning of 1939 the British government were confident that, thanks to their efforts at peacekeeping the previous year, combined with accelerated rearmament measures, world peace was assured for many years to come. When German troops marched into Czechoslovakia on March 18th, after the Slovaks had declared their independence, Chamberlain informed the House of Commons that this declaration had nullified the guarantee he had given in the Munich agreement to protect the Czechs against aggression. On March 29th, however, Chamberlain sent Poland an offer to support her against any action which threatened her independence. This offer could only have been made good with Russian support, and with the signing of the Ribbentrop–Molotov pact in Moscow in August the threat to Polish independence was clear and war became inevitable. Though Joyce hastens to reassure Ma, in her letter of August 30th that 'it don't smell like war' and the 'wretched Germans are in a dreadful situation', she also adds, 'We are fully prepared and the feeling here is . . . calm and ready.'

War was declared on September 3rd and entered its first phase: the phoney war.

# 1939

Well, the first item of news is that Betty is letting me have Wilton while she goes to America! At the moment he is visiting David Winn[1] and as there is but three months between them they are having a grand time together. Their evening bath and previous naked gambol are two events well worth seeing. The Nannies get on, I think, so that, too, is a happy thing. Betty was going to take Wilton over alone, leaving Nanny and she was upset at the idea of him going away from her just now when he's teething and being left with a stranger in Philadelphia while Betty went to Palm Beach with her father. So I did a lot of thinking and asked Reggie what he felt about it and then asked B. if she would leave Wilton and Nanny with me and she said yes. So that's fine.

He really is rather good just now. He walks, as you know, and rolls about a good deal in a nautical manner, making weird noises that are efforts at conversation and blowing out his scarlet cheeks with this effort. Already being with David has done him a lot of good. He is less shy, less fractious and, in consequence, happier. I like that silent Nanny very much. Her devotion to the baby is remarkable and I can't think how Betty could think of losing her. She's so calm and quiet and she keeps him so well and so attractive.

Betty was down here for the weekend and we had several good talks. She's a nice creature under that veneer of worldliness. If Tommy had been an ordinary husband with affection and quiet and if they had led a normal life Betty would be quite different. As it is she has hardened in defence. (I don't say she didn't start with a certain amount of hardness but with warmth that would have changed. As it is it has intensified.) Anyway she is apparently devoted to Tommy and loves Wilton in her own rather detached fashion.

Of one thing she is determined: and that is that her child won't be

[1] Reginald and Alice Winn's son.

spoiled as she thinks Tommy was. This may lead in the opposite direction. I don't know. Anyway, I feel it is essential for that baby to have cosiness and warmth at this stage and I believe that Nanny and I can give it to him. I'm leaving him with Alice for a while as it is such an admirable arrangement but when he comes here he'll have the double room as his nursery and Lefty's little room as his night nursery. It can just be done. Betty, of course, is paying Nanny and I'll manage the rest with possible assistance from Pa.

Aunt N. wasn't well last week and lost her voice as the result of her cold. This necessitated cancelling an engagement in Plymouth and of course the papers got hold of it and made the most of such an opportunity. She's quite all right now and is probably off to St Moritz on Wednesday or Thursday with Uncle Waldorf.

Last week saw the estate ball. As usual it was 'Fancy Dress' but, out of the ordinary, the family wore costumes too. Reggie and I were sitting down to our frugal meal at 7.30 when a message arrived from Cliveden to tell us that the family were dressing up. We hadn't anything in the house but about 9 we went upstairs and looked in our cupboards. The result was pretty horrible I must confess and you'd have hated to see us! To start with we powdered our eyelashes and pinked our noses to look thoroughly dyspeptic. (We were alike in every detail.) Then we parted our hair in the middle and slicked it into two undertaker's scallops. Then we had handle bar mustachios and little imperial beards, parted by protuberant false teeth. Wing collars, bow ties, morning coats, white flannel trousers rolled to look *just* too short, plaid socks and black shoes. Oh yes, and glasses and hats.

Lefty would have appreciated our appearances but I think you would probably have wept to see us. I must confess that we did look pretty unattractive. I don't know what we were meant to be but we were quite funny and almost unrecognisable. Arthur was his usual extraordinary Pantomime-ish dame. Rose was a washerwoman. Blyth took a prize as a baby! And Bert Jeffries had another as an ingenious two-way facing old woman. I can't explain it more than that. He was built out to look as if he faced both ways and wore two masks . . .

Of course in the end, we found the family *hadn't* dressed up except for the children. However we didn't mind.

I stayed here all last week but am up to London tomorrow. It's strange, balmy weather. I saw a snowdrop yesterday.

(we were alike in every detail.) Then we
parted our hair in the middle and slicked
it into two Undertakers scallops. (See picture!)
Then we had handle bar mustachios and
little imperial beards, parted by protuberant
false teeth. Wing collars, bow ties, morning
coats, white flannel trousers rolled to look
just too short, plaid socks and black shoes.
Oh yes, and glasses and hats.

Lefty would have
appreciated our appearances
but I think you would
probably have wept to see
us. I must confess that
we did look pretty unattractive
I don't know what we were
meant to be but we were
quite funny and almost
unrecognisable.
Arthur was his usual
extraordinary Pantomime-ish
dame. Rose was a
washerwoman. Blyth took
a prize as a baby! And
Bert Jeffries had another
as an ingenious two-way
facing woman. I can't
explain it more than that He

*January 9th, 1939*

Well, what do you think of the news about Ginny? Isn't it fun? Tony [Thesiger] is thirty-two, tall – rather on Reggie's lines but holds himself better – has humour, gentleness, charm, *money*, and is absolutely perfect for Gin. He has lived for ten years in Burma, looking after his family's tea and teak business. His pa and ma are elderly and live in Cranley Gardens, Kensington, where they have been for thirty-four years! Virginia is meeting them and is in a tizzy about what to wear, how to be, etc. You wouldn't know the girl! She's aglow all over and looks so pretty and radiant and is so gentle and romantic and altogether heavenly. She came down here yesterday for the day and night while Tony fulfilled an old engagement of a shooting party in Hampshire. It all happened on Thursday evening about 6.30, I gather. She went around to his flat after a tea party at Madame Van Swinderen's[1] and there it happened. I haven't liked to press the point too much but I rather think he said 'Shall we get married' and I know her answer was in the affirmative.

She is quite dazed and can't believe it's true. Never thought she'd fall in love and of course, has, like a ton of bricks. You'll love Tony. Reggie took to him at once and so did I. Dorothy Graham couldn't believe it when Gin told her that he was quite well off and said that no *nice* young man ever had more than £500 a year. Nor do they as a general rule. But Tony's the exception. At the moment he is living in a very grand flat in Arlington House, Arlington Street, just by the Ritz. But it's only a small bachelor service place and the lease is a short one.

The plans, so far as I can make them out, are as follows: A 'white' wedding about the first week in March. (Unless the old folks think things about Lent in which case it will have to be before March 1st.) No bridesmaids but a row of small boys. Honeymoon at Norah Smith's villa near Pisa in Italy? Possible extended trip that might include America but this last is largely a dream and she doesn't know whether T[ony] can take time off for so much. What else do I know? He's got a Bentley car and plays good golf. Sings a good deal (in the car) – mostly unknown songs, Gin says, that men know, with sort of Winchester choruses about 'old Johnny Bradleum' kind of things. Says he'd like concerts he thinks but doesn't know about them. Doesn't mind V. being C.S. Is thoroughly tolerant, gentle, honest, sweet, head-over-heels in love with the girl and silly enough to play

[1] English wife of Junkheer Van Swinderen, Netherlands Ambassador.

crazy games like Lefty – you know – can do nonsense and what Gin calls 'play bears'.

Gin says he's as lazy as she is and likes the theatre and dancing as much as she does. She doesn't know what he reads and says he has no tiresome views on politics or religion. In fact he's OK.

Think he sounds nice?

Oh, something else: he loves his old parents. Was at Winchester. (I've said that before, perhaps?)

Have I told you that Barbara [Bevan] plotted the whole romance when she first met Tony in India two years ago? Such schemes rarely come off but this one has. Last June she said to me that a young man called T. T. was coming home after ten years in the East and that she believed he'd do for V. so when she and Johnny took a house near North Berwick last August for a month she asked them both to stay, having previously had them both to dinner and seen that they seemed to get on quite well.

And all the autumn it's gone on steadily and I knew the girl was feeling something foreign and was *so* tactful about it and now she says she was holding herself in so as not to get hurt in case it was all a dream and how *could* I have noticed anything?!

She came down here yesterday armed with a large photograph and we talked of nothing else but the engagement. Norah and Maria[1] motored over after lunch and we went over it all again and Gin had to go and visit R. Winn, just returned from his appendix operation, and tell him all. Till last night, she says, she hadn't been able to sleep a wink but this quiet cot did the trick and she slept like a log.

It's rather sad for her ma. You know how she dotes on Gin. Of course she is absolutely delighted at the same time and loves Tony; but it will be a wrench and lonely. However these things will happen and the joy of Virginia's happiness and the realisation that Harry [Graham: 1874–1936] would have been so pleased is going to be a big help.

Meanwhile I can't do a jot of work or think of anything else.

Can you imagine it? – Tony has never heard V. play the piano! I don't even know whether he knows she does. They've met mostly for lunches and dinners and twosomes at theatres, I believe. She spent three solid hours having a permanent on Wednesday and got engaged on Thursday. Now she says it must have been a premonition that made her get it done and out of the way before the excitement began!

---

[1] Norah was Maria Brassey's mother.

It isn't announced yet; but after this afternoon's tea party they'll put it in the papers, probably on Wednesday.

I don't remember what else has happened.

We went to a BBC concert party on Friday night. Stephen Potter* is *the* coming man in the 'feature' department and his wife is an artist – a good 'un too. We originally met them with Phyllis* and Phil Nichols,[1] before Christmas. They live in a tiny eighteenth-century house in Chiswick Mall, just a few doors down from Mrs Benson's Walpole House.[2] There were about ten of us for supper in the drawing room. White, with white curtains and one scarlet-patterned chintz chair and two white-covered divans that must have been beds in disguise. Three of her pictures, in light wood frames, hung on the walls and there were books and a hot fire and spring flowers and delicious Austrian food. We just sat and talked and later people did turns. I've, quite accidentally, evolved a new one. It happened the evening we dined with the Nichols's to meet the Potters. I'd come up from a Women's Institute meeting where our lecture-demonstration had been on 'Useful and Acceptable Gifts'[3] and had been a first-class subject to be funny about anyway and the lady who did it that day was a classic example for copy. Well, I told them about her – with illustrations – and then forgot about it, but on Friday night they said, 'You must do the Women's Institute woman' and after breaking the ice with 'Princess Margaret Rose' I launched, quite unprepared, into this WI demonstration. And, as sometimes happens, I got carried away, I said things I didn't even know I knew and was really quite funny. Sitting in a corner by the fire was a tall thin man in glasses, about forty-five, who turned out to be Herbert Farjeon,* who wrote that very witty revue *Nine Sharp* that is just coming to an end after a phenomenal run. He is now engaged on another to follow it and after I'd sat down he asked me who had written the 'sketch' I'd just done as he thought he could use it in his revue! So I told him it was just made up as I went along and he asked me if I'd come and see him about it. So on Wednesday I'm toiling up to St John's Wood to lunch with him and his wife to meet Charlotte Leigh[4] who does the sort of thing I do, but professionally, and I'm to do it again. At the moment my mind is quite blank and I don't remember a thing I've said so I'm going to try and collect my thoughts and

[1] Philip Nichols was married to Phyllis Spender Clay. A diplomatist, Minister to the Czechoslovak Government in London, 1942–47, he was knighted in 1946.
[2] In Chiswick Mall. Mrs Benson was, before her marriage to Guy Benson, a director of the London Assurance, Lady Violet, second daughter of the 8th Duke of Rutland, and widow of Lord Elcho.
[3] For Joyce's description of the WI demonstration, see pp. 58–9.
[4] Charlotte Leigh appeared in *Nine Sharp* and was to be in *The Little Revue*.

write them down before I go on Wednesday. Rather fun even if it doesn't come off. Driving home from Chiswick at 12.30 a.m. through thick fog was not the right ending to a very pleasant party. However we found this district quite clear and got to bed by 2.

---

*January 23rd, 1939*                                               Parr's

D'you remember I told you something about meeting Herbert Farjeon at a party and doing a sketch about a Women's Institute lecturer? And he asked to see it on paper with a view to doing it in his new revue. Well I went to lunch with him and Mrs Farjeon in their attractive house in St John's Wood last Wednesday to meet Charlotte Leigh who does the sort of thing I do, in revues. I did the turn and it seems they *do* want it for the new show in March! What's more I told him I had a friend who wrote songs, etc, etc, and the result is that he is coming to lunch with Virginia on Friday to hear some of them! It may come to nothing; on the other hand it may turn out to be a start for both of us. I forgot to tell you that Mr Farjeon actually wanted me to come into the revue but I didn't think I'd be good on a stage. I may do alright in a small room; but the stage is quite different. Anyway he wrote to me and said that if ever I did want to I must let him know at once whether tomorrow morning or in five years' time! Nice, that. He's a most charming man. About fifty, very quiet, intellectual and with something very attractive about him.

I've really very little news because I wrote you such a fat letter last week. Nothing has happened since then. On Thursday I had Prof. and Mrs Katay, Austrian refugees, for the day. They are staying with the Walford Davies's and are charming. He is part Jew; she is not at all Jewish. They have lost *everything*. He is a choirmaster, conductor, organist, about fifty-five. She is thirty-eight I should think, rather pretty with red-gold hair and vivacity. Her spirits are indomitable but he is a broken man: his three best friends were murdered in Vienna. It is all so ugly that one can hardly believe it to be true. And of course, in Science, it isn't. But they, poor devils, don't know that, though someday I suppose they will. They speak little English and I have no German but somehow we managed quite well and had a pleasant time together. Walking in the woods at Cliveden he looked up at the bare beech trees and said very haltingly: 'This – make well soul ill.'

It is heart-breaking to see them. What is their future? They can't be employed here except as domestic servants. They are going to such a post next Thursday for a month. But it *can't* work. He isn't strong enough and she isn't a servant. They had two houses in Austria and maids of their own, I suppose.

━━━◆◈◆━━━

*January 30th, 1939*                                              Parr's

I'm writing this against time for I've got to go and meet Dorothy Gillespie[1] off the lunch time train in a moment and there's so much to say that I don't know where to start.

Well, first of all you may be interested to hear that I've had a serious and even imploring offer to go on the stage!

You know I told you all about Herbert Farjeon taking my sketch of the Women's Institute woman for his new revue in May? Well, now he wants me to actually do it. *And* to sing Virginia's songs. I'm still a bit bewildered by it and if it didn't seem madness to refuse the offer I'd dismiss the whole thing, only Mr F. said so many nice things and seems convinced that I would do well on the stage that I'm putting the whole problem to God and waiting to see how it all works out. You see I don't particularly want to go on the stage nor do I want to lose my lovely *Observer* job. Mr Farjeon believes I could do both by having a radio in the theatre! You see, the revue wouldn't begin till 9 p.m. and he'd arrange for me to have a late 'spot' in the first half and another in the second so you see I think it could just be done. Meanwhile I'm writing to Mr Garvin to ask him if I may come and talk to him about it all. He may be dead against it and if he is then I'll give up the idea, for radio comes first with me and always will. *I love the work.* However if he says I may try it and it works out in all the ways I'll give it a try.

Surprisingly enough both R. and Daddy want me to!

Mr Farjeon isn't a bit theatre-y. He's actually very intellectual, an ardent pacifist – in fact he was a Conscientious Objector in the last war – and I'd love to work with and for him. He is the author of the revue. I don't know who'll produce it. I've told him that I don't think I'm the right type for the stage; that doing amusing turns in a drawing room to an appreciative audience is quite a different cup of tea to doing it in a theatre. Anyway the point is to try me out at rehearsals and if I'm no use to get rid of me and no hard feelings on either side.

━━━◆◈◆━━━

[1] Schoolfriend of Joyce's.

To my own news. First of all R.'s job *is* certain. And he starts with Oliver Lyttelton[1] in about two weeks. It is so nice, isn't it? Then, I've decided to do this stage thing! I do wonder what you think about it all? It's taken me ages to get it straight in my mind but at last I've come to the conclusion that, after all, the experience would be of great value to me in lots of ways. To my great surprise Mr Garvin *and* Uncle Waldorf are both in favour of me doing it. Somehow I was sure they'd frown on it, but no. I went up to St John's Wood on Friday to talk it over with Mr Farjeon and I must say I could hardly have felt less enthusiastic about anything. There was a thick and heavy fog; I had a cold and felt horrible and couldn't imagine being funny at all. I told Mr F. how uneasy I felt about it and he was very understanding and nice and told me to go away and think it all over for another two days. My cold got alright again, the sun shone, Garve approved, as did Uncle W. – and I said I'd do it.

It means signing on for three months with a two-week notice option for either party. It means joining Equity! It means having a small radio installed in Mr Farjeon's office at the theatre where I can go any evening after 6 till it is time for me to get ready. It means taking the 11.45 from Pad. every night. It means getting an extra car or conveyance or some sort, for R. can't wait up to meet that late train and I can't get up in time to take him to the 8.30 – which it will probably be with the new job. It means lots of inconvenience and yet I think – R. does too – that it would be nonsense not to try it.

Mr F. has an idea that my real future is on the Ruth Draper kind of platform! He visualises running matinées for me and Elizabeth Pollock[2] (imitates) – and perhaps one other single turn. *That* would be fun, for it wouldn't cut into my life at all. There is bound to be some discomfort with this adventure but if it turns out successfully it will have been very worthwhile and if it is a failure I can always count it as experience.

Mr F. wants me to appear three times. Now he isn't so sure about Gin's songs as he thinks they may be too slight for Part II and he has no room in Part I. I feel badly about that, for the very reason I originally considered the plan was to do the songs. I'm to do this Women's Institute act, alone; appear in a musical sketch that is *charming*. It's called 'Looking at the Lightning' and is about a very

---

[1] Chairman of a mining company in North Wales, and Controller of Non-Ferrous Metals, Ministry of Supply, until 1940. Later he held important posts in the War Cabinet and in Churchill's 1951–55 Government. He was created Viscount Chandos and became Chairman of Associated Electrical Industries.
[2] Actress and mimic. She appeared in *Nine Sharp*.

hot night at that unbearable moment before rain falls and the storm breaks. In the sketch it does break and the relief is tremendous – the lovely smell, the relieved sound of falling rain, etc. That's about all. It's for three girls' voices. And the third thing is to be either another single item for me or a duologue with a man. There's an idea – I like it – of doing 'Conversations at Parties' and I'm trying to write one down about a couple of pros – a writer and a broadcaster (!) discussing each other's work with that mixture of humility and egoism.

The money is about fifty dollars a week. Not a lot in American theatreland but it's about right for an unknown in London. The whole thing is run on a co-operative basis. Everyone inside the theatre gets £5-0-0 and then, over it, a percentage on the takings. I like the system; it's so obviously fair. My percentage should come to a bit over £11 – which is about fifty-five dollars.

And that's about all I know at the moment about it.

Both Daddy and Reggie have encouraged me to do it and so I feel I'm at liberty to do so. I don't think I'll call myself Joyce Grenfell as that might confuse my radio life! So I'm trying to decide what to be.

Joyce Phipps?

Jane Phipps?

Grace Gunshell – as I once was, by mistake, on the telephone! (*I love it*; but don't worry, I won't.)

or Jane Wilton?

Talking of Wilton – I haven't seen him since last week because of my cold. It's quite gone this evening so I'll probably get to see him tomorrow or Tuesday.

By the way, he comes here on the 14th.

If I'm doing this revue I think that perhaps T. and Betty ought to take him as my hours will be so strange then and I'll see him so little.

We start rehearsing on March 20th and open four weeks later – April 20th. (Hark at me!)

Aunt N. got back from Switzerland this evening and we are dining up at Cliveden to see her in about an hour.

Spring poked a nose in today. We found violets, snowdrops and primroses this afternoon. It was a delicious day. R. worked in the garden all morning.

---

*February 12th, 1939*                                                    Parr's

As I write this Tony and Virginia are sitting on the yellow sofa in the sun. It's nearly lunchtime – Sunday – and they are reading. The more we see the lucky man the more we like him. You will, too,

I'm sure. It's just under a month now to the wedding.[1] What are you giving them? We're getting some symphonies on records – they come in sets and that's what they want.

*Next day*. It maddeningly was lunchtime and I had to stop writing. We spent the afternoon playing tennis in the indoor court and the rest of the time reading, playing Racing Demon and listening to the radio. Tony fits in beautifully. He appears to be perfectly happy in our milieu and enjoys doing nothing just as we all do. Virginia is a new woman and I've never seen her happier.

Wilton moves in tomorrow and at the moment I can hear Rene [Easden]* over my head giving the room a good brush out.

As for my career? At the moment nothing more has happened. It will be uneventful now until March 20th when we start our rehearsing! Mr Farjeon wrote last week to say that he thought I should make two definite and important solo appearances. To do two monologues. One is to be this woman who lectures on Useful and Acceptable Gifts and the other – ? Well I hoped to do the schoolgirl but Mr F. has written a fairly serious song for Hermione Baddeley[2] to sing and that is about a schoolgirl doing her homework so he says he'd rather have something else from me. I'm trying therefore to make another monologue for that type of girl. Perhaps she can be a Brown Owl at a Brownie's camp? I'm not sure yet. In the meantime I've worked up quite a good one about a mother entertaining her two children in the drawing room after tea. (Based on Alice and all the mothers generally!) She is showing a fourteen-month-old child a book: 'Car-car? John-John say car-car? CAR?' Etc, Etc, Etc. I've got another character, Susan, aged about four. She is bored with the baby and a little jealous. My main aim at the moment is not to do anything *remotely* like Ruth. Not easy, because I find she knows and does everything. But this very English mother is, I hope, something different. Then I've another idea – an English chaperone on the beach. And perhaps a little spinster who runs a fancy goods shop in some country village. I'm going to do a lot of work on all these this week before the Farjeons come down for the day next Sunday. Then I'll try them out on Mr F. and we can see how they go. It's all rather fun, don't you think?

I'm so glad you were such a success at the Damrosch party. Perhaps you'll get lots more as a result? You'll have to make a definite season otherwise you'll spend all your profit and time training to and from

[1] Virginia and Tony were married on March 9th, 1939, in St George's, Hanover Square. Joyce's letter to Ma describing the wedding is, unfortunately, missing.
[2] Revue comedienne of great versatility. Known as Totie, she was the sister of Angela Baddeley.

NY. Isn't it fun, though, when things begin to hum? It's all part of activity in mind; I'm sure of it. It's what ought to happen all the time.

———◦◉◦———

*February 20th, 1939*                                                    Parr's

A good letter from you a few days ago. I'm so glad you were such a success at the birthday party and got all those exciting offers. I quite see why you refused the Rainbow Room but surely there must be other openings – radio? concerts? Anyway, it is most exciting.

Mr and Mrs Farjeon came down yesterday for the day. It was sunny and clear and lovely and after lunch we went for a long walk down by the river and up in the wood and by the house. By the river we found violets, snowdrops and primroses growing in the disused garden of old Rose Cottage.

My plans for the revue were discussed at length and we finally decided to let me do only my own stuff and not sing in the sketch as originally planned. This is, of course, much chic-er. To appear quite independently and quite alone is far more important than if I took a hand in the other parts of the revue. At the moment I'm going to do the Women's Institute woman in the first half and a thing which I'm calling 'Mothers' in the second. It is to be five very brief sketches of mothers. So far I've got an ordinary young English mother showing a picture book to her baby. Then there's the American wife of an Englishman bringing out a daughter. And I've got a v. silly smart mother who is still rather vague in my mind; and perhaps a 'tired mother'? And I'm going to end with that hideous village woman I do with my tongue stuck in my lower lip[1] – they may be rather fun if I can work them up well. I intend to get on to them this week and write down what I feel at the time. One must have a foundation to go on; to learn by heart –

I rather imagine I shall be wearing an evening dress and not disguise – anyway I hope so.

Wilton is here. He moved in last Tuesday and is now thoroughly established in his 'suite' upstairs. He takes a certain amount of time to get used to places and people and I was very tactful with him for the first few days. Now he is used to me and the house and all is well. He's a very attractive child and full of initiative and alertness. Nanny is so nice and quiet and good with him and her

---

[1] Eventually became the sketch, 'A Terrible Worrier'.

devotion is really quite wonderful. So far all goes well between the kitchen and nursery except that Winnie, my widow-cook, being herself the mother of two, thinks she knows more than Nanny about what he should eat. I'm doing my best to smooth out that little riffle and I'm sure it will be all right for they are both such nice women.

----------❦----------

'Street Acre',
St Nicholas-at-Wade,
Kent.

*March 18th, 1939*

We are staying the weekend with Tom Jones. It's a v. attractive little house about ten miles from Sandwich. The party is: T.J., his daughter, Eirene, Mr Merryfield, a sculptor, and ourselves.

We had a cosy cottagey breakfast and cleared the table and then went for a leisurely walk into the village for daily papers and some candy. It snowed on us, we didn't stay out long but popped into the church which is v. old and lovely. A nice big light Norman building with some good tombs and, to my surprise, a plaque in memory of Lady Bridges.

Back here to do the X-word and read Chamberlain's speech. I may be wrong but I don't feel any of the tension or war fear that we felt in September. No one seems excited but there is a determined calm and a confidence that is comforting and, I think, inspiring.

I did my two days' Wilton service last week. From 10 a.m. on the 15th till 8 p.m. on the 16th I took charge and I may admit that I was all in by the time I'd done. It's the potting that wears one; all those buttons and his resentment at the idea anyway. And the meals. Every mouthful has to be engineered into his mouth without him noticing. The first half dozen are easy; then he gets bored and only by the most brilliant diplomacy can one clear the plate. He was very good and extremely attractive and I loved him. But all the same I believe I'm glad I haven't got one of my own. Too much responsibility, too much time taken by the little ungratefuls. I'm enjoying Wilton like anything and I hope his visit lasts a long time but I'm still glad I haven't got any myself.

I potted him successfully at 10 p.m. on Weds night and he was very alluring in his half asleep battle to withstand my efforts. Very pink and tousled and smelling like good toffee. I crept into bed a little later (I was sleeping with him) and sank gratefully to sleep without having wakened him, but my night was not to be as simple as all that! He woke up at five to three and stayed awake talking and grumbling for an hour and a half. I changed him, put him down, tucked him up, begged him to sleep, all to no use. When he was ready to sleep he slept; and not one minute before!

I can't say I was sorry to see Nanny get back, I can tell you. I *did* enjoy the following night's undisturbed rest.

Otherwise I've no news.

Rehearsals start next week! Dear heaven! I lunched with Virginia and Tony at Claridges last Tuesday. A happier couple or a more at ease one it would be hard to find. They've already slipped into the right kind of matrimonial peace. Gin was looking very smart in a grey and red checked jacket. They left for Italy next day.

---

*April 1st, 1939*                                                        Parr's

I've only had one rehearsal so far and I must confess that I was scared. However it went alright. I've discovered the difference – the essential difference – between amateurs and professionals: amateurs must get support from their audience or they collapse – lose their power. Professionals are complete and don't care whether they are listened to or not.

That, of course, is an exaggerated account. But you will know what I mean. Until one is so certain of oneself that one is quite oblivious of the audience one ain't no good. I'm trying, now, to get that certainty. And it isn't easy. It isn't only a question of lines and 'business'; it's a complete conception of the part as a whole.

It is all very interesting and when I can see, from a C.S. point of view, that I contain both myself *and* the audience and that there are no outside difficulties of any sort then I shan't be scared.

The rehearsal was really only a run through of my stuff and I wasn't very good. Afterwards I felt so depressed that I couldn't imagine why I'd ever considered taking the thing on at all. However by the next day I'd fully recovered and Mr Farjeon rang me up about some time detail for the next rehearsal and said he was full of confidence for me and that I was fine, etc, so that I felt better. I am now a member of Equity! I couldn't sign my contract till I'd joined so I went up to Kingsway, sought out Equity's office and by paying a small sum became a member of Equity.

On Monday I've got to go to *Vogue* to be photographed! That's at 12 and then I've a call for 1.30 so I don't see a chance of eating. I'll take a sandwich with me.

I don't yet know what I'm wearing but of course I'll let you know when I do.

*Monday*. Spent the whole morning made up in yellow movie paint for photographs at *Vogue*'s studio! The pictures promise to be distinctly glamorous. I was taken from all sorts of angles and in what may be quite becoming attitudes. Mostly head and shoulder studies. My 'straight' dress for 'Mothers' is probably going to be copied from that lime green crêpe one Nancy Tree gave. For the Women's Institute woman I shall dress up properly.[1] Ear-phone hair, gold-rim glasses and a beige knitted suit, fitting badly across the bottom! I shall look *hideous*, I hope!!!

——◆——

Nannau,
Dolgelly,
N. Wales.

*[Undated – second week of April]*

I haven't actually done my stuff on the stage nor in front of the rest of the company but I'm going to do it on Tuesday next. It isn't very long now! Only a week from next Thursday. And what a week it's going to be. Sat, 15th, a dress dress-rehearsal for lighting etc. 16th, dress rehearsal, 17th, ditto, 18th, ditto, 19th, charity preview performance, 20th, opening, 20th, *midnight* performance for the stage – actors and actresses. 21st, show, 22nd, mat and evening!

——◆——

Little Theatre,
John St.,
W.C.2.

*April 20th, 1939*

I'm writing this in the stalls on the day before we open. It's 4 p.m. There's a musical rehearsal going on on the stage. Four of us had lunch at a little pub near Charing Cross, then a walk in the sun along the Embankment Gardens where the tulips and daffodils are a riot

---

[1] This costume was cut after the first performance and, at Cyril Ritchard's suggestion, she wore a simple evening gown.

and it's one of the most attractive little gardens I've ever met in London.

Last night was our charity performance. The theatre was full with a very chic audience. It was a preview – a sort of glorified dress rehearsal and they paid as much as five guineas for stalls!

Well, I spent the day just not thinking about it at all. Mrs Rawson was giving me some help and I wasn't too bad really. In fact I was so free from wobbles that I felt something must be wrong! I went to a movie in the afternoon. Got to the theatre two hours before it was necessary and had a leisurely make-up, following a tasteless meal at Lyons.

There were two telegrams for me at the stage door – Mrs Grenfell and Aunt Pamela and Uncle Bill [Phipps].

I stood in the wings for all the numbers before mine and absorbed the feeling of the stage and the audience. It was, suddenly, just the moment before I had to come on. (Through a curtain in the middle, wearing my grey chiffon, the coral coat you gave me for Christmas and a viridian green handkerchief.) Someone started clapping and I got a nice little welcome. The bright lights cut me comfortably from reality, and do you know I got a feeling of power – that I could do just what I liked and the audience would like it too! And, gosh, they did!!! I got *lots* of laughs – found I could time them, too, which *amazed* me. Of course they were an indulgent audience. All the same, they did like me and if I say it as shouldn't, I was, in my small way, a sort of hit!

However we have still to get over the first night.[1] That's tomorrow. We've got a dress rehearsal tonight. Virginia and Tony are coming and incidentally they have sent me *the* loveliest first-night present, an eighteenth-century brooch, paste surrounding an amethyst. It's a dream. Aren't they nice? It was waiting at the stage door for me when I got here this afternoon.

I wonder when I'll have time to write you fully about it all. Half of my life is now temporarily shut off: home and husband. I'm living at Aunt Pauline's [Spender Clay]* very very comfy quiet and cosy flat in Ennismore Gardens,* where there is a competent Swiss maid who brings me breakfast in bed, washes and presses my clothes and generally cares for me. All this since Sunday. Reg joins me tonight.

Oh, the heartbreak of the theatre! After last night's performance they have had to cut *lots* of things, and people's best bits – or so they've thought – have had to be slashed. Oh, the *feelings*! Ego

[1] *Little Theatre.* April 21st, 1939. *The Little Revue* by Herbert Farjeon; Music by Walter Leigh. With Cyril Ritchard, Hermione Baddeley, Ronald Waters, Sheila Douglas-Pennant, Joyce Grenfell, Charlotte Leigh, George Benson, Betty-Ann Davies. Produced by Hedley Briggs.

uppermost in every single case. Dear, dear – I'm dressing with three other girls. (There are only three female dressing rooms in the whole theatre. Hermione Baddeley is alone, then (in order of grandness!) comes us four – and then the others all in a dormitory together underground.

Just off to get a meal before this evening's dress rehearsal . . .

I've got what is known as 'butterflies' in the stomach, tho' mostly under control.

———◆———

*April 23rd, 1939*                                                Parr's

Well – it seems as if the inherited talent isn't too bad! I just can't believe any of it. I seem to be a hit – and yet I'm not much good, really. However, they seem deluded and I'll not let down the illusion, if I can help it. Here are the chief cuttings – Alice has sent you the best one I believe – James Agate in the *Sunday Times*.[1] He who is always such a sour old puss. Just another proof that it wasn't me at all; just Mind disguised in a grey chiffon frock and your coral red coat.

I'll try to tell you all.

Last Sunday I left here with my suitcase for Aunt Pauline's flat in Ennismore Gardens. I was low. Why did I ever consider doing such a ridiculous thing? Me on the stage? Pooh. Church with Daddy in the morning, then lunch with Aunt Margaret [Phipps]. Rehearsal from three till midnight! Back to the flat – by far the nicest in London. My room had peach walls and chintz, a wide window on to a blossoming garden and perfect quiet. Also its own bathroom.

Wolfe used to be Phyllis's maid but now housekeeps at the flat. She brought me my breakfast in bed. Then to Woolworths to buy things I needed at the theatre – towels, hairpins, mirror, pins, extra comb, a piece of flowered American cloth for my table, blue, etc, etc.

We had a dress rehearsal that evening, my first. Charlotte Leigh, who is charming, helped me with my make-up. She plays character parts and is v. funny. Actual age about thirty-two. She's intelligent,

[1] 'These monologues are the best thing in their kind since Miss Ruth Draper, the difference being that Miss Draper's have been sometimes too long, and Miss Grenfell's are too short. I have the greatest possible admiration for Mr Farjeon, not to mention Miss Hermione Baddeley, for allowing Miss Grenfell to come within a thousand miles of this theatre.'

quiet, dependable, rather plain but attractive and got plenty of nice humour. Her brother[1] composed the music and it's good. I dress with three other girls. The Little is so tiny that only Hermione Baddeley dresses alone. Even Cyril Ritchard,[2] our male star, must share with George Benson.[3] Next in order of grandeur on the female side come Charlotte, Betty-Ann Davies and me. The other girl in our room is Peggy Willoughby, chief of the glamour girls, very nice, quiet, married but divorced with two children. The room is about fifteen feet by ten feet and it's not exactly spacious when we get the others doing 'quick changes', with Daisy, our dresser, in it as well. She is a Cockney with a pale bony face and kind eyes. We call her 'dear' and she calls us 'dear' back! Betty-Ann Davies is about my age, small, slim with a gamine little face rather like Luise Rainer[4] only less soppy looking. She fascinates me because she's such a mixture. Her language is terrific; she looks rather glamorous in a slightly Shaftesbury Avenue way and yet thinks only of gardening! Rushes from the theatre each night to catch a goods train down to Kent where she has a little house with her insurance-selling husband and her mother. Smokes a lot, likes a drink, is impervious to the ordinary standards I've got used to and yet atones for it by being genuinely warm-hearted, intelligent and mad about her garden. All last week, after rehearsing for six to eight hours, well into the night, she'd rush home in order to be up at 9 to plant out her seedlings! She has made a hit with her song about a school girl doing her prep. It makes me weep every time I hear it.[5]

So far I've been experimenting over my make-up and it seems I've still got to use more rouge as the red of your coat takes the colour out of my face and I'm in a terrific spotlight.

As I wrote you I was to have worn a character costume for my Institute woman but after that first rehearsal we decided that if I could get away with it, it would be much better if I wore evening dress. So in order to make it look as if I was wearing something different I first wear your coat and then, for 'Mothers', go on without it in

[1] Walter Leigh first worked for the theatre at the Festival, Cambridge. Composed incidental music for plays; for pantomimes, comic opera and revue. Died July 1942, aged thirty-seven.
[2] An Australian, married to Madge Elliott; first appeared in London in 1925; since then many musical comedies and revues, including *Nine Sharp*.
[3] Appeared in other Farjeon shows, including *The Two Bouquets* and *Nine Sharp*.
[4] Austrian actress, in Hollywood for 1935. Her films included *The Great Ziegfeld* (1936) and *The Great Waltz* (1938)
[5] One of the original Cochran's Young Ladies, Betty-Ann Davies appeared in several revues including *Nine Sharp*, and in plays, notably Emlyn Williams's *Morning Star*. Succeeded Vivien Leigh in *Streetcar Named Desire*. Died, 1945, aged forty-four.

my grey chiffon, carrying a yellow-backed book and a coral-pink handkerchief.

For the first night I covered myself in wet white – arms, neck, etc. But it's such a business and ruins all my own clothes going home afterwards so I've given it up. Of course it's very becoming but too much bother.

We had a small audience on Monday and I found the whole thing *much* easier with lights and a dress. To bed about 12.

Wednesday night we gave our charity preview in aid of some clinic or psychical or moral research or some such cause. We had a full house and all wished each other good luck as we wandered around the back of the stage awaiting our appearances. Mrs Rawson was on the job for me and I wasn't at all nervous really. At last it was my turn. I come on through a curtain in the middle of the stage having been announced something like this by a compère: 'In case we have lured you from your village institute Miss Joyce Grenfell is here to tell you all about how to make Useful and Acceptable Gifts.' (That's not it but it's more or less on those lines.) I got a nice little round of applause and then began my act which got lots of laughs! I hadn't expected so many and had to wait quite a long time to let them get over before I went on to my next remark.

I came off to a really grand hand. And I assure you I couldn't have been more surprised. My second appearance caused a nice little clapping to break out again and I found they seemed to enjoy my 'Mothers' too. Incidentally, I'm going to get hold of copies of my scripts for you but at the moment the old ones are so far removed from what I have since evolved that they aren't remotely accurate. I hardly like to say it but I was quite a hit. I'm very humble about it all because I *genuinely know* it's got nothing to do with the human me. After the performance Mr Farjeon came round to see us and said some nice things to me that made me glow. I was home about 1 and wasn't a bit sleepy so I read some Ferber[1] till about 2. Thursday was another lovely day – we had solid sunshine all week. Rehearsals, cuts, and re-arrangements of the programme took some time. It's a heartbreaking business the whole thing – a song, perhaps, in which one has hoped to score a success is ruthlessly and probably rightly, cut out. There were many long faces but I felt so nice inside that I couldn't be very gloomy with them. We had yet another dress rehearsal that night and I was appalling. I'm not just saying it. I was awful and what is worse, I dried! (Term meaning forgot my lines.)

[1] Edna Ferber, a very popular American writer. The films *Cimarron* and *Showboat* were based on her novels. As a playwright she collaborated with George S. Kaufman on *Dinner at Eight* and *Stage Door*.

It was a hideous moment but just about the best thing in the world that could have happened to me, for it made me realise that one must be on one's toes the whole time. It was partly due to tiredness and partly to knowing Virginia and Tony were in front and wondering what they were thinking. That's a fatal attitude. One mustn't give any thought to that. I've learned that lesson at any rate. Gosh, I was low after that rehearsal. Virginia and T. came around and R. arrived to fetch me. We went drearily along to a dim café in the Strand for food and it was desperately gloomy. They had found the show disappointing and nothing had gone right on the stage. I was scared blue; supposing that happened on the first night. Ugh. Ugh.

Back at the flat with R. I began to feel a bit better. Had a hot bath, fell into bed about 1. Next day was Friday, *the* night. I spent an hour in bed after R. had left for the City and then down to the theatre for an 11.30 call. I wrote you a note from there, written in the stalls while hanging about. And I told you about Virginia's *lovely* brooch. I'm crazy about it. At 1 o'clock there was a break and Charlotte and I went to the Villiers, a pub-cum-restaurant near the theatre for lunch. Pritch, the pianist – we have no orchestra, just two brilliant pianists and a drummer combination – came too, and we nervously forced ourselves to eat food we didn't in the least want. I only craved long iced drinks of lemon, rather sour. But I did eat some lamb and cabbage. It was then about 2. I thought I'd get my hair washed and a manicure and Charlotte wanted a manicure so we went to a telephone booth in Charing X station and rang up Selfridges where, miraculously, my Miss White could do me and there were manicurists free for us both. I slept peacefully under the drier and enjoyed the soothing manipulations on my hands. Then to the post office in Selfridges to send telegrams to the company. I sent them to Mr Farjeon, Hedley Briggs,[1] producer, Walter Leigh, composer, Charlotte, Betty, Ann, Peggy Willoughby who dresses with us and to Vida Hope, a new girl[2] and Jacqueline le Geyt, who was also making her first featured appearance. Then to the flower department where Charlotte bought some bunches for various friends and I didn't buy a thing and then to the restaurant where we ate a huge tea. I drank three breakfast cups full, ate a toasted bun and some coffee layer cake.

Then, on top of a bus, to the theatre, only we were too early so we went down to the Embankment Gardens and sat in two very

---

[1] Directed both *Nine Sharp* and *The Little Revue*; designed sets and costumes. He was also an actor and dancer.

[2] Then aged twenty. She had been a journalist.

comfy deck chairs in the sun for half an hour. Wasn't it nice of Charlotte to stay with me all this time?

By the way, do you remember where the Little is? It's right back of the Adelphi, sort of behind the Tivoli. We got into the theatre at 6.30, the curtain was rising at 8 as it was the first night. (Ordinarily we go up at 9.) The theatre was full of excitement. Telegrams were arriving and flowers. I had seventeen bunches and twenty-seven telegrams!

I've stuck them all on the wall over my dressing table at the theatre. Such lovely flowers they were too. I gave most of them to the dresser, took some back to Wolfe at the flat and kept some hardier tulips and Bertie's little Victorian posy for down here. Cyril Ritchard wrote me a note saying something to this effect: 'Welcome to this peculiar profession, Joyce dear, and may you have a personal success.' Nice of him, I thought. Bertie Farjeon's telegram read: 'I know just how you are feeling but you needn't.'

Well, I did my little bits and all went well. The audience was nicely stiffened with family and friends.

Most of 'em came around afterwards and I received them in the street for there just wasn't an inch of room inside the theatre. The stage door is in a sort of cul de sac alley and it was a warm night so all was well. They were all very relieved that I had been alright, poor things. Daddy says he now knows the full meaning of the words 'Strained Relations'!

After most of them had gone I took Alice and Reg, my Reg, Daddy and Maria up to my dressing room and then they went and we ate our sandwiches and drank tea before doing the whole show *all* over again for an audience of stage pros at midnight. Ivor Novello[1] took the front row of the stalls and roared at my stuff! This was the most appreciative of all audiences and any group would be dull after them. They are out to enjoy themselves and, at the same time, to show that they can be generous to their fellow artists and give them a hand!

After it was all over – R. sat through both performances and enjoyed the second even more than the first – he came around to collect me and we bundled our flowers and ourselves into a taxi for the flat. As I was leaving some unknown youngish man, a *bit* cissy, rushed up to me and poured out nice things about my 'controlled understatement', etc, etc! I'm so bad at receiving bouquets. All I could say was, 'Thanks awfully.'

Bed at 4.30 a.m.

---

[1] Actor, manager, dramatist and composer. His musicals, *Glamorous Night, Careless Rapture, Crest of a Wave* and *The Dancing Years*, were all tremendous successes during the Thirties. He had known Ma and on one occasion had sent her some Parma violets which, to impress her schoolfriends, Joyce pretended he had sent to *her*.

Awake at 9, to breakfast with Aunt Pauline, Rachel and David [Bowes-Lyon]. They were v. nice and had to go about 10 to catch trains. Then R. and I leapt on the papers. He'd ordered every one published! And they were terrific reviews. The whole show *is* grand and I'm delighted that they realised it.

Lunch with Virginia and Tony and then the evening papers with more lovely notices.

Yesterday was Sunday and more wonderful reviews. Church in the morning and lunch at Cliveden where there was an extraordinary party of all Kennedys,[1] Wiss, Lord Mildmay, Helen,[2] Jim [Brand], Betsy,[3] some stray young men and the Winns. Everyone was v. nice. Uncle W. is thrilled by the whole theatrical set-up!

Back here in the afternoon to write thank-you letters. Broadcasts to hear in the evening and bed at 10.30. Now it's Monday. I've been at this all the morning and must go out for a walk soon. I go up to London on the 6.22 this evening, having had my high tea here first.

Well that's about all I know. Wilton and Nanny will sail on Wednesday, May 3rd in the *Queen Mary*. I hate to see him go, as you know. All the same if he's got to go it's best that it should be now, while I'm too busy to miss him very badly. He's angelic and growing so beautiful!

I had a v. nice letter from Betty, thanking me for looking after W. and explaining everything – Tommy sent us 250 dollars which was nice of him and which came at a very opportune moment. It's just as well I'm doing this show for R.'s new job means less money than before, you see.

That's all I know.

I'm quite dazed. Happy and grateful to God. It's all very strange until you realise that all things are possible to him.

———◆———

*May 1st, 1939*                                          Parr's

Well, I've done it for a week now and it isn't too bad. There are low moments when one feels one couldn't *possibly* be funny. But when I smell the scenery and see the lights I get a sort of circus horse

[1] Joseph P. Kennedy, American Ambassador, and his family. His daughter Kathleen married the Marquess of Hartington; his second son, Jack, became President of the United States.
[2] The daughter of Lord Mildmay of Flete, Devon landowner and therefore a Plymouth friend of the Astors.
[3] Betsy Perkins, daughter of Chiswell Perkins, Alice Winn's brother.

instinct and all is well. From a C.S. point of view it is particularly interesting. You see, the others seem to regard the audience as their potential enemy. Now Mrs Rawson said to me that the audience was part of me and I'm sure she's right. We are both there for joy. This has helped me quite enormously; also the truth that everything *is* now and not to be got through or discovered. It's all complete.

We had full houses every night last week and wonderful matinées.

The people in the theatre were very sweet about my lovely notices and weren't a bit annoyed to discover I really was an amateur. I have to keep on my toes in the dressing room for there is a burden of superstition to be dealt with – or ignored!

I had tea with Celia on Thursday between matinée and evening performance. She's going into a new play quite soon. The baby is very sweet. Tiny but like Peter.[1]

Aunt Marg. and Nicholas [Phipps] were 'in front' at the matinée and loved it. Nick said he couldn't get over how professional I was! That's a compliment from a hardened old pro like he is!

I just don't think about Wilton's departure. He really is the most enchanting child and we find him so companionable and endearing. R. adores him and they are too attractive together. However it's only right that B. should have her own child. I'm sure she's right to contest T.'s claim for some of Wilton. He has forfeited *any* rights he ever had. I'm sure Betty will let him see Wilton whenever he wants – she's said so both to Daddy and me – but as for giving him legal rights she won't do it. And rightly.

But to more pleasant subjects.

Bertie Farjeon and wife came down yesterday for lunch. He wants me not to break my contract at three months! But I won't promise a *thing*. I've told him I'm going to America in the fall and that is a certainty and that I *might* possibly stay in the revue till the end of September – if it runs till then, which it ought to, I think. Then he wants me to go into the next year's revue with much more to do! Some singing and a higher position in the bill! I won't promise this either. But it's too good to ignore. His idea is then to launch me into the matinée world doing a varied programme – monologues, and songs.

This is all fairly vague and I may never consider it but it is certainly flattering and Reggie is all for me doing it. He is so funny. Did I tell you in my last letter how he reminds me of you, always asking

---

[1] Celia Johnson had had a son, Nicholas, in the New Year. Sadly *Sixth Floor*, by Alfred Gehri (English version by Rodney Ackland), at the St James's, was not the success everyone hoped.

if anyone has said anything nice to me and being furious if they haven't!

We manage to see more of each other than I'd ever expected. He fetches me late at night and I take him to the early train because I find I prefer a nap in the afternoon to a late sleep in the morning. (I can't rest if I feel there are things to be done like letters, ordering the food, etc.)

Garvin, my boss, was at Cliveden last night and said he was so pleased to hear of my success. So was Dede Lyttelton.[1]

————◄●►————

*May 4th, 1939*                                                    Little Theatre

We had a matinée this afternoon and Ivor Novello and Dorothy Dickson[2] were in front. They came around afterwards to see Cyril Ritchard and I met them and they said the nicest things. Ivor Novello said, 'It is *Joyce*, isn't it?' and I said, 'Yes, Nora's daughter' and they said they loved my stuff and that I was very good, etc, and both said I must write and tell you that they'd seen me and liked me and said nice things about me! And they sent their best love.

Wilton left on Thursday. It was one of the less pleasant events of my life. He was particularly alluring those last few days. Very funny and sturdy and solid and smelt good. Thank goodness he's gone now before he can talk. He really is the most angelic little boy; you'd adore him. I think you'll have to be very extra tactful with Betty about seeing him this summer but if and when you do go north, later on, you must see him.

No more now. It's just about the interval and the room fills up again. At the moment they are all on the stage in the first act finale.

————◄●►————

[1] Dame Edith (Dede) Lyttelton (created 1929 for public service); wife of the Rt Hon. Alfred Lyttelton; daughter of Archibald Balfour. An aunt by marriage of Reggie's stepmother, Hilda (née Lyttelton).
[2] Originally a dancer in her native America; appeared in many musical comedies and revues in London. Played Peter Pan in 1925 and 1926.

Well, I've been doing it for almost three weeks now. They've been very quick weeks and I must say I'm enjoying it. The only thing I don't like about it is not seeing enough of Reggie. That is a bore. He swears he's quite happy reading and gardening and it is he who encourages me in it all the time. All the same, I do miss him; and I suppose that's really something to be glad about. It would be horrid not to miss one's husband.

Tuesday night was Aunt N.'s dance. Reggie dined with Laura [Grenfell] and came on with the debs. I had sent my white tulle crinoline to St James's Square by Rose from Cliveden and went straight from the theatre in a petticoat under an evening coat and dressed properly up in the spare room. It was a good party but much too crowded. When I got there – 11.30 – you literally couldn't move anywhere.

There was plenty to see. Kents and Gloucesters and a sprinkling of the star debs. Dinah's dress was hideous. I can't imagine who chose it for her. Blue taffeta, very tacky and the wrong, rather strong blue with an even stronger, wronger, blue piping around the panels. She looked pretty nevertheless. Alice Obolensky,[1] or what-ever-her-name-is, looked like a Chinese pagoda in lacquer red. Very attractive and queer but definitely oriental. Who else? Phyllis [Nichols] was in very gay red and green stripes, Alice was in yellow and Wiss white satin. I'm not good at knowing how to take compliments and everyone was so nice to me. They seem to come in their hundreds to see the revue and all say the right things to me!

It was so crowded one really couldn't see people properly. I don't know why it was so full – all the usuals were there and very few new faces. The flowers were wonderful and in the little green drawing room there were nothing but gardenias. Bowls *and* trees of them.

Reg and I waltzed together, had supper and went home about 2.30. It wasn't over then but we were v. sleepy.

---

[1] Alice Obolensky (née Astor), married to Prince Obolensky, and later to Raymond von Hofmannsthal.

*June 5th, 1939*                                          Little Theatre

Gilbert Miller[1] was in the other night and said nice things to me. I
told him I was your daughter and we had a conversation about us
all. Bea Lillie[2] was here on Friday and she didn't realise I was me
until afterwards when we met in Hermione Baddeley's dressing room
and she screamed and said: 'You're not *that* marvellous woman?' and
I admitted it. She said she'd loved the whole revue and thought it
very funny. And so it is.

I brought Charlotte Leigh, of the company, down here with me
last Thursday for the night and she adored the cottage and Cliveden
and the country in general. We had a grand day and walked in the
woods and saw the gardens looking wonderful.

Saturday was the great rally of all Bucks Women's Institutes and
their guests, the Associated Country Women of the World. They
arrived about 1 and stayed till the evening. How I hated missing it.
That was the first time I've really had to miss anything I've badly
wanted to do because of this job. The rally was a big success, Maria
tells me. I was there on Saturday morning and helped a bit with
the tea. It's a remarkable fact that the county institutes contributed
580 *dozen* cakes for the tea! All home made and they looked very
delicious.

Aunt N. spoke [in the Commons] in the afternoon so did Edward
Halifax.[3] There was a huge party up at the house for the weekend.

Tomorrow is the Theatrical Garden Party and we're all going to
it and running a side show.

So now I must stop. I'm almost due on in the second part –

We are very well – and happy.

———◆———

*June 12th, 1939*                                              Parr's

You still haven't told me what you think about the prospect of the
revue going to NY in the spring, with me in it. I hope you will soon
as I'll have to come to some sort of decision about renewing my

[1] American impresario. Put on a great many successes, particularly at the St James's.
[2] Beatrice (Bea) Lillie (Lady Peel) first appeared in revue in London in the Twenties
and Thirties; later had her own one woman show, and played Mame in the play,
*Auntie Mame*. She was born in Canada.
[3] 3rd Viscount. Viceroy of India, 1926–31; held leading positions in the Conservative
Party. At this point, was Foreign Secretary in Neville Chamberlain's Administration.
Became Ambassador in Washington in 1941; created Earl in 1944.

contract and for how long, etc, etc. In case you didn't get my letter with all this in it I've put to you the alternatives of coming over this autumn – having quit the revue – or sticking to the revue and coming over in Jan or Feb if they take this proposed combination of the last and the present revue to NY. I can sign on for as little as eight weeks and, should this plan not come off, I can always come to you for the spring anyway. The point is this: do you think I should stick to the revue and risk the NY production, coming to America *anyway*. Or should I quit the revue in about September and come to America for a month? Reggie is in favour of the first plan. He is willing and agreeable to the next eighteen months being somewhat upside down from a quietly domestic point of view as he thinks I'll need all of that to equip me for a future of solo work *à la* Ruth.

She, by the way, got to London last night and telephoned me this morning. We are lunching on Thursday and she opens her four-week season this evening. She did a number of performances in Oxford and Cambridge last week and now has taken a little house in Alexander Sq – somewhere near the Fulham Road – where she'll be for the rest of the summer.

It was *very* hot all last week. Really hot for England. On Tuesday we all attended the Theatrical Garden Party at Ranelagh. Our stall was a penny rolling game at which we made over £23 all from pennies. How it reminded me of my youth! All the stars looking hot and playing friendly, the children from Italia Conti's Corner disguised as Kate Greenaway girls or summer spirits in wisps of sea green chiffon and bare feet, selling tickets. Ivor Novello was a picture in full Tyrolean costume, knees and all. Noël Coward[1] was doing the Grand Giggle and I saw Dorothy Dickson dancing with some beautiful young man in a dansant tent. Talking of young men – the stage is certainly a hotbed of the queers. It's very distressing. They are *all* that way and it's most unattractive. If I had a daughter who wished to go on the stage I'd do all in my power to prevent her until she was twenty-four or had got such character and background of her own that she had standards against which to measure all the floppiness she'd meet with in the theatre world. It's their complete lack of standards that I find so depressing. They just don't think; whatever is easiest and pleasantest they do and all romance is divine. They never look behind it to see if there is anyone to get hurt by their fun. I find them a warm hearted, gay crowd and I like them in small doses. But they don't think and they don't read and they accept the third rate

[1] In the summer of 1939, Coward was principally known as a playwright. *Present Laughter* and *This Happy Breed* were recent successes. His earlier play, *Design for Living*, was revived in London at the Haymarket. Coward, like Ivor Novello, had been an old friend of Ma's and knew Joyce as a girl.

too easily for me. However I'm in a very happy position at the Little
for the girls in my dressing room do not all apply to the cases I've
quoted and one of them, Charlotte Leigh, speaks my own language
and that's a restful pleasure, I can tell you.

---

*June 20th, 1939*                                                  Parr's

I've still not made up my mind about the future. To have a career
or not to have a career – that's the question. At the moment I
don't feel as if I wanted one; but tomorrow I'll probably change
my mind entirely. I think that what I'll do is this: stay in the
revue till about October. Then leave, write myself some new stuff,
enjoy the autumn down here and then, if the show goes to the
US in Feb., go with it and if not, go anyway to visit you. I shall
probably know more about everything after a week or two for it
seems there is one Guthrie McClintic,[1] or some such name, who
has been to see the show twice already and who puts on such
things in NY. He wants to talk business with Farjeon and it looks
as if the NY plan really might come off. Anyway it's more
concrete like this. As I've said before, I can't and won't make
plans but let things develop naturally.

---

*July 3rd, 1939*                                                   Parr's

A letter from you this morning saying you were melting in the heat.
It seems impossible when I'm writing this with a fire burning and a
sweater on even though it is July. Something v. curious has happened
to English summers. They just don't exist anymore. We had three
really glorious weeks at the end of May into June but since then
there's been practically no sun and if not cold then cool. However

---

[1] American director, husband of Katharine Cornell, who appeared in many of his
productions, which included *Romeo and Juliet*, *The Barretts of Wimpole Street*, *Wingless
Victory*, *High Tor* and *Candida*.

while I'm working I don't complain for I like it not to be hot when I must travel and perform.

My big news is that by the time you get this letter, and all wars barred, I will have done my stuff before the King and Queen! Lady Halifax[1] has asked me to do it at Eaton Square on Monday, July 10th, when they entertain a very few friends of the K. and Q.'s to dinner. It's a really small party – sixteen. All their own personal friends.

It's a professional engagement of course. I've not been allowed to tell anyone about it over here because Lord H. being the Foreign Minister entertaining his sovereign, some might think he ought to have invited them to meet him and as it's purely private it must be kept quiet. So be careful who you tell, won't you? Perhaps it's best not to say where I'm doing it. Just that I'm doing it before the K. and Q., and not where.

I don't yet know what I'm going to wear. I've got a white lace that is becoming and a pale chartreuse print of Nancy Tree's that I adore but that isn't new. Anyway I'll let you know about it next week.

Tom Jones is undergoing a v. serious operation this week and he sent me a very touching and lovely letter in case 'this is farewell'. It's had me down, for I really do love that man. He's been *so* good to me and is such a really wonderful person that I just can't imagine not having him to tell things to and to ask advice from, etc. However, there is only one operation and that is God's, so he'll be alright.

I must stop now and go up to Cliveden for lunch –

---

*July 11th, 1939*　　　　　　　　　　　　　　　　　　Parr's

Well, last night at 11 p.m. I curtsied in the rather Victorian drawing room of 88 Eaton Square and performed before the King and Queen of England! Tra la la.

I wore the lime green dinner dress Nancy gave me at least two years ago because a.) it's very becoming and b.) I'm at home and

[1] Lady Halifax (née Dorothy Evelyn Augusta Onslow) was the daughter of the Earl of Onslow. Created Extra Lady of the Bedchamber to Queen Mary in 1926, she was now a lady-in-waiting to the Queen. She and Lord Halifax lived at 88 Eaton Square.

happy in it. The King and Queen sat in two armchairs facing me, she in white with two gardenias in her hair and such a beautiful necklace of pearls and diamonds. He wore tails and a thick cluster of medals. The party was really rather cosy and they turned out to be a very appreciative audience: Halifaxes, Hambledens, Allendales, Airlies, Vyners, Taw-taw Gilmour, Arthur Penn, Fevershams.[1] That's all. Reg came to the theatre to collect me at 10.45. The management very kindly put the running order differently so that I could get away earlier and I was off, make-up changed and into the waiting taxi within five minutes of leaving the stage.

When we got to Eaton Square there was quite a little crowd in the street. They always get to know the royal movements in some mysterious way. The butler took us up to Lady H.'s boudoir and there was a mirror and powder arranged for me. Then Anne came out of the drawing room and said they were nearly ready and was I, and took Reggie back into the drawing room with her and I was left to await my summons. I'd said I preferred to perform first and be presented afterwards, but R. had a chat with them before I came in.

I did exactly what I do at the theatre – Women's Institute Woman and then the 'Three Mothers'. They laughed a great deal, I'm glad to say, and it was fun performing for them. When I'd finished I was presented and they asked me all sorts of questions about stage life. Did I get tired? Bored? Were the rest of the company nice? And he was most interested in back stage life; she was amused by the WI woman and said she knew the type so well and couldn't I next make her lecture on cooking. They could not have been more friendly or appreciative and I just went down under their combined charm, and great surgings of loyalty kept going up and down my spine as I looked at their two sweet little faces.

And *how* nice the Halifaxes were! After all, I was doing it as a professional engagement and even if I am a friend, an awful lot of people would, perhaps, treat one as the entertainer; but not them. I was given the most appetising supper on a little table in his study after the K. and Q. had gone, and Billy and Patricia [Hambleden] and Anne came down and gossiped with me while I ate it and Lord

[1] The appreciative audience: Billy and Patricia Hambleden; Viscount Allendale and his wife Violet: the Earl of Airlie and his wife Lady Alexandra Coke, daughter of the Earl of Leicester; the Vyners – the second son of Lord Alwyne Frederick Compton, assumed his wife's name in 1912; Victoria Laura ('Taw-taw') Gilmour, Lady-in-Waiting to the Queen, wife of Sir John Little Gilmour, 2nd Bt, who would be appointed Minister of Shipping in October 1939; Arthur Penn, Treasurer to the Queen and previously Groom-in-Waiting and Extra Equerry to the Queen; the Earl of Feversham, at one time a Lord-in-Waiting, was married to Anne Halifax.

H. was so very nice about the whole thing and said that my turn had
been quite perfect and thanked me so gratefully for coming! Wasn't
it heartwarming?

The whole party was extremely secret because quite unofficial, so
there are no mentions of it in the papers and it's not in the Court
Circular. All the more exciting, I think.

The girls in my dressing room at the theatre were so sweet and
excited for me and those of the men who were in the know wished
me 'all the best in the world', etc, etc. I'll have a lot to tell 'em when
I get there tonight. I'm writing this in bed after breakfast the morning
after, so if it's illegible, you'll know why.

In the taxi on the way home Reg said that Laura [Grenfell] had
asked us to come on to a small waltzing party that she and about
forty young friends were having in a house just across from these
flats. We were feeling rather awake and excited after our evening so
we went there and had a lovely time. Lady Verney's[1] party – just
eighteen couples to waltz. Plenty of room, delicious supper and a big
cool room. After a while they asked me if I'd perform, so for the
third time in one evening I did my stuff! Only bits of it this time
though. There was a young man with a guitar who sang Spanish and
Italian songs rather charmingly in the dark; and then more waltzing,
and so to bed at 3. A most enjoyable evening.

---

*July 18th, 1939*                                    4 St James's Square

There is no end to our royal life; now we are bidden to the Court Ball
tomorrow night in honour of Prince Paul, Regent of Yugoslavia.[2]
Needless to say we are going. I'm wearing my white net crinoline
yet again and it still looks lovely. Aunt N. is lending me her turquoise
tiara and ear-rings, etc, so I'll be all set.

There doesn't seem to be much news. T.J. has had his second
operation today and is much better, I'm glad to say. I mean he's
come through it alright which is the important thing.[3]

We had our 100th performance last night. That means just over
three months. My contract is now at an end and the feeling of
freedom is quite intoxicating. I don't in the least mind doing it now
– not that I ever did – but I did not like the feeling of being tied up

[1] Lady Verney (Janette), an Australian, was the wife of Lt. Col. Sir Ralph Verney,
who had been Secretary to the Speaker since 1921.
[2] His wife, Princess Olga, was the Duchess of Kent's sister.
[3] Tom Jones lived another sixteen years, dying in 1955, aged eighty-five.

for so long. Charlotte Leigh and her brother asked R. and me to join them and the Farjeons for supper last night but as R. was going to Gavin Astor's[1] twenty-first ball at Hever Castle tonight . . . he didn't stay up.

Our supper was at the Criterion where we sat talking over eggs and bacon and coffee until 2.45 a.m.! Very pleasant it was too.

And that's about all I know. The Eton–Harrow match resulted in a win for Harrow – first time since 1908. And neither R. nor I[2] were there to witness the tragedy as he was busy supervising the removal of his office to a new building and I had a matinée.

———◆———

*July 25th, 1939*                                          Parr's

A letter from you today written at Newport. Wilton sounds wonderful. I do wish I could see him and smell him and feel him. I'm glad you hear good accounts of the new nurse. Yes, I daresay the change is a wise one. It never does if the nanny doesn't entirely like the mother.

Last Tuesday I had supper with Daddy who was going away to Torquay (!) for his holiday the next day and he took me to the theatre afterwards where I found the whole concern in a *state*. The King and Queen were coming that very evening! You can just imagine the excitement. We were all thrilled and a little nervous for they were to sit plum in the front row of the stalls. There are no boxes at the Little. When I'd performed the week before I'd said that I thought they'd probably enjoy the whole revue and that they ought to see it some day. I never thought they would but, gosh, within a week there they were! Of course, everyone said I'd done it. But I expect they'd have come anyway. They brought the Prince Regent of Yugoslavia and his wife who is the Duchess of Kent's sister. The whole party roared from start to finish. It was grand. My stuff seemed to go well, I'm glad to say, although they'd seen it before. By judiciously moving the scenery a little, we managed to make a crack through which we might watch the royal faces. It wasn't quite wide enough to see both the K. and the Q. but when she got excited and leaned forward we saw her well. He was always visible. There

[1] Gavin Astor was the son of Waldorf's brother, Lord Astor of Hever, the owner of *The Times*. His twenty-first party was at Hever Castle.
[2] Reggie and Joyce's fathers both went to Eton. Reggie's father hired a coach every year which served as a meeting point and source of refreshment for all the Grenfell family and friends who attended the two-day match.

was a continual queue to look through the crack; dressers, stage hands, the fireman, artists and stars.

They didn't see any of the company in the interval. But Bertie Farjeon saw them and heard of their enjoyment. It was a purely informal visit and as such they were treated like the public except that at the fall of the curtain we *all* assembled on the stage and when the curtain rose it stayed up while we sang the National Anthem. The King and Queen laughed hard at my stuff, I'm glad to say. I studiously avoided looking anywhere near them; you know how it is.

The next night we were among the 800 other guests bidden to Buck House for a ball in honour of Prince Paul and Princess Olga. It was the same as last year and I wore exactly the same clothes, blue tiara and all. We adored it and stayed till 4 a.m. I got a broad smile from the King and a few words from the Queen. Then I had quite long conversations with Prince P. – David Bowes-Lyon introduced me – and his wife.

Really we do lead an amusing life, don't you think?

It's been another good week. Full houses, amused audiences having good times. Just what it all ought to be. I'm getting much less flustered by it; not that I ever was, very. But you know, I don't even have to rush to WC just before I go on any more! In fact I can sit and write letters and go up when Billy the call boy calls me and not have to hang about worrying until just before I go on.

Beau Hannen[1] was in front with Athene Seyler last night. I didn't see 'em but hear they liked me.

(Don't I talk a lot about myself these days? It's the stage as does it.)

———◦———

*August 1st, 1939* Parr's

I had a summons from Paramount last week on Nicholas Hannen's recommendation for a comedy part in his film but when I got there they found me too young and too – ! pretty!! I didn't want to do it. (Sounds like sour grapes; it isn't though) but it was madness not to look into it thoroughly. I put it to Mind to keep me in my right place and evidently – and gladly – it was not there. There's something sawdusty about the picture business. A blurring of edges and a soul destruction.

[1] Nicholas ('Beau') Hannen, distinguished actor; Athene Seyler's husband. Athene's daughter Jane Ann was married to one of the company, George Benson.

However it was nice of Nicholas Hannen to suggest me.

This is a week of closing up. Aunt N. leaves Cliveden for Sandwich on Friday, Uncle W. goes to Jura that night and the Winns leave Taplow the same day. I can't tell you how much I'll miss Alice. It will be very lonely without her. Thank goodness for Maria. The Winns are going to Jura first, then to Balmoral! Jakie and Michael are probably going to live at Greenwood Cottage[1] this winter which is rather cosy. Aunt N. talks of opening Cliveden again over Christmas but I doubt it. You know there's a big economy drive? Cliveden closed *indefinitely* and gardeners cut down and all sorts of changes being made. Taxation. It's silly really because it cuts both ways; Uncle W. has to employ less people so the Gov. will have to deal out dole if they don't get employment.

———◆———

*August 8th, 1939*                                                   Parr's

Aunt N. left on Friday and Cliveden is now shut up indefinitely. They've pensioned several people off and cut down about twenty employees. Paying such enormous income taxes as he does, makes Uncle Waldorf have to economise very drastically and that throws the burden on to the country. But there it is; Cliveden is now shut indefinitely.

———◆———

*August 14th, 1939*                                                  Parr's

All the stuff from Tommy's flat was sold last week to meet the rent and among it were nearly all my best books (signed G. B. Shaws, etc) and our dining room furniture, drawing room furniture and some linen! Some day when he makes his pile I shall expect my young brother to make some sort of recompense. Actually I don't mind so much about the furniture but I do mind a lot about the

[1] Greenwood Cottage on the Cliveden estate had always been used to lend to friends of the Astors. Joyce and Reggie had spent two summer holidays there before moving to Parr's. Joyce had also known it as a child. Between 1915 and 1917, after her father had been invalided out of the Army and gone to work in America, Ma, Joyce and Tommy lived there.

books. I don't know what happens if T. ever comes back to London. They'll pounce on him for masses of money for Income Tax and this flat rent; for of course the content nowhere nearly went to meet it. Mess. Mess. Brrrr.

I don't think I know anything else. WI this afternoon.

There seems to be more possibility of the revue going to NY in Feb of next year. Three separate people are interested in it and Mr Farjeon's giving first choice to the Theatre Guild people, I understand. At least its Guthrie McClintic who's interested and he's Katherine Cornell's husband, isn't he?

Otherwise no news of any sort.

Just a nice quiet life, thank you, and the usual European rumblings which are frightening if you stop to listen to them but which have gone on so long now that one really can't keep up being on tenter-hooks. I've no ideas on the subject and no hunches; nor have I heard any gossip. The ghost of last year's tension is hovering about a bit and the old people pull long faces but everything is really just as usual and the country is full of holiday-makers and I'm darned if I'll let myself get hypnotised this time.

Of course, from a C.S. point of view we know what is real and what isn't! However the world is material and will ever be so and Mrs E. [Eddy] says that 'even now the world is becoming the arena for conflicting forces'. And she's right; it is. So all we can do is establish our knowledge of truth and so weaken the lie of error.

*Where are the pictures of Wilton?*

---

*August 22nd, 1939*　　　　　　　　　　　　　　　　Parr's

I suppose you know all about Betty's marriage? We had a cable this morning telling us briefly that she and Edward Reeve were married yesterday and the cable address was Bar Harbour. Were you surprised or did you know about all this before? I hope he is a rich young man this time! I must say I'm amazed at her speed but I suppose if one looks at it cold-bloodedly, there's no reason to wait and I daresay she was lonely and insecure and wanted something settled. I shall be most interested to hear details.

What of Wilton? (*And where are the photographs?* I do think you might send them over when you know I'm longing to see them.

Now don't be so lazy. Get them off to me soon, please.) I hope he's going to have a nice step-pa.

We are presumably in a crisis but I'm darned if I'll let myself get all het up like I did last September. My present method is to avoid all newspaper talk and print and never to listen to radio news bulletins. It may be ostrich-like, but it makes me happier and therefore nicer to have around. If there's a war there's a war and that's all there is to it.

Meanwhile Reggie has been sent by his firm [British Non-Ferrous Metals] to look into their mining interests in Flintshire, N. Wales. He goes this afternoon for three or four days. He'll probably enjoy it, for between office hours he can look around at the country and the change will do him good anyway.

If there isn't a war and you really can afford it, it would be lovely to see you over here; but I'll be over for absolute certainty between Xmas and Easter, so don't waste your money. If there's a war you wouldn't be allowed to come, I don't suppose, because they don't want to have to cope and feed any more than they actually have to. But war probably won't happen. It seems impossible to conceive of as I write, for it's a hot summer day with a delicious breeze and all seems so peaceful out here.

---

*August 30th, 1939*                                                    Parr's

Well there's no further news but it don't smell like a war to me. Anyway we'll see. We are fully prepared and the feeling here is good – calm and ready.

The wretched Germans are in a dreadful situation – No food, no news. I'm afraid there may be internal conflict and that won't be exactly a picnic.

There's no news from Parr's.

(A wasp buzzed around my head and I flicked at it with a sheet of blotting paper and it vanished; but where to? I keep 'feeling' it on my leg and down my neck. I can hear it, too, but there's not a sign of the thing!)

We are very well and calm and happy.

*P.S. Where are the pictures of Wilton?* You are mean.

*September 4th, 1939*          Parr's

Well, well, so it's a war.

So far it doesn't look or feel like one, except very slightly, but I daresay that by the time this reaches you we'll have had a taste.

The entire populace goes about with gas masks tied by strings over one shoulder. Sugar is unobtainable in Maidenhead but that is only because the transport has been delayed while the evacuation of children, pregnant mothers and the blind took place. Fortunately we have enough to go on with.

Right up till Friday I was sure there wouldn't be a war and even now I find it hard to believe. We'd been playing all week to tiny audiences and on Thursday evening Charlotte and I came out of Lyons after eating our supper to find posters saying that all ARP [Air Raid Precaution] workers were ordered to report at once. This shook us a bit and we turned up at the theatre half imagining there would be no evening performance. But there was. Luise[1] was coming down for a night and the following day and we met at Paddington to get the late train. Reggie met us and said cheerfully that Hitler's sixteen-point plan had been broadcast and we all went to bed full of hope. And slept like logs. R. went off on his early train as usual. I slept till 10.30 and woke up just in time to hear the first news bulletins. 'We regret to announce,' said the speaker as if he was speaking of the tiresome wet weather, 'that the international situation took a grave turn during the night.' Such coolness is the greatest help, preceded as it always is with the chattiest sort of 'Good morning everybody'.

Luise and I were sort of pooped by the news and spent a shiftless morning in our wrappers, only bathing and dressing just in time for a lunch we didn't want. All the time we were quite undepressed; merely amazed. After lunch I telephoned Reggie to find out whether we were playing that evening, and after trying to get on to me, having got in touch with the theatre, he finally telegraphed me that we were. This was about 5.30 and the train to London left at 6.40. Rene had gone on her holiday the day before, Mrs Jaycock[2] had gone home as usual at 2.30, and I had to shut up the house, leave some food for Reggie and get down to the station. I was sure we shouldn't be playing so I hadn't changed from my skirt and shirt. A scramble followed, we closed all the windows and drew the curtains, lured

---

[1] Luise Blackburn, dancer; came to London from America in 1926 with a troupe called the Hoffman Girls who appeared at the Hippodrome. In 1930, between jobs, she appeared with an amateur group, the Bright Spots, with Joyce at a charity concert in the Pump Room, Tunbridge Wells.

[2] Mrs Jaycock was Joyce's 'daily'.

Gary in from the garden to do watchman duty in our absence and we were just going to get into the car when the back door bell rang. I rushed to it and there was an evacuation officer with a small girl in school clothes. 'Here's your child' he said and told me her name and was just going when I had intelligence enough to say I had room for two children so he went back to his car and returned with a second. Situation! Here was I with two small girls of twelve, a cold tongue and some uncooked potatoes in the house and no maid and a train to catch! Thinking swiftly and deciding that it didn't matter if I missed the show or not in times like this, I ran up to Mrs Jeffries's house to see if she would oblige by minding my children for the evening, but found her door shut and her neighbour, Mrs Martin, said she was down the road looking after Bert's mother, old Mrs Jeffries. So I then decided to go up to Rene's house, tell her all and beg her to come back from her holiday. (I knew she wasn't going away and she lives but 200 yards up the road.) She was out but her mother said she'd certainly come back and not to worry. She was shopping in Burnham and would go to Parr's as soon as she returned. By this time our train was due in but as they were said to be running late owing to the vast evacuation scheme we gambled on catching it. We went to the station, leaving the children to settle themselves and find their own way. I drove via Burnham in case we should meet Rene on her return and we did. So I told her what had happened and, angel that she is, she said she didn't mind a bit missing her holiday and would pop up the hill and look after the children right away. So we left in high relief. Luise was coming in with me to collect her passport, money and steamship ticket as I didn't want her to stay in London alone and she wanted her stuff with her. Our train was one and three-quarters of an hour late at Taplow! So we crawled into Padding-ton with only just time for me to tear along the crowded and almost dark platform, go out into the street to find a rare taxi and arrive at the theatre by 9.15. I'm on at 9.30. The blackout in London was complete and I'd never realised how dark a lightless town can be. We crept along at about five miles an hour. I may add that it was pouring with rain.

I threw my clothes on, smeared on some make-up and just had time to collect myself before I was called. The house was minute; about forty. They behaved grandly and made as much noise as they could; in fact they worked harder than we did! Bea Lillie (sixth visit) and Phyllis Monkman[1] were in front. So was Reggie.

It looks as if that was my final appearance for I couldn't get to London on Saturday, altho' I believe they played. Today, of course,

---

[1] Musical comedienne and dancer; particularly popular in the West End between the wars. Took over Joyce Barbour's part in *The Two Bouquets*.

no theatres or movies are open anywhere. I've written to Bertie Farjeon to let him know that even if the run is resumed under some new management I shan't be able to join it. There's too much to do down here and anyway I can't go to and fro every night in blackouts.

Aunt N. and Uncle W. have again offered Cliveden as a Canadian Red X hospital.[1] Whether it will be wanted or not is still uncertain. If it is Aunt N. says I will be needed urgently as she won't be able to devote her full time to it as she is now an MP and will necessarily have to be in London for a good deal of the time. She has decided we must have a new car as the old one can't last much longer so Hopkins[2] is going into it for us. She is giving it to us! Isn't she thoughtful? What's more, she's giving me a bicycle! I ordered three lovely ones for her in Maidenhead this morning.

But where was I?

Oh yes, Friday still.

Luise and Reggie and I met at the theatre and got into the same taxi we'd taken from Paddington. They were impossible to get that night and Luise had very sensibly made him wait for us. We got to Paddington about 11.20 and caught the 10.45 that had not yet left. There wasn't a light anywhere and we had some difficulty in finding room in the crowded carriages. We found places and as we got accustomed to the gloom could see our fellow passengers. There was a young mother in the corner, nursing a tiny baby. Her husband sat opposite with a two-year-old boy asleep in his arms. I thought she looked pretty tired so I offered to hold the baby and discovered it was only born three weeks ago. I suggested she lay down, for there was room, and she got some rest that way during a very tedious journey in a train that stopped at every station all the way down. I discovered from the husband that they'd left Rochester – danger zone – earlier that evening and were aiming for some relations at Lent Rise near Burnham. They planned to get out at Burnham and walk but we discouraged this – two babes, a wet night and a suitcase on a mile and a half walk didn't seem a good idea for so recent a mother. When we got to Taplow I drove them and Luise to Lent Rise, dropped them and then returned for R. who had started to walk carrying Luise's case. Bed certainly felt good that night.

---

[1] During the First World War the covered tennis court at Cliveden was converted into a hospital to house 110 patients for the Canadian Red Cross. Taplow Lodge, next door, was used to accommodate staff, and the big house at Cliveden served as a convalescent home. Nancy Astor had spent a great deal of time working at the hospital, but now her duties in Parliament and in Plymouth, where she was Lady Mayoress, forced her to find others to carry out the tasks she had performed for the hospital in the earlier war.

[2] Hopkins was the Astors' chauffeur.

Next day R. had to go to London again, for what reason I don't remember. I spent the morning buying stuff to blackout our windows, hooks to hang 'em by, and the rest of the day making them. Luise and I sat out in the sun, hard at it all afternoon. Gwen Cooke and Margaret Wallis, my girls, went to Burnham to 'look at the shops'. They are from Godolphin and Latymer Secondary School at Hammersmith. Scholarship girls. Gwen has red hair and an enchanting disposition and manners. Betty is gayer, smaller, fairer and has more go but less dependability. They are both darlings though, and no trouble at all. In fact they are very useful and make their own beds, dust their room (they are both in the best room!) and help Rene lay and wash up their meal things. I've arranged for them to eat with us for lunch and tea, but to have breakfast and high tea/supper in Rene's little sitting room. So far their school has not organised any timetable for them, but they have to go down to Taplow every morning and report at the church school by 10.30.

Gwen's father is in hospital and has been for five years. I don't know what with. Betty's is a builder's foreman. She has two young brothers, John and Peter. Peter is only eighteen months old. They come from nice homes and have been so nicely brought up. They look after themselves and could hardly be less nuisance. I'm very lucky. Some of the locals have got quite fierce little East End children with wide vocabularies and no finer manners. The keeper's wife has a pair of real little street arabs who arrived with sole-less shoes and no change of clothing of any sort. I gave one of these a ride back home today, having found him a very long way away, almost in Taplow village. He'd just wandered. I asked him if he was enjoying it at the Smiths and he said with awe: 'Mister Smiff's got *five* dawgs. E's gawn huntin' today but e's only taken one but he's got a double-barrel gun.'

The whole countryside is alive with children. They must all wear labels and gas masks and one comes upon them in little groups all over the place, making friends with the locals and comparing facts about ages, forms, and athletic prowess.

Alice's house is full of eighty-one babies under five! They have a staff of seventeen to look after them and need every single one. It's a government orphanage and seventy per cent of the children are illegitimate. The Winn young are at Greenwood Cottage and Alice and Reggie are at Cliveden for the moment. Mike and Jakie were both called up last week and Aunt N. says that Jakie looked just like an hors d'oeuvres in his khaki. We saw Michael and he was heart-rendingly handsome in his.

Reggie has applied to join the 9th Lancers but hasn't got any real information yet. Things are pretty busy at the War Office so, thank God, it may take time.

Reg Winn is on the reserve of the Grenadiers and hasn't been called either, so far.

David[1] is said to be doing Secret Service stuff and Bobbie's joined an anti-aircraft unit! (Searchlights).

And that's . . . about all I know. There is an enormous searchlight on the polo field at Cliveden which necessitates a unit to maintain it, so we've a generous sprinkling of khaki around here. It's springing up all over the place.

We all go around with identity labels tied to our clothes and our gas masks in hand otherwise, so far, we don't know it's a war. The petrol is going to be rationed but isn't as yet. The radio programmes are all of gramophone records at the moment so what I'll write about I don't know. Nor do I know whether my job persists or not. If it doesn't I'll be in somewhat of a hole, but I hope it does.

I've put in quite a lot of time lately giving a hand down at Taplow Lodge with the settling in of the eighty-one babies. There are actually eighty-two tonight, for Aunt N. discovered an eighteen-month-old boy in Kentish Town whose mother was having another this week and had seven more besides so she bundled him into the car and brought him down to join the rest.

I don't think I know any more. Cliveden is said to be housing some treasure from the British Museum but I don't know if that is true or not.

We are extremely well and happy and, gosh, how busy. I never seem to stop.

R. thinks this will be a short war but people said that in 1914. I don't know.

Haven't the [C.S.] lessons been marvellous lately?

Now, don't worry about us. If we're blown up we're blown up and it couldn't matter less, life being what we know it is. Anyway we shan't be. This is said to be a safe area.

———◆———

*September 11th, 1939*　　　　　　　　　　　　　　　　Parr's

So far nothing much has happened.

We had an air raid warning – our first – last Tuesday morning about 7.30 a.m. It was a foggy day and rather cool; the sirens certainly

---

[1] David Astor. Later, he joined the Royal Marines.

made one feel rather peculiar but nothing more. I went into the children's room and suggested that they might as well get up. We all did; there was nothing else to do. Hearing the distant thud of guns gave us a queer feeling too but it was so remote that one remained detached. The children had their breakfast, so did we, and then I drove R. to the station and the All Clear was given as we went along. It had been a reconnaissance flight by German planes and they'd been driven off. But the rumours! Lee at Cliveden had spoken to the odd-man[1] at St James's Square who said there'd been a two-hour raid over Southern London. Later we heard the planes had got as far as Reading and were driven off – all complete lies! And that warning is all we have experienced in Hitler's war – so far.

Aunt N.'s present of a new car started us off very cheerfully. It's a dream. Pale grey with a thin red line and red leather inside. It goes beautifully and we're simply enchanted with it. The old Ford limped away and fetched a mere twelve pounds towards payment on the new one.

The bicycle has come too and is extremely shining and streamlined. I've done a certain amount on it and find I've retained the cycling instincts from my youth. Wiss was down here for three days and we did some riding together.

*The Observer* job folded quietly last week. I had a really charming letter from Mr Garvin who said he hated having to do it: 'It makes me miserable to have to write this and so many other letters like it. You have done the "Broadcasting" delightfully. You have been a favourite of mine in the paper, as everyone knows. May you resume in happier times.'[2]

So that is that.

Meanwhile I'm perfectly OK, having stuck to the money I'd saved for the American trip. As long as I can, I shan't touch it for I'm still sure I'll be over next year.

As you know the revue has closed but Bertie Farjeon writes that he may open it up again and I think I may join it. You see, R. has applied for the army but – this is grim but fact – there is no room until a few have been wiped out. So the sensible thing is for him to go on with his job as we've got to eat and without it we shan't. The job is actually one of the exempted ones, being connected with mines which are badly needed in war time, but needless to say R. is dying to get into a uniform and be in things. But not yet. His office has been moved to North Wales and he'll have to join it by the end of this week.

---

[1] In large households the odd-man was employed to do all the heavy fetching and carrying.
[2] Wartime papers were so small that many features had to go.

Jakie and Michael are both at Cliveden with two days' leave. They look so fascinating in their khaki that one can hardly believe they are such babes. Poor Aunt N. is minding it all a good deal. She says the last war didn't really matter to her personally but this one is different: her two youngest ready to go and Bill in Egypt and David – I don't quite know what David is doing as a matter of fact.

So far nothing spectacular seems to happen but one hears of occasional losses and the U-boats seem to be active on the seas.

We are all rather mystified that the enemy haven't done any night bombing at all. Can it mean that they are not equipped for night flying? In which case our task is comparatively simple for we have got really magnificent defences. Virginia says the balloon barrage over London is the loveliest thing she ever saw. When the sun has set and the city is dusky the balloons remain rose pink for quite a time, high above the grey buildings. She came down for the weekend, having got leave from her driving. She's been hard at it for a week – 9.30 a.m. till 8 p.m. daily. She's on the personal staff of the Women's Voluntary Service and finds it interesting but very tiring. She enjoyed her two days' calm down here.

I'm so glad you really aren't worrying about me because it's a great joy to think of you leading an ordinary life in Tryon. That's the truth.

———◆———

*September 18th, 1939*                                    Parr's

Not quite so much time to write this week. The revue reopens on Wednesday the 20th as a Non-Stop! As the restrictions for all places of entertainment in the West End say that shows must close by 6 p.m. we are opening at the curious hour of 1.15 and running through to 6. I can't imagine who is likely to patronise us at such hours but as our prices are now way down we may attract the person who otherwise would go to a movie. I've not yet been to a rehearsal but we assemble tomorrow, Tuesday, and hear about alterations, cuts, etc. Of course this new time is perfect for me as it means I get home by 7.30 in the evening.

A piece of good news – from my point of view but not from R.'s – he's not been passed fit for service because of his varicose veins. You can imagine how I feel on the subject but of course with that fighting tradition in his family he feels a bit low about it and was very surprised when they refused to pass him. For the moment he is sticking to his job and is, therefore, off to Wales on Wednesday where his office has been evacuated to. I don't know how long he'll be away; probably until he can get some war work in London. I intend going up and down as long as I can. Rene is here to keep an eye on my evacuees so they are alright by day and I'll be here to see to them by night. Virginia is probably going to reopen her house in a few days' time and she's asked me to stay with her if I want to but as long as I can keep this house open I'd rather be here.

It gradually begins to feel more like a war. The news bulletins get more serious and the Cabinet's belief that the affair will take at least three years has sobered us all a bit, I think. Of course it was uttered to assure the Germans that we mean business; all the same it's a grim prospect. The sinking of the *Courageous* today[1] has depressed us a bit. R.'s cousins Harold and Victor G. were both on it but not, we imagine and hope, on this particular journey.

Alice went with her Reggie to the C. of E. service on Sunday and was shocked to find some villagers already in mourning for relations lost in the war – reference to this from the pulpit made her realise their black was not for a civil death!

The lessons are so wonderful and so applicable to the situation that one reads with increasing wonder and awe. I know that none of this is real and that there's only the now and that is harmonious and eternal.

Aunt Nancy is suffering a certain amount from self-pity but to give her her due she fully realises it and knows she won't be of use to anyone until she gets herself right. Poor little thing, she gets so knotted up and busy and of course it must be hell to see Mike and Jakie looking like a pair of newly-born hors d'oeuvres in their beautifully fitting uniforms. They look desperately young and they haven't had any life as yet.

You'd better be tactful if people ask you what we think about America being so selfish and isolationist! If this was a local war, fought for gain or territory we'd be mugs if we even hoped for US aid, but we're fighting an idea that menaces the world and America is not the least likely spot for the growth to spread to. And therefore we are fighting America's war for her and I think it's disgusting. All last September she called us names and spoke sanctimoniously about sacrifices, etc, and now, when we are in some sort of a position to enable us to combat the menace (which we certainly weren't in 1938), she just sits back and says she's not going to soil her fingers in something that doesn't concern her! It makes me *sick*.

However I expect she'll come in when we've done most of the

---

[1] HMS *Courageous*, 22,500 tons, sunk by a German U-boat off the west coast of Ireland, was the oldest aircraft-carrier in the Royal Navy.

hard work, just as she did in the last war, and then with her resources and freshness will claim she won the victory.

No sign of food rationing yet, although certain things aren't always obtainable because of traffic dislocation and not because of scarcity. Petrol is cut from the 23rd. We are allowed but five gallons per month! We figure it will get us to the station and back and that is literally all! Already we've been without the car for two days in an effort to save and it's amazing how quickly one gets adjusted to walking and bicycling! R. biked into Slough to fetch his dog from the vet's, on Saturday. (She'd been shut up for three weeks.)

So that we shan't be jolted into a new mode of feeding when rationing does come in I'm breaking into it gently. We now have meat but once a day and no butter for toast, only for cheese at the end of supper. We've cut down cream already and don't have a sweet at dinner – just fruit and/or cheese. We find we prefer it anyway!

My little evacuees continue to thrive on country life. They are good little things about the house and help Rene a lot. She likes having them, too.[1]

Luise and I took them blackberrying last week and we picked six lbs. Rene subsequently made three lbs of jam and gave us a blackberry flan and a hot stew of them too! She's turning into a grand little cook. We've been without Mrs Jaycock for some days now and find we manage very well. Luise and the children look after their own rooms, I do ours and R.'s dressing room, dust all the passages, the stairs, hall, drawing room and dining room and lay the table for lunch as well as clear away all other meals. It's a routine that soon becomes a habit and one just does it as a matter of course. It still takes me ages to dust but I'll have to learn to be quicker, for the train I'll take leaves about 11 in the morning. Luise is still with us. She hopes to sail on the 27th but we read today of US liners being held up by the crew's striking for 250 dollar bonuses for going into war zones! So maybe she won't get off then. I shan't mind if she doesn't; nor will she.

I must go to bed, I'm so sleepy after a day of sun and air, having washed my hair and dried it in the garden and then played tennis with Aunt N. all afternoon. R.'s done a great deal of work to the garden in the last few days and now it's ready for the winter.

No more news, don't worry about me being in London by day. The Little Theatre has an enormous underground air raid shelter in which we propose to continue performances during raids!

---

[1] The evacuees, Gwen and Margaret, only stayed with Joyce for three weeks. The authorities moved them, with their school, to Newbury to be further away from the danger of bombs aimed at London.

Much love and you needn't worry about us.
I'll miss R. dreadfully but still it's grand to know he's in this island.

---◆---

*September 24th, 1939*                                              Parr's

Nothing very much seems to happen in this war and it is these periods
of inaction that are perhaps the most trying. Hospitals are grimly
empty waiting, fully staffed, for emergencies. The streets in London
are full of special constables in tin hats; overhead are the balloons,
looking gay as a children's party, and the fronts of most buildings
are wearing a padding of sandbags.

Well, I'm back on the stage and in Non-Stop, too! We begin at
1.15 and do three shows until 6 p.m.

My appearances occur every one and a half hours and last for four
minutes each! I'm only doing the 'Institute Woman' as there's no
time for the 'Mothers', and anyway they are too subtle for the sort
of audiences we now get. Wednesday's houses weren't too bad and
they've improved since then so we are hopeful that we may be able
to run. If we each get our £5 salary with no percentage we'll feel
lucky. Tho' I must confess it is hardly worth my while, for out of
that £5 must come:

    10/- for my season
    3/- underground
    10/- tips
    30/- Income tax

Which leaves me £2-7-6d! per week. However that's something in
these days.

If we really get going in a big way we'll make much more of
course. Anyway, we'll just have to see.

---◆---

*October 2nd, 1939*                                              Parr's

I'm now alone down here for R. is still up in Wales where he looks
like being for some time to come. As you know he's been failed
medically and of course I was thrilled. But now all his Grenfell blood
has bubbled up and he says he's got to get his legs right in order that
he can join up and get to France! So he's written to the doctor to ask
if there is any treatment available to cure his veins and the doctor

says there is. Injections of some sort. Of course R. can do nothing while he's up there as the injections can't be done away from London and he can't leave Wales till he can get work in London so you see there's no immediate hurry. And even when the treatments start I shouldn't think they'd be quick in results. Reg wrote me a long letter about all this, explaining his feelings and telling me he felt as Julian Grenfell did when, as he lay dying, they told him his brother Billy[1] was on his way to France and he said: 'Thank God there'll be no gap.' All of which would sound terribly over-dramatic if it didn't come from R.P.G. who is hardly of that sort, as you'll agree. He feels there must be no Grenfell gaps – as if it really mattered actually! – and so he's got to get himself cured in order to be used as cannon fodder. Oh well, I can't help being sort of proud of him to want to do all this.

We did quite good business in the theatre last week: we are the only intelligent entertainment on in the West End! There are some genuine, naked Non-Stops but ours is the same witty revue that it was in the summer and is therefore the only show for the discerning audiences!!

I wonder if you heard Winston last night and if you thought he was as good as we did?[2] I particularly enjoyed his obvious relish in mispronouncing the word Nazi as if it smelled bad.

A batch of Tryon Bulletins came today and I must say I longed to be suddenly transported to Little Orchard where I'm sure there's lots of sun and autumny air and the view of the mountains. It's lovely here and not a bit like a war; but there's just a something everywhere that prevents one from concentrating on anything much. I sew without ceasing! In the theatre I have already finished a blouse and a small girl's frock and am halfway through the pants to match the child's frock. This is for evacuees – if wanted. At home I've made a woollen dress and am now making a pale blue, *very* thin, wool nightdress for really cold winter nights. It's a sheer stuff, very soft and not a bit stuffy, as you might imagine. The model I'm making is just like the kind Granny used to wear.

I can't sleep alone in the house. Rene has moved into what was Lefty's dressing room.

So far I haven't had a minute in which to feel lonely. I'm called at 8, have breakfast about 8.45, then help with housework (I do my own room entirely and dust several others.) At about 9.45 I take the dogs out for a run – me on the bike. We go up to Cliveden and all around the paths, long garden, etc. I leave for London at 10.30. In

---

[1] Julian and Billy Grenfell were sons of Lord and Lady Desborough, both killed in the first war.
[2] In Chamberlain's War Cabinet Winston Churchill was First Lord of the Admiralty.

the evenings I get back here at 7, bathe, dine – in the drawing room before the fire – write my letters, do the X-word, hear the news, sew, read the morning papers – finally, about 10.30, go to bed. So you see I don't have much time for moping. I've spoken to R. twice on the telephone but with the revised rates it's too dear to do very often. The new income tax is a nasty shock. Whew! 7/6 to the £. Ah well, it's worse for the rich.

---

*October 9th, 1939*                                                    Parr's

I've no very new news. We're still going on in an uneventful way though by the time you get this things may have begun. We'd be silly if we thought this war could continue for ever in this quiet way. Reg is still up in Wales at his work and I'm still going to and from London each day doing three shows at the Little. It's very hard work but we're lucky to have it. If the trains won't fit in with my hours I'll probably have to stay in London and if I do I'll go to Virginia's where Maria Brassey is already established. She [Virginia] has an air raid shelter in her basement so you needn't worry on that score. She and Maria are both driving for the Women's Voluntary Service and Maria comes home for weekends.

The WVS uniform is very pretty and Gin looks most attractive in hers. It's a good bottle-green tweed suit and overcoat with a wine-red shirt. I did two troop entertainments last week. The first was on Wednesday when I went Somewhere in Berkshire to entertain Michael's regiment [the Berkshire Yeomanry].

The other entertainment happened on Saturday – Somewhere in London. Cyril Ritchard, from the revue, ran it and several of us from the show and Bea Lillie did it. It was very gay. I did my W. Institute woman and then the 'Tattooed Lady'. (It's my theme song this war!) Once again it went like anything and I had to do it four times. Bea was very funny but filthy! She chose her programme rather badly I thought when she must have known the majority of the audience would be troops. A very chic and decadent little number by Noël Coward called 'I went to a Wonderful Party' had literally no point unless one knew it was about Mrs Corrigan,[1] Grace Moore,[2] and a

[1] A lumberjack's daughter from Cleveland, Ohio, Laura Corrigan was the wife of an American steel magnate. She rented the Grosvenor Street house of Edward VII's friend, Mrs Keppel, hired her butler, Rolfe, and soon became a well-known London hostess.
[2] American opera singer who became a film star in *One Night of Love*.

lot of toughs on the Riviera. However her renderings of 'Rhythm', 'Nanette' and 'The Three Little Fishes' were heavenly. Sam Maxwell is a major in the regiment we were entertaining and afterwards he drove me to Paddington through the blackout and was it black! It's awful. Sitting for an hour in a very slow train lit with only a dim blue bulb is no fun. I think one could knit by it but reading's out of all question.

And that's about all the news I know. Reg writes frequently and we telephone each other every week – it's too expensive to do it more often. I miss him a lot, as you can imagine. He's up there indefinitely which is good in one way as it means the postponement of his leg treatments and therefore his fitness for a soldier. We are well and happy.

---

*October 15th, 1939*                                                    Parr's

Last Monday I went to see Mrs Rawson. I felt all muddled inside, wasn't sure whether I was in my right place in the theatre, didn't know how much longer I could face commuting from here in the bad weather, etc, etc, etc. Generally caught up in the world thought of confusion and inaction. Well, I told all to Mildred and felt a whole lot better. She advised moving up to stay with Ginny, continuing in the theatre until something better came my way and was generally clear and helpful. Incidentally she is first class on the subject of what C.S.s should be and do now. The old formulas don't work: reading the lesson, denying the ego, etc. She says we are here to prove the allness of good and instead of rushing to read and be solaced by the 91st Psalm we must actually *be* the secret place of the most high. We must be the Truth personified just as Jesus was.

Well, I left her feeling tidied up and then decided to cut my ropes and be mobile. What did it matter really where I was? All this took some getting to for I adore my home and have strong beliefs in 'things' that belong to me. You know how it is.

Meanwhile several other things have happened in the theatre. We are ceasing to be three times daily Non-Stop on Thursday of this week and are going to do two complete shows a day, at 2.30 and 8.30. Worse really, for the other way at least gave us our evenings free. However, there it is.

I've not got much other news. The war drags on. All England is shocked and hurt by Lindbergh's[1] extraordinary broadcasts. The man's a mental Nazi, and after seeking solace in the freedom of England to turn against democracy and say that is not what we are fighting for – it's just disgusting.

Aunt N. has been at Plymouth for ten days and got back here on Friday. The losses to Devon families from the *Courageous* and *Royal Oak*[2] tragedies are terrible. Aunt N. knows one mother who lost three sons in the last war and her fourth when the *Courageous* went down. And yet she's sure this fight is right and would give more if she had them!

It's a beastly day; pouring rain and a high wind. I had lunch up at Cliveden but have managed to escape dining up there. No one seems to understand that I *like* being alone. If I can't have Reg I don't want anyone else and I love being quiet down here with my radio, knitting (scarves for the Navy) and my fire. It's all too rare these days and is going to be rarer. Weekends only. With the additional night work, week time entertainments will have to be cut out and that means Sundays. Oh well, it's a form of war work.

---

*October 29th, 1939*        Parr's

If you knew just how much I've been thinking and aching for Tryon these past days! I don't know why unless it's the local Tryon weather and faint indication of Tryon autumn colouring. Anyway I *long* so to be there.

At the moment I'm not really living; merely existing. Reggie is away from me and I'm at the theatre so much that I lose all remembrance of ordinary life. However I'm bound to be in my right place if I realise my oneness with Mind. And I do try. This darned old war may not yet have started in the front lines but in private lives it's having a horrid and upsetting effect. But that, of course, is the function of mortal mind; to stir up and disintegrate. I know quite well that the real and true are eternal and unchanging and that is what one must cling to in these topsy-turvy times. You can't imagine what

---

[1] Charles Lindbergh had been to Germany and Russia just before the war, and was very impressed with the German Air Force. Therefore he was pessimistic about the Allies' chances. He believed in Nazi philosophy and hated democracy.
[2] In October a U-boat got into Scapa Flow (though it was heavily defended) and sank the battleship *Royal Oak*, a considerable blow to Royal Navy prestige following only a few weeks after the sinking of the *Courageous*.

a comfort it is to know that you are leading a more or less normal life in Tryon. I think of it and glow!

What news have I?

Our second week of twice-daily has gone well. It's pretty tiring, I must say, but I sleep like a log after it and haven't lost weight so don't worry about me. I'm in the theatre so much, among so many people that it's giving me a Garbo complex and I just have to be alone. And I have been all the weekend and loved it.

I left immediately after lunch, went for a long walk alone with the dog. Came in, washed my hair and since have just gloated over the silence and solitude.

I wonder if you've seen Elliott yet?[1] He wrote me that he'd spoken to you on the telephone. Do try and see him, please. He's so darned lonely and not a bit happy – he probably never will be but you can be a help just now. I know it; *so do try and see him*. I'm so fond of him, you know, even though I disagree with much he believes and know that his moods are dreadful and that he is his own worst enemy. The fact remains that he's a very sweet person and more in need of warmth than anyone I've ever known.

Dinah [Brand] hasn't been well, is in a nursing home at Oxford, something on the bladder; sounds uncomfy, I must say. She's better but has got to stay there for a while yet. Aunt N. is so good to her and goes rushing down from all over the place and when you know what her life is like you'll realise it isn't easy to pop down to Oxford just like that.

Living with Gin continues to be most comfy and so cosy.[2] She's insisted on me staying in bed for breakfast and I must say I didn't oppose the suggestion for long. It's lovely. I lie in bed till about 10.30 reading, writing and just lying. I get lunch somewhere and then have to be in the theatre by 2. Charlotte Leigh and I go out for our meal between shows and that's just about all that happens in the week!

There really is no news of anything else. No war news; no home news. I've read nothing, knitted one scarf for the Navy, am halfway through a second. Being down here for the weekend is so heavenly. The time flies and it's now nearly 10 at night and that means that in about twelve hours I'll have to be getting ready to leave for London.

I came down late last night. I've adopted a more comfortable method of travelling in the blackout. I pay excess on my ticket and

---

[1] Elliott Coleman, an American professor and poet, was a family friend. He had been at Oxford but the outbreak of war forced him to return to America.
[2] For a time Joyce stayed with Virginia in London during the week, travelling to Parr's only at the weekend.

travel First, bribing the guard to lock me in and to wake me up at
Taplow. Then I lie full length and stare up at the solitary blue bulb
that lights the carriage and soon doze off in spite of constant stops.
We stop at literally *every* station along the line.

I think I'll go to bed now.

I'm very well and not depressed although somewhat annoyed by
the personal discomforts of this war!

My love to you and please give some to Lefty and tell him I
know I'm a pig not to write and that I really do mean to but don't
get time and will he, *please*, send me the long overdue and much
promised pictures of Wilton that you have repeatedly failed to
send!

*Please.*

I told you I'd been promoted on the billing didn't I? I come very
high up now!

Now, please, go and see Elliott if he can't get down to see
you.

---

*November 6th, 1939*                                              Parr's

Two big fat letters from you in two days. And one has only taken
nine days to get here so the mails are looking up.

We're gradually resuming normal theatre business doing three
matinées a week now instead of twice daily. A quiet week on the
whole. Good houses and gay audiences, particularly in the latter part
of the week. I went to several of the National Gallery Concerts. (Did
I tell you about them?) They are run by Myra Hess, the pianist.
There's one every day from 1 to 2 in the lunch hour and the entrance
is one shilling. I think the artists are paid a very small fee and the rest
goes to the Musicians' Benevolent Fund. There are thousands of
people aching for music at a price they can pay and these concerts
have filled a big demand. I love them. The Nat. Gal. is now denuded
of pictures but the other art sits just as happily under its roof.

I've been very America-homesick of late and just longed to walk
into Little Orchard and see you. But I'm not low: that's true. I really
am not.

I didn't get down here till 8.30 last night. But as we had no matinée
today I've had a lovely quiet time here by myself.

It was a pouring wet morning but I didn't care – I just wanted
some air – so put on an old macintosh and a beret and plunged into
it for an hour or so and got soaked. Since then I've washed my hair,

had lunch, written to R., to you and now, alas, it's time to go and change before having a cup of tea and catching the train to London.

Hermione Baddeley is still not well and we are still without her – a pity because there is definitely a public who won't go to a show if the star is off and as the news of her illness is in the papers it isn't too good for business. It's her own fault really for leading such a mad life. You can't work all day and evening and then sit up all night. And she likes to drink. It's a great pity.

Well, that really is all I know. I'm very well and cheerful and its marvellous knowing that R. is coming down in under two weeks.

D'you know I've discovered something I never knew about myself? I miss male society! I don't like not having a man about the place – and the theatre is hardly full of men – if you get my meaning. There's literally only one real man in the company and he is George Benson, height five foot six inches and happily married to Athene Seyler's daughter![1] So I'll welcome the return of Mr G. in a big way.

I've no gossip and I know this is a dull letter but there it is. Gin and I were *so* Tryon-homesick yesterday. We had a long reminiscence and tried to imagine just what you were doing.

I went to see Nick Phipps in *The Gate Revue*[2] on Friday afternoon. He's written some amusing numbers in it and does some of them himself – very well. Isn't it strange to think of him and me being on the stage?

No more.

I'm very well and happy –

PS WHERE ARE THE MUCH-PROMISED PICTURES OF WILTON?

I don't believe you read my letters or you'd know I've begged, asked and beseeched you to send them. Why not? *Please.*

---

*November 26th, 1939*     Parr's

No letter in two weeks. I suppose we'll have to get used to this sort of service; it'll probably get worse. Anyway I shall always write each

---

[1] George Benson had toured with Nicholas Hannen and Athene Seyler in Egypt and Australia. The marriage to Jane Ann, Athene's daughter, broke up. He married again, very happily, to Pamela White. Became a successful actor, mainly in character parts.

[2] At the Ambassadors. Had transferred, with cast changes, from the Gate Theatre.

Sunday as usual and mail it on Monday. One can't know when ships are sailing so it's just chance that one makes a fast one. I daresay you find that you get two from me on the same day at times.

R. is now settled in the new job at the Foreign Office[1] and his hours last week were 9 a.m. to 4 p.m. This week they'll be from 3 p.m. to 10 p.m. which is nicer really, for we'll have our mornings together and he can come up to the theatre – Whitehall is so near – and collect me in the evenings. We are now doing our London life from Ennismore Gardens and I'm glad to say we've forced Aunt Pauline, much against her will, to take £5 a month from us. This will pay for our linen, washing, breakfasts and lighting and telephone calls, but doesn't do more – she was all against it and said that if we wanted to we could send something to the fund for Polish refugees but we didn't feel that was quite right, so, after discussing it all at length with Rachel, we decided to send the £5 in cash in a registered letter. We feel so much better about it this way. After all, there is a war on and one can't go on being guests for ever. This arrangement makes us feel far freer and we like that. The flat is extremely cosy and comfortable. Steam heat is never to be sneezed at anyway. We have our own bathroom and Gertrude, who used to be Barbara Bevan's housemaid and who is very nice indeed, is there to cook breakfast and look after us. We expect to be there most of each week and as R.'s free day varies he may have to stay for some Sundays. He's had two inoculations for his veins and the doctor says it will only take eight weeks to do. I don't see that he'll ever be able to do really active service even if they are cleared up because this is only a patch work anyway and they will probably recur after a little while. He finds the ciphering quite amusing and hard work.

We had a matinée and between shows I went up to St John's Wood to have a meal with the Farjeons and discuss any new stuff I may be going to do. We've decided to put the old schoolgirl in place of 'Mothers'. This to take effect on December 11th when Totie Baddeley returns and Edward Cooper, who is taking Cyril Ritchard's place, joins the company.[2] Cyril is going into Pantomime. He'll be a great loss, I'm afraid. He got the offer when war broke out and theatre business was dead so he had to take it as it's big money. Manchester. He'll be badly missed because not only is he a draw and first-rate at his job but he's nice to work with and has a pleasant personality off as well as on stage.

[1] While being made fit, Reggie was in the Deciphering Department at the Foreign Office.
[2] Cyril Ritchard went into *The Sleeping Beauty* at the Palace, Manchester. Edward Cooper later played the lead in *Rise Above It* with Hermione Baddeley until an injury caused him to withdraw from the show.

Ivy St Helier[1] is still with us and is improving but will never be right in Totie's stuff. She's very friendly but I've had almost no chance of talking to her – I told her I was your daughter and she said she remembered you very well!

On Wednesday night, just as I was making up, Jimmie Smith telephoned to say he was home for twenty-four hours' leave and would R. and I join him and Dede [Lyttelton] and Billy & Patricia [Hambleden] at the Café de Paris[2] after the theatre. R. wasn't at the flat when I telephoned him but I left a message saying I was going anyway and that I'd explain if he felt too tired but that I hoped he'd come. (He didn't! He got back at 10 p.m. and couldn't face the idea of going out again, so went to bed.) I hadn't been out anywhere since war started and it *would* happen that I'd get asked out on the one night when I was wearing an old reddy-brown skirt, a striped blue lined shirt and sweater and shoes with rubber soles! So helpful for dancing, of course. Anyway there it was and off I went in this costume de sport to see life at the Café de P. Of course the 'no-dress' rule has gone and people wear just what they want to. There were a very few full evening dresses, several tea gowns with high necks and long sleeves and more afternoon dresses with feminine white touches! all the girls have gone womanly since war broke out and have wafted themselves on to pedestals, complete with natural nails, un-curled hair and light make-ups. I must say they are quite right. The contrast to the manly figure in uniform is as it should be. The boys, they were there in dozens, looking about fifteen each, broke one's heart. We sat in the gallery, feeling quite the next generation. Down below, on a space measuring little more than eight feet by twelve, they danced and danced. The place was jammed. Looking down from the gallery one felt pleasantly remote and I must say I was glad to be. There was a sort of homesick feeling about it all to me. It was ugly; it was touching; it was dreadfully earthly and it seemed so wasteful to see these babies dancing and drinking in the Noël Coward era manner with a 'let's-eat-drink-be-merry-for-tomorrow-we-die' look on their faces. This is *not* the way to face the war. It should be done in searching for and finding what are the realities. But maybe they are too young for that yet. I find I fly to music and poetry these days. I've been haunted by Walter de la Mare's lines:

[1] Her best known part was Manon La Crevette in Noël Coward's *Bitter Sweet*, His Majesty's, 1929–31.
[2] On March 8th, 1941 two high-explosive bombs fell on the Café de Paris building; thirty-four people were killed, fifty were injured, many seriously, and thirty were treated on the spot.

Look thy last on all things lovely
Every hour. Let no night
Seal thy sense in deathly slumber
Till to delight
Thou hast paid thy utmost blessing;
Since that all things thou wouldst praise
Beauty took from those who loved them
In other days.

There's been so much about beauty in the lessons lately. The more music I hear the more I know it is the nearest to spirit of all the arts. I went to a wonderful concert at the National Gallery on Thursday evening at 5.30. A string orchestra, the Boyd Neel,[1] were conducted by Sir Henry Wood. A perfect programme of Tchaikovsky, Bach and Elgar. We came home on Thursday night and had Friday here. R. worked in the garden all day and I lazed indoors, reading and listening to the radio.

Saturday – yesterday – we had good houses for both performances. R. took Charlotte Leigh and me to supper between shows and then he stayed at the flat in order to work today and I came down here on the late train. Church this morning, Laura Grenfell for lunch. Walk afterwards in a high wind. Tea with the Winns then R. arrived on the 5.30. Since then we've been tucked in here before a rosy fire. We are now replete from a huge supper, ending with cheese and celery. The Prime Minister is due to broadcast in five minutes.

The war is horrid and I hate it. One has feelings that it is going to be quite worse quite soon; but that impression is probably due to the fact that I am, at the moment, 'under the weather'. R. does not feel as I do; so let's hope he's right.

We are both well, busy and happy –

WHERE ARE THOSE PICTURES OF WILTON?
?????
Did you remember his birthday. Nov 24th.

---

[1] Founded by Dr Louis Boyd Neel, the orchestra played at the Salzburg Festival and at Glyndebourne. Boyd Neel returned to medical work in 1939, and was engaged in fitting artificial limbs.

*December 3rd, 1939*

Sunday in London. Because I'm doing a troop concert this evening and as R. is working today it wasn't worth going down to Parr's alone last night. It's a cold grey Sunday.

We had quite a good week in the theatre. I went to some *lovely* concerts at the National Gallery, beginning with an all-Bach one on Monday to which I went with Myra Hess. We sat at the back and popped out to congratulate the artists after every item. Myra is the whole thing behind these concerts. They were her inspiration and succeed so wonderfully because of her energy and spirit. She plays at least once a week herself on top of all her other work. I wish you knew her; she's one of the most attractive people in the world. Gentle, humourous, gay, quiet, intelligent, kind, and above all this the world's greatest woman pianist. Jewish of course, but, for once, not Jewish looking. I always feel that when she plays she does so in a sort of 'this-is-what-my-race-is-really-like' spirit. And does the job perfectly.

Reg and I lunched together most days and Ginny joined us on Wednesday, looking so pretty in her WVS uniform. Tony is due for a full week's leave on the 11th. They are both holding their breath till the time comes. I must say this war is extra hard on the newly married; particularly when they are so enormously in love as Tony and Ginny are.

R. had Friday off again so we went down on Thursday night and spent the next day at Parr's. He took a gun and Nan and went over to White Place where he felled a couple of rabbits and a pheasant. I spent the whole morning washing my hair; such a boring job. I resent spending an hour with my head in the fireplace – but it does save money to do it at home.

———◆———

*Christmas Eve, 1939*                                    Parr's

What else have I done? Helped cut sandwiches at the National Gallery for the buffet at the concerts.

Been shopping with Myra Hess.

Seen the Deanna Durbin movie and loved it.[1]

---

[1] Probably *Three Smart Girls Grow Up*.

Lunched with the Grenfells at Chesham Place – Frances and Katie both very large now – their babies due in Feb.

All the Winns – all except David – came to the revue on Thursday afternoon and seem to have liked it.

And that's about all I remember. I'll add to this after Christmas.

———◆———

*December 31st, 1939*                                    Parr's

Snow on the ground, fog and it's cold! Virginia, in a series of coral and yellow sweaters, is on the sofa with some scarlet knitting; R. in thick corduroys, is deep in an Edgar Wallace in the green armchair, and I'm practically in the fireplace, wearing blue suede bedroom boots lined with sheepswool, writing to you from the yellow armchair. It *is* cold. Particularly after the steam-heated luxury of the London flat. We got down late last night and except for going to church I haven't been out. R. walked his dog down to Burnham and V. went as far as the post box with a letter to Tony and now we're making a Sunday nest and it's good. If *only* weekends lasted longer. You just catch your breath again and it's time to get back to work. I've been more or less speechless for some days. Sort of aftermath of a cold and somewhat worrying when you consider my livelihood. However Mrs Rawson was wonderful and I did all performances almost comfortably, and after today's rest I'll be quite alright for tomorrow evening. It's a horrid feeling and one wants to whistle loudly or bang something just to break one's own enforced silence. Actually the whole thing has been rather wonderful, for I arrived quite speechless one evening and was able to speak pretty well when I got on to the stage.

It's been a quiet week.

(Virginia, now in a book, has looked up to ask who I'm writing to and sends you lots of love. She's in excellent form, looking pretty and well and is much relieved because Tony has at last got his commission which means he ceases to be a slave and becomes an officer, with at any rate *some* creature comforts.)

R. left here last Monday – Christmas Day, and I followed early the next morning. I dined up at the house and it was all a little sad and strained. After dinner Jakie and Reggie Winn did some really good charades, Bobby was the clergyman and Aunt N. was the Little Jew. She was inspired and very funny. All about Rosie and how the London Rothschilds hadn't been so pleased to see them when they got back here from Poland. Before the home entertainment we'd listened to Gracie Fields and she was *so* moving in her gaiety and infectious spirit of happiness. I wonder if she was relayed to America? It was from a troop concert somewhere in France – for the RAF.

This week has been largely work and speechlessness. I did a nurses' Christmas Party at the Elizabeth Garrett Anderson Hospital (singing, word-gaming, etc, for one solid hour alone, was the start of the voicelessness). It was a success and I've been invited as a special guest – not entertainer, mark you! – to the nurses' own private party on the 4th! So I'm going. Miles away up the Euston Road but they were so nice and seemed to find me funny.

I've been to the Nat. Gal. concerts a lot and on Friday went to the rehearsal for the joke New Year's Day concert – the Haydn Toy Symphony is going to be done by all the stars. It's a children's nursery school thing really; trumpets, drums, triangles, cuckoos, quails, nightingales and rattles. The Isolde Menges Strings are being the orchestra and Myra Hess and Irene Scharrer are cuckoos, Moisewitsch is a triangle, old Elena Gerhardt[1] is a drum! etc, etc, and I – suddenly – I am going to be a nightingale! Myra asked me to go to the rehearsal and then asked if I'd like to blow the water whistle nightingale – so I am! We laughed so at the rehearsal that we ought to have nothing left to giggle at at the performance. The nightingales have a nice straightforward part with one extremely exacting passage of sixteen bars to be done in one breath! We do it very nicely – Mr John Simmonds – pianist – and me. The Toy Symphony is the finale of the whole concert. It's all very much on the light side and includes the Schumann Carnival being played by ten famous pianists in turn! A movement each.

We had a slackening off of business in the middle of the week but it pepped up yesterday. Between the matinée and evening shows the girls in our dressing room gave a sherry party and at one moment there were twenty-seven people in our very small room! I provided the cakes – pure gold they were, from an American shop in Park Lane. Delicious. R. gave us a bunch of giant daffodils to give the spring touch and we all went shares on the sherry. It was a successful if noisy party – we only invited the company.

I saw Aunt N. in church looking v. pretty and she asked us up for lunch but we got out of it!

No more time to write to you before supper and I don't suppose I'll have time afterwards so I'll stop.

Much love and let's hope 1940 is better than 1939 has been.

[1] Isolde Menges, Irene Scharrer, Benno Moisewitsch, and Elena Gerhardt were all distinguished musicians of the day.

*1940*

On April 9th, 1940, the war entered its second phase. The phoney war ended and Hitler's *Blitzkrieg* offensive opened with the German invasion of Norway in April, the invasion of the Low Countries on May 10th and the conquest of France by mid-June. British reverses in this part of the war were immense: failure in the Norwegian campaign was followed by the retreat from the beaches of Dunkirk between May 26th and June 4th. The country was defenceless and apparently on the point of being invaded. On July 10th the *Luftwaffe* made its first heavy bombing raid on southern England, heralding the Battle of Britain, fought between July and September for air superiority over the Channel coast. Though this battle was lost by the Germans, they nonetheless continued bombing London and the large industrial cities until adverse weather conditions in December forced the raids to cease.

Like most people in England, Joyce had learned to live with the phoney war. Its end jolted her into living from day to day, in constant fear of bombing or invasion. She writes in her autobiography: 'Music was particularly important in the terrible (beautiful) spring of 1940 – continuing days of cloudless blue skies and more and more tragic news.' Myra Hess's concerts at the National Gallery gave joy to many, including Joyce, and nourished her love of music. But the blitz ended Joyce's visits to London and the concerts: she worked in a troop canteen in Maidenhead and as a Red Cross welfare officer in the Canadian Red Cross Hospital at Cliveden. In June Reggie was passed fit for service by the doctors and joined the King's Royal Rifle Corps in Wiltshire.

In her letters to Ma, Joyce frequently criticises America's isolationist policies with regard to the European war. And, in North Carolina, Ma did all she could to publicise the plight of Britain by organising a campaign for all her influential friends to write to their senators urging material support for the British war effort. The results were mainly in the form of money to purchase supplies for specific organisations.

# 1940

Darling Ma

Well, the New Year's Day concert at the National Gallery was a whole parcel of fun. We were conducted by Sir Kenneth Clark[1] who had never done such a thing before. He is really head of the Nat. Gal. and pictures, not notes, are his forte.

The audience of 1280 enjoyed themselves from the sounds they made but none of them had as much fun as we did in the orchestra.

What else do I know?

Oh *yes*. David Niven[2] suddenly appeared at the theatre last week. We fell on each other's necks. I don't quite know why I was so glad to see him but I was. (After all I used to think he was an over-funny young upstart, didn't I?) But he was sweet and I was somehow very pleased to see him. The RAF have refused him, because he's thirty and because he is not absolutely fit because when he was very small he had an operation on his neck somewhere near the jugular vein and this does something still to his circulation and means he'd go unconscious in deep dives from heights. He's furious. Now he's hanging on, hoping to get a commission in his old regiment, I think. He's coming to the show again next week and we're going to have some supper.

London is full of young Canadian soldiers. You see them every-where – They have 'Canada' written in block letters across their arms and all have that unmistakable look of space about them that few Englishmen wear. We see them in groups at Lyons where all the waitresses vie with each other to serve them. I suppose the ones at Cliveden in the last war looked young. These are babes in arms.

---

[1] After the National Gallery he became head of the Independent Television Authority. Later celebrated for his *Civilisation* television series, he was made a life peer and died in 1979.
[2] Under contract to Samuel Goldwyn in Hollywood when war was declared, David Niven eventually joined up in March 1940 as a subaltern in the Rifle Brigade. He and Joyce knew each other through the Astors. They had also met in the US in 1934.

Reggie's legs appear to improve under treatment – I'm sad to say! – and he thinks he'll pass fit by the end of Feb. But even if he does it'll take ages to get him trained so there's no immediate worry.

*January 22nd, 1940*                                              Parr's

We're having the coldest weather known to living memory and it's fierce. All the pipes in this house are frozen solid and we've spent the weekend up at Cliveden. I'm just down here for the morning to pay the books, repack clean clothes, etc, and I can't begin to tell you how icy it is. I'm right on top of a large fire, wearing socks and boots, a vest, two sweaters and a pair of woollen pants and I can hardly hold my pen because my fingers are so frozen. Plumbers all over England are doing a roaring trade but there aren't enough of them to do the work and the Great Unwashed are legion. It must be really dreadful for the very poor; it's bad enough for the middling. Uncle Waldorf's bathroom at Cliveden has, so far, escaped the freeze so we've all queued up to use it, and of course the central heating is on full in order to save the other pipes so it's very comfy up there. Here a pipe has gone and its sudden demise called forth a Niagara that flowed steadily all one night from the tank in the roof to the ceiling in Rene's cupboard, where it maliciously wetted every sheet, towel, blanket, and bath mat in its path. Rene has got everything dried out at last and Webb, from Cliveden, has turned all the water off at the main to prevent further trouble so one can't wash or go to the john and it's most tiresome.

Last week was mainly music – and lovely it was too. I did a couple of full mornings' work at the National Gallery canteen, heard a concert every day and went to several movies.

I don't believe I've any other news. Aunt N. is in good shape and you know there are moments when I believe she really does understand what C.S. is about! Last night she attacked me about Daddy not coming to see her and said a lot of foolish things about him – disloyal, etc, etc. It didn't even make me rise because I knew that he wasn't any of those things so I let the tide roll over me. This morning she apologised and said she hadn't slept at all last night and now saw clearly and felt quite differently about it!

I got down on the midnight last Sat. and the nightwatchman let me in and I crept up the stairs to the Orange Flower[1] where there was a huge fire blazing and a thermos of malted milk waiting for me.

---

[1] One of the principal bedrooms in Cliveden.

now waiting for a decision. They've got
as far as Fougasse ; now they repose
on the Editors table for a final
judgement. If they come off I'll send
you copies.

And that's all we know.
Apart from the cold — which is bad —
we're fine.

Much love

Joyce

This is me —
even in London.

January 22nd, 1940

Presently there was a knock on the door and Aunt N. came in, little face all cold-creamed and her funny stocky little figure wrapped round in a pink satin dressing gown, to see if I was warm enough and if the fire was alright. She *is* touching you know. *And* maddening. Like quicksilver – here one minute and way over there the next. But she's so angelic and thoughtful of me that I'll never feel anything deep down but the greatest affection for her.

Elly Cunningham [an American friend] has just sent Virginia and me six pairs each of the most lovely Saks silk stockings so we're very well stocked now and I, personally, have a dozen pairs put away for later use.

———◆———

*January 28th, 1940*                                             Parr's

I've been to the Nat. Gal. most days last week and the Beethoven Quartets concert on Wednesday was wonderful. I'm just discovering Beethoven and it's an awe-inspiring process. He's beyond anything of the earth. Virginia has given me a bound score of Vol. II of the Quartets and I've seldom been more delighted with a present. There are to be two more Quartets played on Tuesday of this week and both are in my book so I'll take it along to follow from.

I do love music – more and more and more. The only thing I'd sort of like to have a child for would be to watch it grow up with music. But it might hate it so I wouldn't care to risk anything so awful!

Our weather continues to be bad. Very cold till Wednesday then a partial thaw, followed by rain that turned, by stages, from sleet to hail to snow and now, on Sunday, we are in a completely white world with the roads very tricky and the skies still dark and full of snow – Jakie has just come over from Windsor and says that his windscreen froze over at every 100 yards. I don't know how we'll get to the station tomorrow – I abandoned all hope of getting to church this morning and it's worse now.

Myra was playing Brahms's Second Piano Concerto yesterday afternoon and as I had a matinée and couldn't hear it she let me go to the full orchestral rehearsal at the Queen's Hall in the morning. It was thrilling. The hall, quite empty, the orchestra busily concentrating on the job in hand and Myra playing like an angel. It was far more fun than any real performance could ever be – one could feel the thing growing.

———◆———

Well, the next day we awoke to find deep new snow – a foot – on top of frozen old snow and the roads were almost impassable. We managed to get down to Parr's in the morning, where we collected clean clothes and saw Rene and then, after twenty-five minutes' effort, we managed to turn the car around and get back to the big house for lunch. The station had told us earlier in the day that all trains were late so we telephoned them again before going down to try and catch the 1.40 ([Neither] the 12, nor the 11 had been in by then and they said we'd probably catch one of these earlier ones if we came down.) It was icy on the platform but the GWR [Great Western Railway] had thoughtfully banked up a roaring fire in the waiting room and we hugged that for half an hour. At 1.45 the station master telephoned Reading for news of trains and they said they hadn't seen or heard of anything coming our way so we dashingly decided to use up some of our precious petrol and go to London by car. There were two lonely people in the waiting room, both anxious to get up too, so we offered them lifts and they came with us. Driving up wasn't too bad as it hadn't begun the evening freeze yet; but it wasn't wise to hurry so we didn't get up till 3.15. In this flat I searched for my torch – without which one never moves in the blackout as the only way to stop a bus or a taxi is to flash the light on the ground in front of the thing you want to stop. But it wasn't here and I was sure I'd had it on Saturday, so I rang up Myra Hess's niece, Beryl, to see if I'd left it at the Queen's Hall when I was there for the rehearsal two days before.

I found that Beryl wasn't well so had moved from Myra's house because the housekeeper was also sick and there was no one to look after her. I traced her to her sister's house and she knew nothing of the torch but was very worried because Myra, who had played at Bristol the day before, was coming up by train to London and there was no way of stopping her from trying to get home to Golders Green, which was impassable. Beryl had arranged a room for M. in central London but couldn't let her know. So of course I said I'd go to Paddington, meet the train and deliver the message. We knew the trains were late so we guessed that an hour and a half – that is 4 o'clock – would be about the time she'd get in. So accordingly at 4 I arrived at Paddington to take up my watch by the indicator (to tell us which train came to which platform). Myra's train wasn't in till 7.35! And I *so* nearly missed her and if it hadn't been for some strange prompting that made me suddenly say her name aloud as I passed through what I thought was a taxi-full of people I should never have found her. But she was in it! And as it was blackout time and she wasn't expecting anyone to meet her it was sort of a miracle that we got together. She was terribly grateful to me for waiting so long. I must say I hadn't minded it at all because I made such friends with so many people all waiting to meet trains. There were two very young porters who promised to help me in the search; and a Welshman whose wife had been visiting her family in Cardiff; and a know-all man from Rickmansworth who had strong but foolish opinions on every subject. We had a pleasant political discussion which warmed us all up. My sole legacy from a three-and-a-half-hour wait in the bitter weather was stiff legs from marking time in order to warm my feet!

Well, that was Monday. I just got down to the theatre in time and although we had a dreary and little house it was sort of fun because Robert Donat[1] and Montgomery[2] were in front.

Thursday's was a lovely concert – the Boyd Neel String Orchestra. I took Rachel and Virginia to sit with Myra and we had such fun all in a row at the back, behind the curtain. For the concerts are given in a round hall in the N.G. [National Gallery] out of which four big rooms open in cruciform. If there's a big audience the curtain is pulled back. There wasn't a big one on Thursday, so we could relax in our private room.

One of the things they played that day was Capriol Suite[3] – remember Anthony Bernard playing it? *Pieds-en-l'air*. It always reminds me of Aunt Phyllis. And they also played *the* most beautiful Bach thing that was quite new to me. Ricercare, I think it was called.

———◆———

*February 11th, 1940*                                        Parr's

I'm *thirty* since I last wrote – it was yesterday. I'm very glad I'm no longer very young but thirty is quite an age. Whew. I must say I often feel all of it; tho' there are moments when I distinctly don't. It doesn't matter anyway.

I wrote you a very long letter last Monday and I've had no real news since then. Tuesday was a huge day at the National Gallery.

[1] Robert Donat, best known in the theatre for his performances in *Precious Bane* and *A Sleeping Clergyman*, and under his own management in *Red Night*; in films he had made a great impression in *The Citadel*, and *Goodbye Mr Chips*.
[2] Robert Montgomery, American film actor, played in *The Last of Mrs Cheyney* and was in England, in 1940, to make *Busman's Honeymoon*.
[3] By Peter Warlock.

We had 1,280 people and they ate 1,500 sandwiches, heaven alone knows how many dozen dozen rolls, buns, slabs of fruit cake and chocolate biscuits. Myra was playing duets with Irene Scharrer and Elsie Suddaby sang. All Bach. It was wonderful.

We've had better houses all the week and [they] ought to be up still a bit more next for our 'Last weeks' bills are out and that seems to add a spurt of business. It's pretty certain that we'll be off on March 16th, and I still haven't plans of any sort. An agency wants to book me for cabaret but I've said No, firstly because it would be hell to do my very subtle stuff in restaurants and secondly because I want more stage work first before I'm reduced to cabaret. (If ever.)

I worked in the canteen at the Nat. Gal. twice last week – 9.30 a.m.–2 p.m. On Tuesday after the concert I went back to Golders Green with Myra and her niece. Such a cosy afternoon with tea in front of the fire in her music room, followed by another performance by Howard Ferguson[1] of his lovely sonata that I first heard on New Year's Day up there. It is completed now and is *magnificent*. A great piece of music, full of inspiration and emotion and truth. Really very remarkable.

Such a wonderful Beethoven concert on Friday at the Nat. Gal. two Quartets, early ones. I've discovered that by following with a score these become just a hundred per cent more thrilling; and clearer.

———◆———

*March 3rd, 1940*　　　　　　　　　　　　　　　　　Parr's

Did you send me the *Ladies Home Journal*? Two copies – Feb and March – blew in last week and I think they must be from you. So thank you v. much indeed. You can't imagine how we *all* love to see American magazines. D'you know my *New Yorker* goes from me to Myra Hess, then to Aunt Margaret [Phipps], on to Ann [Holmes],[2] back to Nicholas and finally to the Red Cross!

Well, my big excitement is that I've been asked to appear in the big Royal Command charity matinée on March 12th for the Red

[1] Howard Ferguson, a lifelong friend of Myra Hess, organised the National Gallery concerts for her. A distinguished composer, he also edited all Schubert's piano works and *Keyboard Music*.
[2] Ann Holmes was Joyce's cousin, daughter of Margaret and Edmund Phipps. John and Nicholas Phipps were her brothers and she was married to John Holmes, who served in the navy.

Cross. Not only to do my monologue (schoolgirl) *but* to appear as Lady Bull to Godfrey Tearle's Sir John[1] in a specially written finale by Clemence Dane.* She's built my little part *specially for me*! Seems she's a fan and insists on me for the part!! Really the incredible things that do happen to me. The finale begins with Sir John and Lady Bull at home in their large library where they are entertaining the local county and their evacuees and their mothers. The movie that Lady B. had arranged to show has fallen through so she has engaged a conjuror instead. Groans from the disappointed company. But it turns out that the conjuror is Leslie Howard who conjures up Peter Pan (Dot Hyson) and Hook (Gordon Harker) and, well, everyone on the stage really! Peggy Ashcroft as Juliet, Fay Compton as Mary Rose, Donat as Mr Chips, Lilian Braithwaite as Queen Elizabeth, Sybil Thorndike as St Joan, Robey as Falstaff, etc, etc, etc.[2] And in the middle of this galaxy is me. Here is how Clemence Dane describes the part: 'Lady Bull rises. She is young, shy, charming with a breathless apologetic manner and a delightful smile.' And she wrote the part for me! Golly!

All I have to do really is make a speech about wool! You know: thank the knitters everywhere for doing so splendidly and then I tell 'em about the movie and the conjuror.

It's not a very long part but it is important and I'm on the stage all the time. I've no idea what I'm to wear – whether it's day or night in the sketch. But *me* and Godfrey Tearle. Really! The things that do happen to me!

There are to be five rehearsals so you can imagine how busy I'm going to be with the last week at the Little and then the final week of all at Golders Green. We close on March 16th and I couldn't feel sadder about anything. It has been such fun; and I love my friends in it – Betty-Ann, Charlotte, Peggy and dear Daisy the dresser – and George Benson and Cyril, etc, etc. There are sides of the stage life that don't attract me but on the whole I *love* it!

And to think that a year ago I'd never even set foot on the boards. Well, I am glad I took the great risk – because it has taught me a lot and – well, because I love it.

[1] Godfrey Tearle, one of the heads of the profession. Had done much classical work, and had recently played in *The Flashing Stream*, by Charles Morgan.
[2] A clutch of names of the time: Leslie Howard, chiefly in films at this point, one of a distinguished family of actors; Dorothy ('Dot') Hyson was daughter of Dorothy Dickson, and later married Anthony Quayle; Gordon Harker was a Cockney comedian, who often worked with Will Hay; Fay Compton, recently Ophelia to John Gielgud's Hamlet; Lilian Braithwaite, a grande dame of the theatre of the period; and George Robey, a music hall comedian, billed as 'The Prime Minister of Mirth', who also played in operetta, Shakespeare (Falstaff). Knighted the year before, he died in 1954 aged eighty-five.

Totie Baddeley got German measles and is still off, so that for a week I've been the star of the finale, coming down the steps hand-in-hand with Cyril for the curtain. It's been a very gay week in the theatre and (sh-sh-sh) Totie hasn't been missed much. The girls who do her parts are so good and then of course Cyril Ritchard is back from Pantomime and he is a pillar of strength and makes up for everything.

I don't know much other news. We've been very quiet, seen no movies this week. Lovely concerts at the Nat. Gallery and I did two mornings' *very* hard work in the canteen. But as I slept in the afternoons it worked out alright.

You asked me the other day whether we had enough money. And the answer is Yes. R. is making about £400 and I've got £175 saved – was to have been my trip to America, alas – so that we are perfectly alright. I'll try and do odd jobs in the summer if I can. Maybe some broadcasts? A film?

Today is the day of the gala matinée and I'm spending a quiet morning in bed before going down to the theatre at 1.30 to get ready.

Our last week at the Little was complicated by absences from the company. Charlotte got German measles, Peggy Willoughby got tonsilitis and Totie Baddeley – who has no sense of duty towards her neighbours – just didn't choose to play on Wednesday night as she'd rehearsed all day Wednesday! – with the result that we had to cancel Wednesday's performance entirely. Money handed back, the audience turned away at the doors. All very sad and quite unnecessary if only Totie had turned up.

The next day we put on an admirable performance with under-studies – including me in one of Charlotte's parts, The Lady Organiser at a charity dance matinée. Fortunately the whole thing is read anyway so I did not have to learn a part. Charlotte always plays her as an elderly sort of Mabel Grey but I had fun changing her into a benevolent and obviously simple-minded ditherer with just a shade of the older kind of C.S. prac. about her! I seem to have been fairly funny. But I prefer doing monologues. However it was very good for me to have to do it. I played the part for five performances.

We had two rehearsals of the Clemence Dane Finale at the Palace last week, Thursday and Friday. My 'husband', Godfrey Tearle, is nice and friendly, but it is slightly alarming all the same being in such exalted company.

\

Well, it was a terrific day for me. I stayed in bed till about 12 then Gertrude gave me some mushroom soup, cold sausages and baked potatoes here and then I bused up to the Palace Theatre and got there about 1. (The show began at 2.15 but you know how I am.) I was put into Dressing Room 15, high up on the third floor, and was to have shared it with Angela Baddeley, Gladys Henson (Leslie's wife) and Joyce Carey (Lilian Braithwaite's daughter)[1] but luckily it ended with Joyce Carey and myself as Angela B. was sick and Gladys Henson dressed at her own theatre just down the road. Actually Totie Baddeley blew in for her change but wasn't there long. So it was peaceful and roomy. I put on a very careful make-up. The Palace is so huge after the Little that I used just about double of everything and larded it on to my eyes and eyelashes. The boy called the half and I was already fully dressed so I sat by and talked to Joyce Carey who is charming and very friendly. Her dresser used to be with Edna Best[2] and we had a lot of chat about the other stars she'd worked for.

The quarter – then the five – and I decided I'd wander down to the stage for I was on No 3 to do my Women's Institute. Madge Titheradge,[3] dramatic in white crêpe and diamanté was preparing to go on and speak the Prologue. A dresser hovered over her and Walter Crisham[4] (who used to dance with Dorothy Plunkett) and his partner did a few practice steps on the darkened stage.

The curtain rolled up with a whirring noise. (It's even more exciting to be behind it than in front of it – the sudden lights and the feeling of a crowded auditorium.) Titheradge did her bit – gave her all in fact, on the subject of England, England, England. (Actually a v. well written piece by young Christopher Hassall, a poet.[5] I thought she gave it too much.)

Crisham followed with his dance and while he took his call before the curtain I got ready to come through the tabs just behind him. (The organisation was wonderful. No delays at all and when you

---

[1] Angela Baddeley, Hermione Baddeley's sister, concentrated on straight parts, classical and modern; married Glyn Byam Shaw, actor and director; Gladys Henson was currently in Emlyn Williams's *The Light of Heart*; and Joyce Carey had recently played Gwendolen in *The Importance of Being Earnest* with John Gielgud.
[2] Edna Best is always associated with Tessa in *The Constant Nymph*.
[3] Dramatic actress, born in Australia; in her young days appeared with Lewis Waller; was Peter Pan in 1914; throughout the Twenties and Thirties had many successes.
[4] Actor and dancer, born in America; appeared in *The Gate Revue* and several other revues subsequently.
[5] Wrote the lyrics for several Ivor Novello musicals, and verse-prologues for many such occasions as this one.

know that at least sixty people, mostly stars, took part and most of 'em brought their own managers, dressers, lighting men, etc, etc, it was a miracle of smoothness and all carried out in the face of overwhelming difficulties.)

I got a nice round of applause when I came out and it went well. Without being told to, I cut it considerably because I know the horror of endless turns at such charity matinées and I'm sure the audience is grateful for small doses. Anyway my policy is always to give 'em too little so that they feel not quite satisfied and wish they'd had more! Leslie Henson followed me. (Incidentally: before the show started he came up to me and said he wanted to thank me for my lovely work! Wasn't it nice? I at once told him how much I loved his work and we had a very cosy two minutes.)

I went up to my dressing room after my turn and made the change into Lady Bull.

I told you about the part, didn't I? Lady Bull: she's entertaining the county and the evacuees and the movie she planned to run for them fails to turn up so, at the last moment, she gets hold of a conjuror. He is Leslie Howard. It's not a big part, but it's very important to make it matter. I think it was alright. Anyway Daddy and R. seemed pleased. (They paid a guinea each to see me!)

And I know how much you like to hear all the dewdrops so I'll tell you that Cyril Ritchard was standing at the back of the stalls and he told me afterwards that I had an entirely commanding personality on the stage and much charm and sweetness and that I was easily heard and held the stage whenever I spoke! So there. Now DON'T go and tell all Tryon about this – sh-sh-sh –

Well that's about all. Oh no, there's another really very touching dewdrop – Robert Donat, no less, came and introduced himself (what a nice man he is and so modest and natural) and said that he'd sat next to Aunt Nancy the night before and my goodness how proud she was of me! I don't quite know why that has touched me so but you know how she is and to think of her proud in public – well, I think it's so sweet. Particularly as she always says to *me*, 'When are you coming off the stage? Come on back and look after the Women's Institute and the hospital, etc, etc!!'

Beau Hannen was very sweet and friendly to me. I had some chat with George Robey and I introduced myself to Bebe Daniels and Ben Lyon[1] who came at the eleventh hour to substitute for someone else. They asked to be remembered to you both. Evelyn Laye[2] was

[1] Husband and wife. Appeared first in their native America, and in films; settled in England. Broadcast regularly (including *Hi-Gang* and *Life with the Lyons*).
[2] Musical comedy star, born 1900, who was currently appearing in *Lights Up* at the Savoy Theatre.

friendly, and Bea Lillie (who was a big success singing 'Weary of it all').

I by no means was the heroine of the day but the point is that I got by in my first straight part and I enjoyed it enormously. Two people have asked me if I'd ever consider going into a straight play and I answered: Certainly, I'll try anything. God certainly does do the most extraordinary things for me, doesn't he?

Edith Evans did a wonderful scene from *The Way of the World*. I didn't see her to speak to.

To return to Donat: he met Aunt N. dining with Ronnie Tree and didn't hear her name. They got on like houses afire and she said all you can imagine on the subject of Hollywood and film stars and when she'd gone he said to Ronnie: 'Who is that volatile and attractive woman with the political interests?' Don't you love it. I can't wait to tell her!

It's 12 o'clock and time I got up.

Golders Green is being great fun and a fitting end to our run.

———◈———

                              48 Wildwood Road
                              (Myra's house where I've come to tea
*March 17th, 1940*            and stayed for supper.)

Well, I'm 'resting' now (i.e. out of work) only since last night but I'm already homesick for the theatre and the eight o'clock call and the smell and my friends and – oh everything, so it looks as if it's got me, doesn't it?

I wrote to you on Wednesday and the rest of the week was full of Golders Green and finishing up. On Wednesday afternoon I came up early and was met at G.G. station by Howard Ferguson, who is a great friend of Myra's and who is a composer, Northern Irish, about thirty-ish and nice. He lives by himself in a little house in this road, looked after by his old nanny, who is as big as a minute and bent but smiling. She's called Pooh and obviously adores him. Her niece aids her in the housekeeping and it's a cosy household. He gave me a wonderful meal; created the omelette himself and it was a French one and excellent. Brie cheese, raspberry jam and fruit cake. Afterwards we talked of books and music and poetry and he then played me, at my request, his own piano sonata, only recently completed.

———◈———

*March 24th, 1940*              Parr's

I'll probably get a letter from you tomorrow so I won't say *much* about Tommy's plan except that it's a blow to Daddy; and me. After all, this is a very curious moment in which to become a citizen of a country that is behaving as America is just now. I suppose it is – and it is – entirely his own business. Nevertheless it's an awful shock to Daddy.

I last wrote to you on Sunday a week ago from Myra's – (*not* MOYRA – MYRA!) house where I spent the evening. On Monday I came down here where R. met me. We had a long walk in the afternoon, he did a lot of digging in the garden and went back to London at 9 in the evening. I suppose I needed the rest from the theatre because when I let go and rested I was quite floppy. Lovely weather with a wind and all the trees are budding and this garden is full of crocuses. I did very little all the week. Dined with the Winns one day; Enid Lawson called on me; otherwise I just slept and read and walked a bit and it was pleasant. But I miss the theatre *so* badly!

I'm going up to London on Tuesday where I've got four days' work to do at the Nat. Gal. canteen. There are lots of good movies to see and R. and I are going to see some of 'em this week.

Ginny and Tony came on Thursday and we've been extremely cosy. Coal shortage – we get but one sack per week! – made it necessary to eat in the drawing room, so we moved the dining room table in here and while it is a bit crowded it's very warm and we're enjoying the innovation. Rene is a wonder and continues to do everything aided, slightly, by me.

Today Gin and I went to church, then Cliveden. (R's been on night duty till today.[1]) Such a party at Cliveden! To start with, Lord Castlerosse[2] – you never thought he'd get there did you? – then there was Mrs Luce (Clare Boothe who wrote *The Women*),[3] and Joe Kennedy [US ambassador] who, in my useless opinion, is a cheap Boston Mick and doesn't know his job. He shakes hands with one hand in his pocket and he's tacky and, I think, a poor representative of America.

At this point I'd like to tell you quietly that there is a growing anti-American feeling over here. I deplore it and mind it, but I do see why it is. It's all a question of morals. There sits America, selling

[1] In the Foreign Office Deciphering Department.
[2] Author of 'Londoner's Log' in the *Sunday Express*. A friend of Lord Beaverbrook and Winston Churchill, he was the son and heir of the Earl of Kenmare. Grossly overweight, he died in 1943, aged only fifty-two.
[3] Clare Boothe Luce, author of *The Women*; produced at the Lyric Theatre in April 1939. Wife of Henry Robinson Luce, proprietor of *Time* and *Life* magazines.

huge quantities of materials to Russia all the time Russia was fighting the Finns. All America is doing in this war is growing fat and rich and playing the Johnny-Know-All. After-Munich and Finland it is a bit much for England to take. (I've said all this before; but here it is again.) Of course there are large groups of people who feel as we do but that's not enough and doesn't make up for the moral cowardice of the rest. And that's what it is.

Well, I'm very sad about Tommy – not – and do understand this – because he is going to become an American but because he's chosen this moment to do so.

Oh *dear* –

---

*April 15th, 1940*          Parr's

Friday was a record day at the Gallery. We worked like beavers in the canteen. Whenever Myra plays we know it will be a big day and this was certainly a Big Day. We made over 1,700 sandwiches – and would have sold more if we'd had the bread. I began by making fresh tomato and cheese but when I'd done five loaves – with a pal to butter while I spread – I then did two fish and cress loaves singlehanded. By the time the concert started I was whacked; as were the rest of us. But it was the Horn Trio that I'd heard rehearsed and it did the trick. Heavenly music it is.

---

*April 22nd, 1940*          Parr's

Yesterday suddenly brought us the summer; not just the spring but full-blown hot summer with bees and butterflies and amazed wasps blowing about the windows.

By the time you get this I hope that the problem that is facing me at the moment is settled because from where I now stand I cannot see what is the right thing to do. As usual I am trying to leave it as honestly as I can to the Almighty to show me the way. It's this: I was planning to go out on tour, leaving about the first week in June. It was to be a ten-week tour but I was only signing on for four weeks, with a fortnightly basis clause to come into operation after that. Well, it seems that the hospital here is going to open about the last days in

May, and Aunt N. is more than a little anxious for me to be here to get the social side of the thing in running order for her. She has got to have someone to do it and she particularly wants me because she thinks I could do it and because I would be so convenient! If I cannot do it she must get someone permanent to be on the spot and it looks as if she would have to use this house for the purpose. She says, and I'm afraid she is right, that it would be impossible to have this house, known to be a Cliveden house, right on the edge of the hospital, remaining empty except for weekends when Reggie came home. From a 'career' point of view the tour is probably not of vital importance to me. It would be excellent experience but as I would continue to do the old monologues it wouldn't be anything very special. On the other hand, I have as good as signed my contract with a Mr Ridgeway who is running the tour and he was very keen to get me and has given in on a whole lot of points in order to have me. I am to be 'featured' as a leading player and as I have been a sort of success in the revue it would have been a good thing to have been with it on tour. Reggie says that although I have not actually signed my contract I have given them plenty of evidence in letters for them to insist on me carrying out the tour. Of course I can bring a lot of patriotic sentiment to bear but I don't want to. Gosh, I wish I knew what was the right thing to do. If I don't go on the tour it means that R. has a home; an important factor. If, on the other hand, I go out it means a break here and I don't want that. Aunt N. has offered me a small wage to do the job, otherwise I couldn't consider it because my real reason for touring was to make some money and I stood to make quite a lot. Aunt N. quite understands that I want to continue on the stage and though she does not approve because she thinks it makes people so egotistical (!) she is fully aware that my taking on this hospital job would only be a temporary measure as I am going to do something for Bertie [Farjeon] in the autumn. Once the hospital business is got going it ought to run itself. I understand that my part would consist of getting together entertainment committees to take over certain wards, etc. This could be done in the first three months of the hospital, I imagine and hope. After that, with an appointed chairwoman to carry on, I could fade out and only come back occasionally from here.

But I don't know what is the right thing to do.

Obviously I could do this job; on the other hand I have as good as promised a little man to go out on his tour. Am I justified, even on patriotic war grounds, in letting someone down. Of course Aunt N. says I'll be letting her down if I don't do it and that I do owe her something after all. As indeed I am fully aware. Only God can make this clear. I have written off to Bertie to ask his opinion. He is not actually running the tour; he's merely sold his stuff to Ridgeway.

So there you are; that is my problem and it takes a lot of looking at, doesn't it![1]

*May 12th, 1940*                                                    Parr's

Thank you so much for your cable[2] – I suppose it's no good telling you not to worry about us but I do say so anyway because it's no good and anyway we are *alright* even if we do get blown up and you never see us again! So there. We ARE ALRIGHT – as you well know, and this bloody lie of war never can be true so don't let's be deceived by it for an instant. By the time you get this we may have been bombed about but I've a sort of feeling that I'll always be OK and of course in truth I shall. So loose me and let me go, won't you? We are all in Mind, and nothing can possibly separate us from the love of God and that's all that matters.

At this moment Virginia and I are sitting out in the garden with the radio sending us a Praising God cantata by Bach. Reggie is spraying his roses and Nan, the retriever, is wandering about. There are just too many clouds and it's just not quite warm enough, otherwise it's perfect. You couldn't guess there was a war on. It's a very peaceful Sunday. We listen to many too many news bulletins but that's a passing fever and as soon as we are used to the idea of the fighting in the Netherlands we'll give it up. If this last piece of aggression doesn't awaken America then nothing else will. It's amazing how long it takes to stir her idle conscience. All the same I see new signs of responsibility in her from the various magazines we get. But she's being too slow.

Aunt N. is a continual surprise to me. There are moments when I really do believe she knows what C.S. is about! I've come to this conclusion: it is that she *knows* about it but doesn't always put it into practice. She was *so* good and clear on Friday when I lunched up at Cliveden. Amazing woman.

There's a certain satisfaction with the new Cabinet and Winston as

[1] Joyce did not go on the tour of the revue. The Canadian Red Cross hospital was opened in July 1940 with 480 beds and a research centre. As the Astors spent a large part of the war in Plymouth, where Lord Astor was Mayor, the day-to-day running of the hospital was delegated to other hands, and Joyce found herself increasingly drawn into hospital activities.
[2] Ma's cable presumably expressed anxiety about the situation at this point. The German army was advancing on the Western Front, and had invaded the Low Countries on May 10th.

PM. But Aunt N. wishes Ll. G. [Lloyd George] was instead! There was a serious school of thought who felt he was the one man to get us going but he is seventy-seven and I think it is probably as well that it isn't him after all.[1]

Last Wednesday Reggie and I dined with Lord & Lady Kennet[2] because her son, Peter Scott,[3] was home on (Navy) leave from the Norway campaign.

We had such a pleasant evening with the Kennets. They live in the house J. M. Barrie once owned on the corner of the Bayswater Road exactly opposite the Round Pond in Kensington Gardens. It's like a country house with a garden full of tulips and cherry trees in flower. We had an excellent wartime dinner and afterward six or eight youngish friends of Peter's came in and we did turns – I never stopped, it seemed to me.

It's so funny the way you and I swap material! You do the schoolgirl and I do Aunt Irene[4] singing 'Go tell Aunt Nancy' before & after lessons with Jean Darewski.[5] I also do the little Japanese tea lady and I've turned her into really rather an amusing monologue. (Bombs permitting I hope to go to Bristol on the 23rd to broadcast it.)

---

*May 19th, 1940*                                   Parr's

Well, the war goes on, the news is awful and the tenseness worse but I've learned so much in C.S. and it has helped me enormously so that I no longer feel so down. And after all I am one of the lucky ones; my husband is at home and I've no children. One hears nothing but rumours about everything and personally I've abandoned the news except for once a day. I can see no point in sitting round a radio six times a day even when the news is good. As C.S.s, our job is to keep our thoughts clear and that isn't done so easily if we are being bombarded with error all the time.

[1] On May 10th Chamberlain resigned and was succeeded by Churchill. His Cabinet included Herbert Morrison as Minister of Supply, Duff Cooper as Minister of Information and Lord Beaverbrook as Minister for Aircraft Production.
[2] Lord Kennet of the Dene, 1st baron; created 1935. Formerly Sir Edward Hilton Young, MP, Minister of Health, 1931–35. He held many official positions. His wife, Kathleen, had been married first to Captain Scott (of the Antarctic). As a sculptor she made many public monuments.
[3] The son of Captain Scott and Kathleen Kennet, artist and Founder and Director of the Severn Wildfowl Trust.
[4] Joyce's aunt, a Langhorne, married to Charles Dana Gibson.
[5] Singer who is said to have offered to train Joyce's mother on hearing her sing.

One thing I do hope you know: that is that we are alright no matter *what* happens. I'm ready to meet ANYTHING because I know what is true and what isn't. Being bombed can't be fun – they say the noise is so awful – nor do I look forward to any of the horrors of war but if they come, remember that I'm able to face them in the armour of God, so please don't worry. I believe it's far worse for you over there in safety than it is for us here.

We both went up to London last Monday and on Tuesday I worked at the Gallery and after the concert went up to Wildwood Road to spend the afternoon with Myra. She has been very hit by Holland's invasion and surrender. I think I told you that she had many great friends there and that her musical career had begun there when she was seventeen. You know it's very difficult to help anyone humanly about that sort of thing. Sympathy is something I suppose; understanding and tact are helpful too but only Science heals that sort of wound and you can't throw it to people. I think it's harder to present it for hurt than for sickness, don't you?

On Wednesday we had 900 people at the Gallery to hear Myra play the Bach Fifth Brandenburg Concerto with a motley assembly of strings. It was a heavenly concert and did everyone so much good. The Mozart the day before had been very nostalgic and delicate – its poignancy had had me almost blubbing in contrast to the bloodiness of the world. But Bach – there is sanity and the confidence and certainty that heals. Everyone felt it. Myra was amazing that day because she was very low about the news of Holland's surrender and obviously was not in the mood to play a joyful piece of music. But she has that kind of greatness that puts herself entirely to the side and lets the music do its work through, and in spite of, her. Everyone was saying how wonderful it had been to hear such great music. It was. I felt better for it.

(My writing is bad because I've played tennis all afternoon. I think that always makes me write wiggily for some reason.) Jakie was over yesterday, Michael today. Both are still in England, I'm glad to say. We think Harry is in action now and R. minds that a bit. And Patrick Campbell-Preston [Frances Grenfell's husband] too – in Belgium.

So far the casualty lists aren't published but we think they must be pretty long. Gosh. The *waste* of it. And to think that if America had bothered to take her head out of the sand and face facts before this, maybe it could have been avoided. I feel bitter about it, don't you?

Well, we're still here! I feel that I am learning more and more every day and fearing less and seeing further and further into reality. It's no good talking about the war so I shan't do it. We manage to do a great many things and enjoy them.

I came to London on Friday as I didn't feel much like being alone at Parr's and R. had work in London. Went to the Gallery for lunch and spent the afternoon in the Sloane St C.S. Reading Room. Emerged feeling much better. Daddy says the whole thing is hypnotism or I mean mesmerism. One gets whole waves of depression followed by let-ups and it wasn't till I got on to it and saw that error cannot project itself anywhere or through any possible channel that I began to beat it. Daddy put me on this view. By the way: news. He's been elected 2nd Reader with Ralph Schofield's wife as first and they start in July.[1] It's a very popular election and Daddy was elected the first ballot – an event that is extremely rare at First Church where they have to have a two thirds majority. Daddy's pleased as Punch in some ways; awed in others. Anyhow he's fully alive to the job to be done and he'll do it well I'm certain.

R. and I had a salad here on Friday night and later he and David [Astor] listened to the King's broadcast[2] but I funked it, feeling it might make me sad. So I took myself for an evening stroll in the Gardens but it wasn't much of an escape because every house for miles round had the radio on and all windows wide open so I was pursued wherever I went by the King's voice.

*Monday.* Your cable has just been forwarded to me by Rene and I'm staggered to think you heard me last week![3] If only I'd been better – darn it. I went much too fast and the whole programme wasn't very good, was it? But how exciting. Thank goodness I didn't know beforehand or I'd have been in a state. I'd *no* idea the programme was going out on short wave – makes me think I should have been paid more! Do write me all details. How did you happen to hear me? Was it a fluke or did you remember from a

---

[1] Christian Science has no clergy. The Sunday services are conducted by the First Reader, while the Second Reader has the responsibility of reading the Bible passages. Usually a man and woman alternate these roles and they are reappointed at regular intervals.
[2] The situation was tense. The fall of France was imminent; the evacuation of Dunkirk was about to begin.
[3] This was the broadcast recorded in Bristol on May 23rd in which Joyce did her new monologue about the little Japanese tea lady.

letter that I'd said I'd be broadcasting on the 23rd? I'm longing to know.

Yesterday was Sunday. R. was working so Daddy and I went off to 11th Church because we were lunching with Virginia afterwards and it's her church. Marvellous service. Yesterday was a day of national prayer and churches all over England were packed with prayers. It's strange how we all turn to God in our hour of need.

<hr />

*June 3rd, 1940*                                                    Parr's

I've just washed my hair and now I'm sitting out in the garden drying it under the sun. A perfect June day and as peaceful as Tryon. Not even a practising aeroplane in the sky – in fact you couldn't guess a thing about the war. Every day is a day gained and when I think that it was nearly a month ago that I was jolted into living from hour to hour, not knowing just what horror to expect, and to find that I'm more than alive now – well, it's encouraging. I went to see Mrs Rawson last week and she was terrific. She's so absolute, so confident, that she heals just to be with her. She made me read the second book of Chronicles, chapter 20, verses 1–25 in connection with the times. Do look it up. When they were troubled they sought the Lord and he said, 'Don't fuss; this isn't your battle anyway, it's God's. – Do be quiet and stand and listen.' So they got together and praised God like mad and *sang*; and *then* won. Which being interpreted means that God doesn't know a thing about the battle and as we're under his law we'd better stand still and recognise the fact – do a bit of expressing love and praising truth. Mildred was particularly interesting about the God we have chosen. Ours is Love – the Germans' is Hitler, the world's is success, etc, etc. (By 'ours' – I mean C.S.'s.) Therefore love being literally all, one can only abide by love's laws. This week's lesson looks good. I've just done three sections and I found that bit about 'multifarious forms of creation which before were invisible will become visible'. That may not be exactly accurate – but you know the bit. In the September of Munich – 1938 – that came into the week's lesson and it suddenly became quite, quite, clear to me. I believe it to mean that one will *literally* see things – that the destruction of present things – which is what happens in air raids and wars – won't matter. There are 'multi-farious forms' waiting to take their place. That's not clear either but still, I daresay you'll see what I mean.

In spite of his legs Reggie says he's *got* to be a soldier and he's trying to get into the King's Rifles – or some such name – which is where Francis Grenfell[1] began his military career. I don't mind much – I mean I fully appreciate his feelings and if it makes him much happier then he must do it. Training will take at least three months and by then – well, we're either all dead or on the way to beating the Germans – because we hear they must beat us in two months or never. Getting all those men out of Flanders is indeed a miracle. Harry is back, thank God. But John Erne[2] is dead, John Cowdray[3] has lost an arm, the young Duke of Northumberland[4] is dead, Charlie Hopetoun (Linlithgow)[5] is missing. His wife – Mary Kenyon-Slaney's daughter – had a baby daughter last week. It's all foul. And if America had come in or helped with arms it need not have happened. It is incredible that they don't see it *yet*. This *is* their war and we're fighting it – ill-equipped, when we could have equipment if only they'd wake up and do something. One's mind reels at their blindness. Let's hope by the time you get this something will have roused them.

I came down here on Monday of last week because we'd been in London over Sunday and I wanted to fetch clean clothes, rations, etc, and see how things were here.

I gardened and took Nan for a walk and it was alright but rather lonely – for the first time I've ever felt that. It's the war – Next day it rained ceaselessly so I took an early afternoon train and went back to London. Myra was broadcasting at 8 so I stayed in till she'd done and then R. and I met for supper at a rather dim restaurant in Knightsbridge. I worked at the Gallery on Wednesday.

———◆———

*June 9th, 1940*　　　　　　　　　　　　　　　　Parr's

I had four letters from you last Monday – the first for ages. So I'll answer them separately. The one mailed on May 7th, suggests that

[1] Reggie's uncle. He was the first officer to be awarded the VC. Both he and his twin, Rivy, were killed in the First war.
[2] 5th Earl. His father, Viscount Crichton was killed in action in 1914.
[3] Weetman John Churchill Pearson, 3rd Viscount Cowdray, Captain in the Sussex Yeomanry.
[4] 9th Duke. Killed in Belgium aged twenty-eight, he was succeeded by his brother, Lord Hugh Algernon Percy.
[5] Lieutenant, Scots Guards; prisoner-of-war; succeeded father as 3rd Marquess of Linlithgow in 1952.

you and Dorothy[1] and Lefty should come over to help. It's a generous idea but I don't think it's altogether a good one. First of all, I doubt whether you could get permission to leave America or enter England. Secondly – there's the question of what you all could do. Nursing? Not as a C.S., do you think? No, I don't think you'd be nearly as much use here as you obviously are being in America with your grand write-to-your-senator scheme. (We are all very impressed with that.)

I'm not being ungracious when I say that you aren't wanted – I don't mean it personally! But the point is that they are trying to clear the place out a bit and, unless one is actually a combatant or doing work of national importance, one really is better away. I feel all the time that I'm not pulling my weight because, so far, there isn't enough for me to do. However, that may change any day now. In some ways I'd love to have you here; on the other hand I can't stress enough the joy it is to know that you are where you are, leading as nearly a normal life as it is possible to lead in the circumstances. I've written that often before and I repeat it again because it is true and a great comfort to me to dwell on.

It's still boiling weather – just about the most perfect summer I ever remember. Isn't it ironic? (or should it be ironical??). Anyway it's HOT. Wasn't Dunkirk terrific? And it followed the day of national prayer. I've got a firm certainty of victory – altho' I'm braced to face any hideousity before it's attained. However I'm so sure that 'clad in the panoply of love human hatred cannot reach you' that I really don't much mind anything.

---

*June 24th, 1940*                                                      Parr's

Well, we're still here. Reg. joins the 60th on Tuesday and as they are [line cut out – presumably by censor] I really don't feel too badly about it. Of course it's beastly having him leave but then – there's a war on and I'm one of the lucky ones to have had him so long. Frances Grenfell's husband is missing.[2] We *hope* he's a prisoner but it's rather a faint hope. Reg tried to get into the Bucks with Harry, as I told you last week, but because his name had to go before the King when he applied for the 60th (it's the King's Royal Rifles. Very special.) and because he was accepted it seems it would not be

---

[1] Mrs Dorothy Baker, an American, a great friend of Ma's.
[2] Their fears for Patrick Campbell-Preston's safety were unfounded. He returned.

done to transfer. At any rate not for the moment. So he's off
tomorrow.[1]

*June 30th, 1940*　　　　　　　　　　　　　　　　　　　　　Parr's

We had our first air-raid alarm last Monday night. R. and I were at
St Jas. Sq., sleeping in the best double room with Alice [Winn] in
the dressing room next door. We'd dined with Joe Stephenson[2] and
got to bed fairly early. R.'s uniform had arrived and he tried bits of
it on in front of the mirror. About 1 we were wakened by the sirens
and they really are the most beastly noise – like an hysterical woman
wailing. Much too frightening, I think. We sprang out of bed and
kept our heads about not turning lights on. R. put his greatcoat on;
I had a dressing gown. We woke Alice up from a deep sleep and
then, armed with our gas masks, we went down to the cellar, meeting
three housemaids on the stairs and Lee in almost full evening dress
in the passage! Aunt N. soon arrived in a Jaeger dressing gown armed
with *S. & H.* [Science and Health] and *Miscellaneous Writings*. Rose
followed her, armed with things she valued. It was all rather funny,
I must say. The air raid shelter at St Jas. Sq. is so far below ground
that it's freezing cold and very damp! We didn't stick it very long
because Reggie and Lee reported that there was no gunfire to be
heard, nor bombs falling so we went back to bed, planning to descend
at the first sign of trouble. I was glad to have R. with me on our first
alarm. It's such a foul noise – otherwise one doesn't mind the event,
so to speak!

The All Clear didn't go off for four hours and when it did it woke
us from a deep sleep – second time. Daddy conscientiously stuck the
full four hours out sitting in a deckchair behind Alice [his house-
keeper] in another, down in his basement!

R. got up into his uniform and I must say he looks really attractive
in it. After breakfast we went out to do some shopping for him and
get him photographed. His train went at 11.20 and I saw him off at
Paddington. It wasn't very nice but having him in England is such a
comfort that I really shouldn't complain. Alice and I came home
here. I met Hubert Smith at Taplow and asked him if there was any
work to do over at the farm[3] and he said they were hay-making and

[1] While being treated for varicose veins he had first worked at the Ministry of Eco-
nomic Warfare and then joined the Deciphering Department of the Foreign Office.
[2] Sir Joseph Stephenson, later a judge.
[3] Hubert Smith,* Cliveden's estate manager; lived at White Place.

I could help so at 2.30 I crossed the river, wearing an old divided skirt and a worn Aertex shirt, with my head tied up in a scarf and for the rest of the afternoon I hay-maked. But not in the ordinary way. Oh dear no. It was much more fun than that. Bill was given a Chrysler two-seater on his twenty-first birthday twelve years ago. Remember it? Well, now it is entirely paintless, bonnetless, brakeless, roofless, floorless and hornless but it still goes – in bottom gear. It is equipped with a giant wooden comb-like device that is fixed on in front. You drive the car along rows of raked hay and this arrangement collects it up. When you have enough you steer off the row into the open and deliver your load in a part of the field near the rick (to unload you merely reverse; in fact that is the only means of stopping anyway!) Then a man in another car picks it up and delivers it to the rick. I was at the job till the field was swept clean and I can't tell you how enjoyable it was. Hot and filthy work, for the car isn't clean and hay is dusty, but very satisfactory. I had tea with Hubert and Diana at the farm and afterwards helped to 'shake' a field of mixed crops for feeding. This was hard on the arms so I only did it for an hour. I slept mighty well that night, I can tell you. Alice and I both went over to the farm the next day, but alas the scooping job was done and we had to shake beans and hay till we about dropped! We had lunch in Hubert's garden between jobs. I was so sleepy when I got home about 4.30 that I fell off while I was having a cup of tea! But I woke up so refreshed that I got on my bicycle and took Nan for a run, stopping at Aunt N.'s garden to deadhead all the roses.

———◈———

                                        St Paul's Waldenbury,[1]
                                        Hitchin,
*July 7th, 1940*                        Herts.

There really is no news. Reggie is quite settled and loves it. He writes quite a lot – for him – and we've spoken on the telephone. My plans are still quite vague. In fact I haven't any! I leave here tomorrow to do a concert for Enid [Lawson] near Beaconsfield tomorrow evening. I have another in London on Thursday – for the Red Cross in a private house. A woman in First Church asked me. I don't know

[1] Home of Rachel (née Spender Clay)* and David Bowes-Lyon, and reputedly where Queen Elizabeth the Queen Mother was born, although there has been some dispute about this. Later in the war the house was turned into a convalescent home for troops.

what it will be like. But I do all I'm asked to because I feel it's the one war work I can do and if it's wanted – so much the better.

*July 14th, 1940*　　　　　　　　　　　　　　　　　　　　Parr's

Thursday morning I did some odds and ends of shopping and then at twelve, went to the War Office to find out about doing entertaining for troops in far away camps where they get nothing in the ordinary way. It seems that there is a great deal of room for entertainers who can convey themselves to go to these remote units and break the monotony. The difficulty is that there are no pianos in these places so I want to get hold of a girl who can play an accordion well enough to be a solo turn on her own as well as be an accompanist for me. Not easy. The War Office like the idea and now I am trying to find the girl with the accordion and I'm to go along and report next week. Since I got enthused over this idea Bertie Farjeon has come into the picture again and wants me to get together some new material to be tried out at the Players Theatre[1] in August. The plan is to have two late nights a week called *Farjeon's Late Joys* and to try our stuff for his new revue that he hopes to present in October. I should like to do this and it is just possible that I might be able to do the troop thing first.

*July 21st, 1940*　　　　　　　　　　　　　　　　　　　　Parr's

Last Tuesday I worked at the Gallery all the morning and it was a huge day. We had 1200 people in to hear Myra and Isolde Menges play Beethoven sonatas. After the concert Myra and several others and myself all sat on in the artists' room talking for ages. It is so cosy the way we all use the National Gallery as a home.

Wednesday I worked at the Gallery again and in the afternoon I came down here in order to do a concert for the nursing staff down at Alice's old house.[2] I managed to get Elsie Suddaby to come over

[1] Club theatre specialising in Victorian music hall numbers. Then in Albemarle Street; later 'underneath the arches' in Villiers Street.
[2] Alice Winn's home, Taplow Lodge, now housed the nursing staff of the Canadian Red Cross Hospital at Cliveden, the orphans who previously lodged there having been moved further away from London.

and sing to them and as she is the best soprano in the country and accompanies herself quite beautifully they were indeed lucky to have her. I wasn't a bit sure at first whether they were going to like my stuff nor whether they would find me funny. But it was alright; they did. They were sticky and needed warming up but we managed to do it and by the end of the evening one of their majors was teaching us an action song that got us so hot we nearly burst. I hope to be able to arrange similar informal parties for them down there from time to time. The nurses are a very nice crowd and the doctors are alright too. Some of the girls are very young and they have a very high average for looks. They still wear those bright blue dresses with gilt buttons and could hardly look smarter. The hospital is officially open.

Thursday Elsie was here all the morning and we made music singing duets together and then at twelve we struggled through the rain to be shown over the hospital by one of the doctors who was all out to do anything for us after the evening before. Gosh, it's nearly seven, and I am going up to Cliveden in half an hour so I must fly and finish this later.

Here I am back again. I wish you could see the hospital. It is the most wonderful and complete thing I ever saw. I do hope it doesn't get bombed; it really would be a pity! I don't really remember the last one but from what I hear this makes it look like a matchbox. It is the most permanent looking thing too. I cannot believe they could ever have the heart to pull it down after the war. It ought to remain as a special children's clinic or something similar. I spent Thursday afternoon sewing peculiar-looking garments for the Red Cross. Diana Smith runs a weekly sewing bee up in the steward's room at Cliveden.

Friday? Well now, what did happen on Friday? Oh, I know. I took four young Polish naval cadets who are spending their holiday up at Cliveden over to Windsor and Eton. They are such nice young men – between the ages of twenty-one and twenty-four. They know absolutely nothing about their families. They were cruising at the time Poland was attacked so managed to get away but the fate of their families is lost to knowledge. Their grim determination to pursue this war to its end does one good to hear. I suppose one should not relish revenge but in these days of passive resistance on the part of the French and the curious lack of fighting incentive from the Jews it is a relief to find strong young men who want to smear the Nazis over the earth and who would undoubtedly enjoy the process! I never thought I would feel this way; but if you were here I believe you would too. This enemy has got to be destroyed and it is no good America thinking she is immune from the far-reaching tentacles of evil. I am told that some sections of Americans – probably those who react favourably to Nazi propaganda – are convinced that we must be beaten and therefore feel justified in withholding aid to England on the grounds that they would be too late to be of use anyway. I hope you do as much as you can to counteract such twaddle. We will *never* be beaten even if the Nazis take England. the truths for which we stand will go on in the Empire and we will continue the war from there. I am sure you say all these things to everyone you meet so there really is no point in me urging you on. I wonder if Roosevelt will bring the US in when once he is returned. I hope so. I suppose financial aid is a sore subject in view of the War Debt but as this is a question of the survival of what both England and America hold dear I think that the US ought to send us millions if she won't risk her manhood.

⎯⎯◆⎯⎯

*July 28th, 1940*                                             Parr's

It isn't bad here just now, with a sudden return to summer and, so far, no invasion. Aunt N. says that the women in her constituency who are under a good deal of bombarding are magnificent, one old girl of eighty not even complaining that her home had been demolished; was merely grateful to be spared and had nothing but praise for our wonderful forces. The spirit everywhere is good. The fact that we are all together on this island is a comfort for us all.

You would be amazed at the ordinariness of our lives under the war conditions. The food problem is not at all bad and the shops are full of things. Whether they will continue to be so is a different question but the fact remains that for the moment we are definitely alright and sleeping, eating, shopping, reading, movie-ing, working at our jobs and generally living. I have a feeling that you visualise us all living with white drawn faces under the most appalling strain. Well, that is probably the case of an airman's wife, poor thing, and may well be so for a sailor's. But for me and Ginny and Maria and Alice it is not a quarter as bad as you obviously seem to think it is. It isn't exactly fun being separated from one's husband and friends but it isn't as bad as all that and we are all prepared to face far, far worse things in order to win this war. So take heed, Mrs Flynn, and quit worrying and having mental pictures of me gassed or bleeding or whatever it is you indulge in. So far I am not; and so far I have learned enough to know that it doesn't matter a damn even if I am. What about this week's lesson? Truth.

Last Monday I escorted a party of six nurses and four Polish sailors on an expedition to Oxford. I asked the boys if they could sing us a Polish song and they were shy and said no but all of a sudden one of them said something in Polish and they burst into a four-part folk song of some sort and most terribly moving. I don't believe any of them had sung it since they had left home and they were all quite stirred by it. One of them picked grass throughout and another kept his eyes shut. We were quite silent when they had done and soon they sang another. I can't tell you how touching the whole thing was. Four young men sprawling on the grass by the river with Christ Church behind them and the day sunny with huge rushing clouds. The nurses had taken off the jackets of their navy blue suits and were wearing bright butcher blue shirts. It was a lovely sight and I shan't forget it. I felt very quiet. Here were four young Poles whose country has been slaughtered but whose spirit lives on to fight with the British navy in order that someday they may restore their land. And the six young nurses come all the way from the prairie country in Canada to help the Motherland in her moment of need. All rather sentimental? But true. The rest of the afternoon was spent in looking at New College and the Bodleian and the Sheldonian and by three thirty we were dry and tired so we went to a tea shop and drank gallons of tea and ate ices. And so home on the five o'clock bus, singing all the way.

What do you think about Noël Coward going to America to do propaganda for us – or what ever it is he is gone for? I think it is a great mistake. Everyone knows his past history and altho' those things don't matter if one is merely writing stuff for the theatre, it is definitely a pity, to say the least of it, that the man who represents this country at a time like this should be famous as a 'queer'. I don't doubt his sincerity for a moment and I know he is passionately patriotic but I am all against the appointment. He has been sent by Duff Cooper.

Thursday I went to the Gallery and worked like a black for we were expecting, and got, a full house to hear Myra and Tertis[1] play Brahms sonatas. The canteen made a record that day and there were over 150 people standing as well as 1100 sitting. My four Poles came and loved it and I introduced them afterwards to Myra who invited them to come whenever they could as her guests.

---

[1] Lionel Tertis, viola player and propagandist for the viola as a solo instrument.

Friday is our Maidenhead canteen night.[1] The place is starting to be known and we are getting bigger crowds. We were rushed off our feet on Friday. Over 200 men came in and the noise and heat were indescribable when we had to black out the room! I'm taking my accordion player[2] there on Friday of next week and we're having what is known as a 'singsong'. I doubt if we'll be heard over the chink of china and the general row, but we'll do our best.

---

Up to St John's Wood to see Bertie and Joan Farjeon. We talked a lot about the new revue and he read me some of the new stuff and I read him my newest monologue. It's called 'Canteen' and it's done in the Ruby Cromer[3] manner with a touch of Freda Dudley Ward's voice in it. The character isn't in the least like either of them but she's very typical of a lot of people, I think. Bertie is really pleased with it and says it's first class and a worthy successor to my first efforts. So that is v. good. I must now try and make another, for I need two. By the way I told him about your lady with the Little Spirit Lamp and he's fascinated. He wants me to do her. *Would you mind if I did it?* Please let me know about this as soon as possible. I want to have her in the hairdresser's maybe, just letting flow a rush of chat about this and that but in particular about the little spirit lamp and the joy it added to travelling. Naturally it's your own idea so you may say don't do it; but I don't suppose you will! Any way I thought I'd ask you.

Aunt N. has a good story about a Canadian she met in the street. She asked him why he'd come over to fight. Was it for England? No. For freedom? No. Did he hate Nazis? Not particularly. Then why had he come? Because he saw the Queen in Canada last summer and by golly he'd come to fight for her.

And I don't blame him. One feels her essential qualities of goodness, gentleness and unselfed-ness. She *is* England – or rather Britain.

---

[1] Alice Winn organised a canteen for troops stationed in Maidenhead. It provided Joyce with the background for her sketch 'Canteen', about a lady of leisure 'doing her bit – or rather not working very hard – in a forces' canteen'. It starts: 'I am *so* sorry but I'm afraid I'm *not* allowed to carry things.'

[2] The accordion player was Eve Clark, the wife of a doctor.

[3] Wife of the 2nd Earl of Cromer, the Lord Chamberlain; Dame Grand Cross of St John of Jerusalem.

We had a terrific excitement on Saturday. I'd gone over at 2 o'clock to get some further details from newly arrived patients and word got around that the Queen was coming to see the hospital. Such brushing and tidying went on; blue jackets were put on; hairs brushed, shaves hurriedly administered, etc, etc. Suddenly there she was, looking enchanting in hyacinth blue with a very becoming hat. Both the little Princesses were with her, also in blue. Little suits with short-sleeved jackets over silk shirts. Princess Elizabeth is going to be lovely. One can suddenly see her as she will be. She's got her mother's smile and Queen Mary's colouring so she'll do. The little one had a large pink elephant brooch pinned to her chest! Goodness knows where it had come from or why she wore it but Marian Hyde (George's widow)[1] who was in waiting told me that Princess Margaret Rose always has some sort of brooch or mascot or something pinned to herself. She's at the plain stage but is full of charm and vitality. You've never seen such a sparkling eye. The Queen was wonderful in the ward. She spoke to every single man and they were her slaves from the word go. The doctors and nurses were photographed with her in the garden and the whole affair was very exciting and gave the hospital a great fillip. It was the first hospital ever visited by the children.

---

*August 18th, 1940*                                                      Parr's

We are having another go of the most marvellous summer weather and the moon is at its height. I don't know how much you hear of our air successes but they have been very wonderful and we all realise what we owe to the RAF at this point. David Lyon tells me that some of the US correspondents over here are afraid of being thought too pro-British if they give the actual figures of our successes in the air so they cut them down a bit so as not to be disbelieved! If that is true it really is fantastic.

By the time you get this letter you will know whether Hitler is going to invade us or not. I cannot say that I agree with Duff Cooper who said in his broadcast last night that we would be very disappointed if he didn't invade us! All the same it would be good to get some sort of decisive victory as well as this air one. The RAF men are a joy to see these days. They go around with a quiet pride that is positively radiant; and so they should. Some of the ground personnel come into our can-

---

[1] Lord Hyde, elder son and heir of the Earl of Clarendon; Marian was Woman of the Bedchamber to the Queen.

teen in M[aidenhead] and they have quite a different something about them merely because they are in that service. R. writes that there have been bombs in his district but that the total bag, so far, has been six partridges and a cow, and as one of their own over-zealous sentries shot the cow in the blackout in mistake for a fifth columnist the score stands with only six partridges to the Huns.

I now have a ward of my own. It is a chest ward which means that many of the men are in for quite a time and so one gets an opportunity of getting to know them. I have one pet in there so far. Danny Forsythe by name from Bear Creek in Nova Scotia. He is a truck driver and very tough and I dote on him.

He is only sixteen years from Glasgow and the accent is thick as ever but one gets an occasional Canadian sound in it. He has what he calls 'bronical asma' and has just had his sinus dealt with.

There is a young and very good looking boy called Holden who has just been told he has TB. He is tucked away at the end of the ward and I am not allowed to go very near him but I got near enough to him to take down notes for a letter to his mother. Oh dear; they kill one. If I can only keep aloof from pity I shall be alright. And I am learning the difference between pity and compassion.

I went to London on Tuesday and did some odd chores for the men in the ward: razor blades, special soap, etc, etc, etc. At one I went to hear Myra play Beethoven at the Nat. Gal. and there was an audience of over 1200. Such beautiful playing too. Afterwards we all sat and talked in the artists' room, for it had been over a week since I had seen her. She is very busy working for her prom concerts and as I am down here so much now we don't meet nearly as often as we did. I must say I miss her for she is one of the warmest people in the world and a real friend. However we do telephone each other from time to time and next week I am going to have supper with her after a Mozart prom. Whenever I tell her of anything nice happening to me she always says how lovely for you to tell your mother. She adored hers and went through a pretty agonising six months before she died knowing that she had cancer and keeping the knowledge from her. She gave up her work entirely to be with her.

---

*August 24th, 1940*                                   Parr's

My life is one long round of hospital, hospital and more HOSPITAL. One gets so bitten with the work, I find. You get to know the men in your ward and they are glad to see you go in and get less shy of you as the days go by. My little corporal, Danny Forsythe, is being sent home because of his 'bronical asma' and for a while he tried to pretend the news was a blow but he couldn't get the smile that was underneath under any sort of control and soon it was all over his face and I must say it does one good to see him. Did I tell you his daughters, aged six and four or so, are called Mavis and Gertrude? He worships those two and can't wait to get back to them and his wife. He and three others came to tea with me today. Bestard is a very young looking forty and has a tragic story. The day before he was due to sail from Canada his wife, his mother and his sister drove down to see him off and had a car smash and all three were killed. He is an odd chap; I imagine part of his oddness may well be due to this nasty accident. He, wisely, refused the leave they offered him to stay behind for a while and see to things and came away at once. He talks ceaselessly of his wife and his mother and in a very detached and almost hard way. One wouldn't dare show any sympathy; he'd close right up, but so long as one lets him go on talking as if they were alive all is well. He constantly refers to the accident though and it is a sort of background for him, I feel. It's as if he has nothing else, poor devil. He's a toughish creature. I think he could get quite nasty if he was roused. I didn't want to ask him for tea but something made me do it and I'm glad I did for he had a nice time and talked a great deal and enjoyed the food.

I have four more soldiers coming to tea tomorrow. You have to treat them just like children and if you ask one they must all get asked. They are also exactly like babes when they get jealous of a sicker patient than they are and say that he is 'swinging the lead' to get more attention. I wonder if it was like this in the last war?

Well, what other news is there?

I went to London on Tuesday, having spent most of Monday over in the hospital. Just to go back a minute to the ward. I find that it takes me all afternoon just finding out what they want me to buy for them next time I am in London or Maidenhead and making lists and talking about the books they are reading or the work they are doing (petit-point or drawing or puzzles) and then there are the letters that must be written to their families if they can't do them themselves. This leaves me no time at all for plain visiting so I go in a bit each day and do it that way. In between times I am constantly biking into Burnham to do a bit of shopping for them. And so it goes.

*Sunday.* I started this letter last night but I came over sleepy just there and gave it up for the time being. I stayed up much too long as it was, reading and listening to the news and when I came out of my bath about midnight I heard the last notes of the warning dying away. I decided to take no notice until I heard bombs or guns and as Rene hadn't wakened I didn't disturb her. The sky was striped with diagonal lights; simply lovely. I imagined I heard a bomb once but that was all and I was soon asleep and didn't bat an eye till Rene called me at five to nine, just before the Sunday morning news. She hadn't heard the warning but was successfully wakened by the All Clear! I expect you get all the news of the bombardments of the coast and I daresay you visualise me in the London raids. So far I haven't been near one and as far as I can see this place is about the quietest on the island. Aunt N. comes back to get a bit of rest from her constituency and everyone remarks on how quiet it is here compared to almost anywhere else. (As a result of this boast we shall probably be blown sky high tonight!) But, seriously, it is a good place to be, I think. Last night I heard the German plane, very high and far away but their engines are unmistakable and we can all tell them. Did I tell you that a friend of mine, whom you don't know, who is an air raid warden in South London near where the big raid occurred a week or so ago, hurried to the scene as soon as he could although he wasn't on duty at the time. He said that the smoke hadn't even cleared before people whose houses weren't damaged were saying to the ones whose houses were hit: 'I've got the kettle on; come in and have a cup.' And that sort of spirit is what wins wars. In some ways I wish you were here just because I know how much you would appreciate the little things of that sort.

---

~~*August*~~ – *No, it's September 1st, 1940*                              Parr's

Quite a lot has happened since this day last year. Curiously enough I feel a lot better about things now than I did then. After all it was the unknown then; now we are in it and it really isn't so bad. Of course I haven't been in London since things began to happen there so I don't yet know what it's like to be bombed.

Down here we have had several warnings and heard bombs falling on an allotment beyond the station at M [Maidenhead], over to our right. Several fell over near where Enid Lawson lives and they made a colossal noise but I don't believe much damage was done. I understand they came from a plane that was being chased by one of ours and had to get rid of his ammunition to lighten his load. We hear the anti-aircraft guns in the London area from here but only very faintly and if there wasn't a war on and one's ears weren't tuned into that sort of sound one wouldn't notice it. Last night the guns in

S [Slough] went off and I saw the shells bursting high up in the sky. It is odd that one feels so little except curiosity. Mark you, I have not the slightest desire to experience more than I have; which is exactly nothing. All the same the nights are exciting from this remote spot and when I open my bedroom windows at night I find it hard not to stay leaning on the windowsill for hours, just looking at the lights in the sky. There are few lovelier sights than searchlights on a starry night. I'm afraid you go through so much for us but, so far, you needn't. I shan't go to London unless I have to until things calm down. There just isn't any point in spending hours in a shelter and one has to be obedient in the towns and do what the wardens say. You can't even go on shopping in the big stores for everyone has to go down to the cellars and stay there till the All Clear. I believe the theatres have had great fun getting up impromptu concerts for their audiences kept after the show is over. Amateurs get on the stage and there is community singing and charades. I can't wait to get to one but I won't be rash, I promise. The seven-hour warning last week held hundreds of people at the promenade concert at the Queen's Hall. The orchestra played on for ages and individuals in the orchestra played solos and there was singing and the whole evening seems to have been such fun that the Q. Hall did a record for the rest of the week! I don't know how long one could keep up such gaieties but at the moment 4 a.m. is the latest any public entertainment has had to go to.

My own news is still the hospital. It keeps me busy and I really have good fun with the men. I was in my ward every day last week and did the men's shopping at intervals.

On Saturday my musical friend Mrs Rowe invited six men to her house over at Cookham Dean for tea. She sent her daughter Grace to fetch three and I took the others in my car. We left at three in the afternoon – a perfect day, clear and burningly blue. The Rowes' house is high on the top of a hill and all the way up there were orchards full of apple trees heavy with fruit and it was a very English and a very cosy scene. The men loved it. We had a huge tea in the garden with an elderly parlourmaid hovering with the silver kettle and all the children helping with the currant bread, raspberry jam and fruit cake, biscuits and Swiss roll. A feast, and they did justice to it. After tea the walking ones took a stroll down the steep garden to see the pig that Mrs Rowe had won at a flower show raffle and see the damson trees blue with fruit. I went with them, led by two bathing suited evacuees that the Rowes have adopted for the war and resuscitated to health with good food and care. (She has six altogether and she and the twin daughters look after them entirely. The youngest evac. is one – the eldest eight.) After this we all went into the drawing room where Grace played the violin to us, followed by more violin music by Mrs Rowe, piano solos by Glory the other twin, and then I did a couple of turns and we all ended the party by singing together. Oh, I forgot to say that one of the men played the piano too and was delighted to be asked to contribute to the programme. He played with rather good harmonies and many broken chords: 'The London-derry Air' and 'The Sunshine of Your Smile'. Throughout the concert all six of the evacuees sat quite still and listened and I couldn't help thinking of the strange way in which good does appear to come out of evil. (Only of course it is really the natural progress of good and hasn't got a thing to do with evil except to shine in contrast.) What I mean is that it was heartening to see that long, rather plain, drawing room with its nice untidy collection of music on chairs and on the floor, Daphne's 'cello against the wall, the music stands, Grace's and Molly Rowe's fiddles, and then the six blue-suited Canadians and the six under-eight evacuees, and to think of the motives behind their being there. The Canadians are here because they believe in the Mother Country and love and feel her cause is theirs. (Every overseas soldier in this country at the present time volunteered to come.) The children were there because someone with a large house and large heart opened both of them for safety at a time when their East London homes were threatened. Both were gestures of love and neighbourliness and both are essentially democratic.

Last week the Paramount News people telephoned to know if I would make a two-and-half-minute propaganda short for the Ministry of Information. The pay would be merely an expenses fee – it was more in the nature of war work than anything, and was to be about a woman who does everything wrong in an air raid.

It is Sunday evening and I am suffocating from a very hot evening and a complete blackout. The evenings are dark by eight fifteen these days. Whew. I am quite alone and have spent a lot of the time curled up in a chair listening to the news and J. B. Priestley.[1] (Who is spoiling his talks with too much intellectual left-wingedness. I am with him up to a point but I split when he wants to level everyone because the upper ones make him mad and not because he wants to see a happy mixture of levels; and that is possible with taxation bringing the rich men into the same circle as the poor. Equality is never possible where enterprise is encouraged and it must always be encouraged in a democracy. The good always get to the top and the less good one will muddle along on the lower slopes. Equal opportunities are essential and they are becoming widely available.)

[1] His popular broadcast talks, *Postscripts*.

I wonder how I can describe my life for you so that you can see I am not going through the things you are imagining for me? At least not yet! Well, I sleep well – except for the one night when bombs were dropped near M. [Maidenhead] and woke me up twice; the second time I found I was very hungry and so raided the larder for ginger cake, a thing I have never done before. I am never hungry at night, are you? But this time I was famished. I go about my ordinary *tasks*; I change my library book and read it and I knit a scarf for Reggie, while listening to the news of an evening, and I ride my bike into Burnham to do the men's shopping, and I go into M. for canteening on Fridays, and I lunch up at the house now and again and get out of dining there when I can, because I like to be here in the evenings to write or read or listen to the radio. I have an occasional sister from the hospital for supper and sometimes the few wives of doctors over here come in for lunch.

And that is what I do. I am well and I don't worry and I read my lesson every day with continued gratitude and I do, or try to do *The Times* crossword puzzle.

Mary Bovet is up at Cliveden this week. I do like her so much. She is very quiet and very funny and a very good C.S. I asked her what she thought about me going on with my stage career, because Aunt N. goes on about it and says I am lost! She was most emphatic about it and said I was doing the right thing and that I had joy to give and that was important at a time like this. So I go on my way with renewed confidence. Anyway the thing won't come off unless things settle down a good deal. It would be madness to try and launch a new show [the proposed Farjeon revue] with raids going on as they are now and people not going out in the evenings because they don't want to get stuck for seven hours in a shelter.

*September 9th, 1940*                                                    Parr's

Reg was home for the weekend and it was heaven. He arrived after tea on Friday looking wonderful: brown and fit and happy and he is obviously adoring his militant life.

We haven't had a drop of rain for weeks and the whole place looks like hay. However it is pouring today and I am delighted to see it although it is very cold suddenly, and feels completely autumnal. The evenings are getting horribly short and by eight we have to be all closed up and blacked out. I must say that is a bore. I took R.

over to the hospital on Saturday and showed him off with pride.

We dined at Cliveden on Saturday night and Jakie was there, also on leave; but he was suddenly recalled and left after supper to join his extremely hush-hush unit who are some kind of suicide squad.[1] The moon and the tide are again right for invasion and these heavy raids are thought to be a prelude to an attempt. All the men are aching for it to start and R. says we could wipe them off by teatime but I cannot say I am in the least anxious for it to start even if we smash 'em. Anyway the entire country is at the alert and the next week or so are the critical ones. I haven't the faintest doubt about the outcome. How could one after seeing the people of this island and their complete unity against the enemy? Even the East End who have had it so badly in the last few days are right on top and ready to go on with the fight.[2] There was a grand interview with a railway man who did an incredibly gallant piece of work in uncoupling some trucks on a railway line after they had been bombed. (I forgot to say they were loaded with ammunition: some of the trucks were on fire too.) The broadcaster asked him what sort of ammunition it was and he answered: 'Well, it was mainly insenitary bombs.' (Incendiary)

Aunt N. and Uncle W. have been down here a lot lately and have been entertaining the officers and their wives and some of the nursing sisters for various meals and I have gone up and helped now and then. They are such a nice lot and as one gets to know them individually they seem to be even nicer. Two of the officers were up there for supper on Tuesday night when Alice and I went up. One of them plays the piano tolerably well and we had some music while Aunt N. sat in the next room and talked to Mary Bovet who was still down here then. I do like her. Before we went home Uncle W. took us up on the roof to see if there were any searchlights but for the first time in weeks there weren't. All the same, it was worth the climb for the stars were all out and the river wound in a dull silver twist at the end of the lawn and you could see the shape of the country.

That really is about all the news I know. I try to save up things to

---

[1] According to Christopher Sykes, Michael and Jakie 'had joined a unit (which they both seemed to regard as a colossal lark) whose purpose was to form small armed motorised groups to provide liaison . . . during the land battle in Britain'. On September 7th the government issued a precautionary invasion warning and many auxiliary units, among them Jakie's, were called out.

[2] In the afternoon of September 7th, an air armada of about 1000 *Luftwaffe* aircraft set out for London. The first wave bombed the London docks, the second flew over central London and then back over the East End. The bombing resulted in heavy casualties: over 300 civilians killed and 1300 seriously injured. The fires raging in the East End served as a guiding beacon for the night attack that followed.

tell you each week but really one sees very few outsiders and there is not much gossip to pass on.

*September 15th, 1940*                                              Parr's

By the way, do my letters get censored? I know they are read but do they arrive with passages deleted? I try to keep it all fairly general and avoid details but I just wondered if they took exception to any of my statements? . . .

David Niven is engaged to Prim Rollo,[1] daughter of Lady Kathleen and Bill Rollo. It was in *The Times* yesterday. She's about twenty-four, pretty in a pink and white way and I think it's a good plan. She's quite intelligent and will keep him guessing just as much as he'll do the same to her!

*September 17th, 1940*                                              Parr's

I suppose you are getting a picture of a flattened Britain? – physically that is. About London – I don't know; I haven't been there once since the battle started and it seems more sensible to stay where I am as I've got plenty to do here, and dead weight sightseers aren't exactly welcomed in the metropolis. My Pa has got a timebomb outside his house and is at this moment awaiting its explosion. Will he have a house to go home to, or not? At present he is evacuated to friends. His reports and Mary B.'s and several other London friends are all the same: magnificent spirit and courage. Not a sign of defeatism anywhere and a growing union of opinion that the Germans must be wiped off the map.

Maria [Brassey] says you see quite a lot of external evidence of the raids but that London, as one knows it, is the same. I love that city and it makes me wild to think of them daring to touch it. But as that very wildness is a feeling they aim to provoke, I'll subdue it and merely cry a little inside. You know this war is making me into a Kipling-y imperialist and a very proud Briton indeed. To see the

---

[1] Prim Rollo married David Niven the following day. She died on May 21st, 1946, in California, after falling down stone stairs during a game of Sardines at Tyrone Power's house. She was twenty-eight.

place filled with overseas soldiers – all volunteers at the moment – gives one a sense of such gratitude that the Mother Country can and does mean so much to its very young sons that they come thousands and thousands of miles to help her win this war. And, oh golly, how worth fighting for she is. God keep England.

I've just driven myself home from a troop entertainment about five miles away and the night was so lovely I was in constant danger of climbing hedges inadvertently, while moon-gazing. There's a gusty wind too and my poplars are making deep sea sounds in it. And they looked like silver in the white light when I drove in through the gate. It was a good concert in a packed village hall and, to my surprise, they liked the sketches. For they don't always, you know. They are apt to be scared of 'em; thinking I'm laughing at and not with them! However they were nice tonight, and I gave 'em two as well as a number of songs including my stand-by, 'The Tattoo'd Lady'[1]; complete with gestures.

Life down here is hospital – and then again more and *more* hospital. I love and cherish my nice ward on all seven days of the week, doing their shoppings and their chores, getting them doing games and puzzles, taking them out for tea occasionally and writing letters, etc, etc. Oh, and doing the flowers, etc.

Last week Myra Hess came down to stay with me for three days to get a rest from the noises of nights in London. She arrived pretty whacked; so did her two great friends, Marjorie and Sazzie Gunn who came too. The Gunns are sisters and Sazzie – derived from a lisping baby attempt to say Sarah-Jane – used to be Myra's secretary and companion in pre-war days. They are ambulance drivers and have been at it since Munich, I ask you, with no leave of any sort till these three days. They've been busy in London as you can imagine and their stories of their cab-driver, truck-driver and ambulance mates are a delight. They, too, are overwhelmed by the grandness of Londoners under bombs. The object of their visit was sleep and recuperation and I'm glad to say they got both. Myra angelically offered to play for the men in the hospital, and Marjorie suggested she might produce her fiddle – she's a very good teacher – and on Friday afternoon in the long drawing room of the big house they played for about forty-five men, officers, sister, doctors and us. The feeling in the room that evening – it was 5.45 to 7.45 – was very, very touching. These young boys from Canada in their hospital blue flannel, the spectacular sky against a wind-tossed, tree-filled landscape and the wide lawn streaked with shadows – it was all in the Gregynog

---

[1] A song Joyce learned from an American soldier in the First World War (and was not allowed to sing at the time).

feeling. And then Myra played Bach and the lovely stillness that surrounded the music; I was stirred almost too much. I had told the wards, individually, about the concert and stressed the fact that it would be serious music, for I didn't want to encourage those that merely wanted diversion of some sort. We had guessed at about ten of the men signing on and about the same number of officers. But, as I said before we got about forty-five really enthusiastic people and M. said they were lovely to play to. She gave us two Beethoven sonatas – Appassionata and, by request, the Moonlight – Brahms A Major for fiddle and piano with Marjorie, followed by Gluck and a Kreisler trifle, and then, of course, and happily inevitably, 'Jesu Joy'. As you know, she arranged it for piano. (It was for organ.)

I must go to bed. The fire is out and it's getting on for 12; I'm still made-up for the concert (a strange sight in private lighting). And I'm that sleepy. I think I hear one of those damnable Hun planes droning high above us somewhere but I expect he'll move off.

It is hard to make you realise what it is like being here in these days. We are only an hour from the city and yet we get that feeling of peace that might mean we were a million miles away. If ever anyone had doubts about the outcome of this war they are long gone, and one knows quite certainly that we have won it – and not only on moral ground. They can, and quite likely may, flatten London. It is horrid and makes one angry as can be; but the point is that London isn't England, and there you are. There's a screw loose in the Nazi make-up. They quite disregard the spirit of man, and that commodity would seem to be doing nicely in these parts, thanks very much. And it is a huge enormous point.

---

*September 22nd, 1940*                                    Parr's

Still no mail from you – that makes about three weeks but as I had your cable I'm not in the least worried. Mails are bound to be delayed because of the bombing and I'll probably get a fat batch all at once – if they haven't been lost in transit. The *Ladies Home Journal, Life* and the *New Yorker* arrive with punctual regularity and so does the *CSM* [*Christian Science Monitor*]. Why, therefore, don't letters come? Censored? I dunno. Anyway I'll be thrilled if and when they do arrive.

I've little news this week except that I now have a paying guest in the shape of one Mrs Robert Luton, wife of the head of the Canadian medical services (military) in this country. They have both been to Cliveden a number of times but I didn't get to know them particularly well. Mrs L. was bombed out of her flat ten days ago, came to C. for Sunday to recover and Col. Luton asked Alice to have her for a few days' further recuperation. (The big house was about to be closed for boiler cleaning and domestic holidays.) Al. was quite willing to do this but felt, rightly, that rest was not what anyone would get who came to share Greenwood Cottage with her and David, for he wakes at dawn and you can't keep a good child down and quiet.[1] So she asked me if I'd take her and I said I would for a day or so but that I had Nicki and Christine Harrison[2] coming mid-week to do a troop concert and I'd need the spare room. Mrs L. has turned out to be a pet and *so* easy that I shan't be surprised to find we're sharing the house for the duration. She's about forty-five, I should guess – the chin *slightly* underhung, sort of thrust out more. She gives a first impression of quite ordinary rather foolish womanliness but that isn't a bit right. Actually she's got a very cosy sense of humour, is very domesticated, most thoughtful and tactful and quite easy to have in the house. And you know how I am so you can appreciate that she is OK!

It is Sunday evening. Rene is out and Mrs L. and I have just had our supper in the kitchen. We had a large bowl of soup, coffee and some fruit and I for one am bursting. (Which just goes to show one eats much too much in the ordinary way.) I've washed up – altho' Mrs L. begged to be allowed to help but I'm so quick at it that I really prefer to do it alone. She does her own bed each day, as do I, and helps me clear the table after meals and really couldn't be more helpful. We seem to feel the same about all the simple primitive things of life – food, warmth, clothes – and that's a good foundation for communal living. The only thing I'm entirely out of practice in is merely feminine chat. Clothes, for instance. It's very odd to suddenly feel that such topics are a waste of breath! I'd far prefer to talk of books or poetry; but to say so sounds mighty precious, doesn't it? You know, I've come over rather intolerant of mere femininity – sort of sitting round. I can feel my mind addling! After all, muscles get stiff if you don't use 'em. All the same, I like Mrs L. very much.

(Our local AA [Anti-Aircraft] guns are busy as bees tonight and Mrs L. and I have just been out in the garden to look at the lights and the night is beyond words lovely.)

This isn't a very good letter. I've written most of it against a radio programme that Mrs L. wanted to hear. She's gone to bed now and Irene Scharrer is playing the 'Moonlight' on the radio.

(The distant warning went off and Mrs L. has rejoined me down-

---

[1] With Michael and Jakie in the army and Alice's old home, Taplow Lodge, given over to the Canadian hospital staff, Alice now lived at Greenwood Cottage. Her son David was aged three.

[2] Christine Harrison was a Christian Science practitioner.

stairs by the fire. Having her a bit tremulous is very strengthening, I find. I'm never scared when other people are. At least I don't think I am! Anyway I'm so sleepy now I think I'll tactfully suggest we go up to bed. The poppings have eased off.)

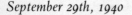

*September 29th, 1940*                                                    Parr's

We get our local excitements in these parts but, so far, thank God, they have been remote – as for instance the plane shot down at 9 a.m. today and so far the pilot has eluded detection in spite of Home Guard Squads combing every wood for miles round. They've been all over C. and after tea up there we climbed to the roof and surveyed the district. Such a lovely evening with rain clouds in the west and a lot of thick blue distance. And a further-off bit of highlife: last Wednesday I went Somewhere-in-Bucks, about fifteen miles off, to sing to the troops and while I was singing and leading 'The Tattoo'd Lady', *forte forte*, no less than seven bombs fell within 400 yards of the house and apart from a window rattle and a vague sense of blast through the room one didn't even notice it. It wasn't till later that we knew what had happened. So you see how near it can be without even worrying one. The nights out here are fairly quiet still although now we hear gun fire – where from I don't quite know – and an occasional crump.

I don't know what the world would do without the Veras and Hildas [Grenfell]. They are both at Granny Grey's empty house for a night's rest and I biked over there this morning to see them and loan them a loaf, for their little London maid had forgotten it. They look dead tired, both of them. V. hasn't had her clothes off for a week and is, as you know, living in Shadwell where things have been bad. Hilda is the quiet persuasive sort who looks harmless but cuts through anything when she's got a mind to do so. And, rightly, it's struck her lately to get the cellars of large rich houses in Chesham Pl. requisitioned by the LCC [London County Council], to turn into hostels for the homeless in East London. She wiped away all difficulties, untied red tape and got the thing going in two days. She's got YWCA workers in charge and is making an excellent job of it. V. is helping to feed 1000 people a day in Shadwell and to evacuate at a rate of 3000 a week. She has been at it ceaselessly and I think she is wonderful. I can't *tell* you how cissie I feel sitting down here doing my potty little job in the hospital, sleeping eight hours a night while V. and the others really do war work and are doing something worthwhile. Cheering up the sick and taking the homesicks' minds off themselves has got to be done, I suppose. All the same, it's a softie's job. As you can imagine all theatrical life has come to a complete end for the moment. Bertie writes from Hampshire, where he digs for Victory and has congregated his family, that he doesn't suppose the theatre will come to again until the whole thing is over. Meanwhile how the wretched pros are to live seems to be an unanswerable problem. Personally I'm alright; I'm now living on the cheque Uncle W. gave me in April. I've *just* and only just had to touch it. Till now I've managed on odd cheques from *Punch* and broadcasting and R. has sent home an occasional dollop. The *Bystander* has just taken a poem – I've written nothing for ages though – this is an old thing. By the way, I'm in no way worried financially. We're alright. Now that I've got a PG [paying guest] the house books are taken care of too! She's very cosy and has a grand sense of humour. We get our own supper when Rene is out and lead a communal life of such feminine equanimity that it's a pleasure to have her. She is inclined to be a bit nervous, which I find very strengthening! I always go in contrasts. Col. Luton comes in for a night every now and then and he is nice too, so all-in-all I'm a very lucky person indeed to have such easy guests. And knowing me you'll appreciate that the Ls must be extra nice. I even got over and controlled my horror at Col. L. smoking in the bathroom before breakfast! And it's only happened once, to date, so that's good. She smokes at breakfast and has quite cured me of objecting to that too. She has borrowed a bike and we go for miles all around the country- side – we blackberried one day; shopped in Burnham, and she's getting almost as much muscle as me and will nip up the hills pretty much as fast as I do.

I don't believe I've any special news. Life is still full of hospital. It's very sad the way you just get to know the men well and they get to relying on you when, bang, they get sent back to their units, quite cured. Or else get boarded and sent home to Canada. Half Ward 11 got cleared out last week. It's filled up though with a nice new lot and I'm beginning to sort them out and make their names match their faces.

---

*October 6th, 1940*     Parr's

My big news is that Farjeon is going to start a revue after all but I don't want you to worry about me being in London because it is going to play at matinées only and is going to the Criterion Theatre in

Pic. Circus and, as you remember, it is entirely underground and could hardly be a safer place. His idea is to start a sort of high-class variety of all sorts. He is hoping to get Edith Evans to do some poetry and he'll have some good singing and some dancing and some funny stuff – me – and contracts will be for a month and then he can change things around if a star happens to be in London for a time between engagements. He wants me to do my old stuff and one new one – the canteen woman. I don't yet know what I shall wear. As in regular variety one provides one's own costumes and I am not at all sure where I can get hold of anything, although they tell me that there is a wonderful woman at Webbers in Maidenhead! Maybe I'll have to try her out. I fancy a grey velvet with possibly a pair of bright blue bows on the shoulders. I'm ashamed to say that I thought it all out in church this morning.

Aunt N. is at Plymouth this week and due home in a few days. I haven't yet told her about the theatre and for some reason I'm quite sillily scared to do so! Such is her power over me!! But, seriously, I don't think she'll mind for I can go on with my work here and go up and down to the show. Besides I need the money and one must manifest activity and supply.

Daddy has sent the Sargent[1] of Granny down here and also Gt. Grandfather in his white linen suit standing on Staten Island over looking the sound. They seem to be enjoying the tranquillity of the county and look lovely: Granny in here on the table leaning against the wall and held in place by the *Seven Pillars of Wisdom* – that being the heaviest tome I own – and Gt. Grandpa in the dining room, merely standing against the wall.

---

*October 13th, 1940*    Parr's

Three letters from you last week and the latest one arrived in ten days by airmail, censorship and all. So now where are we? Your old letters used to take nearly a month to get over, notwithstanding the air mail stamp, and I'd fully made up my mind not to send my letters by that expensive route. But now I don't know?

Oh – oh – oh –

Just wait while I wipe my eyes after listening to Princess Elizabeth

[1] Family portrait of Jessie Phipps by John Singer Sargent. He was born in America, settled in Chelsea in 1884 and became a fashionable society portrait painter. The portrait of Great Grandfather was by Healey.

broadcasting to the children of the Empire.[1] Did you hear? It was one of the loveliest things I've ever heard. So young, so true – so touching in its innocence and wisdom. I do hope you heard it and like me, were moved by it. Whoever thought up the whole idea was a genius; whoever wrote that little speech couldn't have done it better – one's feeling of gratitude for a land that can produce that sort of thing is unbounded and, as I've just said to Mrs Luton, you can't possibly defeat what that little talk stood for. The love and generosity and warmth of it. I'm not easily brought to tears these days – one is beyond that sort of thing – but there just was something about that little voice, so like her mother's, so strong and clear – well it got me alright!

D'you know I've come to the conclusion that we are fighting this war for far more than mere democracy and so-called freedom. It *is* freedom we want but I don't believe we'll get it until we are wakened from what Mrs Eddy calls 'earth's stupid rest'. We've been lulled into a false sense of security, a wrong sense of comfort and we've got to break that. Of course we here in England are having it broken for us, for the old things we thought so safe, bricks and mortar, steel shelters, etc. just aren't there when you turn around to lean on them. Instead we are getting glimpses of the things that really do last. And these are qualities of spirit – neighbourliness, brotherly love, kindness, compassion, spiritual strength, etc, etc. These qualities are on fire everywhere nowadays and the barriers of class and position are coming down through sheer necessity. If we can only cling on to these things – and I feel we shall – this war will have accomplished something really worth while.

One night last week the German planes were over and over this district. I was sleeping solidly when Mrs L. came into my room in a tizzy, poor thing, having been scared to death by a bomb that fell at least three miles away! I didn't even hear it but it was just about the last straw for her; she'd just lain there for two hours, preceding the bump, listening to the planes and getting scareder and scareder. (It's my private belief that she is about to have the C. of L. and she was struck down that day with a particularly violent bout of the curse. This would account for her excessive and quite unwarranted nerves.) Well, anyway, I got up and made her put a dressing gown on – it was very nippy – and I took her down to the kitchen where I came over all domestic and efficient and made some hot Bournvita for us to drink. She was shaking like a leaf but after a while my quite unassumed calm seemed to reassure her and we went up to bed again

[1] In a programme for Children's Hour. This was the Princess's first broadcast on radio.

where I fell back to sleep at once and she says it didn't take her long
either. The point of this little anecdote is to tell you that, thanks to
what I understand of C.S. and a nice solid constitution, I don't mind
the noises. And, as I've said before, having someone with me who
does brings out all the lion in me! Having someone to comfort and
strengthen is fine. I can't tell you how sorry I was for her. She really
did mind and hadn't a thing to combat it with. Of course we have
such a start – knowing as we do what is real and what isn't. And the
mere fact that one *knows* that bombs can't do more than get rid of
mortal man is quite something and does, of necessity, make one's
outlook just that bit different!

News of my theatrical venture is that in addition to Edith Evans,
Cyril Ritchard, Irene Eisinger[1] and me, no less a light than Cicely
Courtneidge[2] is going to appear in this high-class variety. It looks as
if we are going to be at Wyndham's and *not* the Criterion as at first
thought. And we don't open till the 23rd.

I must stop but here is an amusing story Aunt N. told me about a
soldier who was a prisoner in Germany and wrote to his wife a card
to say he was very comfy, beautifully housed and fed; that the care
was superb and everyone marvellous to him. 'Be sure,' he ended, 'to
tell this to the men of the Navy and the men of the Army and Air
Force and above all be sure to tell it to the Marines.'!

I'm very well and looking foward to the theatre.

---

*October 20th, 1940*                                          Parr's

The revue didn't open last week; nor is it opening tomorrow as at
last decided. No, God willing and a few other things, we will present
*Diversion* to a panting public on Monday, October 28th at Wyndham's
Theatre at 2.30.[3]

Reg is home for a whole week's leave! He came on Friday arriving
two hours late in the pouring rain with his hair bitten off at the back,

---

[1] Actress and opera singer; born in Vienna; in the Farjeons' *An Elephant in Arcady*.
[2] Musical comedy actress; married to Jack Hulbert.
[3] *Diversion*: a mixture devised and supervised by Herbert Farjeon. Music by Walter
Leigh. With George Benson, Edith Evans, Walter Crisham, Joyce Grenfell, Peter
Ustinov, Joan Sterndale Bennett, John Mott, Dorothy Dickson, Cornelius Fisher,
Irene Eisinger, Elsie French, Vida Hope, Dilys Rees. Produced by George Benson.
  Dirk Bogarde was also in it as 'a glorified chorus boy', sharing, as Bogarde
recalled, Dressing Room Number 4 with Peter Ustinov. They started a small salon;
Ustinov wrote a play, handing it sheet by sheet to 'an enraptured Joyce Grenfell
who sat at his feet . . . in blue velvet'.

otherwise looking rosy and beautiful and I was very happy. Mrs Luton tactfully absented herself for supper and we had a perfect evening by our own fireside, eating a homely little meal run up by Rene consisting of lettuce soup and salmon fish cakes. It was very good.

Yesterday was Saturday and at 10 we set off for the White Place [home of the Smiths] with Nan quivering on the back seat and there we joined Hubert Smith and a pal of his for a rough shoot. It was decidedly that. I spent a good part of the time rolling under barbed wire fences or wading waist-high through kale; and of all the vegetables that hold water kale is the best. I was soaked by lunchtime but having intelligently remembered to bring a change it didn't matter. Diana fed us off a most excellent and picturesque meal of bread and cheese, beer, fruit cake and apples. Such a sensible thing to do; particularly in these days when meat is a problem and labour over-taxed in most kitchens. (She, too, has a PG.)

Reg loved his day and didn't get in till 7 but I quit at lunch, for there was the ward to be cherished and its shopping to be done. We had a singsong in there one evening last week. One of the Canadians, a six-foot-four Scot, in the Seaforth Highlanders, plays the guitar and sings a bass so we got things going and really made some quite pleasing sounds. Their chief fault, in my view, is that they like to *drag* so terribly and don't really feel they savour the song unless they render it *largo largo*, with a terrific diminish at the end. Like most Americans they can 'carry parts' and we did what they call 'Harmonising' for over an hour and I think they enjoyed it. They need someone to start them; otherwise one isn't needed at all, for once they are off there's no stopping 'em. They have lots of Cowboy songs with endless verses on sentimental themes and some quite amazingly saccharine numbers about their Dear Old Mothers having birthdays that they sing in all serious reverence! What a strange crowd they are. I prefer the men to the officers. There's something sort of uneasy about the officers; it's as if they aren't quite sure of themselves and, in order to prove they are, over-do everything. They've got a certain Americanisation which, because it isn't the real thing, doesn't add to their charm. But I'm referring in the main to Winnipegians, of which there are many at the hosp. In fact the whole unit was formed from there. Mrs L. tells me that they are known for being small town-ish.

Look – just by the way – MYRA's name isn't *Moyra*! You always spell it that way. It's just MYRA. No O!

Tomorrow, God willing, I become an actress once more and from my cable you will have learned of the high company I'm keeping! Edith Evans – who sends her regards – Dot Dickson – who sends her love – Wally Crisham, a 'strange' young American youth who contorts himself in the dance and has partnered D.D. before[1] – dear George Benson – who was in the last show – Irene Eisinger, the Mozart singer from Glyndebourne – and Joyce Grenfell. We are the stars. There are small fry to support us but we are the featured players and each have a poster to ourselves saying:

*Diversion*
a mixture devised by Herbert Farjeon
JOYCE GRENFELL
(or Edith E. or D.D. etc, etc)

I saw the sandwich-men parading in Leicester Square towards Pic. Circ. yesterday afternoon as I hurried through to Paddington and was amused and annoyed to see my name there in six inch letters – red on a yellow ground.

We had the first full-length dress rehearsal yesterday.

The new monologue – 'Canteen' – is said to be a worthy successor to the others and I hope that is so.

God governs and all is harmony so I'm prepared for all to go well but it is maddening to have a cold for the opening! However, it's three days old now and I'm getting Mildred Rawson on the job for me so I've nowt to worry abowt. (I don't feel in the *least* ill; it's just a bit 'nasal' though for talking and singing.)

Irene Eisinger who is about five feet high and sings like an angel is sharing a dressing room with me. Neither of us smoke so that's nice. She's a refugee and has been through it like anything this past year, poor little thing. Ours is the Number 2 dressing room. Edith and Dot share the Number 1 (not that I address either of them by their first names yet but I daresay I soon will! One does, in the theatre).

Wyndham's is a nice theatre and not too big. You know where it is, don't you? Right across from the Hippodrome in the Charing X Road.

Edith Evans is also doing a monologue! Competition! Hers is quite excellent and very touching, I think – about an East End hop-picker

[1] Walter Crisham had been in the charity matinée at the Palace Theatre on March 12th, 1940.

in the train. I was very moved by it. Gosh, what an artist she is![1]
Celia had told me she was remote and hard to know but I didn't find
her so – she's been very friendly to me and she knows I'm a C.S.
too. She is reading a poem by Ralph Hodgson as well as doing the
monologue. This takes some doing and no one except E.E. could sit
on a plain chair, pop on her glasses, and read a long, quite difficult
but wonderful poem called 'The Bull' and do much more than merely
get away with it. Dorothy Dickson does a very funny burlesque of
the girl who did 'A Nightingale Sang in Berkeley Sq' number in
another revue as well as a dance with Wally Crisham and a sketch
with George, by Bertie, called 'Snaps'. It's about a girl showing her
holiday snaps to a young man who has come to tea. It's quite
excellent. Irene sings Mozart and does a coloratura number as well
and George has a good new song, by Bertie, called 'Sing Heigh for
the Open Country' that is a burlesque on the first sort of Norfolk
Jacketted gent who set about his exercise in an earnest and scholarly
fashion with handbooks to aid him. George does it with all his usual
charm and it should be a hit number. The whole bill is really
just high-class variety. It's pretty amazing getting E.E. and D.D.
on the same programme and only a war could get such stars to play
for the pittance necessity offers us. (For me it's not too bad after
the Little's £5 minimum. I'm getting twice that and quite a nice
four and a half per cent on the takings over £450.[2]) The whole
thing is a very sporting gamble on everyone's part. We may flop
off in two days. We equally may do very well, for there is little
other competition and every one says there is need of entertainment – particularly for the various services on their off-duty
hours. I don't yet know the prices of seats but I imagine they are
reasonable.

I have some nice little press items – 'The Inimitable J.G.' *The
Observer* says. And the *Evening Standard* called me 'That Monologue
Queen, J.G.' I feel most odd about the whole thing. At the moment,
by my own cosy fireside, not frightened. Of course tomorrow,
waiting in the wings – well – I don't know! But I do know that if
one can only get it quite clear about being an instrument for joy to

---

[1] One of the leading actresses of her generation (the Nurse in *Romeo and
Juliet*, seasons with the Old Vic, Lady Bracknell, and already in 1940, in *Cousin
Muriel* by Clemence Dane and Epifania in Shaw's *The Millionairess*, which began a
pre-London tour, but never reached the West End because of the blitz). She repeated
the hop-picker's monologue in her one-woman show at the Theatre Royal, Haymarket in 1974. She was a Christian Scientist.
[2] Edith Evans was paid '£10.1s. a week of six, seven, or eight performances, or *pro
rata* for any part thereof, plus 12½ per cent of the excess of gross receipts over £450
a week'.

play through then all is taken care of. I always try to work on those lines and it's a great help.

Reggie's week at home was heavenly. It felt like peace and we both enjoyed it so much. He gardened a lot – picking the entire border to pieces and then replanting it. He had two days' shooting and filled the larder in a most welcome way. Nan enjoyed herself too. On Wednesday I had to sing at a troop concert some thirty miles away the other side of the county. It was a wet night and my windscreen wiper is *still* out of order! However we made it and the men enjoyed it. R. came with me and I was sorry it wasn't a more exciting concert – because we do have some wildly enthusiastic ones. But these lads were all about seventeen and quite indiscriminate, if noisy. On Tuesday we gave a tea party to five of the men from the hospital. We had the usual large meal first – white and brown bread, currant buns, ginger cake, choc cakes, fish paste, honey and jam, and cup after cup of good strong sweet tea. One nice boy gave me half a pound of tinned butter from Canada and that was a big help. Just ask Annie [Ma's housekeeper] to show what 2oz butter looks like and try making it last you a week! (It doesn't; we eke out the supply with 6oz of marg. and it's so good nowadays that one doesn't mind it at all.) After tea there was the usual lighting-up of cigarettes and pipes and the magazines to look through as well as some of my photograph books. Then music. This time we had two quite good voices so we did some tasty renderings of 'Drink to me Only', 'The Londonderry Air' and 'Way Down Upon the Swanee River' as well as 'My Bonnie Lies Over the Ocean'. If I can remember to I'm going to send you the picture of us all taken by R. in the garden before tea.

I took the morning off in bed today and read the lesson very slowly and got a lot from it. If one can only see the *facts* – that life is complete and harmonious. I do at times; and *always* inside I know it.

Did I tell you I now brush my fringe under – instead of up – except at the very outside tips.

---◆---

*November 3rd, 1940*        Parr's

Well, I'm a actress again and how I love it! The notices have been wonderful and even with the increased competition I seem to have been particularly lucky. Of course Reg is delighted and writes me heavenly letters saying that if *The Times* hadn't so obviously put me first on its list he would have sued them for saying I should have left singing to the others and stuck to my own medium. As a matter of fact the singing goes particularly well.

There are yards in the skirt.
The colour of the bows is
still moot — turquoise?
Scarlet? Velvet I think.

October 27th, 1940

Yesterday, Saturday, was a terrific day for us, the theatre completely sold out, every single box, even the ones on the roof where you can't see or hear anything! And it was thrilling to see that great sea of faces and to hear them laugh. For your ear alone, now, mind – they loved me.

Now I'll go back to the beginning of the week and take it all in order.

Vera [Grenfell], Mrs Luton and I rose at 7 on Monday and went in by the 8.28. As usual in these days the train was packed and we had to stand all the way – altho' I got a perch on the edge of a table in a sort of Pullman car. I hurried off to Wyndham's where we were having a run through. (By the way, I can't help thinking of you every time I set off in the morning, for I really do look so unglamorous and I can *feel* you saying, 'Oh *Joyce*.' I carry a basket in which is a thermos and a tin of sandwiches, my library book, my gas mask and other oddments and I wear a very thick comfy tweed coat of rather dull brown and beige herringbone design and low-heeled shoes and my hair tied up in a scarf. Why do I? Because those are my clothes for this winter and I like to take my lunch with me (a) because it's cheaper, (b) because it's cosy eating it in the dressing room and (c) I enjoy that second hot cup of coffee at 3 in the afternoon.

Back to Mon. The run through was more or less alright and then suddenly it was 2.15 and I'd been called and was standing in the wings wearing my new grey dress with my hair all tidy and the fringe fluffed out. Edith Evans did the prologue and I prayed a bit as I always (literally) do every time I step on to the boards and then it was my moment and I stepped out into the lights and got a really lovely welcoming round that was all the nicer because it was public, as only Daddy and Mrs Luton were there as personal rooters! My new sketch is still v. rough; I'm such a slow worker. But it seems to have pleased them and I'm beginning to enjoy it now myself.

My second appearance is at the beginning of Part 2 and I gave 'em those old Mothers but, if I say so myself, they really are quite good and I love doing them. My third spot is halfway through Part 2, and this is my singing turn. I have a piano on the stage and nice Pritch to play it for me. (He was our number-one pianist at the Little and does the same at Wyndham's). The songs went well and since then they've gone even better. It's such fun to be singing Gin's stuff.

After it was over on Monday Daddy came round and escorted Mrs L. and myself to our train at Paddington and, of course we talked ceaselessly of the show and picked it all to pieces but in a nice way. Daddy was pleased and Mrs L. couldn't have been cosier or more motherly. Said all the things you would and was thrilled when people behind her talked flatteringly about me in the interval. I didn't expect

– this is absolutely honest – I didn't expect to get more than a mention in the press because after all E.E. and Dot D. are stars of some magnitude but, believe it or not, I got some lovely notices and, in fact, most of the space. And this makes me feel just a little bad because altho' it's lovely to get it one does hate to see them NOT get it. It's like when Aunt N. gets deflated and sad. It's peaceful but darned unnatural and you'd rather have the discomfort of the other. However I'm extremely grateful and everyone is very nice to me indeed and I'm very happy there and long may we run. Now for your peace of mind let me just tell you that I'm out of London easily before dark. I'm off the stage at 4.05 and I tear upstairs, fling off my dress and shoes, fling on my outdoor clothes without attempting to button or straighten, grab up my basket, bag, a couple of Kleenex and a pot of cold cream and rush for a taxi and Paddington. In the taxi I tidy a bit and clean the face and I arrive with ample time at Pad. I prefer the rush the first end tho'; that's why I do it. It's extravagant to taxi but worth it I think. I get back here about 5.30 and usually go straight to the hospital where I cherish my ward for an hour or so and am always back here by 7.

I've had one or two C.S. snippets with Miss Evans. I shared my picnic with her yesterday and I like her and of course admire her enormously. She was *so* nice and helpful to me about reaching the furthest parts of the house without losing the sense of intimacy necessary to my sketches. The Little was *so* little you see and Wyndham's isn't. I rather think she is a nervous and lonely person and that C.S. is her one anchor. She didn't say so, but I guess it.

Virginia and I have just cleared supper away. Rene is out. Tony is reading and we're waiting for the weekly Bebe Daniels, Ben Lyon radio programme to come on.[1] Gin says please to send you lots and lots and lots of love and she wishes you were here. Wouldn't it be fun!

*P.S.* Gin has just reminded me of a true story that she thinks you'd enjoy. Mary Shirley, friend of ours, heard from a friend of hers who gave a lift to a soldier. They were discussing bombs – as we all do.

'My auntie had quite a nasty experience the other night,' the soldier said. 'She was sitting in a shelter when it was hit by a 250 pound bomb.'

'Gosh,' said Mary's friend. 'How *awful*. What happened?'

'It blew my auntie's head off.'

The description of such an occurrence as 'quite a nasty experience' is wonderfully English isn't it?

[1] Called *Hi-Gang*, it ran from 1939 to 1941.

I forgot to tell you that the *Bystander* sent down a photographer two days ago to take the Actress in Her Home! If the results are any good I'll send 'em of course. Can you believe any of it's me? I can't.

This is my only afternoon for really getting down to it in the hospital and I made a day of it – 2.15 to 5.45 and ready to fold at the finish.

I'm now doing shopping for no less than three wards – each has thirty-five men in it. It's Christmas that agitates them now. What to get for the home folks, how to get it and how to send it. So I take early trains to London these days and buy endless souvenir hankies with views of London stamped on them, gloves, books, Xmas cards, stickers, etc, etc. It takes a long time to do but I think it's worth doing and is just about the only war work I know I can do quite well. I've just come home with a list the length of your arm and it's all been paid-in-advance so I'm off in the morning for a session at Selfridges and Woolworths before the theatre.

*Diversion* continues to do nicely and we are all most grateful for it. Bertie is going to put on a new edition at the end of five weeks and he's asked me to be in it definitely.

While I was in London on Friday a billeting officer came to call in search of billets for two officers, so it looks as if I may be forced to yield up my spare rooms. (You have to if they insist.) Rene did her best to protect me by saying she'd read somewhere that solitary ladies didn't have to have soldiers in their houses! But the officer soon disillusioned her.[1]

I'm enclosing a superb piece of verbatim reporting – a message from Myra (a lovely message too) after she'd been to see the show. I thought she was coming round to visit me in the interval but she misunderstood and waited till the finale when of course I'd left for the country. We had a long conversation on the telephone the next day and she said all the sort of things you'd love to hear but which I really haven't the face to repeat. As a matter of fact one thing was so nice and as it is obviously a tribute to God I'll tell it to you: she said I had a very subtle quality that she was hard put to analyse but that was lovely. And you and I know what that is – just plain God. Gosh, how *do* people do anything without Him? I dunno. Maria [Brassey] says that when she's in East End shelters and things are really frightening it is staggering the way people turn towards those who know something of and believe in God. Not only C.S.'s – just anyone who has faith in Spirit and Truth. Ain't it true, just. Gosh.

The weekly papers came out with nice notices for me and there have been some amusing caricatures.

[1] Joyce got her first two officers billeted soon after the New Year.

We've done good business all week – much better than the week before – and of course Saturday was a riot. I had a lovely reception and got asked for my autograph, twice, outside the stage door! How's that for fame?

---◆---

*November 17th, 1940*        Parr's

We've been on for three weeks and done very well. Saturdays are riots and yesterday was the best of all. Part of the show was broadcast direct from the theatre and is said to have come over well apart from the men in my ward who obviously – from their looks of blank amazement today! – didn't think I was in the least funny and can't yet discover what it's all about. (I did the new 'Canteen' sketch.) Daddy was in the theatre and I'm so glad because it really was a lovely house and I went better than I ever have before. In fact when I finished my songs – this is my third and final appearance – I had such applause that Miss Evans, who was waiting to come on next, had to stand and stand in the wings. I felt badly about this, but it was very exciting and I can't deny that I was very pleased indeed. And of course dear Daddy, whom I saw afterwards, was beaming from ear to ear with parental pride.

Well, the war goes on and one doesn't see its finish although one knows that each day brings peace just that much nearer. We've had some very noisy but harmless nights. I think the Bloody Hun uses this way as a route somewhere more important – anyhow he's over us quite a lot in a tiresome way, although I really can't complain as I sleep quite undisturbed most of the time. The news of our naval success at Taranto[1] was a very nice piece of alright and we were justifiably delighted by it. There is a sort of almost affectionate contempt for the Italians. One laughs at them – a thing one wouldn't dream of wasting on the Germans. Not that hate or reprisals do any good – all the same I'd like to see every single German mown down and exterminated – every bloody one of them! So there. And I wouldn't be above a nice spot of prolonged torture for the top boys. I can't really think up anything quite harsh enough! Not that I need bother; they'll get their own hell and they are heading for it and paving quite a path for themselves.

It's Sunday today and my only free day and never long enough.

[1] One of the Italian Navy's strongholds, it was successfully bombed by carrier-borne British aircraft. It was eventually occupied by British forces in September 1943.

I've got Helen Kirkpatrick staying here. She is the foreign correspondent on the *Chicago Daily News* and exactly my age. She's an old friend of Elly Cunningham's[1] and was at Smith with her. She couldn't be brighter and is also extremely courageous, going out on bomb stories with demolition squads and on to rooftops with the fire services and altogether quite a remarkable person.

Helen is the only woman in a large man's world of reporters and that they think very highly of her as a person as well as a journalist is a tribute indeed. She's become very well-known over here and contributes quite a lot to the *Daily Telegraph* as well as to her own paper at home. She is a great friend of Nancy and Ronnie's [Tree's], the Duff Coopers and all the world, and has been 'taken up' by all sorts of people but remains nicely unimpressed and quite an old cup of tea among the girls. Talking of *la vie sociale* Helen tells me that Lady Colefax[2] has remained in London throughout the blitz, canteening and sleeping in public shelters and altogether being very human and rather wonderful. So even the strangest people turn out to be dependable in crises.

Nancy came to see *Diversion* the other afternoon and it wasn't till I took my final bow that I spotted her in the second row. There wasn't time to see her afterwards for I always fly away for my train as soon as I'm off but she very sweetly sent me a telegram and I was much touched. I can't explain what I mean in this letter but her home is now often the scene of much important entertaining and it is funny to think of somehow. I don't quite know why! But it is. Your sister doesn't know about it and that's even funnier!! Bother the censor but I can't say more.[3]

It's a funny thing the way the hospital varies in one's eyes. *Most* days I love it and feel as if what I'm doing is of use. Then there come boring days and the whole Canadian population look unattractive and un-British and one can't think what all the fuss is about. Something one ate, no doubt! This, in a slight degree, has been one of those days. I fully realise it is all in my own thinking and that I have a personal sense about the place instead of free, un-selfed

[1] An American friend.

[2] Sybil, wife of Sir Arthur, an eminent lawyer. With Lady Cunard, she was one of the two leading hostesses of literary and political London.

[3] As Chequers, the Prime Minister's official weekend residence, was easily identifiable from the air and therefore vulnerable to German attack, an alternative was found in Nancy and Ronnie Tree's house, Ditchley. Here, according to Clementine Churchill's biographer, Mary Soames, 'The Trees welcomed not only Winston and Clementine and their essential entourage, but also their official guests' who all enjoyed the Trees' pre-war hospitality. In this way Nancy Tree became the most important political hostess in the country, but for security reasons very few, including Nancy Astor, knew about it.

love. My wig, you can't let down on C.S. for an instant. Not even in the little things. I didn't go to church today because I thought a walk would be so lovely – it was a heavenly day. I didn't have time – or didn't make time – to do the lesson. Ah me! One lives and learns.

There is a v. young party up at C. this weekend. We've been asked up but said NO. I wonder why I dislike young parties so? They make me feel all prickly. At least the ones at C. do. The gramophone goes incessantly; the young lie about on their collarstuds and it all combines to make me seek solitary seclusion in the big outdoors. I was up there this morning seeing Bobbie who has returned from the hospital and is getting on and *so* glad to be back at home.[1] I sneaked in and up the back stairs and bolted when I came down. Why? I really can't analyse it unless it is that I wasn't awfully happy at the young parties there in my own day. It never was quite my cup of tea, was it? I never was a gal for sitting around doing nothing and you know I do think the young are boring. Or, once again, I'll qualify that by saying the young at C. are. The more I see of people brought up in the easy way the more I lean towards socialism. I needn't worry; we're hurtling in so called – or comparatively – easy stages towards it. Things will never, can never, *mustn't* ever be the same, as they were before the war.

---

*November 23rd, 1940*      Parr's

By now you should have had my cable and in about four hours will have heard my broadcast. It was recorded; I did it this morning. Gosh, I do *hope* you heard it – it was specially for you and I sang 'I'm in Love with a Gent' for everyone in Tryon.

Just in case you *didn't* get the cable or hear my broadcast I'll tell you what it was all about. Mr Ogilvie[2] replied to my letter telling him what you had said about thanking people in America (I've sent you the letter) and yesterday he sent a representative from the BBC to ask me if I'd do something. So of course I said yes and this morning I made a record for transmitting at 7 p.m. your time. I said thank

---

[1] In the middle of October, Bobbie Shaw, who was serving in a balloon barrage squadron in Kent, was severely wounded when a bomb fell destroying the pub in which he was drinking. While in hospital in Maidstone, he made sure that an edited version of events reached his mother, who believed that the bomb had hit the barrage squadron.

[2] F. W. Ogilvie was Director-General of the BBC, 1938–42.

you and mentioned the Mayor and Trade St and later said you lived in Tryon, North Carolina, and sent messages to all my friends there and finished up with Gin's Gent. That was all; it took about three mins and was very exciting. So was my adventurous method of getting to London. Like an ass, I got into the wrong train at Taplow this morning. I meant to take my ordinary fast one but inadvertently got into a very slow, stopping one that stopped at literally every station on the line. Too much. So when I discovered this I got out at Slough and ran down to the Gt. West Road where I thumbed my way London-wards and succeeded in getting a lift with a nice quiet man in fur gloves and a small, old Ford. He took me a good bit of the way and then I got another lift in a chauffeur-driven car to Kew. There I hared after a bus I saw marked with where I wanted to get to and caught it. This took me to an underground station where I was lucky to find a train actually waiting to go so I arrived at my recording place (Yah! Mr Censor, shan't tell you where and I bet you'd *never* guess.)[1] only five minutes late. It was all the Almighty's doing I can tell you. I might have just sat in that darned old stopper for hours.

We had another marvellous house today, packed from roof to ceiling and madly enthusiastic. Oh! It *is* fun when they are like that. It's been a lovely week as a matter of fact. Sylvia Skimming left on Tuesday and Ann [Holmes] moved in. She came and met me at the theatre and we travelled down together in the usually crowded train. It's fun having her. We've reminisced endlessly about our childhood and granny and Culford Gardens and Chorleywood [Granny Phipps's house].

(Ann has just asked who I'm writing to. She says she sends you a lot of love and says she'll never forget you singing spoof French songs in the studio at 28 [St Leonard's Terrace] and wearing a top hat and slapping your bottom! She says she'd certainly like to see you.)

Families are fun, aren't they? I must say I do like the Phipps side a lot – and oh my, they are easy to get on with, being nice rational creatures and not sensitive instruments who have to be handled with care like some of our other side!

---

[1] It was the Criterion Theatre in Piccadilly, which had been converted into a BBC recording studio.

*December 1st, 1940*                                             Parr's

Of course I nearly cried when I got your cable saying you hadn't heard the broadcast! It is hard, for you would have liked it, I think. If I can find the script I wrote for myself I'll send it to you so that you may read what you should have heard. Oh well – maybe I'll do another some day. I wonder why you couldn't get it? It was on the regular English broadcast shortwave length. I had a letter from you yesterday dated Nov. 4th – you'd only just heard about *Diversion* when you wrote it so news does take a time nowadays, doesn't it? We've been on for weeks and of course it feels longer; it always does. We continue to do good business and the audiences are very enthusiastic; particularly on Saturdays. Yesterday's was terrific! They enjoyed everything and yet there was discrimination in their applause. V. pleasant to play to, they were. It's Sunday today and I haven't been to church. Instead Sylvia Skimming and I have just done the lesson together in front of a big fire and it was very restful. There comes a moment when I just can't go on getting to places! Every day I travel so far that on Sunday, now and again, I just can't face the going to church and when I feel that way I indulge a bit and stick to the fire. It's mighty cold and yesterday we had a pea souper in London 'tho of course it was glorious out here when I left. Miraculously the trains weren't very late and it didn't deter our audience in the slightest *and* it did deter the Nazis. We've had very quiet nights out here of late except for Friday when our cannons had been at the enemy almost ceaselessly from 8 to 12. The nasties dropped flares on parachutes to light up their objectives but as these lit up nothing but the woods and meadows and were very soon shot out by our boys no harm was done. Sylvia, Rene and I stood out in the freezing starry night and watched. It was a very pretty sight and not in the least bit alarming.

John Phipps came to supper with Ann and me last Sunday night and we got onto the subject of Phipps women. Ann and J. both averred they were terribly handicapped because of their self-sufficiency and capability. But I'm not sure – John says it is essentially un-appealing to be so complete! Ann says all her fun has always been spoiled by a prim Phippsy inability to swing easy if anything looks like being the least bit unorthodox. I know what she means; I curl up inside. Ann says she would often love to hold hands but she just can't! John says our rigidity is a blight to a party!! It really was a funny conversation. Ann was sad to think of the colour her life lacked because she'd always been so *'bien'*. I said little because I realised the entire talk was about matter and it didn't! But I know what they mean and personally I like it. From a human point of view sex appeal is probably an asset. But it's such a handicap if it gets to be important and does interfere with clear thinking. Maybe it is because I am so happy with my Reg that I don't really take much interest outside. Of course it's gay and comforting to know that one is found attractive but it must stay on a very light footing, that attraction, or look at the 'ell it leads to! Once again thank God for what I know! And for what I've been through too, to learn it. I remember Mildred Rawson telling me that no one can float in C.S. True, ain't it?

I'm going up to Cliveden for lunch and it is time I went and did something to my face. More later.

*After lunch.* Too much to eat of course and a very mixed bag of guests. I sat between David A.'s nice friend Dr Gillespie and Reg Winn. Stephen King-Hall[1] was there; the McNaughtons[2]; Edward Hulton[3] who owns *Picture Post* and his editor called Hopkinson[4]; Tom Jones and daughter Eirene. I can't remember the rest. Oh, Irene Ravensdale, who sent you her love. When one hasn't been to C. for a while its strange restlessness smites you, I find. Too much goes on. Too many people, too much talk, too much food. The fires are lovely, so are the flowers and it is fun in some ways but oh, how glad I am to get down to my quiet little drawing room, with my books and Brahms First Symphony coming into it in clear tones and Nan asleep at my feet, and a thick wintry landscape outside. I suppose John is right when he says our Phipps-womanliness is disheartening to a man because we appear to be complete in ourselves. I'd love to have Reg here; but I ask nothing further. I've got the rest inside. Even his love, I think.

What of the week? Well, we've had nice audiences and business is good. I've got to know the Misses Evans and Dickson better and like them enormously. Dorothy D. reminds me *so* much of you. She even has a pair of glasses with one side off! I am happy up in my snug little room with Irene Eisinger.

George Benson left the company a week ago to become a soldier and we miss him a lot. His place is inadequately filled and some of his work so badly done that it's been cut and now I've had to put in my old Women's Institute lecture to spin out the programme. We are having an all-new show on New Year's Day and I'm in the throes

[1] MP (Independent Nationalist) for Ormskirk 1939–45. He founded the National Newsletter in 1936, and the Hansard Society in 1945.
[2] General Hon Andrew George Latta McNaughton, and his wife Mabel. He commanded the 1st Division Canadian Overseas Force, 1939–40, and later became GOC-in-C, First Canadian Army.
[3] Managing director of the Hulton Press which also published at various times *Farmer's Weekly, Lilliput, Housewife, Eagle, Girl.*
[4] Tom Hopkinson, author and journalist. As well as *Picture Post* he edited *Lilliput*.

of composition for Bertie wants two from me. Gosh. Rumour has it
that La Lillie may join us but I'm hoping she won't. We're a very
happy little unit as we are and nice and amusing as she is socially,
they say she's a devil to work with and throws her stardom about. I
ask you! With Edith E. and D. Dickson sharing a room and being v.
human, to have one of Bea's calibre lord it would be a bit much.
However I'm counting that chicken long before it's hatched. If she
comes I shan't get a song spot in the next edition so there's more to
it than would first appear! For of course she must have her spots and
there isn't room for us all to have three appearances as at present. So
I hope she's out.

(The Brahms is *so* lovely. I'm stopping to listen for a sec.)

---

*December 8th, 1940*                                          Parr's

News is nil this week. Days fly by and I can't distinguish one from
the other as I look back. One entertaining thing stands out though:
on Thursday I went into Edith and Dot's room and found them deep
in it about the Shulamite woman who came into the lesson last week.
I joined them and we had a fine time, disturbed only by the call boy
urging us on to the stage as our turns came round. It seems Dot's
parents are C.S. and she was 'raised' in it. Now at last she is beginning
to take a look at it again. It seems that the Almighty plotted to put
her and Edith in one dressing room. In the ordinary way a most
unlikely arrangement.

---

*December 15th, 1940*                                         Parr's

I've just spent the entire afternoon making a giant Christmas card –
four feet by two and a half – to decorate my ward. Its background
is made from a piece of wallpaper left over from R.'s dressing room,
white with little green stars. It is 'framed' by a tasty red crinkly paper
frill and an edging of lace (paper doilies) and a surround of artificial
holly tied with scarlet velvet ribbon. The lettering is silver outlined
in red. Can you imagine it? It looks extremely festive and is to hang
or be supported somewhere near the entrance to the ward. While I
was making this Reg was sticking my notices into my clipping book.
He takes charge of that book and has made an impressive job of it.

He came to the show on Sat for the first time. I'm glad to say I went *extremely* well; in fact I stopped the show which is always fun and more so with him there to see it all. He loved it and was as thrilled as I was.

Reg and I had a very cosy day and it was so peaceful and ordinary, gosh I'll be glad when this war is over – BUT NOT till we've won in a big way.

Wiss is at C. for the night looking very blonde – she's 'dipped' her front lock and wears it very glamorously in a sort of messy curtain. Only one eye shows and I think the whole thing is a big mistake. However she's happy about it. Her wrists are laden with clanking seals, lockets, etc, on bracelets and it would drive me bats. But, once again, she's happy about it. She's a cosy old cup of tea though and I'm fond of her.

*December 22nd, 1940*        In the train to Swindon

This week's letter is being written under considerable difficulties in a train. Life at this moment is so bung full I just have to snatch any odd times there are for letters and mere living – I'm on my way to spend the day and night with R. at his camp; to perform for his troops this evening and attend his officers' ball afterwards. *Très gai* – it has meant getting up in the dark – for the blackout holds till about 8.30 a.m. these days – and catching a train at Maidenhead. Being an officer's wife I get a travelling voucher and can go first class for half fare – very nice. The train is stiff with people and I'm enjoying my 'first' corner in comfort while the common herd stand in the corridor! Oh, it is nice to be luxurious at times.

We've spent the whole week rehearsing and playing and I've sandwiched a bit of shopping in for the men and done a broadcast and generally rushed. The broadcast was a singing one. I sang Gin's 'Gentleman' and 'The Tattoo'd Lady' and before I sang the last I was allowed to say I was singing it particularly to my friends in Ward 11 at a Canadian Hospital Somewhere in England. They were very pleased about it – I saw them last night when I went into the ward. I forgot to say that quite a lot of time has been spent decorating the ward. We've got a good sized tree, lots of red and green ribbon garlands across from lamp to lamp, each lamp a cluster of silver bells – all products of Woolworth. The sisters on my ward are very enthusiastic and have done a lot of it themselves with their own money. It makes a lot of difference if the sister on your ward co-operates. Both mine are particularly nice and helpful and very popular with the men so that the whole thing has a very happy atmosphere indeed.

I've been the least bit uneasy about my new monologue and on Friday when I did it at a public rehearsal (to the rest of the company) I was sure it wouldn't do. It's a good idea but it hasn't shaped well so I've scrapped it at the eleventh hour and last night on the train from London to Tap. I wrote a new one about an assistant in a small town lending library that I really have got some confidence in – she's so darned nice and simple, and the trouble with 'Question and Answer' was that neither the discouraging questions or the nitwit girl were in the least cosy and I just couldn't love them. That's why they wouldn't grow properly. But my library lady is cosy as can be and I dote on her. I almost know her by heart already. I shall do a bit of work on her in this train, I expect. I find trains *lovely* to work in. The wheel noise is an incentive to work against I think and then there's something so detached about being taken somewhere with no effort on your part that your mind clears at once and ideas pour in.

*I'll add to this later –*

*December 23rd, 1940*
My gosh the cold! You've never known anything like it and R.'s camp, set in the Wiltshire downs, is probably the coldest spot in the land. He arranged for me to stay with a charming couple called Davies who have married quarters in the camp. They did wonders in a paper-thin walled bungalow but really there is nothing to be done under such conditions. Fires roar and bottles glow but the air surrounding them remains icy – literally. R. was very sweet and I love him. It's beastly the way this war keeps people apart. He met me at the station in a borrowed car and we went straight to the Davies's where I hung out my velvet dress to prepare for the evening. Then for drinks before lunch with some Major and his wife. After-wards we had our lunch at the King's Arms in Swindon – very excellent roast pork.

I'm finishing this letter at home – I wrote the second part in the train this morning but it got so full I had to stop.

The concert went quite well and I was OK. R. was pleased, the night was frigid, the party was gay and it all went well. I'd like to write more fully but if you could see all I've got to do this evening and the time I've got to do it in you'd understand this dreary note.

Christmas wasn't a bit itself this year – thank goodness – for with separations and all it would have been worse if it had been.

After church I went to my ward carrying a trayful of little presents for all my friends therein. Each one wrapped and tagged with the man's name. Just Woolworth presents – soap, shaving cream, soap cases, sponge bags, etc, etc. The up patients were just about to sit down to their Christmas dinner at one long table spread down the centre of the ward and decorated by Sister Millar with red and green candles, etc, and little paper cups for candies. I handed out my presents and then to my amazement and pleasure I was 'presented' with a silver plate engraved with my name, Ward 11 and the hospital! I have seldom been more touched. It was so entirely unexpected and unnecessary and therefore all the nicer. Sister Leashman made the presentation and all eyes were glued while I opened the package. Tears rushed to me rather and in response to 'speech' I just said what I could in a jumbled way – thanked them enormously and said how grateful we were for their presence here this Christmas. I also said it wasn't a real Christmas because it was so full of separations – separations for them as well as for us actually in this country – so we'd just make it as good a day as we could, have it off the record, so to speak and then have proper Christmasses as soon as Peace came. After this I was cheered; then I cheered them back, solo. Then we sang 'Auld Lang Syne' followed by cheers for the King and cheers for Canada. By this time it was 1.15 so I left for lunch up at Cliveden. The party up there was almost entirely composed of strays.

We sang carols after lunch until the hour of the King's speech. After this Laura [Grenfell] and I came away. I wrote letters by this fireside while Laura had to take my car and do some WVS job of collecting toys from the Kents' house at Iver[1] to deliver to the poor children in Slough. At 6 we put on long frocks and went over to the hospital to help Aunt N. with her Christmas party to the 300 up patients in the old recreation room. A local jazz band – good – played for an hour and the men sang, Aunt N. did a Cake Walk with one of them, I sang 'All the Things you Are' (easily my current favourite) and there was a Father Christmas with joke toys for the men and finally a meal of hot dogs and coffee and Christmas pudding. In the middle of all this I sneaked off to my ward where I knew there would be at least eight bed patients left out of it all. There were many more than that I found and after talking to them a bit I asked Sister Millar, on night duty, if she thought they'd like a sketch and we decided

---

[1] The Duke and Duchess of Kent lived at Coppins, Iver, Bucks.

they might, so I made a little circle of semi-up patients and performed for them.

By the time all this was over it was 9 p.m. and I left to go up to cold supper at C. Such a good meal it was too. Afterwards we sang quite a lot of old songs with me at the piano; then there were charades with Reg Winn and Jakie in the leads. After this I was called on and I did 'Canteen' and tried out my new 'Local Library' one. It went well and they were all nice about 'Local Library'. Then Laura and I left to get to bed before starting off early the next day for London and our jobs. We had superb houses on Thursday, Friday and Saturday and we took our first edition off yesterday.

Dress rehearsal on Tuesday, lighting rehearsal, tomorrow – we open on Wednesday, New Year's Day at 2.15. I do hope we are a success – it's *such* a good programme. We ought to be. I'm going to wear my tulle crinoline, now dyed black, to sing in. But don't worry, it's quite lovely with a very expensive and beautiful bunch of deep bright red roses in front. From Marshall & Snelgrove's flower dept. and costing nearly 25/-.

For the monologues I've got a blue velveteen dress rather like my grey one with the red bows, but this one has large sleeves. Sort of double puffs, if you can imagine them, and the bows are apple green. It's very pretty. I do the hair like that, too. Up at the sides with a loose, low bun.

Fougasse[1] and wife on Thursday. Vivien Leigh and Larry Olivier on Friday! Didn't see 'em but they came to pay their respects to Dot and Edith afterwards. My friend Elsie Suddaby was there the same day. Oh, it's been an endless rush of exciting audiences. Good fun.

That's all my news. I washed my hair this evening. Laura and I got our own supper and washed up and now we're listening to Bach's Christmas Oratorio.

You know Aunt N. is so sweet and takes such care of me. I can't describe quite how I mean but she is solicitous and auntly and kind.

Now to bed.

P.S. I was at the Nat. Gal. on Friday morning to hear Myra play in the Brahms horn trio rehearsal. *Lovely*.

Do let me know if you get the *Tatler* pictures I sent you last week – or if you don't and I'll send 'em again.

Happy New Year.

---

[1] Fougasse, otherwise Kenneth Bird, comic artist and editor of *Punch*, 1937–49.

*1941*

1941 was another year of setbacks for the Allies. British troops were expelled from Greece and Crete, Yugoslavia fell and Axis forces occupied the whole of the Balkan peninsula. British naval strength was heavily taxed in the Mediterranean and the Atlantic and by the end of the year about 9 million tons of allied and neutral shipping had been sunk. However, the US Lend-Lease Act, which came into force on March 11th, kept a steady flow of supplies to Britain, regardless of her ability to pay for them in dollars. In December the Japanese bombing of Pearl Harbor brought America into active participation in the war. By this time some German detachments had penetrated into the suburbs of Moscow, Hitler's offensive against Russia having started on June 22nd, thus turning his war aims away from the immediate invasion of Britain.

Through Joyce's letters this year, the role of Cliveden as a centre of political entertaining is seen to be in decline. The 'Cliveden Set' was generally thought to have been pro-German during the Thirties and Lady Astor's spirited clash with Churchill in the House of Commons when he condemned the Munich agreement during the debate which followed Chamberlain's return from Germany was not forgotten; now her continued and violent attacks on the Coalition Government both in Parliament and in the press made her generally unpopular. The guests at Cliveden largely shared Lady Astor's views; it is not surprising therefore that, as described in Joyce's letter of July 6th, they were the 'malcontents'. There were very few 'young parties' like in the old days; the young people were serving in the forces. The guests now tended to be old and disgruntled, and included, in the first half of 1941, Hilaire Belloc, then aged seventy-one, and George Bernard Shaw, aged eighty-five, and according to his letter to Lady Astor accepting her invitation, 'three quarters dead'.

# 1941

January 5th, 1941                                                          Parr's

Darling Ma,

Well, *Diversion 2*[1] is safely launched and has been acclaimed by the
critics as 100 per cent better than *Diversion 1*, and I must admit it's a
first-rate show. My new sketch, 'Local Library', is thought kindly
of and both Ivor Brown and Agate in the Sunday papers have
said complimentary things about it and me.[2] (It is a good one too!
And written entirely by the Almighty in a brief journey by train
from Pad. to Tap. one dreary Saturday evening after I'd decided
to overthrow the Interview sketch I'd been working on for so
long.)

Edith's new numbers are all good and she is particularly 'strong'
in all she does and of great value to the show. And so is the rest of
the company. In fact Bertie says that the chief fault in this show is
that it has too many stars and I think he's right.

Gosh, won't it be fun when this mess is all over and we come to
Tryon and I do all my numbers for you? My repertoire is growing
rapidly. I have seven working sketches and more in the process of
completion.

As you can imagine the new show has taken up most of my time

[1] Wyndham's, January 2nd, 1941. *Diversion No. 2*: a revue by Herbert Farjeon.
Music by Walter Leigh. With Edith Evans, Bernard Miles, Joyce Grenfell, Peter
Ustinov, Dorothy Dickson, Walter Crisham, Irene Eisinger, Joan Sterndale Bennett,
Johanna Horder, Dilys Rees, Vida Hope.
[2] Ivor Brown was editor and dramatic critic of *The Observer*. James Agate having
praised Peter Ustinov wrote in the *Sunday Times*: 'Equally true and just as biting are
Miss Joyce Grenfell's studies of modern manners in both canteen and drawing room.
This country has waited long for its revenge for Miss Ruth Draper's "Showing the
Garden". Miss Grenfell supplies it in that lesson in which an American mother
would have her daughter learn by heart Shelley's *Ode to a Skylark*. There can be no
more delicious moment in modern light entertainment than that in which this
exponent of American culture says: "No dear, I don't know what it was if bird it
never wert." '

and thoughts this week and I've little other news. The cold has been beyond any joke. I wonder when we'll learn to take it seriously over here and do something about it? Already half my pipes are out of order and even with a really big fire in here, woolly underclothes, sweaters, fur-lined bedroom slippers and a rug wrapped round me I am only just warm. And not a bit more than that. In fact my left hand, having nothing to do but hold the pad in place while my right takes exercise with the pen, is frozen. Brr. I hate it. Friday's train home was an hour late and the platform at Pad. was quite unbelievably cold. I now travel everywhere with a rug and it is a help. Fortunately the dressing room at Wyndham's is a haven of heat and both Irene Eisinger and I agree about keeping it snug and we enjoy it a lot.

I performed for Colin de la Mare's Home Guard fund over at Penn last night,[1] the only pro in the programme and I can't begin to tell you what a difference I feel with my acquired pro polish. The audience relaxes with one at once – they feel one's certainty and it does interest me so much to notice all these phases. The compère last night was Cecil Ramage, Cathleen Nesbitt's husband.[2] She was in front but I didn't see her to speak to.

Almost my favourite moment in the evening was when I discovered I'd left one evening shoe behind and had to perform in my lamb-lined boots under a red velvet frock! I explained the situation to the audience who enjoyed it as much as I did. But I didn't feel exactly dainty.

I've pushed aside prejudice and fallen for trousers. Only, let me add hurriedly, in the privacy of this house. But they *are* warm and I do enjoy putting them on after my bath in the evening. Blue wool, with a jade green sweater and red jacket. Not so sightly as you might imagine, for the truth is I am not constructed for such garments. However I'm snug and that's the point.

Much love<br>Joyce

———◆———

*January 19th, 1941*                                        Parr's

On Friday I gave Tom Jones and Edith E. lunch at the Garrick Restaurant in Irving St. At least E. E. didn't eat anything but just sat.

---

[1] Colin de la Mare, son of the poet, Walter de la Mare; director of Faber and Faber.
[2] Cecil Ramage, actor and barrister-at-law. Had been a member of Parliament briefly. Cathleen Nesbitt, leading English actress, was the original Yasmin in *Hassan*.

(She never does before a performance!) It was very pleasant and before she arrived (very late having forgotten about it till 1.20!) we had a cosy tête-à-tête and a good gossip. Afterwards it was rather like two puppies sniffing round each other. The great are a bit like that at first meeting I've found. They look and sniff and question a bit and probe and retire. Edith is just T.J.'s drop, I think, but there was no time for him to discover this at a first meeting. She is a strangely shy and unsure person and that has a sort of endearing quality about it. That she, easily our greatest actress, should be timid and almost quaky is a source of continued surprise to me. It isn't that she isn't sure of herself as an actress. Oh *no*. She knows all about her work and that's why it is so darned good. It's about herself as a woman that she strikes one as being less sure.

Myra enjoyed the revue very much on Tuesday. I talked to her about it the next day and she said very nice things. Stephen Potter, though, has said the nicest thing of all and one that is true and so I'm not shy of quoting it. He said in his note written the evening of the day he came to *Diversion 2*: 'I think one of the things I like best about your bits is that you seem to be on the side of the people you are acting – it certainly is one of the reasons they are so good.'

And that is what none of those asses the critics, nice as they are to me, can *ever* see. They say I'm 'devastating', 'icy', 'bitter' and even 'ruthless' but it just doesn't happen to be true. I'm on the side of the people I'm doing or I couldn't do them.

---

*February 2nd, 1941*                                        Parr's

Lying in the bath on Friday night with the radio on to a programme called *The Curtain Goes Up*, about theatre questions, I heard John Gielgud being interviewed and asked if he thought theatre was make-believe or reality (or should be either of these things) and he said it was half and half to most actors 'but to brilliant people like Ruth Draper and Joyce Grenfell it was make-believe'. (We 'people' the stage, it seems!) I nearly fell down the drain in my pleasure at such a tribute from such a person.

---

Your cable has come and I'll pretend I haven't opened it till tomorrow.[1] Thank you. It was fun to have it.

And, lovely surprise, here is Reg back again for the day and tonight! He took part in a military exercise in this district this morning and as he came by motorbike and could therefore get back under his own steam he got permission to stay the night and leaves at 6 a.m. tomorrow. He has stripped off a few of the layers he wears for this mode of travel but it might amuse Lefty and Tommy to know his outfit so here it is:

A thin wool vest, then a navy blue silk alpaca sweater *under* his woollen khaki shirt; then a double brown alpaca sweater *over* his shirt. Then a lambswool lined leather waistcoat. (No, I've missed out his battledress top, made of wool in the shape of a golfing jacket, army issue.) Then a rather large green tweed shooting jacket and finally a voluminous army raincoat. His legs are covered by two pairs of thick hand-knitted socks over knee-long stockings and over this, rubber Wellington boots. Add a scarf and fur-lined leather gloves, the whole topped by a camouflaged tin hat and you have the complete picture. He brought a birthday cake made by the cookery school at his camp and a lovely little watch – my own having vanished, probably having been dropped in a taxi during one of my daily rushes after the show. He also brought a rabbit he'd shot yesterday but the thing hadn't finished bleeding so we had to leave it in the tank where it had travelled with the cake!

We lunched up at C. One of those mixed groups that just add up to nothing. Shiny Tennant[2] looking like a rather dry bird: I think he is without teeth; maybe that is the reason for the decreasing size of his face; Michael, Jakie, Bobbie – well, I'm off the boys as a whole just now because I think they are messy and uncontrolled but I've got such a weakness for Jakie that I can almost forgive his strange coarseness. Where does it come from? Do you think it's one of those Freudian converse things? That Aunt N.'s horror of the senses has produced this in the boys? Of course I think Aunt N. has a fairly dirty mind. I'll never forget her saying to Wiss when we were both about eighteen that she didn't want us to go to shoe shops alone as it wasn't right for the male assistants to touch our ankles! One can hardly believe it now. But it was true. I always feel she's shocked but fascinated by sex. Bobbie is very nice to me these days but he

[1] Ma's cable: birthday greetings for Joyce.
[2] American C.S. practitioner.

hasn't outgrown his sadistic teasing habits (and that is no exagger-
ation, for he seems to delight in torment).

I don't know why I go on in such detail about all this but there are
times when the atmosphere of C. strikes me as being so darned
poisonous that I have to get out at once. The odd thing is that I
sincerely believe Aunt N. thinks the house has a rarefied and good
air to it. It's always struck me as significant that Uncle W. escapes
to the somewhat chill but ever happy atmosphere of his Munnings-
hung[1] room upstairs!! But this is a waste of time and paper. Don't
read it aloud, will you? I've made a reality of something that just
doesn't exist but I'm sure you know what I mean and won't misinter-
pret as other people would do.

*February 10, 1941*
My thirty-first birthday. Coo!

Rene overslept and instead of calling R. at 5.30 a.m. she knocked at our
door at 6.45. A wild rush – he'd shaved last night so he skipped that and
I helped Rene get his coffee and toast. It was still dark when he left but so
*lovely*, stars and a cock in the distance sensing the day we couldn't yet see.
He went off looking like a Mr Noah, quite square with all those layers
on. (Oh, I forgot one vest – a thin silk one, the foundation of all the rest!)
The headlight from his bike shone in front of him as he swayed up our
little drive and his outline was very sweet and comic.

No ears showing. (Balaclava helmet.)[2]

He says it's fun to ride a motorbike and heaven knows he couldn't
feel a breath of anything through his outfit.

It's the most lovely day – clear blue and sunny and the birds are
quite dotty. When I tell the Canadians spring has started they just
laugh; they can't conceive of such a thing before May but all the
evidence is here – snowdrops, hazel catkins and *warmth*. (Of course
we may still have snow and blizzards; but for the moment it's good.)

Edith E. is coming here for the night tomorrow. I've been writing
again – when I've got the things tidied up I'll let you have copies.

*P.S.* I *always* carry my gas mask!

I'm all dressed up today to be a Birthday Girl – I'm wearing my
neat black, white collar, and my best coat swathed rich in silver fox.
For once I do look quite actressy!

————◈————

[1] Sir Alfred J. Munnings, President of the Royal Academy, specialised in pictures
of horses and racing. Hence Waldorf Astor's fondness for them.
[2] Reproduced overleaf.

I can't do that 'on account' Invasion 2.

Reg has just gone up to take the first bath and din following almost at once so. I'll add to this later. Tomorrow (birthday) Daddy is giving me lunch and I rather think I may get some cake to take into the ward to break the monotony.

Monday: Feb: 10<sup>th</sup> 1941

On 31<sup>st</sup> birthday. Coo.
Rene overslept and instead of calling R. at 5.30 Am she knocked at my door at 6.45. A mild wretch — he'd shaved last night so he skipped that and I helped Rene get his coffee & toast. It was still dark when he left but so lonely, stars and a cock in the distance. During the day we couldn't yet see. He went off looking like a Mrs Noah, quite square with all those layers on. (Oh, I forgot one vest — a thin silk one, the foundation of all the rest!) The head light from his bike shone in front of him as he swayed up on little drive and his outline was very sweet and comic

no ears showing. Balaclava helmet)

He says its fun to ride a motor bike & heaven knows he couldn't feel a breath rare thing through his outfit.

February 10th, 1941

Still no letters from you. It must be about three weeks since I last heard – but I expect I'll get a great wodge all at once quite soon.

I woke up on Tuesday to a completely blank window. I don't think I've ever seen such dense fog. Edith [Evans] had planned to come down for the night but when I'd crept into Paddington half an hour late I thought I'd better warn her of the hazards and may be she'd come another day. However by lunchtime the whole thing had lifted and the day was lovely, so about 5 o'clock we left her garage in Wilton Place and drove down in her enormous comfy actressy cream-coloured Chrysler. We had a very quiet cosy evening: dinner in front of the fire on a little tea table followed by talk and the photograph books. She *is* an extraordinary person. There she is, easily England's greatest actress, as uncertain of herself and shy as a girl at her first party. And always. Not just this time. She's got a very good *doing* sense of humour. That is, she does funny things and enjoys funny things. I'm not sure how safe she is about the sort of Lefty jokes we all like. And she's strangely unintellectual. In fact she dislikes things intellectual and says so. I'm with her there – up to a point. But of course it's the intellectual people, as such, that we don't like – not the things they are intellectual about. She isn't well-read nor very knowledgeable. Funny, because I would have sworn she was. Therefore it looks as if her acting is of the native intelligence kind with more than a touch of genius to it. She is very human. That is her trouble, I think. The frailties of man worry her and concern her. I can't say the same; but then I've been brought up in C.S. She finds it hard to see *why* certain things persist when she's worked and worked over them. I don't know her well enough yet but someday I'll tell her that it is only when we are still and resting in God's action that things get cleared up. You can't help liking Edith. She's got a childlike quality about her, a sort of naivety that is rather endearing. And then she thinks she knows (which I suppose we all do) but I'm sure she hasn't got the answers right!

Next morning she and I walked up to see Aunt N. T.J.[Jones] was there and later we compared amused notes about Aunt N. doing her stuff for the great actress! There was a good deal of the authority about her that morning. Neat mauve outfit, pink on the cheek and a light in the eye as she talked of nursery schools and children's rights. They both know G.B.S. He was half shared between them for a while. [T. E.] Lawrence was introduced to the conversation. It was all very well done and had I been Edith it would have left me with a clear impression of a dynamic little woman with a way with her.

Which, after all, is just about right, isn't it? Ah me, even the travesty harks back to its original! Later Edith drove T.J. and me back to London.

*February 23rd, 1941*          Parr's

I've just lost my first two officers, who have been moved elsewhere, and gained two more who arrived in states of deep exhaustion from the far north last night. They fell into baths and beds about 10 and I caught a glimpse of them this morning. Not very glamorous: a Capt. Graham who is small, dark, shy and spotty. The other is a 2nd Lieut. – name of Miles. He is larger, dark and a bit flat-faced. My sole complaint to date is that one of them smokes in the bathroom. That is altogether unforgivable and will have to be dealt with if it recurs! They are surrounded by batmen in big boots who will have to be lured into sand shoes for our peace. It's a Somerset Reg. and said to be nice. I was asked if I'd take in a married couple but I couldn't face a wife about the place so I said I'd prefer two officers, unattached. As in the first instance, I see nothing of my boarders so it's not too bad. If these are here for long I think something will have to be done about turning the dining room into a sitting room for them, as I cannot keep my heart steeled when I think of the horrors of their having to live at the horrible mess (Dropmoor) for all their leisure hours. But we'll see.

*March 1st, 1941*          Wyndham's Theatre

Several friends have been to see *Diversion*. Aunt N. blew in for half the programme on Thursday and I haven't seen her since to ask what she thought but T.J. tells me that Bobbie, who was with her, was 'extremely pleased' with me. Particularly as I had more applause than Dorothy Dickson! It was a full house that day but just the dreariest imaginable. Audiences don't realise how much they can contribute to the fun! It's like tennis – you must get the ball back occasionally if it is to be amusing. Some audiences play like mad and then it's heaven! Others merely sit; and that makes the work ninety per cent harder for the actors.

I've tentatively started writing a few things I remember about my

life but you know the odd thing is that I find it *such* a depressing
pursuit that I think I'll have to abandon it. All the lovely times are
clouded over with a Saturday-afternoon-gloom. I think that is because
it didn't *end* happily because of you and Daddy and the divorce. One
feels, vaguely and unreasonably that all the fun was a cheat because
of what followed it. Which is, of course, nonsense. Don't think I still
feel anything in the least sad about it all. I quite honestly don't because
I see you being happy in a new and true way and Daddy having
found a peace of his own. It's just that St Leonard's Terrace – 28 –
has a sort of haunt to it for me that has tainted the happy times there.
The final break-up seems realler than the gay silly times before hand.
Which is sad; but not in the least important! Personally I find each
year increasingly better. You learn to drop unimportant things and
'objects that before were invisible become visible'. It is increasingly
enjoyable, this life, in spite of the sadnesses by the way.

I'm afraid you may think I'm low by the foregoing. I assure you
I'm not. I've learned a bit about letting the past slip off and I'm
growing daily more grateful to God for the little I know and understand.

I've eaten my sandwich lunch – bacon and celery, *delish* – and
drunk my coffee while Katy, the dresser has 'done' our tables. From
below the window I can hear signs of the pit and gallery queues so
our usual promising Saturday has begun and it's three quarters of an
hour before the curtain rises.

I think John, the call boy, is just about to call the half hour so I'll
stop this for the moment and write more later in the afternoon.

My new officers are still mysteries as one has gone on leave for a
week and the other has taken to his bed with a cold. He is a small
dark man with spots and burnt eyes like holes in a blanket. Dull to
talk to; but then I must confess we've only made conversation
concerning the impossibility of finding a house nearby for his wife
and two babies. I will NOT have 'em *chez moi*! There are limits to
kindness and hospitality.

---

*March 23rd, 1941*      Parr's

Reg came home last Friday for forty-eight hours. He is working very
hard indeed these days and was glad of the breathing space. His camp
is a training one and also a clearing station so in his capacity as
assistant adjutant he has a lot of official and boring jobs to deal with.

He arrived about 7.30 on Friday and telephoned from Tap. station to announce the fact, just as I was stepping into my bath not having expected him for an hour. So I hurriedly dipped and dried, flung on some underclothing and a dressing gown, then my fur coat, and took the car down to meet him. We had a cosy supper and he didn't draw breath telling me all his news. Next day we went up early by the 9.46 for him to see a man about his income tax, his family and to lunch with Gin and me at the Ivy before the matinée.

Gin was in *fair* form only, a little spring melancholia on her. How well I know that complaint, don't you? When the beauty of everything seems almost unbearable in contrast to the bloodiness of the rest! She and I always agree that the saddest thing in the world is after tea on an early summer day when you can hear the sound of people playing tennis in the distance. Gosh, I hope we hear that again though, and soon.

R. and I stayed in on Saturday evening and went early to bed. Sunday was just one of those magical days when spring comes completely for a few hours and intoxicates you. There was thick fog till 11; then it swooshed off and showed up a perfect, blue, still, warm, wonderful day, full of birds and first daffodils and damp brown bits of garden spiked with growing greenery and lumpy buds on bushes and a smell of newness everywhere. I went into the hosp. before lunch and then we walked together up to C. for lunch.

Reg and I were so overcome with the beauty of the day and the fear that we mightn't use it to the full advantage that we almost wasted it wondering what to do with it! We came home early after lunch and then decided to drive over to Maria's [Brassey] and call in on her and Norah. We found them gardening; it was just the day for it. We put a stop to their energies and we sat under a black and budding mulberry tree in the sun and cracked some good jokes. So it went till teatime when we came home and I put the kettle on, Rene being out for the afternoon. Then Reg got out my press cuttings and began to get them in order, throwing out the dull ones and sticking only to the ones that said the really extra nice things! He took so long reading and deciding that we never got to the paste stage and had to leave it till next time. The awful Sunday evening hour arrived; he went up to change back into his uniform, Rene came in to cut him some sandwiches, I drove him to the station and he was gone. It had been a lovely weekend.

On Monday Celia [Johnson] came to stay. She is working in this MOI film that I'm to have a little part in and she started at it on Tuesday. She says it is remarkably different from the theatre but quite amusing to do, altho' she cannot see how one can ever build up character or get continuity, for they work in such staccato little bits.

On Tuesday I went to London wearing last year's navy blue suit, white muslin blouse (old) and my new spring hat for I was going down to stay the night with Kathleen Dewar[1] after the show to do some performing for her in East Grinstead. I lunched with Daddy that day who was in his usual fine form. He told me not to tease you about Tommy! *Tease* is hardly the word!! But anyway I won't. We lunched at the Garrick restaurant which is pleasantly near the theatre. It's old fashioned to the point of being picturesque and it has plain food cooked for a predominantly male clientele.

Mrs Dewar sent a shining rich black car to collect me at 4. It was a perfect afternoon – the match to Sunday – and I enjoyed the drive in a pathetic slum child way, peering out at everything and actively enjoying the richness of my conveyance. Mrs D. lives near East Grinstead so we went the old familiar road as if to Ford. I felt so homesick for the days that really never will come again. War or no war the Ford we knew is gone for ever. Remember those Easters – chairs in the oval garden among the polyanthus and the sound of the birds in the early morning? I got down to Dutton Homestall – the Dewars' – at a few minutes to six and just had time to powder the nose, go to the lav. and adjust the hat, before whirling off to the plastic surgery hospital where I did two fifteen-minute performances in two wards. The cases are mainly young airmen suffering from bad burns received when their planes have caught fire and they've had to jump. I won't go into it too much. Suffice it to say that I was moved beyond words to see these great tall young men so disfigured, so crippled and oh, golly, so uncomplaining. How right he was, Winston, when he said of these boys: 'Never was so much owed by so many to so few.'

The equipment at this hut hospital was deplorable and I may, later, be writing more fully on this subject as the need for instruments, equipment like beds and blankets is awful and I've got a half-hatched plot to get you to do something for it instead of canteens, of which there are, now, *more* than enough. But I'm trying to get in touch with a Dr O'Bryan of the Rockefeller Institute who is over here for the very purpose of finding out what is lacking medically and remedying it, so that if he can cope with the demands I shan't bother you. If not – well, we'll see. Austin Lamont[2] sent me a cheque for £16-odd pounds last week to use as I best thought fit and I've sent that off as a preliminary. But I understand that it isn't so much money that they want as actual staff, increasingly difficult to obtain over here. I did the men's ward and the officers and quite successfully refused to let the horror of it all sink into me till I'd done what I'd

---

[1] From South Africa, wife of John Arthur Dewar, Director of John Dewar Ltd, whisky distillers.
[2] An American doctor.

come for. Then, I must confess, I felt very churned up. Mrs D.'s house is a convalescent hospital for officers and among these is a v. young Australian called Richard Hillary who has moved over from the plastic place to finish his treatments and to convalesce. He has been given entirely new eyelids, forehead, nose, upper lip and chin, and from the set of his jaw and ears and the bones of his head you can see he must have been a really handsome young man. He is no longer that. And his hands are burned to the point of deformity. He is air force, of course, and *full* of spirits. Rather busy being a bit of dog still – a night-club boy and a devil but his blue eyes can't hide his real feelings. He was shot down at 25,000 feet, baled out on fire, fell unconscious for thousands of feet when the air brought him to and he had enough sense to pull the parachute string. He fell into the Channel where he floated in torture for three hours. Then, despairing and in such pain, he began to let air out of his 'Mae West', which is a sort of life-belt jacket, and at that point was picked up. He has been through every sort and kind of agony but is now mended – but no more use as an airman because of his hands. His courage is terrific and the act of being a devil breaks the heart. He said to me: 'I only like women over thirty, preferably married, with dark hair and olive complexion.'! He is twenty. Wants to write and is even now working on an autobiographical novel.[1]

After visiting the plastic place we rushed back to the house and bathed and changed and then had sandwiches and drinks before going to the officers' club in E. Grinstead where I was to perform to a large room full of perfectly well officers and their girls who ought b—— well to have paid good money to come and see the show! I don't know why I did it really. It's a waste of time. Yes, it went particularly well; they were a marvellous audience but I don't think it's right to ask professionals to perform for love to a lot of hale and hearty officers living in civilised surroundings and not needing entertainment. Needless to say, I didn't voice any of this to anyone. Working in the hospital was *so* worthwhile that the other just didn't count. After the E.G. concert several people came back to Mrs D.'s house for supper and dancing to the gramophone. I've never seen liquor flow as it did. Excellent supper too. The house is pretty tacky. One rather nice genuine old corner of what must have been a small manor house; the rest a huge pseudo-Tudor affair on a big scale of awfulness – Knole sofas and stained glass. This last is the hosp.; I stayed in the small

[1] *The Last Enemy*, Hillary's autobiographical novel published in 1942, was an account of his training (he was a Spitfire pilot shot down in the Battle of Britain) and his time in hospital. Hillary was killed in 1943 during a practice flight, having read *The Mint*, T. E. Lawrence's then unpublished book about life in the RAF, lent to him by the artist, Eric Kennington (see October 1st, 1938; p. 54).

corner where Mrs D. lives. She is obviously, and wisely, enjoying the fortune and doing plenty with the money. She is toughish, I'd say, but with the proverbial golden heart. Her daughter is a particularly nice gal with the most perfect manners and thoughtfulness. Jakie stays there occasionally and is, I rather thought, looked on with favour from that quarter. But mainly by Mama. Daughter yearns for a beautiful blonde young god out East. Penniless, alas.

She is v. friendly, Kathleen, and is doing a great deal down there for the soldiers, sick and well. One can't help liking her good nature and warm heart. I saw all over the house next day, met the officers, found young Hillary snoozing in bed being unsophisticated even then, poor little boy. He made my heart ache, he really did. I danced with him the night before and felt positively middle-aged in my maturity!

The same lovely shiny car drove me back to London next day through another golden day. I went to the Nat. Gal. at lunchtime to hear Denis Matthews[1] play Beethoven sonatas. It was superb. He is a young airman with a gigantic talent – and that isn't my description either, it's Myra's. She is just back from a very long and successful tour all over the country. I went to the Queen's Hall yesterday to hear her rehearsing the Brahms Second Concerto with the London Philharmonic Orchestra. It was a treat. I love to sit in that great empty hall, having the concert all to myself. Rehearsals are more fun than the performances, I think. M. played at the top of her lofty form and I enjoyed every minute of it.

At the Dorchester on Wednesday evening at 6, there was a large cocktail-cabaret affair in aid of the Free French Forces and John Gielgud[2] asked me to be one of the turns. (Edith was another; and B. Lillie, and Delysia[3] and Zena Dare,[4] etc, etc.) They sold over 500 tickets and it seems to have been a success 'tho we found the audience unyielding to a nasty degree. I had the doubtful pleasure of opening the programme – being the youngest. It was alright; but I was much put off by having, quite unnecessarily as it turned out, to use a microphone. You cannot visibly do monologues with a mike. On the air, yes. But not otherwise.

---◆---

[1] Concert pianist. He played in the RAF Orchestra, 1944–5.
[2] John Gielgud was appearing as Dearth in *Dear Brutus* at the Globe.
[3] Alice Delysia, French actress and singer who first appeared in London in 1914, and continued to do so.
[4] Distinguished actress, sister of Phyllis Dare. Appeared in two Ivor Novello musicals, and, much later, as Mrs Higgins in *My Fair Lady*.

I saw two things yesterday that made me roar with laughter and long for you to share 'em with. The first was a sort of Mrs Adelaide Bragg Gillespie woman; fifty to sixtyish, squat, plump and in a black astrakhan coat and a little perched hat. She was in a terrible hurry and she'd run a few paces, walk, run a bit, walk; and when she ran she held a plump little hand spread across her bosom. I watched her through the back window of my taxi; going down Brook St.

The other sight was rather similar. A *very* fat schoolboy of about ten like a comic strip character, tossing a toy parachute into the air and running after it to catch it as it came down. I saw him from the taxi too, and his concentration and wobbling movements made me giggle out loud to myself. Both these things sound desperately boring on paper but I think you can imagine how good they were in the flesh.

---

*March 30th, 1941*

Well, I didn't get very far with this letter in mid-week, as you will see. So much time is wasted in trains and at the theatre. But it isn't consecutive stretches; just snatches and you really can't write letters that way, although I sometimes have to. Celia has been here till today and I've loved having her. We've laughed a great deal with each other and been what I call Lefty-silly which is the best sort of silly there is. We suddenly took to talking to each other as if we had no roofs to our mouths and while I know it was pointless and probably unkind we found it intoxicating and our tritest remarks took on a piquancy that gave us enormous pleasure. Occasionally we stopped and remembered that we were both over thirty and of average intelligence but it was no good. We squealed with laughter at each other's jokes and belched when we felt like it and generally had a lovely un-repressed two weeks. I daresay our rather long days ending in dressing gowns and supper by the drawing room fire tended to make us relax more than we otherwise might have. Except for Ginny, who is Queen of Sillies, Celia is the only friend I've got who is as un-selfconsciously silly as I like to be. And that's saying something.

Here are two items of news.

(1) That I've done a day's filming.

(2) That *Diversion* comes off on April 19th – if not before – and

that on the 21st we go to Oxford for a week where we hope to 'do well'.

*April 6th, 1941*                 Parr's

Reg is home for a week's leave, goody, goody. *And* I've got Thursday and Good Friday off! So that's pleasant.

Less pleasant is the news of the latest German aggression on the wretched Yugoslavs – and I expect it will get worser an' worser. Damn the bloody Germans, one and all, women and children, babies and men!![1] How long, oh Lord, how long? It is an exceedingly cold wintry day and the bad news doesn't help. However, from a purely self-centred point of view, R. and I are beside our own fire and he is doing my clippings into my book and the radio is giving us a really lovely performance of the St Matthew Passion. So lovely that I have to stop writing and listen properly at times!

Well, I've finished the [MOI] film and enjoyed it all and now I'd like to make a full-length picture because I *think* I understand the medium and could do it. To start with I am able, through the training I've had in monologuing, to make up everything from nothing and where I'd thought it would be impossible to forget the hordes of men doing various jobs all around one, it wasn't a bit. You get surrounded by your own imagination and as Celia said you've only got to think it for it to show. Where you have to stress on the stage you minimise for the camera. Of course I've only four days' work and all of it simple. Nevertheless I do believe I could do the work. Heaven knows what I look like though – I haven't seen any of the rushes. I'm going to see the whole picture this week, I think.

*April 13th, 1941 (Easter Sunday)*          Parr's

Did I tell you in my last letter that R. is to be made a Captain? I know the news came by telephone last Sunday but I think that was after I'd finished your letter. He is to be Garrison Adjutant which is a good job

[1] On March 25th a coup d'état in Yugoslavia nullified the previous government's pact with the Axis powers. As a result, Hitler launched an attack on Yugoslavia on April 6th, and the whole country was overrun within a week.

and means he'll be kept where he is for a bit at any rate. And with so many people going overseas I do thank heaven for that. Of course it is an office job but as he isn't fit for a full-time up-and-doing post because of his legs, he does feel he's pulling his weight in doing a necessary piece of work that he knows he can do well.

In church today I couldn't take my eyes off Aunt N.'s right profile. She really is *so* pretty. It is, bar none, the prettiest profile I know and time can't touch it because it is so beautifully constructed of bone.

I'm very lucky to only have officers billetted on me when it might be mothers and East End babies. (How horrid I sound!) But the fact of anyone being in one's house is a constant irritation and I've got to do something about it! I mind the fact of them being here uninvited! Coming in as if they owned the place, closing their doors at night with a careful click that wakes one up, smoking, smoking, smoking, and talking *forte forte*, to their batmen when they are called at dawn. It is pure thoughtlessness, for when I've asked 'em not to converse in the hall late at night they've apologised profusely and not done it again. They are bachelors both of 'em and probably spoiled at home by doting mamas. I rage inside at their absolutely harmless and unintentional little offences but it all goes when I'm met face to face with the rather gauche offenders who so obviously don't know they are an annoyance to me merely because they are in my house! It is petty on my part and just one of those things sent to try us and I shall and will get over them. But they drive me dotty at times and I'd like to say 'Shoo, out you go' and have the war over for ever! (Who wouldn't?) Their batmen *try* to be quiet but their feet are large anyway and their army boots are an additional spread. The result is quite touching. One hears a painful tapping in the stone hall and it is a batman progressing on his toes. But with a sole an inch thick you can't bend the boot much. And then there are, of course, nails.

They *try* to knock on their officers' doors as discreetly as they can but a mere touch of one of their knuckles on the thin wooden door is like a blow with the flat of one's own hand!

(I may say I'm exaggerating my troubles just to make a good letter. They aren't as bad as that. Not *quite*.)

---

*April 20th, 1941*                                                    Parr's

Your cable came and was lovely. I expect it all sounds much worse to you being so far away. Physically poor old London has had it a bit but spiritually she survives and it is impossible to tell you how

and I must admit I do not look forward to
seeing them exhibited!! But there you are; its the
penalty of fame......

Nicholas came to see me on Friday looking
quite extraordinarily nice in his uniform. He's
just become an Officer. There is no questing
that the army becomes people; and does their
health good.

We've had so-so houses all the week
and then suddenly yesterday we were right
back to the wonderful capacity houses and a
glorious performance! Quite inexplainable.
Reg. came straight to London from his camp
where he surprised me at the theatre and we
drove down after the second performance at
about 7 with the Car packed solid with
Mrs. C. and the Col. and Francis.

It is now nearly 4 and the Passion is coming
to a close & I've got to get tea for 7 people! So I'd
better stop hadn't I?

I've got such an exquisite hat to go with my
new stone-oatmeal tweed suit Uncle Lo gave me
the stuff for. It is v. becoming. Pale felt to
match the
suit and very
spring like.

(It's hard to
convey the
droop of the
brim!)

much love

Joyce

April 13th, 1941

amazing and wonderful the Civil Defence people have been. The mess cleared up so quickly and efficiently and the buses and trains working magnificently under all sorts of difficulties. Of course one of our greatest gifts is that of improvisation and that's just as well! After listening to today's lesson I rejoice to know a bit about reality. Thank God.[1]

What have I done since I last wrote? Well *Diversion* came to an end – in London – yesterday and we have just a week's more work at Oxford before finishing entirely.

------◆------

*April 23rd, 1941*                                            Ditchley*

Well, both Edith and Dorothy arrived on Sunday after I'd finished my letter to you. I met them at Taplow at 4.30 and Sylvia [Skimming] made the tea while we drove back as Rene was out. It was a pretty April day with all the new greens clashing across the countryside against sudden thundery skies lit with brilliant bursts of sun. Quite my favourite time of the year. We had a good tea and the 'girls' seemed to be glad to be out of London. There was sun in the room and daffodils out of the garden and the red roses Bertie had sent me on Saturday for the last performance, so it looked quite gay and is, anyway, quite the happiest room I know.

Next morning we had a leisurely breakfast in dressing gowns before the drawing room fire and then there was packing for me to do and a journey into Burnham to fill up with petrol and do some last-minute shoppings for the ward before leaving them for a whole week. (They were flatteringly concerned about this!) I took Dot to see the hospital for a brief second and at 12 we all piled into my little Ford with all the luggage.

An excellent lunch with Celia at Merrimoles, the house Daddy built for her and Peter.[2] Lots of children – her Nicholas and her widowed sister-in-law's (Dunkirk) four. On to Oxford after lunch,

---

[1] German air attacks had eased off due to bad weather during the winter months of 1941 but started again in March and continued till mid-May, when the bulk of the *Luftwaffe* was sent east for the coming invasion of Russia.

[2] With twenty rooms (including eight bedrooms), Merrimoles was built near an old barn of that name on the Flemings' Oxfordshire estate at Nettlebed. Paul Phipps designed a neo-Georgian house of red brick, but completion in 1939 was delayed by the appropriation of various supplies for rearmament projects.

equally slowly and very drowsily after food and sun. Straight to the
theatre with our stuff, then I parked the car and we all went in search
of tea at Fullers. Ox. is packed like a drum and on that sunny
afternoon the crowded streets looked wonderfully un-warlike and
cheerful.

We ring up at 7.15 and I was surprisingly nervous – like a first
night. The New is a colossal theatre and the lights are real old
fashioned white limes that completely blind you but give you a
sensation of theatrical glamour quite lost in small theatres. We had a
big house and went well. My songs were particularly liked and the
applause went on long after I'd left the stage. I'm doing much too
much in this version I think – and that's not modesty but artistic
sense! Three monologues, four compères and the songs – never off
the stage. I'm wearing a variety of dresses.

We drove out here afterwards with our make-up on to save time
and Nancy [Tree] had the most delicious supper of creamed chicken and
corn for us. It is angelic of her to have us and it makes the whole
difference to our week having this exquisite haven to come home to
instead of straggling with the surging masses and limited accommodation of Ox.

Needless to say that rumour about Nancy having a baby is complete
nonsense. She said it to tease Aunt N. and Alice! She is a very
sweet, kind and cosy person and, I think, rather a lovely one. She
spent all yesterday morning gardening in a pair of corduroy
trousers and a lily-green linen shirt, looking *so* pretty and young.
It was a dream day. We had our breakfasts in our rooms – ah,
luxury! And then meandered in the sun all the morning looking at
the gardens and the wood and drinking in the flowers and the new
spring sights. Delicious lunch followed by individual siestas. Mine
was punctuated by *The Times* X-word puzzle – when I could keep
my eyes open. Tea at 5 and we all went in at 6 in Nancy's Ford
wagon.

Isn't life funny when you think here I am with Edith and
Dot, playing to vast houses at Oxford, getting fan notes from
undergrads and feeling just the same *inside* as I did when I was
small!

Both she [Edith] and Dorothy were delighted with Ditchley and
well they may be because it really is beyond words lovely. I don't
believe I'd fully realised just now wonderful it is until this visit.
Nancy's warmth and kindness are reflected throughout that lovely
house and it ought to be for ever preserved as an example of what
money can do and yet not harm a place! It was a mighty comfy visit
and made the whole difference to our week. I had cosy bedtime chats
with N. whom I love.

Did I tell you that Noël C. was in front last Friday? He told Dot he'd found me good.

---◆---

*April 29th, 1941*                                                    Parr's

We closed at Oxford on Saturday and it was very gay and crowded. Reg came over twice – on the Thursday with his colonel and on Saturday with a pair of majors. On the Friday night a little cluster of undergrads came to call on me, headed by Jim Brand. The university had come up that day and they had hurried in to see the revue. I was appalled to find that these handsome young giants – Frankie Margesson,[1] etc, etc, – were the *sons* of my friends! That makes you think! True, they are but babes of eighteen but all the same they are now 'Varsity students and almost men! They had enjoyed the performance and came to say so. They then escorted E.E., D.D. and me to the car, carrying things, lighting the way with torches and finally grinding us out of the carpark with many instructions. They were charming and quite unaffectedly enthusiastic. Can it be that, at last, the young are going to admit enjoyment? What *progress* this is.

---◆---

*May 11th, 1941*                                                    Parr's

The week has been more or less routine hospital, shopping and walks for the dog, a little writing, a little (a very little) reading and more hospital. I've taken in another ward so that gives me seventy men to cherish – no idle task, I assure you. The new lot are 'operatives' therefore iller, therefore less cheerful, therefore, probably, more in need of attention. They require less shopping but more time spent on them talking about their homes and families and children. I find I have to do quite a lot more thinking before I go into Ward 3 than into my own dear gay Ward 11. We've got a particularly gay lot in there just now and the jokes are legion and the conspiracies to tease the much-loved Sister Millar go on endlessly and everyone has a wonderful time.

On Tuesday I took Eve Clark down to Rachel's to perform to the seventy men in her convalescent home. It was a highly successful

---

[1] Frankie Margesson, son of David Margesson, now Secretary of State for War.

concert and ended with a free-for-all rendering of every known song. Of course the thing about entertaining the troops is that they really only want to sing themselves. We've worked out that about six solos by us and a couple of monologues are all they will take before joining in with us!

---◆---

*May 18th, 1941*                                              Parr's

It's warm today and for the first time. It's quarter to six after tea and I've just come in from a strenuous afternoon in the hospital. Rene has gone up to do her shift at Alice's canteen and I'm alone in the house with Nan lying out on the lawn in the sun and a heavenly quiet over everything. I'm so afraid Aunt N. may suddenly recollect me and telephone down a bidding to supper! There is no possible legitimate excuse, so I'm sunk if she does.

   Daddy was here until Tuesday and it was heavenly having him. I don't remember consciously enjoying him so much before! We did the lesson together and *The Times* X-word and we took long talky walks and called on Guy[1] at the stud and Lee up at the house and it was very pleasant.

---◆---

*June 28th, 1941*                              In the train to London

I'm on my way up to London to hear Daddy do 1st Reader – it's his last Sunday. This is being written in a very crowded third non-smoker and started in Slough station.

   This past week has been mainly domestic but culminated in a Big Event – Bea Lillie's appearance at the hospital.[2] I started getting busy about it on Monday – rounding up the local, hospital talent for the first half of the programme, arranging where it was to be held, ordering the microphone, etc, etc. When Friday finally dawned it was a grand day, warm and sunny but not unbearable in the sun. There is a very attractive garden courtyard at the hosp, with a green lawn about tennis-court size (? No, a bit smaller.) And all round it a

[1] In charge of the famous stud at Cliveden.
[2] Cliveden being a Canadian Red Cross Hospital, a visit by Canadian-born Beatrice Lillie was a Big Event.

wide cement path and deep flowerbeds. At one end the patients'
lounge opens on to a narrow terrace and three shallow steps down.
This was our stage.

The up patients sat on grey blankets on the grass. Bed patients
were wheeled along the cement path, into the corridors that surround
the square and into the patients' lounge (isn't lounge a horrible
word?), which meant they were behind the stage. I wish you could
have seen it because it was quite one of the prettiest sights I've ever
seen. All the men in white shirts, scarlet ties, blue trousers. A good
sprinkling of sisters in their bright blue. Officers in khaki. Altogether
about 400, I think. Aunt N. and the grandees all sat in the place-
marked chairs. Bea wore a purply blue dress with silver embroidery
around the neck and sleeves, and had her large white feather fan of
course. Sister Muriel with hair lacquered a deep blue black was 'at
the piano'. Mother Lillie came, too, wearing ground-length black
and showing quite clearly where Bea gets her looks from. But let's
get back to the concert. I was over at the hospital at 5 o'clock which
was in good time if you consider that the show was timed for 7.30!
I wore a lime green linen frock I've had for three years, white shoes,
and had Nancy T.'s rose-red Schiaparelli jacket in case I needed it. (I
didn't.) Having rounded up the talent, arranged with Sister Meadows
what music we'd use for the community singing at the start, arranged
for the mikes, plotted the programme on paper, etc, at last the
auditorium began to fill up and by 7.10 there wasn't a great deal of
space left. We started singing about 7.30 and I did 'The Tattoo'd
Lady' as usual and it was well received. Then Aunt N., the Col,
[Luton] etc, Bobbie, Anne Islington, who had arrived for the weekend, Alice and the rest of the 'important' public came in, and we got
on with the programme. An orderly sang the 'Mountains of Mourne';
a lieut., a patient from the officer's ward, whistled very well; a
nursing orderly recited two comics! (they were too!!) A patient sang
'Lazybones'; another did a comedy song; a third patter-danced in his
huge army boots on the cement steps and just about made sparks.
He was a French Canadian and said to be quite batty. The boys
thought him v. funny and he went big. A sister sang 'The Sunshine
of Your Smile'. A very ill little Scotchman due to be sent back to
Canada sang a very touching 'Danny Boy' to his own concertina
accompaniment. And then, finally it was Bea. I may say that the
anticipation all week had been terrific – I'd been building it up from
day to day and when Friday arrived it was at a high pitch. I had
hardly stepped up to the mike and said, 'And now – Miss Beatrice
Lillie', before they burst into clapping and whistling (which in
England means approval and not the bird, in case you've forgotten).
After that it was all hers. And I hand it to her for giving a superb

performance. She did all the usuals – 'Rhythm', 'Nanette', 'Three Little Fishes', 'This is My First Affair', 'Fairies in the Garden', etc, etc; and finished up with 'Black-eyed Susan' *and*, believe it or not, 'Oh Take Me Back to the Land of Promise'. It certainly took me back. Way back to the last war. I've always remembered it, even the words. I had the longest-in-hospital patient, a twenty-year-old boy called Shields, on crutches, give her a bouquet of Aunt N.'s best carnations, delphiniums and some fuzzy mauve flowers, tied with red, white and blue ribbon. The Colonel called for three cheers for Bea and then, very nicely I thought, for me, for getting it all up; we had the King and it was over. I was by this time ten good years older than I'd been when the concert started. Oh the responsibility!

The concert was considered a huge success and I must say it all went beautifully and *looked* so lovely that it was well worth the effort. After it was over we were all invited over to the Sisters' Home for food and once more the weather did its bit and we had the most delicious food out of doors in the garden. Later Bea sang again and Sister Muriel Lillie rendered selections on the piano. Ma Lillie sat about and looked proud. Bea sang one awfully funny new song with the opening line: 'She's lying in the gutter and she *loves* it.'

This all went on till after 11 and everyone had a fine time. I was asked to perform but was quite firm for once and I know I was right. When you've got someone like Bea there let her be everything.

*Later: on the way back.* Daddy read better than ever. He reads with such certainty and with a clarity that makes even the familiar passages seem fresh and new. He looks so good too! His face beams and his bald head gleams and his big bow tie all go to make up the most cheerful sight. And he enjoys it. You can hear that from the vitality of his reading. I teased him a lot about his fans – and he really has hundreds. He is fully aware of the dangers of personal sense in these things and has all that in its proper place. I really do wish you could have heard him. I'm quite sure there must be dozens of gals in 1st [Church] who worship from afar; and small blame to 'em. He's superb.

---

*July 6th, 1941*　　　　　　　　　　　　　　　　　Parr's

It's really too hot to write anything intelligible and I warn you this won't be a very bright letter. It's just after tea, which I gave to Celia, Peter and their son Nicholas, two, who have now left for Nettlebed

and home. I've washed up, taken off the shoes and am now lying on
the sofa with, it must be admitted, a delicate breeze playing on my
toes and making things mighty delightful. My poplar trees are
swishing in sea-like sounds and the wheatfield in front of us – the
one that used to house horses and then cows – is a heavenly sight of
movement. The ears are in the inbetween stage – no longer green
but not yet yellow. A sort of metallic bronze grey. Quite lovely.
And there isn't a cloud in a bright blue sky. No one can complain
about this summer. We've had a solid month of perfect days and
there seems no reason for it to change. Which it probably will do
tomorrow!

The Flemings make a very attractive trio. Peter is burned a magnificent copper brown from his time in Greece and Crete. He's been
quite ill with malaria since he got back but is recovered now. Celia
is so happy to have him home that she positively glows. And
Nicholas, who is sound in everything, is a continual joke to them
both. He and C. lunched here while Peter ate with the stars up at
the house. (Various heads of various professions and departments.
Probably grousing. That's what they usually do there. Al. [Alice
Winn] and I have renamed it the house of malcontents. It's sort of
sad in a way. It's all the people who've missed the 'bus being cross
about it. I suppose it's hard when once you've been the top to have
to be content with scraps. It's their own fault – our relations, I mean.
And in particular our female one. She's got too big a mouth and
switches her faith from one to another which is quite permissible
only it's done so blatantly and so violently that it just doesn't do.
Never has had much judgment about people anyway in my view. If
only she'd give up the public job and stick to the good works. But
there it is, she won't. She's in good form and looks lovely. Today
in church she was wearing a white straw hat, rather tip-tilted, and a
printed blue and white patterned silk suit.) I've been reading the book
about Sir James Barrie that Denis Mackail[1] has done and I wonder
if anyone will be able to write such an honest and dispassionate book
about Aunt N. without filling it with contradictions and impossible
(apparently) views?

You could with perfect truth write on one page that she was kind
and on the next that she was unkind. But in all fairness I don't believe
she knows about being unkind. There's a sudden thickening of
sensitivities and she pours salt on an open wound. Grandfather was
said to have done the same and at the same time been kind as well.
A peculiar mixture. I've an idea that the worst fault she has is power.
It comes from a dominating personality and of course money. That's

---

[1] *The Story of J. M. B., a Biography* had just been published.

a terrifying combination! Lesser people couldn't do the good she does, for her gestures are wide and benefit the majority. It's the strange lack of being able to sense atmosphere that baffles me. And the complete disregard (almost) of popularity. I daresay it's a sign of weakness but I definitely do *not* like being not liked. I don't want to be adored but to be tolerated. To be approved of is balm to the soul but not necessary. But to be disliked and to be a nuisance is one of the things I can't say I'd fancy. And yet so convinced of her point is Aunt N. that she has the courage to plod through all hostilities to achieve what she has set out to do. And that does take courage. Of course she has the reformer's zeal to help her out. I've come to the sad conclusion that I really prefer peace (in the house or surroundings, I mean) to battling courageously for things – that is unless I think they are really worth fighting for. Then – oh boy – I'd fight the world.

---

*August 10th, 1941*  Parr's

I've just finished listening to the Queen. Did you hear her? I thought it charming and just right. The touch about thinking of Americans knitting on their porches was good, wasn't it? I expect she wrote that speech herself. She always does when it's something dear to her – as this thanking of American women undoubtedly was. I do hope you all heard it well.

This has been a hectically busy Sunday. After church I went straight to the hosp to help Sylvia Skimming and Diana Smith set out the exhibits for their handicraft show. The entries were judged yesterday and today a lot of people were invited to see them and take tea afterwards. We worked like blacks, all of us, from 12 to 1.30 and then on foot solid till 4.45 when in truly *Ladies Home Journal* fashion I 'poured'. Four of us were at two tables pouring away. Such a wonderful tea too, with chocolate cake and a Canadian speciality called Matrimony Cake, consisting mainly of dates and shortbread crumbs. Golly, it was good. The whole thing was a big success with a big crowd and a prize-giving and a press photographer to get pictures to send to Canada. Sylvia and Diana have been at it for days, getting in the entries, writing labels, etc, and they have done a wonderful job in getting the men enthusiastic about handwork any-way. By the way it is no longer called handwork – it's got a fancy name now – Occupational Therapy!

After the visitors had gone we helped to clear the tables and wash up the tea things. Then Sylvia thought it would be a good idea to take the exhibits into all fourteen of the wards to show the bed patients who hadn't been able to see them set out.

Thursday I took a party of four men from the hosp to Maidenhead to see Bette Davis in *The Letter*.[1] Did you see it? Much too good, I thought. I was glad they gave us a cheerful comedy and a newsreel of the Quintuplets[2] to follow it. Friday was a foul day and it didn't stop raining till 5 o'clock in the afternoon. I helped Al[ice] take in the stores at the canteen in the morning and went to the hospital in the afternoon. At 5 I went to do the shift at the canteen and that was heavy-ish going till nearly 10. Al. has established some firm rules about cleanliness and we always scrub all the tables, counter and shelves every night before leaving so it's quite a chore getting the place tidied up before we go home. I'm always ready for bed on canteen nights. I don't have a special night but take over when needed, which I much prefer.

Yesterday was Saturday and Aunt N. came home for lunch before going over to Nancy T.'s for Sunday. Al. and I went up to C. for lunch and Al. was *so* funny keeping the conversation off the dangerous topic of jobs she hadn't done while Aunt N. was away and that would make Aunt N. furious if she knew! One is the inviting of two Virginian clergymen who are over here as ferry pilots and stationed nearby. Ten days ago Aunt N. told Al. to get them over and she hasn't! We got nearer and nearer to this subject all through lunch and Al. got quite panicky! It's so funny to think how two grown-up women like ourselves fear the wrath of a little firebrand of sixty!!

I left here at 9 on Tuesday and went straight across London to Waterloo to catch the train to Salisbury where Rosemary Crawley[3] was to meet me. I'd come down to perform for Rosemary in the enormous camp where she works as an important ATS [Auxiliary Territorial Service] officer.

The concert was in a huge RA [Royal Artillery] gymnasium. The backbone was the extremely efficient RA orchestra of some twenty pieces complete with a poker-backed conductor in dark blue dress uniform. The stage was an extemporised affair six feet high and approached only by a flight of three very steep steps from the back. The band took up most of the stage so one had to creep around the edge of the thing with no balustrade and I must say I didn't like it

---

[1] Adapted from Somerset Maugham's play.
[2] The Dionne quins, all girls. They were Canadians.
[3] The wife of Cosmo Crawley, brother of Aidan Crawley who was later an MP.

much. The other talent were: an ATS private with a charming
crooning voice and enchanting shy pretty face who couldn't say her
R's and who sang down the mike songs about 'Dweams' and 'Fools
Wush In'. There was a comedy reciter (Stanley Holloway's stuff) and
a tap dancer in a snow-white flannel suit and shoes. I was the Guest
Star. Fortunately I went quite well.

I must confess that I rather enjoyed the complete efficiency and
slap-uppedness of this very military concert. The gym was so clean
and well looked after. There was much heel-clicking and saluting
and the front rows were occupied by Cols and their ladies in full
dress. (The Cols', not the ladies.)

The Crawleys, on their way back to Clarendon, drove me over to
Florrie St Just's where I was staying. Here I found a certain number
of troubles! Poor Florrie[1] – the boiler had burst; the footman, subject
to brainstorms, had had one and vanished in F.'s car. The cook who
was supposed to have recovered from concussion caused by a fall off
her bike hadn't; the kitchen-maid's mother had died; a dog had just
made a vast and unexplained pool on the carpet and finally (though
we didn't know this till later) Olive Baring who was also staying
there came in at 1 and was locked out! She bayed like a wolf on the
lawn and her daughter Olivia heard her and crept down the stairs
expecting to be pounced on by the brainstorming footman at every
step. But all was well and all the wretch had done was to crash the
back of the car into a tree in the drive. Of course he alibied himself
neatly next day by saying he didn't remember anything about it. (He
is now under dismissal.) I slept like a log and missed most of the
excitement.

I was to connect with the London train. I was here for lunch, oh
blessed spot. Home *is* best. I was in the hospital all afternoon and
then biked up through the rain to tea at C. where Aunt N. has the
Shaws – G.B.S. and Charlotte for two weeks' change. I took the
venerable author for a tramp afterwards and we penetrated a path in
the woods below the Rule Britannia theatre that I've never seen
before in all my years here. It was a wet walk but he didn't seem to
care. Eighty-five he is and shows it a *little* but not much. She's older
and very bent, poor thing. R. came that evening. We did nothing by
our own fireside with much pleasure. Next day we shopped in
loathsome M. and then spent an idle day doing v. little about the
place.

On Sunday I got up in trousers and an old red shirt and we spent
the morning in the garden. I dug up bits of the border and R. did

---

[1] Wife of 1st Baron St Just, formerly Edward Charles Grenfell, Director of the Bank
of England.

some very drastic pruning of the creepers, bushes and roses on our
vast property!

------◄◉►------

  *August 24th, 1941*                                             Parr's

Two letters from you this week, both written from East – or is it
South? – Hampton.

  I hope something gets fixed up about Wilton for you all. Lor',
doesn't it make one look fair and square at divorce where there are
children! Tom must feel an awful ass to have muddled his life so. It
reads dreadfully sadly to me somehow: you all staying on the outer
edges in order to see the child. He must be very attractive. I'd love
to see him again. Do send me pictures. Daddy loves them so. Do
you ever talk to him about his Grandpa? Gosh, *isn't* it a wasteful
mess! But then so is the war . . .

  Monday started off quite calmly but ended in a flurry. I rushed off
to the canteen where I washed up solidly from 6.15 to 9.30! As a
matter of fact, I prefer washing up to being at the counter. It's a nice
one-track-mind job and requires no mental effort. And as the other
helpers have to do a certain amount of washing up in their own
homes and I don't (so far!) I feel it's a good thing to do. The shift on
Monday is a very cosy one: Mrs Hopkins, Mrs House, Mrs Irvine
and the latter's two daughters, Brenda and Barbara. We had a
particularly heavy night at it on Monday and I washed up over 300
cups. Tuesday? Went to Burnham in the morning with Al., who as
usual kept me waiting for half an hour! I never knew such a creature
for unpunctuality and disordered thinking! I love her dearly as you
know but her ways drive me to desperation and I'm sure that one of
the reasons she is always so tired and exhausted is that she doesn't
co-ordinate herself before starting to do anything but dashes at it
unprepared and wastes her energies that way.

  On Friday I lunched up at C. to say goodbye to Aunt N. who was
going off to Jura that night for a well-deserved ten days' quiet. The
G.B.S.s came down here for tea; or rather I went up in the car and
fetched them down.

  After visiting my wards I went up to C. to pour the tea in Aunt
N.'s absence. She has invited all the staff from the hosp in relays to
meet the G. B. S.s ever since they first came down and there was a
little group up there yesterday. It takes a bit of an effort to get the

great man started but he finally puts on his act and sends the Canadians home with popping eyes.

I spent the evening here indulging myself yet again. (It was the rain that induced this mood.) I read a whole A. A. Milne novel called *Two People* that was no sort of effort. In fact its simplicity and sweetness cloyed by the end. (Only don't ever tell R. I said so. He is a staunch A. A. Milne fan and won't hear a word agin him!)

—◆—

Lunch up at C. with the Shaws. The more I have seen of them the more I like them and find their company stimulating. Which is no uncertain tribute to a pair of octogenarians. When he is not putting on his act, not being the naughty contradictory small boy who must take the opposite view – then he is a charmer and what he has to say well worth hearing. I've had several quiet meals with the two of them. We've talked of books; of Barrie; of music; of Elgar; of the stage; of Mrs Pat[1]; of the English countryside; of eugenics; of food. Mrs Shaw is inclined to deafness which means that each conversation takes time and must be executed *FF*,[2] which makes most utterances sound worthless. Incidentally they both have asked tenderly of you several times and Mrs S. says she sees you as if it was yesterday; in fact it was twelve years ago.

I hope Tommy gets the envelope full of old photographs (not many, eight or ten; maybe less) that I found last week and which I mailed yesterday. The ones of me were unbelievably awful. Like an egg. How *could* you have allowed me to scrape my hair like I did? Alright, I know you had no alternative, me being the forceful character I was! But golly! How come I didn't see then what I see now as I look on the frightening sight? I assure you I fluff everything out nowadays to counteract any suggestion of egginess!

And Stephen Potter came down from Manchester, if you please, in order to do tea with the great man and later to ask him to do his

---

[1] Mrs Pat Campbell (1865–1940) for whom Shaw created Eliza Doolittle in *Pygmalion*. Shaw fell passionately in love with her when he was fifty-six and she was forty-seven. Their letters were later published and formed the basis for the play, *Dear Liar* (1970).
[2] FF: *fortissimo* (very loud); as in the sketch 'Canteen'.

own autobiography over the air! I'm afraid G.B.S. won't do the programme because he says he's too old; which being translated means his teeth don't fit and make rude noises that would be particularly exaggerated on the air and his vanity wouldn't stand for such a thing. And I think he's right. It wasn't quite the disappointment it might have been for S.P. because he hadn't realised just how old G.B.S. had become and he began to think, after talking to him, that maybe the old man was right to decline. He *is* older; but golly he's still incredible for eighty-five. Looks so wonderfully pink and white and so fresh and beautifully dandified. I do like attractive old people, don't you? Both the Shaws take trouble over their appearances and are well-rewarded by looking pretty and soignée. She is very bent now and a bit deaf and loses interest quite easily. He is less combative but still as anxious to be naughty and contrary as ever. We had a pleasant little tea here on Friday and I took a picture of Stephen and G.B.S. together which ought to be quite good. As all my G.B.S. books were sold up when Tommy failed to pay his rent – (don't ask me how bitterly I feel on that subject! Wow!!) I had no signed editions at all so I asked him to put his name in the rather rare and beautifully handbound leather copy of his autobiography, *Shaw Gives Himself Away*.[1] He did so with grace. I also contrived – by the dirty method of getting him to try this pen! – to get him to write his name down on a separate sheet of paper which Rene has since cut out and pasted into her book.

---

*September 7th, 1941*                                                    Parr's

On Monday afternoon I took it quiet, preparing for a heavy session in the canteen. It was the night before the men were going on an exercise and that always means a big attendance. My Monday night team is: Mrs House, Mrs Irvine, Brenda House, Barbara Irvine and me. We have a high time and giggle quite a lot and exchange a series of clichés that some day I mean to write down. Such as (Mrs House): 'You do feel like somethink hot to drink after a long day' or 'I always say a fire cheers you up' and 'You can do a lot with a smile, I always say' (Mrs Irvine). Have I told you about the canteen at all? Where it is? It's in the Old Dairy and is actually made from a row of converted cow stalls with a small kitchen that is a converted outhouse. The

---

[1] Published by Gregynog (1939). This house ('Centre for Arts') in Wales published handsome limited editions.

walls are white, the floor is stone, the curtains are checkered red-white
and it is always cram-jammed with men from 6 p.m. to 9 p.m., radio
roaring and a steady demand for tea and sandwiches. There is a
minute box of a room with four writing tables in it that is always
crush-full of letter writers and cigarette smoke. The other ladies
appear in their best afternoon silks but I'm a messy worker and
always wear a pinny. The leader of the shift – me on Mondays – has
to get to the canteen by 5 p.m. to get the kettles boiled and the
sandwiches cut in order to open by 6. The other ladies have husbands
to feed before they can get away so one usually does the opening-up
alone. We have very few conveniences and have to boil all the kettles
for the urns over a stove and a primus. All of which takes time and
is tiresome. We usually each take a job and stick to it. Mine is apt to
be dirty-cup collector and washer-upper. The others do plenty
of washing up at home and delight to do the counter jobs and as I
hate the niggling money mathematics involved at the counter I'm
only too happy to stick to my sink. We sell tea, 1d a cup; coffee
1½d a cup; sandwiches – meat paste, lettuce, cucumber, sardine, or
if there has been milk left over Rene turns it to mild cheese. These
are all 2d each. Doughnuts are 1d; pie is 2d; cut cake is 2d.
Cigarettes are rationed to ten per man. They have been rationed as
low as three per man but distribution seems to have evened up a
bit and we are issued with more by the YMCA. Candy is rationed
to a bar per man and is rather short at the moment. In fact it is
only the few first lucky forty or fifty who get any just now. But
this is only a temporary shortage we think and it is the first we've
had.

Before we leave the place each shift has to clean up. This means
scrubbing the tops of all the little tables – about fifteen – all urns,
utensils, etc, and washing out all the cloths.

I'm on this evening and I'm writing this out in the sunny
garden while I sit awhile in preparation for a long five-hour stand
around.

---

*September 15th, 1941*                                   Parr's

I think you asked me some questions in your last letter. Just a sec.
while I look through to see if there are . . . No, not one. Well it must
be the letter before that. Hold on while I fetch it from the letter
drawer and see. Well, in a letter of August 14th you ask what
magazines I like best. You are sending me *Harpers* and the *Ladies*

*Home J.*, *Life* and *Time* and I love them all. Could you, do you think, drop *Time* though, and substitute the *New Yorker*?

*September 21st, 1941*          As from Parr's

You ask what it means about Rene being called up. Well, everyone has to register as their age group gets called. (So far I'm in the over thirty lot and that hasn't been touched as yet; but it will.) After registering you are liable to be called to an interview and then either drafted into munitions or the ATS or WAAFs or nursing and if one happens to be doing a full-time job that the authorities consider worthwhile you may be left where you are. The chief idea of the whole scheme is to mop up all those girls who are doing literally nothing of any sort first. When these are used up they'll pounce on domestics like Rene and voluntary workers like me. Even though I do a large number of possibly worthwhile jobs they won't, in all probability, consider that enough and I'll have to go into something else, full time. One can only wait and see. If Rene goes I expect I'd have to shut the house or else find some aged foreigner to housekeep for me. The alternative is to let this – which I'd loathe – and move up to a room at C. which I'd hate. But there's a war on and one cannot plan.

What did we do all week? On Monday we pottered about and R. took Nan and his gun, while I went to the hospital, and they returned with five partridges and two pheasants. (All but one of each went up to C. for the pot). We dined at home and played racing demon and rummy. On Tuesday we went to London for the day, parting on arrival at Paddington for R. to go shopping on his own and to see his family and for me to do the hospital shopping.

We met Norah and Jimmy and Maria [Brassey] at the Ivy at 1 p.m., and there we had a very good lunch, saw some celebrities and then went to Wyndham's Theatre to see *Quiet Weekend!*[1] a simple, domestic comedy that pleased us all. Noël C. was at the Ivy and he called out to me and when I went over to his table he said a great many nice things to me about My Work! The shaming thing is that it pleased me and yet I hold a thoroughly low opinion of his taste and standards. How frail is one's ego when it can glow with pleasure at praise from someone one disapproves of.

On Wednesday – let's see now. I went to the hosp in the morning

---

[1] Comedy by Esther McCracken. Revived at Wyndham's and then at the Playhouse with much the same cast in 1944.

and R. got at my new veg bed for me and transplanted some winter lettuces and generally pottered. In the afternoon we walked Nan. It was a delicious hot but definitely autumnal day. We had early tea and then locked up the house and took Rene into Maidstone with us to see *Pimpernel Smith* with Leslie Howard.[1]

Thursday: Hosp. for me in the morning, garden for R. After lunch, as usual, we did the X-word puzzle over our coffee and asked each other what we'd like to do with the afternoon. Much time is pleasantly wasted this way we find. About 3 R. decided to do even more gardening and I went to wash my hair which I later dried in the garden beside him. We dined at C. that night. Uneventful and too cold. Like the v. rich, Aunt N. is panicking about not having enough coal, so we had no fire until we all shivered so realistically that she gave in and Dinah was allowed to light it. But it all fell in at once and gave no heat at all so we might just as well have left it alone!

Friday: R.'s last day and a nasty cold grey one in sympathy. I made a hurried round of my wards and got home as soon as I decently could. We lit our fire and had lunch beside it and then we did the puzzle and it was time to pack. We took the 4.18 from T. [Taplow] and had to change on to the express at Reading. Our train was late and we had the nightmare of being kept just outside the station and seeing the express come in ahead of us! By much scrambling we caught it but it was a bad moment. Huge crowds in the train; there always are now. No seats anywhere. But we managed to get some tea in the restaurant which lasted nearly till R. had to get out and I was lucky enough to get a seat from there. It was horrid leaving him but he plans to get a forty-eight hour weekend quite soon in October so that's to be looked forward to.

---

|                           | As from Parr's                  |
| *September 28th, 1941*    | but actually up in Shropshire   |

Rene is called up and *has* to go on October 11th. I've been to the Min. of Labour and done all I can but it's no good and she has got to go. I've written off in answer to advertisements, put my name down with agents all over the country and now I'm just waiting on the Lord to do his bit. When I came back from Virginia's on Monday and found the bad news waiting for me I must confess that I was

---

[1] Updated version of *The Scarlet Pimpernel*, in which Leslie Howard played a professor of archaeology who rescued refugees in war-torn Europe.

knocked out by it and saw everything through a gloomy blue haze. Poor Rene's chin trembled when I broke it to her and altogether it was AWFUL. Daddy, with whom I lunched on Friday, has pointed out to me that I am perhaps relying a bit too much on Rene and not enough on God! And I daresay there's some truth in this. But you know I've come so that I never have to think about any details because Rene does all that for me. She is maid, secretary and friend, and my heart sinks to my knees when I think of being without her. She's a creature of immense character and unswerving loyalty and I've been very lucky to have such devoted service for five and a half years. The only trouble is that I'm like a man without legs all of a sudden; Rene has been every prop to me. She deals so intelligently with everything and really and truly I cannot think of a single thing I'd alter in her.

We are both laid low by the parting, although now I am getting numbed to it and she says that if once she makes up her mind to a thing it's made up. So we'll weather it and I only pray to God we get together when it's all over and can resume the partnership. Meanwhile I'm combing the island for older women. I'm open to almost any one, but I'd rather not have a foreigner, if I can help it. There's something a bit un-cosy about a non-Aryan refugee in one's kitchen; I'm a bit insular, I'm afraid! I could do with a mother and child. Bombed out maybe. Well, that's enough of that. Don't worry about me. You know how I am – up at once. Can't keep me down.

*Later.* I've got on to the scent of a housekeeper – one Mrs Ivy Proctor who has *two* small daughters of eleven and six! She lives at Windsor with her mother and is coming over to see me tomorrow. The two daughters are by no means ideal but still if Mrs P. is nice and the children aren't too boisterous I don't see why she won't do for the duration. She was with a magistrate in Hertfordshire till he died, so she may be used to the work. I've no idea what has happened to Mr Proctor. Maybe she's a widow. I heard of her from 'Mrs Hunt's'[1] and wrote off at once yesterday morning, mailing it in Burnham in the morning. So quick was the mail that she had it by 5 in the afternoon and had rung me up at once. She *sounds* nice. Quiet and gentle. Oh Lor', I hope she's nice to see and know! It's quite awful the way a problem like this can fill the entire mind and colour all one's doings. Until I get it all settled I feel I cannot sit still. Rene has changed from wanting a nursing job to going into the WAAFs [Women's Auxiliary Air Force]. She's put herself down as a bat-woman (they have them in all the services now!) or, failing that, as a waitress. Whosoever gets her is lucky.

---

[1] Domestic agency.

Have I told you that I'm doing a series of four, maybe more, weekly broadcasts for ENSA[1] through the BBC? ENSA is the much, and most fairly, maligned official entertainment organisation for all the services. Their headquarters at Drury Lane. They have two 'hours' on the air each week and one of them is on Wednesday at 6.30 and for October Gillie Potter[2] and I are the stars.

---

*October 10th, 1941*　　　　　　　　　　　　　　　　　　Parr's

Oh joy, oh bliss!!!! First your *lovely*, perfect grey dress came and fits as if made for me. I *adore it*. Exactly what I'd have chosen, *thank you*. And then Mrs Proctor is *NICE*! And is coming. She's tall and quiet and used to nice houses. Dark. Looks a bit like a parlourmaid. God is good to me and I think all is OK. She and Rene are chatting as I write. *Thank God.*

She is tall and rather sad looking until she smiles. I rather think she has been through it a bit. Her husband has deserted her and their two little girls and she has to support them both on what she can earn. I am not prepared to carry the full load but she assures me that they eat very little, poor things, and that the elder Miss P. is ever so useful about the house. Maybe we can train her young! She is eleven; the other one is six. I haven't seen them yet. Rene has to go to her medical board on Tuesday and Mrs P. comes in on Monday afternoon. I have got to be away all that day and until lateish in the evening as I'm broadcasting. This is probably a good thing as it will give them time to settle in without me and then I shan't have time to sit and think about Rene's departure. Which I must admit I do not look forward to.

I had a very early lunch on Tuesday in order to be at the hosp by 1.30 as I was taking a party of three to the movies in M. and the programme starts at that hour. We followed the show by tea here and rounded off the evening by a view of the big house and a box of candies to be shared among 'em from Aunt N., who had just returned from Devon that day. I dined up there that night. Just Al, Bobbie, Dinah, Jim, Lady Vesey and me. One soon gets out of practice with the family I find and when they suddenly reunite it is a very strong dose and takes quite a lot of digesting. The thing I find the hardest

---

[1] ENSA: the acronym for Entertainments National Service Association, which was directed by Basil Dean.
[2] Front-rank patter comedian. He invented a mythical town, Hogsnorton.

to endure from them is their abnormalcy! Not one of them fits in to the ordinary world. I think maybe the Brands are an exception. But while it is refreshing to be with oddities for a while I find it gets me down in the long run and I very much trust the Lord will enable me to live down here and not force me to be an inmate up there. Which sounds darned ungrateful I know. It isn't that. It's just that there is no ease, no rest, no peace up there. At least not for me. Aunt N. is particularly sweet these days and sort of sad. Daddy tells me that David turned up at First the other Sunday and came around to see him after the service. He had tears in his eyes and was obviously moved by the whole thing. I don't suppose he's been inside a church for a mighty long time. The tragic thing is that I daren't tell Aunt N. or she'd make an issue of it and scare him off and yet there is nothing would make her more happy than to know that D. had been. What a strange mess the world is in.

---

*October 19th, 1941*                                    Parr's

Well, Mrs Proctor is nice; so are the two Miss P.s. They arrived last Monday while I was up in London doing a broadcast and Rene handed over to them and helped them to settle. I got home about 9 p.m. and found the children still awake with curiosity to see me, and their mother looking pretty in a blue and white printed overall waiting to give me some supper. The children are very well brought up. Truda is eleven and Shirley is six. They are nice looking and the little one is very pretty with curls and pink cheeks and an irrepressible giggle. The first days of readjustment were got through and it wasn't absolutely easy on either of us because she was very anxious to please and therefore flustered a bit and I kept saying, 'Rene did this or that' – which wasn't very tactful. However it's a week tomorrow since they came and we are what is known as 'getting used to each other's ways'. She is a good cook and a terrific cleaner and I like her as a person too, so that the Lord has once again provided.

Mrs P.'s meals, while quite delicious and I must admit more tasty than Rene's, are apt to be a bit late. But that will improve. The children attend the local village school and like it well. I was in London (another broadcast) on Wednesday, which was their first day at it, and when I got home I heard Shirley calling to her mother from her bed: 'Mum, have you shown the lady what I made?' and I had to be shown a cardboard doll with a separate paper dress that she'd created that day at school! So it is all rather cosy and the girls love

Nan and she tolerates them and Mrs P. is looking less and less harassed and making cleverer plans of her work so that she doesn't have to fluster at all.

---

*November 2nd, 1941*     Parr's

Last Tuesday was my big broadcast.[1] It went well I'm glad to say and I've had some very nice letters from strangers as well as several from friends. Last Monday I had such a funny letter of abuse from a schoolgirl, taking offence at my poor old schoolgirl sketch! She took a firm line and said, pompously, that no schoolgirl outside of a school story ever spoke so un-grammatically and gushingly and that, obviously, I must be very old or had never been to school or at any rate I didn't know what I was talking about! She ended by saying she must therefore ask me, in the name of art, not to continue to perform the sketch! Which goes to prove how lifelike it must be to touch off a humourless little high-school gal in Northampton like this. I wrote a long, kind and slightly patronising answer back in which I quote the dictionary's explanation of the word 'satire'. I hope that she answers me back. It was a stimulating correspondence. I did concede one thing to her. She accused me of making the creature a Sixth Form girl where as she is, clearly, a much younger one. I agree. The sketch got called the 'Head Girl' in the Little Revue and I was lazy about rewriting it. So far all the letters about Tuesday have been in praise. Daddy had one from a C.S. friend of his Oxfordshire days who said she'd once seen Ruth but that I was 'beyond even that'! Now you ARE NOT TO breathe that to anyone because, in all sincerity, I know in my heart that I am NOT. I'm not bad; in fact sometimes I know it's quite good. But I have never approached the width of canvas, nor could I sustain the thing as Ruth does. Some day, if I stick to it, I might be able to attempt something on the grander scale. At the moment mine are all glimpses compared to her full view. As a matter of fact I think monologues ought not to be very long.

To digress for a second: I've had what I think may be a good idea. To do a maid who is continually quoting her last place. 'Mrs Harpington-Gore always had reel lace on her undies', etc, etc. That's a bad quotation but it's a good idea and came to me while I was

---

[1] This was Joyce's first solo broadcast and lasted twenty minutes. It consisted of seven sketches and was produced by Stephen Potter.

easing in Mrs Proctor and trying to curb myself from saying: 'Rene did this, Rene did that.' It struck me then how maddening it must be and I reversed the situation in my mind. One could have fun with the maid describing the awfulness of Mrs Harpington-Gore's bedroom, etc, etc.

Reg is home this weekend. It was his birthday yesterday and he and Alice went shooting over at White Place with Hubert. I had chores to do for the hospital in the morning so I walked over later with our lunch, crossing in the ferry, and it was such a romantic day: the woods going gold, the sky wild and grey and sudden sharp bursts of dazzling sunshine. The river was deserted except for the ferryman who had tethered a punt in mid-stream and was fishing while the down-stream rushed by spotted with fallen leaves, curling and turning on their way down. I had Nan with me. She sniffed the river air and had to be forced away from swimming. It really was too cold but she's so water-minded that she thought I was silly. The guns came into Diana's house about 1.30 and we'd each provided our own sandwiches but she supplemented them with hot coffee and fruit. Such good pears this year. The best of the day was behind us by lunchtime so R. and I came home afterwards and dug ourselves in with a roaring log fire and a delicious loaf of French bread and sticky ginger cake for tea. Mrs Proctor was out for the afternoon and night and I did the supper. She had left us a freshly baked steak-and-kidney pie and all I had to do was heat it up, do the potatoes and toast, make the coffee and serve! I can't tell you how much we've enjoyed having the house entirely to ourselves. This morning R. relit the boiler, which had gone out, and I did the breakfast and everything was in order for Mrs P. to take over when she got back at 11. R. gardened all morning, I went to church. Since lunch we have just hugged the fire and I've written to you. At 3.30 Celia Johnson was broadcasting *The Silver Cord* so I put down this letter and knitted a dreary old khaki scarf for R. instead as I listened. Do you remember the play? with Lilian Braithwaite as the man-eating mother and Clare Eames as the new daughter-in-law?[1] Celia played that part and did it perfectly. My goodness, she's a good actress.

We've just had tea and now it's getting dark and I'll have to go and do the blackout. (What a day when we take it down! That will be about the pleasantest small thrill of all when peace comes.)

My two officers are billeted back on me as from today. Their baggage has been arriving in bits all day and the batman has been undoing it and settling the stuff in all afternoon. He is now sitting down to family tea with the Proctors in the tiny little sitting room.

[1] By Sidney Howard. It opened at the St Martin's on September 13th, 1927.

Mrs P. is a regular homebody and likes things 'nice'. She's always telling me: 'I do like things *nice*.' She's made her quarters very cosy and is very pleased with the place. It's three weeks tomorrow since she came and the adjustment is all in order. She isn't what you'd call polished or stylish in any way but she's kind and cheerful and a little bit shy and I consider I'm very lucky indeed. Little Shirley, who is six, still refers to me as 'the lidy', which seems a pity. She is a dream of prettiness and cuddly charm and all the neighbours say she's a 'proper little Shirley alright and ever so well named'.

Truda is a 'proper little woman', Mrs P. tells me and I'm afraid she really is, with a rather worried little face and a great sense of responsibility. Where Mrs P. is apt to forget things Truda jogs her elbow and I can see that she is the stable one between the other two lighthearted ones.

---

*November 23rd, 1941*         Parr's

*Monday*. Hosp all morning. I'm working even harder than usual there now somehow and I like it that way. There's a big call for women volunteers to the forces and to industry on at the moment and I cannot decide whether the job I'm doing at the hosp is justifiable or whether I should leave it for something else. I do NOT want to go into uniform for a whole variety of purely selfish reasons! Mainly physical: eight in room; rare baths; no quiet, no privacy, etc, etc. I had enough of all that at boarding school when I loved it. But now I really would hate it. But of course if I have to, I *can*. On the other hand there are factories. Purely cissy, I know, but I don't like the noise! But, once again, if needs be I can easily do that.

There is a definite need of someone to do the work I do in the hosp and I know I do it fairly well. But there are older women who could do it too. I know that my gifts, such as they are, do not include technical knowledge or ability to do anything that requires mathematics. I've never done a day's geometry or algebra in my life. On the other hand, I am good with people. They interest me and I get on well with most of them. Aunt N. says there is a big need for gals with my opportunities and advantages to lead girls in the services. If I could be an unmobile ATS or WAAF and do a welfare job among some reasonably local girls I would do so. But I do think it's important to keep this house going for R. or am I merely making myself believe this because I want to live in it myself? I wish I knew. I'm asking God to tell me what to do and trying to be as receptive and honest as I can about the whole thing, but it is increasingly difficult to take decisions these days; just part of mortal mind's muddling tactics! Anyway I'll be at the hosp a bit longer because I've got a lot on there at the moment and nothing else has come up clearly.

*December 7th, 1941*                                                    Parr's

I stayed in London to do jobs for the hosp and to hear Myra play Mozart in honour of the 150th anniversary of his death. Over 950 people flocked to the Gallery to hear her and it was one of the loveliest concerts I've ever heard. She is playing like a bird these days. It's astounding that anyone as advanced, as complete, as she seemed to be, could go on growing and growing. She says she suddenly feels as though, for the first time, she really had an idea of what it was all about! Anyway she was inspired. As I sat and listened, with my eyes shut against the packed rooms, everything seemed to flower. I can't do better than that to describe it. A blossoming.

Afterwards she and Howard Ferguson and I went to lunch at a place called, I *think*, Bellini's somewhere behind St George's Church and a most attractive quiet, pink and gold and cupid-ed place with wonderful food; Paderewski used to dine there which makes it holy ground for Myra. We had a lovely lunch, we three, and laughed a lot and talked a lot and all too soon it was time for me to dash away for the 4 o'clock train home.

Wednesday I went off bright and early to carry out the list of commissions I'd telephoned to the ward for the evening before. Then followed an entire day over there, during which I took on yet another ward so now I've got three, four and eleven to cherish. For the moment I'm satisfied that this is my right place and that I'm doing my right job. I'll just have to keep alert and watch to see if I'm doing all I can. So far I know I am.

On Thursday Reg rang up and said he was being sent to London to do a job on Friday and was coming home for the night here on the way. An unexpected treat. He was mighty sweet! The interesting thing is that he gets more and more attentive as the years go by! It's our *twelfth* anniversary on Friday next!!!

He left early Friday morning and I was in the hosp all morning. In the afternoon Eve [Clark] arrived and we planned our programme for no less than five ward concerts. We started at 5.30 and kept at it till 8.15 so you can see it was fairly hard work.

Saturday, hosp all morning. Virginia came down at teatime to

spend the night and go home next day in a big WVS [Women's
Voluntary Service] van she was transporting to Bristol. Heavenly
to have her here. She slept in R.'s bed as Rachel was in the dressing
room and the officers occupy the rest of the house. And Celia came
over by train from Henley on Sunday for the day so we had a very
cosy girlish time with knitting and the radio.

It's a heavenly day – freezing and blue and gold. I *must* go to the
hosp. Good letter from you just this minute with pretty drawing of
flower piece in it. *Very* decorative and the colour sounds lovely.

I'm very well and busy.

Much love for Xmas and New Year and all.

*P.S.* I'm mad about my pyjamas. *So* snug and so pretty *too*.

---

*December 14th, 1941*                                    Parr's

So it has actually happened. Oh dear, and in what an awful way.
And yet, you know, I rather think the US had to learn a little humility
and though it was a lesson at a ghastly price, the Pearl Harbor debacle
did more to unite the whole country, and sober them up too, than
any amount of rhetoric could do.[1] In some ways I hate the US being
in it. Because one hates to see anyone who loves going through trial
even though, as in this instance, the trial is going to strengthen them,
and make 'em face reality for a change. We all minded badly for you
about Pearl Harbor. It's rather like the way one rather dislikes it
when Aunt N. stops attacking and gets sadly gentle. It don't seem
natural! The US has talked so big for so long and criticised us for
our dilatory ways and bunglings and then, whang, she's caught
napping on a major scale and is humbled and frightened and chastened
and bewildered. Again – it don't seem natural. But already she has
stiffened into the pattern of unity and will do all she has to and more,
and for once, oh blessed day, she cannot say she rushed in and saved
the day for us. Instead, we are on equal footing. A sober and solemn
thought and one for which I'm deeply grateful.

Have I ever given you an itinerary of my days now?

8 a.m.  Called by Mrs P. who closes my windows but doesn't take
        down the blackout because it's still pretty dark
9 a.m.  Breakfast. Coffee, toast and jam.

[1] Pearl Harbor was bombed by the Japanese on December 7th.

9.30 Any brief notes, telephone calls, home chores, orders with Mrs Proctor.

9.45 Car into Burnham, park at the chemist-cum-fancy goods and stationers where the niece of the proprietor serves me and is v. kind and helpful. I buy – probably – writing pads and envs., soap, toothpaste, Xmas cards, nail file, a comb. That's an average list – in various quantities. Then to the PO to dispatch cables, buy stamps, register letters; all for patients. To the greengrocer in search of celery and apples, if any.

10.30 Hosp. Park car in the entrance driveway. Stagger in with my green and yellow basket, also my veg-cum-fruit bag of old leather. Straight to Ward 11 via the back entrance. Here I hang my coat in the sisters' little lav. and go into the ward. Delivery of goods first; then a slow round to each bed for fresh orders and chat, taking notes, if necessary, for outgoing letters if the patient doesn't feel like writing. By now it's about 11.30, so I go down to the main hall and reception desk where I copy down the names of the new English patients and their wards. Then down to Wards 3-4, where I repeat the process of 11. After which it's probably about 1 o'clock, so I come home for lunch and the X-word puzzle, but leave again about 2 o'clock and go straight to Ward 11 again to leave my coat and then start off to call on the new British patients and do odds and ends of visiting. It's impossible to annotate these because they vary so. Maybe I call on the matron in the officers' ward where she's recovering from appendicitis; or do a bit of book lending to a sick sister. Or help the visitors in the Red Cross room with items. Anyway if I'm home by 5 that's early. I've probably had a cup of tea or coffee during my rounds which is a help. So I never have tea here. I sit about till about 6.30 when I take a tub and put on your trousers and scarlet sweater (if I haven't worn it that day! I'm wearing it this minute). Supper around 7.30. After which I write letters, read a bit, knit a scarf, for R. which has gone on since 1939! but got finished two nights ago, and at about 10 *start* to bed and finally get there about 10.45.

There. That's an average day.

*Wednesday*: To London for a day of shopping entirely for the hosp. To the City at 12.45 to hear Pa take the Wednesday, mid-day meeting. He read quite wonderfully and it was a most helpful hour. Afterwards he and I ate at a dreamy City restaurant and then bus'd through the battered ruins around St Paul's and even if it's sacrilegious to say so I must confess that I was amazed at the beauty revealed by the new space surrounding the church! It's clear and open and the ruins are a most lovely pale creamy pink colour and don't remind you of death and destruction. Instead you feel life and freedom. Don't say this to those who wouldn't understand it. Back on the 4 o'clock train.

On Thursday evening when I got in from the canteen there was a huge green cardboard box in the hall, Special Delivery, and it had two dozen roses in it from my darling Reg on our *twelfth* wedding anniversary the next day! That was a lovely and unexpected surprise and did me a power of good, making me feel all pre-war and fêted.

<hr />

It's Sunday before Christmas; a performance (good) of *The Messiah* is coming over the air. We've got a heavenly warm fire, cold grey without, and I've stuck lots of holly on all the pelmet boards and wreathed the mirror in ivy and tufts of holly to be like the carol, 'The holly and the ivy, now both are well in bloom'. Reg, home for a nice long weekend, is sprawling on the sofa in very old tweeds, reading various long-distance letters I'd saved up for him. Nan is sleeping between us. The room looks slightly as if a bomb had hit it but on closer inspection you can see it's really just Christmas. The only people I'm giving to this year are R., Mrs Proctor and children, Rene and the men in Ward 11 (just silly little Woolworth soaps, etc,) but these constitute quite a pile on the piano and their red and green papers and tinselly ribbons look gay. R. has planted lots of daffodil bulbs for me and they are all up at once, so we've got bowls on every available inch. My knitting for the Navy – a plain scarf! – is all over one chair, another has my hospital notebook, a borrowed volume of short stories that I must return and the library thriller on it so that I'll remember to deal with 'em all tomorrow! It's messy but cosy and delights my eye in all its meanings.

This week? The first two days of it were crammed full of cables. On Monday I took blank forms and code sheets with 150 assorted messages on them into all fifteen wards, explained the procedure and price to patients at large and told 'em I'd be in next day to collect and that it would be a help if they could have them ready for me. Mere waste of breath of course, because almost none of them had. I started at Ward 1 at 2.25 and at 6.15 I staggered into the Red Cross room under 175 cables and the money for 'em in cash on me! Of these 175 at *least* one hundred were composed and written out by me. There were several who asked what I'd say if I was them so I soon got into practice and reeled off the number of messages I thought it would be nice to receive if I were a wife or mother in Canada. I spent all of Tuesday evening checking up the forms, numbering them and putting them in piles of eight each, with a pound note fastened to its pile (they were 2/6 each & there are eight half-crowns to a pound). This took hours.

I've had a demonstration recently that has been of peculiar satisfaction. For the first time since we began having them here the officers have been really rather unpleasant. One in particular. He drank – in a big way – and while I never saw or heard him in that shape, Mrs P. did, because he made advances to her while I was away and behaved altogether in an unattractive manner. (Including being filthy dirty and messy in his room.) When I discovered all this – rather when Mrs P. told me all about it, my first reaction was of plain human fury; but fortunately this died down and I gave myself time to work it out and I finally decided that I could heal the situation in the only way possible. The very next day I had to go into the officer's room to take down the blackout (and air it because it smelled so foul of stale cigarettes, dirty clothes and himself!) and I found he'd upset toothpaste and a glass of water all over my little polished table and generally been more than just careless, so I rushed downstairs and blew off at the batman who had just come in. I said this wasn't a hotel and that I wouldn't stand for the mess in my house, etc, and that he could tell his officer I'd said so. That evening when he came in he knocked on the door and came in here and said he would prefer it if I would say things direct to him and not send messages through his batman. He was, of course, quite right but I'd done it on purpose. I can't describe him to you very well except to say that he is very like Bobbie indeed to look at (but doesn't have the same troubles!) and just as flabby and dissolute. I told him about the table and said that I wasn't at all pleased with the way things were going on here. That was all, and *at once* he said perhaps we'd better make a change and that he'd find other billets as soon as possible. We parted coldly but with politeness. This was ten days ago, since which time exemplary behaviour and my heart sank because I thought he wasn't going after all. Maybe though, I thought, this is the way it's to be. He's behaving himself so what more can I ask? And then on Thursday I went down to Somerset to do a broadcast and when I got back the next afternoon there was Mrs P. to meet me at the door, grinning all over with pleasure: 'The officers have gone'! And so they had – to government billets up the other side of the park where their regiment is stationed. My heart leapt up. Grateful to God, am I, for doing such a tidy job with a situation. And the house feels quite different without them. I do think the male animal, without his spiritual qualities, is a nasty messy thing. This was a type I can quite well do without, thanks.

I didn't tell R. about this at all until it was over because I was quite sure it could be coped with in C.S. and if I'd been at all worried I could have gone straight to his Col. and got him moved at once. But I'm glad it happened this way.

——◆——

*December 28th, 1941*                                                      Parr's

*Monday*: R. was here till 4 in the afternoon. I was at the hospital all morning and we lunched here and spent most of the afternoon doing the crossword puzzle by the fire. It was a cold raw day and rather dark. At 4 we went down to Skindles[1] where we had an assignation with the messing officer from his camp who would be passing by there at that time, having been to London in a regimental lorry to collect the men's Christmas turkeys from the market up there. Soldiers were not permitted to travel during Christmas week so R. was able to stay his extra hours because of this method of return. I waved him off, sitting in a deckchair at the back of a lorry piled high, behind him, with crated birds! He afterwards telephoned that it had been a very comfortable trip.

*Christmas Eve.* One last dash into B. [Burnham] early that morning and then to the hosp, and while I was there I suddenly decided that I'd like to give the boys on Ward 4 a little something as well as 11, so about 12 I made another dash into B. and nice Miss Jarret in the chemist-cum-stationery and fancy goods helped me get together twenty-three small presents at the average price of 7½d each. (Everything that used to be 6d is now 7½, you know.) They were things like combs, notebooks, shaving soap, fancy matches, diaries, etc. Back here to wrap each one up separately and tag it with the man's name on it. Sylvia came in for lunch and we both went back to the hosp at 2 to wait for the Christmas stockings to come down from the Canadian Red Cross headquarters in London. I wrote two letters for one of my rather sick patients while I waited; and did some visiting too. At 5 the lorry still hadn't arrived; nor at 6. At 6.45 we abandoned the wait which was as well for the lorry never came till the next day, having been waylaid by Christmas cheer en route! The Canadian Red Cross are quite wonderful to their people. *Every* patient

---
[1] A hotel on the river, very well known in its day.

was given a pair of hand-knitted socks and one sock was filled for Christmas with a notebook, toothbrush, paste, gum, cigarettes, blades, candy, etc. And the YMCA gave 'em each a small box packed with similar presents. So they did pretty well. Each ward had Christmas dinner together – doctor, sisters and patients – and there was much fixing up of tables: placenames, candles, snowmen, crackers and pretties about. I didn't go into the hospital till the evening of Christmas Day because I thought that might be the lonesome time – excitement over, evening fallen and homesickness about!

But I've got ahead of myself. Did I tell you that I'd sent Mrs Proctor and her little girls home for Christmas and that Ginny and I were managing for ourselves? They went off on Christmas Eve about 7.30 and Gin and I got our suppers in the kitchen. I'd fixed a white cornucopia vase with holly in it (*never* seen so many berries as this year) and lit the four candles in my two double branch crystal candlesticks and it all looked so festive and cosy. We had a very delicious sausage meat pie with tomato soup (tinned) and fresh onions in it. And piping hot mince pies to follow. Not, I need hardly say, of my own making! No, Mrs P. left 'em in the oven for me to take out when ready. We went to bed reasonably early after I'd started the Aga and the boiler and done the bottles and we'd laid breakfast and tidied the drawing room. Next day I woke up at 8.15. The T.'s were quite dead after spending four of Tony's seven days in London going to theatres and eating a great deal at every meal in gala places. We'd decided to breakfast very late in our wrappers. I was just going to get up to stoke and then pop back to bed till about 9.15 but, woe is me, the boiler was all but out and my endeavours to save it resulted in putting it quite out! So I had to relight it. But first I lit the drawing room fire. It was *so* obliging and just went from the word go. But the boiler – I was at it for forty-five minutes and your pretty pale blue fuzzy-wuzzy wrapper begrimed all around the bottom. And I was nearly in tears. However at this last desperate stage I started to calm down and know that harmony reigned just as well on Christmas Day as any other and, presto! up she went in flames! I then saw it was 9 o'clock, so I made the toast, fixed the coffee, undid the blackout, washed my face and hands and whipped my hair up and called the T.'s. We had a warm and leisurely breakfast in the kitchen, washed up slowly and then enjoyed long, late baths in the now thoroughly hot water. It was about 11 when we reassembled in the drawing room, all clean and glowing, with the house to rights, and sun shining in at us. Tony went off to his C. of E. church and Gin and I did the lesson. Then I manicured my nails and soon it was time to go up to C. for lunch.

It was a very quiet almost sad Christmas lunch somehow, but the evening was true to form and great fun.

After lunch we three came home and had a cosy fireside afternoon with our books. We made toast by the fire and it was *so* peaceful. About 6 I took a bath and put on R.'s black chiffon frock, with its short skirt, and went over to the hospital, carrying a couple of trays full of little nonsenses for the boys. When I went into 11 there was much bustling and I was presented with my Christmas present from them all – a pair of silver Victorian vases of incredible charm and absurdity. They are horn shaped and quite small; quite heavily embossed with irises all up the sides and, odd as they sound, they really are charming, and I was very touched indeed at their thoughtfulness. In response to 'Speech, speech' I said I couldn't thank them that way but I'd sing instead. Which I did; several times over. And then Sister Anna Millar gave me another box to open; this time from her and the other two girls of Ward 11, Edna Leishman and Connie Clarke, and from the doctor Ben Schoemperlen. This turned out to be a really lovely plated muffin dish; dead plain in modern design and most useful because we hadn't one. If I can remember to I'll enclose the tags that came with the presents. There was also a mixed box of sugar, tea and varied groceries from the boys, made up of things they'd had from home. So I had lots to be grateful for and thanked everyone individually when I went around with my own trayload of little presents.

After Ward 11, I hurried down to Ward 4 and gave them their little things and we sang together and I gave a photograph frame to the best soloist and a little Scotch Canadian won it on his mouth-organ. And finally it was after 8 and I was already late to dinner up at C. so I had to leave.

All in all it was a good Christmas. R. rang up on Christmas afternoon and sounded as if his time was being quite fun too.

*1942*

Because of the irregularity of mail transports Joyce numbered all the letters written to Ma throughout the rest of the war. She continued working at the hospital, adding the new-fangled Occupational Therapy to her duties there, which involved supervising the recuperating men at their needlework. Lyric-writing was another new venture. Up till now Joyce had written all the material she had performed in her sketches; the songs in her repertoire were often written and composed by Virginia Thesiger. This year, in collaboration with Richard Addinsell, she wrote the words to a song called 'Nothing New to Tell You'. By necessity much of this work was carried out on the telephone: Richard wrote the tune and sent it to Joyce. She 'fitted words to it and rang him from Parr's twice daily, with new versions. In London he carried the telephone to the piano and played his alterations to me. I sang my new words to his accompaniment.'

In the middle of the year, Joyce was called up. As an established broadcaster and entertainer her war work was to be 'entertaining', and later in the year she set off for an eight-week tour of Northern Ireland.

With the formation of the Atlantic Alliance, the war this year centred round the Far East and North Africa. Japan invaded Singapore and in North Africa Rommel captured Tobruk, El Alamein and prepared to advance to Egypt. General Montgomery's Eighth Army routed Rommel's Afrika Korps at El Alamein in October, and forced the German troops to retreat. During the winter the battle of Stalingrad marked a further reverse for Germany. The Russians launched a counterattack on November 19th which was to be decisive in draining German manpower and resources and thus gradually forcing the fortunes of war away from the Germans.

## 1942

January 25th, 1942                                          Parr's

My Darling Ma,
We've had such a heavenly week's leave. We went up to London on
Monday morning. Snow everywhere and we were glad of the rug I
took for the train. Fog, too, just to make it worse. We went straight
to the Cumberland where we left our bags in our room – Number
610 up on the sixth floor overlooking Marble Arch. We thawed
rapidly in the delicious steam heat and it was fun being off on a jaunt
like this – sort of honeymoon.
  We went to see *The Man who Came to Dinner*[1] at the Savoy and
quite enjoyed it; but it needs American playing and the words sit
uneasily on the English company. Afterwards we went in to the
Savoy proper to dine and dance. Can you imagine how changed
things are when you go dining and dancing in a short grey wool day
dress and are quite right in it? They've closed the big restaurant on
the river side of the hotel and instead the Grill Room has been
enlarged and the big plate glass window into the courtyard is bricked
in and Carroll Gibbons plays in there. At first we thought we weren't
going to see anyone we'd ever laid eyes on before and that's sort of
sad when you're out for life. But later on we saw several familiar
faces. Stephen Watts, friend of R.'s who used to be film critic on the
*Express* came & talked to us and later Puffin Asquith,[2] looking strange
with wild hair and a navy blue silk zippered tennis shirt, sat at our
table for about half an hour. Lady Ox. is living at the Savoy and he
was en route to bid her goodnight. He's doing quite well in films

[1] Comedy by George S. Kaufman and Moss Hart. With Robert Morley as Sheridan
Whiteside.
[2] Anthony Asquith (known as Puffin), film director; younger son of the former
Prime Minister and his second wife Margot (née Tennant), Lady Oxford and
Asquith.

and is working on some government ones at the moment. About 10 o'clock the company of *Rise Above It*,[1] a revue that came on when *Diversion* came off last year, arrived to occupy a central table in celebration of someone's twenty-first birthday. Hermiones Baddeley and Gingold[2] and Walter Crisham were of the party. We had a little chat with them before we left.

Next morning we lay long in bed and it was most luxurious and how we enjoyed it. A little refugee maid brought us our breakfast – *fruit!*, porridge, fishcakes for R. and rolls and honey for me, and coffee and toast for both. About 10.30 we got up. Oh, I forgot to say that one of my indulgences was lying in bed using the telephone. (You may remember that ours is in the dining room here and that's a great help in economising over calls!) I just lay there and telephoned, while R. marvelled at anyone enjoying such a pastime. I rang up Myra and had a long talk with her. Then I talked to Maria Brassey who was abed in her Edgware Road flat with a bad tooth that had caused her to blow up and look most peculiar. She had a good healing about it and it has cleared up. And then I rang up Bertie and we asked him and his wife to dine with us at the Café Royal that evening at 8. And I got on to Phil Nichols and asked him to do the same.

It was a very successful evening and there was so much to say that we looked up in surprise at 11 when they started turning the lights out on us and we found we were the only people left. We had a wonderful meal – by any peacetime standard. We talked of the theatre and acting and writing and both said nice things about my 'Winter Morning' poem that had been in the 'O' [*Observer*] the Sunday before. And we talked about the *Constant Nymph*[3] and how difficult it was to put over the feeling of being in love on the stage and how well Edna [Best] had done. And how well Celia does it. But very few others. Suddenly it was time to go. A very pleasing evening.

Next day I came down on a morning train while R. went to Windsor for lunch with a man he'd done business with before the war and whom he'd like to work with when it's over.

I was in the hosp all afternoon and the snow was so deep in our drive

[1] At the Comedy, a revue with both Hermione Baddeley and Hermione Gingold, Walter Crisham, and Henry Kendall, who directed.

[2] Hermione Gingold, actress, whose reputation was made in revue; later in films including *Gigi*.

[3] *The Constant Nymph* (New Theatre, 1926) was a version of Margaret Kennedy's novel by herself and Basil Dean who directed. It ran for 587 performances, with Edna Best as Teresa Sanger, Noël Coward as Lewis Dodd for the first few weeks, and John Gielgud for the rest of the run. Dean revived it at the Garrick in the autumn of 1928, with Jean Forbes-Robertson and Raymond Massey. Celia Johnson certainly appeared in love with Maxim de Winter (Owen Nares) in *Rebecca* at the Queens in April 1940.

that I had not dared negotiate it at lunchtime so when I got back here about 4.30 I got Mrs P.'s little girls and we dug a path to enable me to bring the car in and get her out next morning. R. arrived while we were doing this and joined in and then we went all round the garden shaking the heavy snow off the bushes and low branches of the fir trees for they were being bent under its weight. Toast and honey for tea by the fire and we felt lovely and glad to be home again in spite of a *thoroughly* enjoyed two days in London. Which is as it should be.

Next day was Thursday and brilliant with snow and sun. We went to the village for me to do some hosp shopping and then we took a walk in the grounds with Nan leaping ecstatically beside us, gleaming black satin against the white snow. In the afternoon R. took her off and they went shooting but failed to return with anything for the pot but he'd loved his exercise and air and we glowed by our fireside that evening with pink cheeks and a pleasant tiredness.

Yesterday was Saturday and we went into B. [Burnham] for a few oddments in the morning and then slopped through the slush to the old dairy to borrow a saw for R. to cut up an apple tree we'd felled in the autumn for firewood. He then got on the job and stayed on it all afternoon and most of today and the result is a fine pile of logs and heaps of kindling. It's been such a cosy, happy leave and we get so quickly back to normal that it is a bit of a wrench to have to go through the goodbyes at the end. We've played games of rummy for hours on end and read our books and walked and talked and done the crossword and I can't imagine a happier seven days. Golly, the gods were good to me when they met me up wit' Reggie!

It's 6 p.m. now and we've just blacked-out. He is reading and I'm writing to you and it's warm and peaceful in here with jonquil bulbs just ready to burst in a white pottery bowl on the table and a big box of chocolates you sent us on the stool between us and the logs hissing a bit on the fire because they are on the damp side. We're alone in the house because Mrs P. and her girl friend Elsie have gone to meet the children coming by bus from their grandma's in Windsor where they've been for the day.

Much love,
Joyce

———◆———

*February 2nd, 1942*
Written in the train after staying in Bristol with Virginia and Tony Thesiger

Yesterday evening a fellow officer of Tony's came to supper. One Joe

Cooper by name, a musician.[1] He is really a very good serious pianist
but has had to put it aside for the war. He can and does also play jazz
and he's written the most lovely tune that Gin wants to do words for
so that I may sing it in Bertie's new revue – (May; God willing). We
had rather a good idea I think, 'No news is good news' being the general
theme and title line. He played all sorts of jazz to us after supper and
then got in the mood and played Scarlatti, Mozart, Bach, Chopin and
somehow Gin's rather tinny little hired upright took on all the majesty
of a great concert Steinway and I've seldom enjoyed music more. When
it was over Gin and I drove him back to his camp through a moon mist
and got to bed disgracefully late. Gin brought me to the train just now
and has gone off on WVS duties for the rest of the day.

---

*February 9th, 1942*                                                    Parr's

I did a great deal of letter writing for the patients last week. It's work
the Can. Red X are keen for us to do and a job I like and am able to
do. Either one takes dictation, or, more often, makes notes and later
assembles the letter away from the bedside.

Some of the men have casts on their arms (motorbike smashes
almost exclusively) and their enforced inactivity comes pretty hard.
Tomorrow is my birthday; it is also the birthday of one Hodson who
is in a solid cast from his armpits to his toes and has been for weeks.
It is also the birthday of Sister Cascadine of the same ward. So we
are by way of having a party with cakes and a singsong. A good way
of spending one's birthday.

You know one learns a lot in a hosp. Human courage is a strange
and mysterious thing; of course it isn't human really at all. It *must* be
spiritual. One man, called Winters, has his arm in a rigid cast, rather
as if he'd started a Nazi salute and got jelled while his top arm was
raised but the forearm was in the salute position. *And* he has his leg
and thigh in a cast too and has enjoyed but eight hours sleep in two
weeks and is in pain all the time but not a peep has there been out of
him! I wrote a long letter to his wife in Winnipeg last week and he
didn't complain in it at all except to say he wasn't quite comfortable
yet! Funny the way one is cowardly about pain. I am. Not that I've
had much ever. Toothache maybe. I think it's awfully hard to deal with

[1] Joseph (Joe) Cooper, pianist; much later he was the chairman of the *Face the Music*
programme in which Joyce was a regular member. She described it as 'one of the
best fringe benefits that came my way'.

even with C.S. and yet these creatures undergo the most awful times
without complaint. Moreland, on Ward 11 has had to have tubes in his
back for a chest condition (sounds Irish!) and it is hell, I believe, but he
hasn't mentioned it. Just held on to Sister's hand a bit harder while the
doctor dealt with him. You know I talked about Love before. You see
it, unharnessed maybe and purely human, but very strongly in a good
*sister* and a good doctor. It surrounds all their ministrations even if they
don't know what it is. Rene's mother, old Mrs Easden, exudes this
kind of love. Her neighbourliness and her warm goodness make her
the one person everyone around here turns to when in trouble. She
looks like a sack of undulating straw in the shape of a loaf. Her family
adore her and everyone else feels better for a sight of her.

(The news has come on. It is unpleasing. The Japs are in Singapore.
*Bah*.)[1]

I made one or two notes of things to tell you about London in case
I've not done so till now.

All railings are down everywhere, all the parks, squares, etc, and
it's *lovely*.

The Savoy has waitresses now in long buff dresses.

Taxis ask you where you want to go at night and if they don't
fancy the route or their petrol is low they just say they don't think
they'll take you, thanks!

Soap is rationed from today. I've got quite a lot of Christmas pres.
stuff so I'm OK.

Tom Talbot[2] had his third daughter last week.

Lady Alice Shaw-Stewart[3] died.

When you shop you must take a bag or some paper because the
shops are not allowed to wrap any goods that aren't actually messy!
I bought half a pound of nails for a patient today and had to have
'em running loose in my purse.

---

*February 22nd, 1942*                                                    Parr's

To 20 Tavistock St where I found Winifred (Clemence Dane's real
name) feeding about ten people with a meal she'd cooked herself that
afternoon. Steak and kidney pie, salads, sausage rolls, etc.

[1] The Japanese invasion of Singapore was launched on February 8th.
[2] Thomas George Talbot, QC 1954; CB 1960. Counsel to Chairman of Committees,
House of Lords from 1953.
[3] Wife of Sir Hugh Shaw-Stewart, 8th baronet; Lord Lieutenant of Renfrewshire.
She was the daughter of the 4th Marquis of Bath.

The party was: Lilian Braithwaite, her daughter Joyce Carey; Val Gielgud, brother of actor John, and the head of the BBC Drama Department. Fay Compton and some handsome young man whose name I didn't hear but who was either Mr Fay or ought to be if he isn't. A man called John Bryson who teaches medieval history at Balliol; a young soldier called Halsey Colchester, of all unlikely names! Winifred's secretary Olwen and a girl called either Bridget or Janet who has just written a novel about young love that Winifred says is good. And lastly there was Richard Addinsell,* who is a youngish composer of very good light music. He's a somewhat pale, young man with a lovely touch on the piano and he and I made music the entire evening quite quietly in a corner. I can't tell you how I enjoyed it! Every old song there is and he was so taken with the way I sing 'Where and When' that we did it at least six times before the night was out. Fay C. and beau, Val Gielgud and the girl Bridget or Janet left about 1 and we all got very cosy and I ended by performing and we had more food, a delicious wonderful un-potent sort of mulled *hot* wine and we added an electric fire to the coal one and had a lovely theatrical chat in a cosy little ring. Lilian Braithwaite told us about playing in *The Silver Cord* and of the abusive letters she had while acting in it. At last it was time to go and after several times of trying we ended by getting a taxi from Great Portland St (by telephone) and the men Addinsell, Bryson, Colchester – in alphabetical order see? – Miss Braithwaite, Joyce Carey, and I all set off together in the same cab. We dropped each other en route and when I got back to 21, it was 3 a.m.!

---

*March 1st, 1942*                                                    Parr's

I think I told you that one of my jobs is being a liaison officer between the British and Canadian Red Cross societies. This includes looking after the relatives of sick English soldiers. We've got a nice young Englishman in now called Raven who had his leg badly crushed in a gun accident. (The gun fell on it.) He was put on the Dangerously Ill list on Friday and his wife was sent for and arrived early yesterday morning. They have taken the leg off and he is going to be all right, thank God. I've had the wife here. Such a nice appreciative creature. A cinema cashier in peace time; he was hairdresser. She's been through a lot and I was glad to have her here. Mrs P. was off yesterday, so Mrs Raven and I looked after each other last night and this morning. She's very neat and meticulous and nicely dressed. Wears highly polished glasses and has a sweetness about her that is endearing. She had a baby and lost it last year. 'A premature,' she said and went on to tell all the details, which were numerous; none of it can have been any fun for her. Her remark at the end of a long description of horrors was a gem of English understatement: 'Oh I was vexed,' was all she said! She came in for lunch today after being with him all the morning. She'll be there all afternoon so I can't say I find her any trouble. And her appreciation makes anything worthwhile. My golly, you don't mind what you do when people are grateful, do you? I've had some wives who don't even say thank you when the Red Cross have fetched and carried them all over the place. I think expressed gratitude is an important thing to teach children, don't you? I believe English people are too afraid of simple expressions of pleasure because they can & do get turned all too easily into gushes.

On Thursday I went to London to do a lot of jobs and at eleven I had an appointment with Mildred Rawson up in her seventh floor flat on Sloane St. Golly, she's so advanced and so lucid and so truly an understander that I came away on wings. She says we mustn't get mixed up into thinking this is a Christian war. She says that we are *none* of us being in the least bit Christian, that we are trying carry on on the Christian heritage, but that it's a dead thing for most of us, and until we see it again as Jesus told us, we are going to go on having messes. She says that most Christians believe that sorrow is a Christian thing; but Jesus proved it had no part in God at all. We were talking about tiredness and she said to stop *thinking*, because thinking is a purely material step, and let Mind just be in us and we couldn't tire Mind. It's helped me a lot. I wish I could tell you all the good things she said. She believes that all churches as they are now known, all creeds, must go because they are dead wood and that the revelation of truth must be established in *us*. And that the Old Testament can be dispensed with because it simply pointed the way to Jesus and we are now the other side of the pointing, so to speak. '*Now* is the appointed time.'

Then I lunched with Bertie and heard plans for the new revue. May is the month and he's full of good ideas but I'm still not sure whether it's *right* for me to go into it. It's to be a small company and he is anxious to have it as un-West-End, un-sophisticated and un-cynical as he can make it. Hurrah. That's enough to make me long to get into it. Well, I'll have to see.

*March 15th, 1942*                                                  Parr's

I think R. is rather disappointed that I'm not doing the revue. He
likes to read my notices and is so proud and sweet and sort of jealous
for me. He knows I'm right though and has backed me up in making
the decision. I'll feel better when I've heard from Bertie. He's so
sweet and gentle and rather too thin just now and he is counting on
me, I know. But even so, with all these reasons tugging at me, I
think I'm right not to. It's no good going against your instincts. And
even though man's highest conception of right may be all wrong he's
got to stick to it until he gets a lead in the opposite direction. So
there we are.

*March 29th, 1942*                                                  Parr's

Wednesday A.M. I went up on the 9.48 to broadcast. Rehearsal was
from 10.45 and I went straight to the Criterion by underground. It
was a *Geraldo Band-Box*[1] programme and Olive Groves was singing
a Mozart aria and I did the American mother and some old silly songs
and the orchestra played Dick Addinsell's Warsaw Concerto. We had
an audience of service men and women and it all went very well.
Afterwards Dick took me to lunch at the Carlton Grill where we
talked & talked – about radio, music, food, war, thoughts, and finally
decided to try and do a programme on the air together. For your
motherly heart let me hasten to assure you there is nothing that
doesn't meet the eye in the arrangement! He's very sweet and long
and gangling and sort of un-sexed. *Very* shy and C3[2] and not in the
army and sweet and gentle and sensitive but not a beau in any way.
He plays the piano well but with a simple sense of rhythm which
rather suits me. We plan, vaguely, to do all old songs and keep it all
unspoken. Just a brief, straight, sung and played little affair. I'm
meeting him next week to go into it all. After our lunch on Wednesday
I went into the Ladies and had some surprising conversation with the
attendant in there. She said the people who came there now were a
disgrace. Just rich, no class at all. No manners. You could see they
didn't know what to do with their money. Looked right through
her, they did, and it wasn't right for such people to be in a place like

[1] Geraldo: Before the war he was a Savoy Hotel dance orchestra conductor. Became
General Managing Director for ENSA's broadcasting.
[2] Low medical grading, exempting from service in the forces.

the Carlton Grill! In the old days (you could tell they were Good Old Days to her) only the best people patronised the Grill. Lots of titled ones used to come and it upset her dreadfully to see all these new *Socialists* coming in! I tried, gently, to tell her that the new-rich with no manners and black market ways were in all probability NOT Socialists but she wasn't convinced. She was a Conservative herself and she came from a Conservative family and wasn't going to change now, thank you madam. The funny thing is that she is one of quite a number who really don't want a change. Imagine being satisfied with the enormous division in privilege and wealth that used to be? Of course there are those who believe titled people are different from the rest of us and by Rights too! Oh yes, this war had to come, there's no question of that.

---

*May 11th, 1942*　　　　　　　　　　　　　　　　Parr's

R. finished his seven days' leave this morning so everything is a little flat this evening without him. But we had a heavenly week so I really can't complain. It has been such a good leave and we loved it. I can't get over how truly lucky I am to be married to someone I am still dead in love with after twelve and a half years! We have such fun together and I must say, when I see how dull so many of the couples are, I do feel grateful for us and the way we feel about each other. Talking of grateful – was that Macy's soap from you? And the sheet music? Both most, most welcome and I think you are very good to me. If they weren't from you – who? I love 'Deep in the Heart of Texas' also 'How about you'.

I'm fine. Hosp all day today and your letter all this evening so there's no time to miss R.

---

*May 31st, 1942*　　　　　　　　　　　　　　　　Parr's

*Sunday evening.* R. fussing over his new tomato plants, manuring, watering and tying. I'm sitting on a small deckchair in the sun. We're having roast pork for supper and I've popped it into the oven surrounded by potatoes. Domesticity personified. If only there wasn't tomorrow morning ahead of us and R.'s train back to his regiment all would be perfect. It's pretty nice anyway and we've plenty to be grateful for.

*Monday*. R. went back early today. It was a grand two days' leave. Last night – oh, I wish you could have seen him! – I made him tell me about when he had first noticed me; special moments in our courtship. He was most un-cooperative and giggled and said, 'You *know*, hon,' and I had a lovely time forcing him to tell me. He confessed to jealousy of *Henry Tiarks*! and Ian Fleming[1] but particularly of Henry!! Isn't it odd how wrong a person can be? He remembers me specially in a red hat at the Eton–Winchester match in 1928! If it wasn't red then it had cherries on it. I can't remember it in the least, can you? He says it was large. He was so sweet about it all.

————◆————

*June 21st, 1942*                                        Parr's

*(The Longest Day)*
Dick Addinsell's party was such fun. Quite small. When I got there Clemence Dane & Lilian Braithwaite and Joyce Carey were all eating delicious salads with some unidentified men. Diana Wynyard[2] and Carol Reed the movie producer (*Night Train to Munich* & *Lady Vanishes*)[3] came in soon. Noël Coward and Gladys Calthrop,[4] Victor Stiebel, the dress designer and Muir Matheson who is directing the music for Noël's new picture(!!) [*In Which We Serve*]. And a stray admiral who has helped with technicalities for the film. And a general and his wife who had something to do with an army film Dick had done the music for. About twenty people I suppose. We just sat about and talked and there was some delicious and piping hot mulled claret which I sipped at! (It was still cold then!) Later, while I was talking to Gladys Calthrop, Dick started playing 'The Most Beautiful Girl in the World' – which is one of the songs we do extra well together and signed to me to come over to the piano. So I sang it and Noël said *very* nice things about it. Said I sang as singing ought to be done. Carol Reed liked it too, and said so. We also did 'I didn't know what time it was', which is another of our specials. It went

[1] Peter Fleming's younger brother; later the author of the James Bond books.
[2] Leading actress; played Gilda in Coward's *Design for Living*, and starred in the film of *Cavalcade*.
[3] At this time married to Diana Wynyard.
[4] Stage designer particularly associated with Noël Coward.

well. Dick is perfect to sing with – his harmonies are so rich and musical and the whole arrangements he makes are so wonderful that I can hardly sing for listening to them. The big thing of the evening was when he told me he'd written a new song for me. It's quite lovely and I've written – or am writing the words. It's probably going to be called 'That's All for Today' and it's a letter song. It's got a heavenly tune. *How* I'm to end it I do NOT know. We ring each other up twice a day with different versions but so far the right one has eluded me.

Wouldn't it be fun if it was a success? With Dick's Warsaw Concerto fame to start it off. I think it ought to get attention anyway. I don't yet know how we'll introduce it. Radio, I expect. Then records. He's so nice to work with. Very gentle and quiet and restful. And oh so good at his job. The party went on until about 1 and I was late to bed.

---

*July 19th, 1942*               Parr's

I'm in one of those strange states one gets in now and then – Indecision about my right place, etc. R. said he thought – this was yesterday evening – that I ought to go back to the theatre, that it was silly to contemplate taking a paid job that wasn't my profession, that it was silly to think that because I wanted to go back so much it must be wrong and finally that there was still ten days to the opening of Bertie's new show and why not ask him if it was too late? So we rang up Daddy and had his view which is that no one but me can decide a thing like this and that if my only desire is to do right then I'll be protected. So armed with this advice and R.'s backing we rang up Bertie who was surprised but pleased and he said he thought it was too late, that timing and programme, etc, etc, were all decided on and that there was the question of another salary to be considered, etc, and that he'd let me know by tonight. As soon as we'd rung off I wished, rather, I hadn't thought of it all again. But as R. said – give God a chance and if Bertie says it's too late that's OK by us. If he says it isn't then it may mean God wants me to do it! Golly, it *is* difficult to know how much is God's will and how much is mine! (T.J. told us a good instance of this sort of thing. Someone once said of Gladstone that he didn't object to Gladstone keeping the ace of trumps up his sleeve but he did object to him saying that God had put it there.)

I dined with Daddy last week after church and he said it was one of the harder problems to decide what God wanted one to do. It's somehow so awfully unlike me to suddenly up and decide to try and get into the show ten days before the opening that I feel quite irresponsible for whatever happens! I've a hunch that my continual dread of and worry about what Aunt N. will say is holding me back and I must break with it. After all I'm thirty-two years old and it's time I felt free. She has said that if I go back to the theatre while there's a war on she'll never speak to me again! Also that she'd take my house away from me, threats that blackmail one a bit into toeing the line. But as R. says it doesn't much matter if she does both these things and that I must feel free to act as I think right. If only I knew exactly what is the right thing to do. Am I being mesmerised into thinking it is right for me to go back on the stage, giving what I fondly hope may be pleasure? For so long now I've said that there weren't any good enough reasons for me to go back, that fun and money were wrong motives. There you get that old self-torture thing again, though, where you almost superstitiously believe that if a thing is fun it must be wrong! I'm sure that's a bogey I've got to lay. Aunt N. has always had its opposite – that if it hurts it must be doing good!

I'm considerably exercised by all of this and rather ashamed by it too – in the middle of a world where bigger hells are needing healing. Yet it's all part and parcel of the same unrest and indecision. If Bertie says, 'yes, come on' the way is far from clear! I've a couple of broadcasting contracts, a month of YMCA concerts, etc, and the Red Cross to talk with, the hosp . . .

*Later.* Bertie rang up and thank God (no sour grapes, either) he can't fit me in – too late. He wished he could – if only he'd known two days ago. I can't begin to tell you how relieved I am. I feel as if I'd had a sign from God! Something impelled me to take all those human steps and then showed me that it wasn't the right thing. I can't tell you how queer it's been. I think maybe I was trying to plan, was anxious to free myself *humanly* – whereas there is only one true freedom, isn't there? Anyway, Mama, rest assured that your child feels twenty-five years younger and totally at peace. As if she'd had a present and had a weight shifted that was becoming uncomfortable.

I don't thing I'm quite fair to Aunt N. because you know the funny thing is that she doesn't ever *actually* interfere, but one is continually expecting her to do so! It's hard on her really – I'm sort of holding her back by expecting her to be as she always was. As a matter of fact she's trying harder than ever these days. Her ways aren't always mine but she does earnestly desire to know more of truth and to help humanity and she is wiser than she used to be. She even admitted to me quite lately that you can't help anyone until they want to be helped – which for her is quite a step, don't you think? The answer to all this is that I have been afflicted by the whole unreal restlessness of the world and I think I let a lot of it get at me. Quite unnecessary when one sees it clearly. Anyway I'm a made-over person this evening and I'll just let things happen after this. R. was so sweet and so funny about it all. He is being moved, as I told you, and it's NOT Scotland but near where Sim comes from, if you remember where that is.[1] We don't know when it is to be but we hope he'll get a seven-day leave in before the move.

I stopped work about 4 and hurried home to change and catch the 5 o'clock to London where I was churching and shopping with Pa before going to Dick Addinsell's and then to stay the night at Gin's. I got to Cambridge Sq. about 6 and dropped my bag, found Celia there also up for the night and we got talking. A button – *the* button came off my drawers while I was in the bathroom talking to her as she washed before going to see *Macbeth* (Gielgud's new production) and I quite forgot about it till we were hurrying across Norfolk Crescent in search of a pair of taxis and I felt something odd about my hips. I managed to keep 'em up – such little satin and lace step ins, too, my only such pair, and I found I had an ordinary stick pin in my coat so I was able to fix 'em temporarily and it wasn't till after the service when Pa and I went to the Royal Court Hotel that I got hold of a proper pin. Didn't your drawers fall off on the stage of the Hippodrome when you were singing to soldiers in the last war? I've always told it as a good story so I hope it's true.

---

*Sunday, July 26th, 1942*                                        Parr's

On Tuesday evening I biked up to C. to dine with Uncle W. and G.B.S. and sweet Mrs Charlotte Shaw who had arrived that day for a three weeks' visit. She is very frail this year and bent. He is younger than last year and very much more on the spot, I thought. His teeth fit less well than they might and he rattles them ferociously at meals and in excited conversation.

On Wednesday R. is coming up for the night and he and I and Gin and Tony are all going to Bertie's first night and taking Dick Addinsell – whom none of them have met yet. AND, before this, at 4 of the

[1] Joyce getting past the censor. Sim was Lord Feversham, who lived at Helmsley, Yorkshire.

clock in the afternoon, Dick and I are doing my song for Geraldo! He is the orchestra leader here, the one who has lovely special arrangements made for his programmes. So I'll go to bed early on Tuesday night and sleep in pins, etc! We *hope* he is going to build a programme around us. I'll let you know all in next week's instalment.

---

*August 2nd, 1942*                                             Parr's

*Tuesday*: Hosp all day and busy too. This has been a record fortnight. I've taught more new patients than ever before. They are so touching, stitching away. I've just managed to get some lovely, plain, coloured linen traycloths and on to these I put their crests and set them off to work them in coloured threads. Some of them do really wonderful work. Finer than any woman. There's a nice, rather tough, little man called Adams in Ward 3 who has turned out to be a wizz with the needle and has done two badges and a bunch of life-like marguerites on a salmon pink art silk table centre! He says – as they all do – 'If the boys could see me now!' It's quite extraordinary to see the good effects sewing has on 'em. They get an interest and forget their ailments. The docs encourage it, particularly in the cases where the men have to be in bed for long times. Did I tell you about the beady-eyed little man who took on a guest towel to decorate with three innocuous roses? When I came back next day he'd written 'From your loving son Jesus died for sinners' on it in pale coloured silks and quite without punctuation.

At tea time on Tuesday I had to take four visiting docs who were here on a gas course, to have tea with G.B.S. and Mrs as Aunt N. was away in London for the day. The old man, who must have once studied medicine I think, was on his toes and teased the docs about their profession quite unmercifully and with some truth. He said they were on entirely the wrong tack – trying to heal the body and discounting the mind. He challenged them to show the difference between a dead and an alive body – except the spirit. The docs couldn't have got a single thrust back because he was oblivious of anything except his own very brilliant flow of ideas and opinions. When he is '*en bonne veine*' he really is worth hearing. He really does seem younger and more on the spot than last year. She is gentle and sweet and has the only really green eyes I've ever seen. Must have been a great charmer in the old days. Still has it now.

To the first night of Bertie's new show at the Ambassadors

Theatre.[1] It was a warm evening and we all stood about outside the theatre till the bell called us in. It's a very different sort of revue. The opening was lovely – just a bare stage with the scenery stacked at the back, prop baskets (in which costumes travel) about the place, a grand piano on the left with a boy in grey flannels and a tennis shirt just playing softly. Betty-Ann Davies in a white shirt and blue slacks is reciting. It is all very quiet and rather lovely. The whole thing is informal and fresh. The only trouble is it is too sad! He's gone nostalgic and everything – or almost – harks back and never looks forward. It's a little too gentle. His sister Eleanor, who writes with great charm, has had a hand in many of the numbers and I'm afraid she's a bit sweet and it's knocked the edge off Bertie's wit. And yet lots of it is excellent. However one doesn't laugh much and there is quite definitely too much beauty! I never thought there could be but there is. It went on far too long and ended with a nativity play that was well done but so wrong somehow. We were all profoundly depressed when we came out. We went over the road to the Ivy for supper and after we'd got settled I left the party and went back to the theatre to see Betty-Ann and the others. Bertie was in her room looking so sort of thin and sad. Oh, I couldn't bear it. We kissed all around and said how good it was and of *course* people would love it and yet I felt it was doomed. Back at the Ivy we went through the programme and said what we'd cut and golly it was almost all the second half! After supper we went back to Dick's flat and cheered ourselves up with the song!

The press notices of Bertie's show were not v. good. One, a yellow-press paper,[2] ended by saying he came out into the street and looked for a hearse to take him home! *The Times* and *Telegraph* were kinder but agreed that it was all a little too sombre.

*Friday*: Pay day in the hosp. Which always means a lot for us to do as men who haven't been able to afford new work before can do so when they've been paid. I lunched over there and didn't finish till nearly seven. As I came in the telephone was ringing and Mrs P. said Bertie had been after me all day. It was him now. Would I, he asked, help him save the show by coming into it! I said I didn't see how I could now as August was so full for me – eight YMCA concerts, broadcasts, besides my ordinary hosp work. I felt so mean somehow – not to say 'Yes, of *course*' at once. But I just couldn't. Oh Lor' I'm afraid the whole thing is going to sort of peter out. I've nothing new ready and while I suppose I could learn something up I feel strangely

---

[1] *Light and Shade:* Herbert Farjeon's revue, with assistance from Eleanor Farjeon; music by Clifton Parker, with Alfred Reynolds, Geoffrey Wright and Harry Farjeon.
[2] A period expression for the more sensational newspapers.

unfresh and anyhow there is too much to do. It doesn't feel quite
right anyway. But because he has appealed to me so generously I feel
I'd love to throw everything to the wind and do it. But without
being over-modest I don't honestly feel capable of 'lifting' a show
right now. I've been out of the theatre too long to rush back without
careful preparation.

Oh *dear*. He was sweet and said he understood. He thought he'd
just try in case there was a chance, etc.[1]

It was pouring with rain when I woke up this morning. I opened
the back door to see if the paper boy had brought the paper and left
it in a puddle (he's not very bright) and to my horror found that the
*baker's* boy had delivered yesterday afternoon and left the loaves on
the back steps where they were all soaked through! I've had them
in the oven all day, and Mrs P., who had just come in off the bus,
says they'll be alright. I read Ivor Brown in the O. [*Observer*]
and he wasn't any better than the rest about *Light and Shade*, so
I fear me it's got a short life. Agate was even more ruthless in
the *Sun. Times*. Poor Bertie. I think he must now hurriedly write a
new show on the old lines and abandon beauty, except in smaller
doses.

---

32 Cambridge Sq,
London, W2
~~On the train~~ – No, I thought I'd start it
there but I didn't.

*August 16th, 1942*

Mrs Jeffries,[2] who is keeping an eye on Parr's rang me up this
morning to say a cable had come from you so I got her to read to
me. Thank you very much – tomorrow is the night. It's only my
private excitement this time because the press have already been to
the show so there won't be any notices. In some ways this is rather
comforting. On the other hand it is a little drear to drop into a
running concern without a stir. The family – P. side – are rallying
which is cosy. Gin has done me a delicious new song – its tune is in
the Haydn manner, very brittle and eighteenth century and is sung
in a rather stilted, somewhat affected manner – Harry Graham wrote
the words – as set by Gin they go like this:

[1] Joyce did go into the show after all; in her autobiography she says she could not
remember what made her change her mind nor how she got out of the promised
concerts.
[2] Mrs Jeffries was the wife of Bert Jeffries, the chauffeur at Cliveden.

Weep not for little Leonie
Abducted – Abducted – by a French Marquis
Though loss of honour was a wrench
Just think how it
Just think how it
Just think how it improved her French!

—◆—

*August 31st, 1942*　　　　　　　　　　　　　　Parr's

*In the theatre*
Bertie has just been in to tell us that we've only got two more weeks. Sad; but I'm so busily involved with the songs and radio and recording that I'm not so low as I might have been. God works in a mysterious way, etc, and the gap left by the theatre (filled again after *so* long) is already taken care of by all the other activities.

—◆—

*September 13th, 1942*　　　　　　　　　　　　In the train

About 9.30 Dick rang up to say he'd rewritten our dreamy song and by bringing the telephone towards the piano and playing loudly he gave me the improvements. So to bed.

*Thursday*: As I've told you it is very restful being with Dick. He isn't the least interested in me as a gal and that's easy. So I lay on the sofa snoozing and he sprawled on another one with the *Evening Standard*. And then we had tea and talked about poetry and the war. And then I went down to the theatre.

—◆—

*September 20th, 1942*　　　　　　　　　　　　In the train

Yet again in a train. This time en route for Andover where Dick and I are doing a big concert this afternoon to benefit Russia. R. is coming over from his camp. It is pouring with rain and rather warm. Dick

is going to play his Warsaw Concerto and then I'm going to do his
two new songs. The concert is in a cinema where they have sold all
the seats so I hope it will be a success.

You will have had my cable by now. I hope you heard the recording
and like it? The Northern Ireland tour is a very new departure for
me but it seems the right thing to do and is, in fact, rather an answer
to prayer at the moment. Aunt N. has been attacking again and I
suddenly feel I must get away. R. is in favour. He goes north next
week anyway and won't get a week's leave for some time so that's
quite tidy. What to do about the house – ? I don't know. It's madness
to keep on paying Mrs P. and yet if I do want to go back permanently
it's madness to lose her. I've no clear view of things at all and would
like to do this eight weeks and then see. I've telegraphed Gladys
Wynn Finch[1] to see if she'd like to take the house for those weeks.
Let's go back to Monday, though. Monday was THE day, the song.
It started off a trifle poorly by Aunt N. ringing up at 8 and giving
me hell about not being in the ATS [Auxilary Territorial Service]! I
took this calmly but made my decision then to get away. One can't
go on accepting things and not feeling free. Tom Jones came down
to see me at 10.30 in order to get a ride down to the train later. He
was very comforting and understanding and said I must go on doing
what I believed to be right, etc. He said that he thought entertaining
was going to be more and more important this coming winter and
that it was my job and I ought to do it.

(*Later Monday*). Dick and I went down to the studio and heard the
orchestration. We were both a bit disappointed with it because it
seemed so ordinary and of course we do NOT think the song in the
least bit ordinary! Having run through it two or three times we were
then dismissed till *the* runthrough at 7.30 so Gladys, D. and I went
very slowly on foot to D.'s club near Trafalgar Sq where we sat in
restful club dimness while they had drinks and I toyed with a lime
and water. We had an audience of two or three hundred I suppose.
Just before transmission started Dick put his hand in his pocket and
produced a small package saying it was a first performance present.
I was so touched I nearly cried. It was a little round silver scent box
– there's a little sponge fitted to it and you soak it with your favourite
scent and dab it on when you want to smell good. It's got a checkered
chasing all over it, rather like a new golf ball. Plain silver and
beautifully made. About the size of a half crown. Wasn't it sweet of
him? He gave it so diffidently too and I was absolutely delighted
with it.

[1] An American friend of Ma's, married to a Welshman.

The red light flickered on at 8.30 and we were off. Gin afterwards said I sounded nervous in the first few bars (I was too) but that it was fine after that and I must say I loved singing it. Dick played like a dream and gave me the support I needed. After it was over we signed autographs for what felt like hours and then staggered up into a warm still night and walked very slowly, arm in arm, down to the Savoy, giving a minute post-mortem of the whole thing all the way along! At the Grill Room we ordered supper and then did a lot of telephoning to see what people had thought about it. Gin said it was alright and that, truth to tell, she was so pleased to hear the song that she'd sung it *with me* most of the time! Daddy said it was lovely. Dick's sister-in-law said the orchestration was dull but that we were alright although I had sounded nervous at the start. On the whole OK. Dick insisted that I should have a drink to celebrate so I had a glass of red wine that I didn't enjoy just because he minded about it. We failed to find a taxi after this so we started walking north and decided to go to his flat and telephone until we finally did get one. And we were lucky because he got one at once so I was home about midnight.

Next day, Tuesday, I had breakfast in my dressing gown with Gin and To [Tony] and spent a happy time on the telephone to various friends about the broadcast.

I forgot to tell you that it was during the recording that Walter Legge, who is head of the music part of ENSA,[1] asked me if I'd go to Northern Ireland for eight weeks starting next week! And I said yes! So after lunch I went down to Drury Lane Theatre to see details and fill in a million forms in triplicate in order to obtain permits and passports, etc. Back to Gin's about 5 to wash and change because at 6 I was meeting Dick at the St Martin's to see the first night of *Claudia*.[2] I was waiting in the foyer and Manning Sherwin, who wrote 'A Nightingale Sang in Berkeley Square',[3] came up to me and said how much he'd enjoyed the broadcast on Monday and what a lovely song it was and I sang it beautifully. And old Louis Dreyfus, the shark of Chappells', rivals to Keith Prowse where *we* publish![4] also came up and said more or less the same thing. So that was nice and I was glowing when Dick arrived.

[1] Walter Legge produced the record of 'I'm Going to See You Today', with 'Nothing New' on the reverse side, for HMV.
[2] By Rose Franken. Pamela Brown had the name part.
[3] American composer. His best-known song, 'A Nightingale Sang in Berkeley Square' was first heard in the revue, *New Faces* (at the Comedy), sung by Judy Campbell.
[4] Chappells' and Keith Prowse – both music publishers. At this time, before gramophone records became so popular, much of a songwriter's revenue came from the sale of sheet music.

Next morning, Friday, I telegraphed Aunt N. about going to N. Ireland and asked her what she'd like done about the house in my eight weeks' absence. She really is unpredictable. As you know she always threatens me with: 'Well then I'll take the house away from you' and this time just to be different she said: 'Well, it's your house; you must do what you think best with it!' I wish I'd asked for that in writing!! I don't know what to do about the house. Gladys doesn't want it. I had a telegram from her today. Well, we'll see.

---

*September 27th, 1942*        In the train

Lunched with Daddy and we discussed the coming Irish tour. He is in favour of it and it does seem to be the right thing. After lunch I went down to Drury Lane to attend to the details of getting permits.

*Thursday*. Came home in the morning and biked up to lunch with Aunt N. She has a new line now; she's Deeply Disappointed in me! She can't imagine how anyone who knows about God can bear to be near the stage! It goes on and on and I have grown a technique for dealing with it. This is in the main: plain Silence!

To give her her due she now knows I've made up my mind and she is trying to understand it! If it weren't such a waste of time and hers, well, it would be very funny. As it is, I can and do get a laugh from it. It's so *silly*.

That afternoon R. arrived, looking so sweet and well in his battle dress and dark green side cap, because he'd come in a rush and hadn't had time to change. We spent a delicious afternoon and evening just talking and doing things about the house and he was so cosy and I do love him so much.

We went up to bed about 10.30 and as I got into it my hot water bottle had leaked all through, right through the bed on to the floor. Mrs P. hadn't screwed it up properly. We were very controlled though and brought a bed in from the spare room and made it up and were settled down in no time. There are few discoveries I like so little as a leaky hot water bottle.

Next day we both took early trains – in opposite directions.

Now that I'm about to leave the hosp I can begin to see what a tiny little world it is. Annette and Sylvia [Skimming] both find that and it gets you down if you don't keep a private life going fairly actively outside. It's the same of course in any sort of community life. Can't be helped. But if one isn't terribly busy the pettinesses and politics do get at you if you let them. The men are always alright. It's the ridiculous over-emphasis and enlargement of personal problems and gossip that irk one. After two very full and concentrated years at it I'm quite glad of a break. I've had the most charming letters from the Canadian Red Cross in London. Full of nice things. Yesterday morning I went through the wards to say goodbye to my special friends and they were heartbreakingly sweet and I think genuinely regret my going. I hate to leave them – the old lags – because they have been there for months and months and they do like to see one now and then. I've promised to write and go off with a long list of names and addresses.

At the moment I feel rather mixed about it all. I know it's the right thing to do but you know what a homebody I am and the effort to break the shackles is considerable. I'll undoubtedly get to like the company when I know 'em. They don't look very cosy – except the Welsh tenor and he is so agitated about his wife's coming blessed event in his absence that I can see I'll be nothing but a bosom to be unburdened on to.

The contralto, Maud Heaton, looks human and wears reasonable clothes and knows some musicians I know so there's a link there! If *only* Dick comes it will make the whole difference because he is cosy and easy and fun and we laugh at the same things. But I have grave doubts that he will somehow.

It's a beastly wet morning here. I've just had fifteen minutes' conversation with Dick on the telephone about details and Noël's movie last night.[1] It's *terrific*. One of the best I've ever seen. Beautifully photographed, cut, directed and acted and you'll adore it. I cried like a tap all through so what you'll do I daren't think! I came up yesterday afternoon, took tea with Gin and Tony who got back from Scotland in the morning, then dropped my bag at Chesh. Pl. and went on to the Gaumont where Stephen was waiting for me. We sat in the circle, very grand, among all the stars – Vivien Leigh and Laurence Olivier,[2] Gielgud,[3] etc, etc. Dick and Winifred (C. Dane) were next to us and David Niven and Prim were just behind. She's having a baby at Christmas. There is a wonderful performance in the movie by a woman called Dora Gregory who plays a mother-in-law, with a sleeping hairnet on – a lovely character.

[1] *In Which We Serve*, with John Mills and Celia Johnson. Coward appeared and co-directed with David Lean.
[2] Vivien Leigh and Laurence Olivier had been married two years. Their 1941 film, *Lady Hamilton* (US: *That Hamilton Woman*) had been a great success.
[3] John Gielgud was about to open in a revival of his celebrated production of *The Importance of Being Earnest*.

his company.

Don't worry about me. I'm not really in
the least bit down. It's just the
changing that makes me feel unsettled —
the packing & effort.

Much love

J.


I haven't said nearly enough about the clothes.
I do so love them all. Thank you, thank
you. And you mustn't do any more.
    I've invented a new way of wearing
a head scarfe which is SONSATIONAL and
v. becoming. Upside down like this. Point at
the top
I'm need
a couple
of pins
to moor it
    and it's very fetching.
    a bit dressy so I only use it for best.
Square or triangular scarves only and if
fringe edged, so much the better. If you ever
find a fur one that goes into an envelope I'd
love that?

September 27th, 1942

I've invented a new way of wearing a headscarf which is SENSATIONAL and v. becoming. Upside down like this [reproduced opposite], point at the top. You need a couple of pins to moor it and it's very fetching; a bit dressy, so I only use it for best. Square or triangular scarves only and if fringe edged, so much the better. If you ever find a gay one that goes into an envelope I'd love *that*.

———◈———

*October 4th, 1942*             On tour in Ireland

Well, here I am. We crossed over on Wednesday and it wasn't too bad at all. But I'll start from the beginning. I wrote to you on Sunday and Monday. I spent the rest of Monday morning at Drury Lane, finding out details and hanging about. It was raining and I've seldom felt lower! However I lunched with Daddy and felt better. Then took the 2 o'clock train home where I packed like mad and came over badly homesick, like one does, dashed down to the village to get the local doc, who is nice and human and knows I'm a C.S., to give me a certificate to say I'm in sound health to undertake the tour! Sylvie [Skimming] came up to sup and stay the night and was so sweet and cosy and made the whole difference. We went early to bed after I'd had long telephone conversations with Aunt N. and R. and Sister Millar. Next day it was still raining. Really the way nature lays it on! I said goodbye to Mrs P. and Nan did that heartrending thing dogs do – sat and looked sad at me from a corner of the drawing room. I felt guilty and mean. Let's gloss over the horrors of travel – the baggage and porter and taxi, etc. Finally it was all lodged in Gin's front hall and I took an evening dress from the top of the trunk and put it into a little borrowed case of Gin's and set off for the dress rehearsal via lunch at Simpsons with Gin, To [Tony], Maria and Kitty[1] first.

The dress rehearsal was booked for 4 but by a miracle we got it started by 3.30 and were off by 5. Final collection of labels, passports and tickets and instructions for the next day. As I was going to bed I took a look at my passport and inside it was a paper informing me that all books and papers and photographs that I wished to take with me must be censored or I couldn't take 'em. So bright and early next day I telephoned the censorship people and arranged for a caseful of Bible, etc, to be dealt with. At 9.15 I started to try and telephone for a taxi. At 10 o'clock I got one by going out and busing to Selfridges!

[1] Virginia Thesiger's half-sister.

I loaded all my stuff on board and set off for the censorship in Kingsway. Then to Dick's flat to leave my fur coat and hand stuff, for I was lunching with him, then on to Euston to check the big stuff, then back to the censorship to collect the censored caseful and at last at 11.30 to Dick's flat where I just sat and gasped! We had planned to record a couple of new songs before I left – just for our own pleasure – so accordingly we set off and it was just one of those miracle days where we got a honey the first time. In fact we did our 'Drifting' song, which you will adore, really beautifully. Then we took the record back and played it on his gramophone and it was even better than we'd expected. Then to the Belle Meunière for lunch. Melon, chicken, creamed in pancakes, fresh figs and cream. Delicious! By this time I felt quite dazed. R. had rung up in the morning and I'd said goodbye to him then. Somehow eight weeks felt eternity all at once! The train left Euston at 3, of all really poor times. Dick insisted on taking me to the station and seeing me off and was a great comfort indeed, because the rest of the company looked so awful when I saw them again in their travelling costumes.

Just get them: our soprano from Lancashire, forty-ish, helped-blonde with *ringlets* and a colossal shape. She was travelling in a little brown fur and black velvet hat and nondescript black coat. The brunette contralto is, a solid mountain of a gal who I've since discovered is only one month older than me! But she looks a good forty. She is solid, mentally and physically, and wore that day a white satin headscarf insecurely fastened in a turban, an orange hand-knit jumper, black skirt and brown and white diagonal striped overcoat! The little accompanist of uncertain early middle age was neat in brown. The cellist had the hell of a cold and wore a hairnet and a sham fur coat in cocoa-coloured curlycues. The solo pianist was well dressed in tweeds and is a lady. She is also an Irish RC and has a little screwed-up monkey face with completely unfathomable black eyes and a sense of humour and is a help to me in spite of her faith!

The boys – oh the boys – tenor, was travelling in a royal blue turtle neck sweater, grey flannels and honey-coloured corduroy trousers. He is thirty-ish and affable and doesn't tick at all but can sing like anything. The baritone is an emaciated nervous-looking Jew. He too was in corduroys but he had a rough green tweed jacket and was hatless. Alfred Cave, who is quite a well-known violinist, is also our manager where programmes are concerned. He looks like Kreisler and was wearing corduroys and a bright blue tweed jacket. Everyone looked aloof and as if they wished they'd never thought it all up. Me too! However Dick walked me up to the far end of the train and we watched a slightly tipsy and very sweet Scotsman dancing an intricate reel all by himself in the centre of an admiring company. This helped. Dick gave me an armful of papers and we were off. The journey was very long but quite possible. I had to share a box of a cabin on the boat with our soprano but I managed to get there ten minutes before she did and had a good wash in solitude before climbing up to my upper. Here I withdrew behind the shadowy chintz curtain kindly provided by the shipping company and I got in quite a lot of dozing all through the night.

We had a long and boring morning in Belfast being welcomed by the NI [Northern Ireland] representative and being lectured seriously and impressively on security by a young sergeant and finally after coffee and cream cakes in a local café we were put into our own charabanc with our baggage and sent off on an eighty-mile journey right across the island. We arrived at our destination, famous for its Air, at 3 p.m. and at the world's beastliest hotel. Here I had a few brief words with the little business manager we had now had tacked on to us. He tried to make me share a bedroom and I got grand and wouldn't! So I didn't. We had to give a concert that night after twenty-four hours of solid travelling and I must confess it didn't seem a good idea. However I got a boiling bath and two hours' sleep on a bed like a rock garden and after rather a good high tea the world looked less gloomy. The hall was huge and very well done. Lovely stage and lighting and a possible piano. I did all the compèring and my monologues and it didn't go at all badly. Mainly a nautical audience – 700 or so there, I think. We were fed afterwards in the Naafi and were at last back at the hotel and so to bed where I slept as dead till next day at 8. I spent half an hour exploring the town and thought it dull and at 11 we were off again on a thirty-two mile trip to where we are now settled for about ten days, I think and hope.

ENSA runs its own hostel here, very clean and efficient and institutional. Once again the bedroom problem cropped up and we were supposed to share three together. So Gwen Byrne[1] and I went out at once and found a very attractive little AA hotel within fifty yards of the hostel and we've each taken a single room here at our own expense and it's a great success. We eat at the hostel but sleep Alone! My room is tiny but clean and faces the sea and has running water and a very good bed and I'm in clover. We did a concert the night we got here, about three-quarters of an hour away in a little church hall. It went very well and the men loved it. You know we do a classical programme, such things as operatic arias from *Bohème* and *Butterfly* and quite a lot of Mozart and some Handel and a little modern Spanish, etc. I do all the announcing and my own stuff in

[1] The company solo pianist.

two groups. I'd no idea just how darned hard it would be to do all the announcing. You can never sit down and relax.

We travel everywhere in our own old bus. It has seen far better days but it gets there, shaking us to bits in the process. Today we had got to go forty-two miles each way *and* to two concerts when we got there! Which is silly and we are protesting. Last night's concert was in an old barn and the audience was small but *most* appreciative. One realises how very worth while it is to do the shows over here. They are so isolated and something a bit better, like our show, gives 'em quite a lot to chew on.

As I told you, Dick was supposed to come and join us but yesterday I sat down and wrote him a very long letter telling him not to and why. You see our stuff isn't right in this programme. My monologues are tolerated, last night they were much liked, but that's rare, and when I do my silly songs I have to hold back because if I let go as I can do it pulls the shape of the programme into distortion; and that's wrong. If only he and I and, say, a small very good jazz ensemble could go about together we could be a riot. But as it is it would be all wrong for him to come out and oh, how he would hate the communal life and that old bus! As you know I can stand anything and even get enjoyment out of it. But he would *mind* too much all the time and he'd be miserable. So I've written fully to him and told him all the details and I don't think he'll come. These straight musicians, being rather second rate, are very snooty about his Warsaw and our sort of songs and I just couldn't bear it if they were nasty and I think (wrong, I agree), that they might be and I won't have it!

Sunday today. A nice long lie and breakfast at 10 and now I'm writing to you in the lounge of the hotel where there is a fire and it's peaceful.

This is all being an Experience and I'm quite amused by it. If only I had a cosy spirit to laugh with . . . and to think I've told Dick not to come! He is *so* cosy and great fun – But I know I'm right.

*October 11th, 1942* Northern Ireland

Sunday morning and I'm once again writing to you from the very comfy lounge of the hotel where I've been staying for ten days. This time the room is full of holidaying Belfast businessmen suffering from suppressed conversation and only by keeping my eyes cast down perpetually and preventing any possible opening for conversation have I managed to do any writing at all. This has been a strenuous week and really there is mighty little to tell you because we mustn't say where we've been nor what we've done there and that leaves nothing much to report. The average day has been like this: bed till 10.30 which means missing breakfast at the hostel fifty yards away where the rest of the party are staying. A mercy. So at 11 I usually wander up to the Trocadero Tea Rooms and take a cup of coffee and a couple of excellent Irish scones and butter. I have stayed there reading the paper or writing postcards.

Then maybe a gentle stroll to the Post Office to send R. a telegram or get some stamps, then that strange ritual beloved of the women in the company, 'a look at the shops'. They live for this and can and do talk 'purchases' for hours on end. 'I saw a most reasonable little lace dinner frock with quite a pretty little coatee – a – well you might almost say it was a *violet* shade', etc, etc, etc.

(I looked up to see what the sky was doing and got caught up in a corner of conversation.)

I usually come back to the hotel about 12 and read or write till lunchtime. We have this at 1.30 in the hostel and there is a lot of rigid politeness that marks the true middle class of England. A lot of passing the cruet and waiting to start and chat about the morning's doings and little remarks about the food. At lunchtime we are told the time of the call – usually about 5.30, with a meal half an hour earlier. Up till now I've been coming back to my room and sleeping, reading and writing and mending. I've had a cold and not felt very like taking long walks but it's gone now and I'm beginning to want exercise. At the appointed time I go along to the hostel carrying my dress and that long black velvet evening coat you sent me at *least* five years ago and my shoes and make-up and music in a bag. Tea – usually high – and then the bus arrives and we get in and hang our dresses at the back and take our usual seats and are off on an hour and a half's drive to the camp or station or village hall or barn in which we are to perform. We travel with our own piano because the ones we find are in a parlous condition and for a programme of straight music you are bound to have a reasonable piano. As you can imagine the accommodation for dressing is apt to be a bit queer and there is never a mirror, nor a useful light! We've been lucky with stoves though, and mostly get cups of strong, sweet tea with slabs of army cake to welcome us. Then the concert. This starts by Alfred coming on to the platform with his fiddle and making rather a nice little speech explaining how the concerts started in response to many letters from members of the forces asking for good music, etc. He then says it is not a highbrow show and that many of the items will be known to the audience and opens the programme with a violin solo – probably Kreisler. And so it goes on. The tenor sings Handel's

Largo with a fiddle obbligato and then I'm introduced as compère and broadcaster and from then on I announce the items. The sort of things we give 'em are these: 'One Fine Day' (*Butterfly*), by the soprano. 'None but the Weary Heart', contralto. 'On with the Motley', tenor. Lots of Chopin on the piano, the Swan on the cello – etc. Our boys lap it up and yell for more. I'm amazed to find how musically illiterate the US ones are. To them the classics mean Victor Herbert, the 'Road to Mandalay' and the 'Indian Love Call' from *Rose Marie*! You'd have thought that radio would have changed that. They are apt to be tougher to deal with than ours, sometimes very polite but unmoved; sometimes unmoved and restless. It's no good our tempering our wind to the shorn lamb because the whole object of our programme is to give the musical few pleasure and let the rest go hang; and there are always a few who love it. The snag is that we use huge halls and you can't build up a cosy intimate atmosphere in them unless the whole house is with you. And they aren't always! My sketches are received with puzzled incredulity. They haven't the least idea what is going on. You know, it's a funny thing the way a reputation gets made – I mean we are all sold on the idea that Americans are quick. Quicker than us anyway. But it's a very surface quickness – backchat and glib wisecracks. But it doesn't tick at all deeply in the majority. And some of the officers, regular army usually, move mentally in heavy snow shoes and you despair of ever getting through to them at all! There are few lower forms of life, in my mind, than smart businessmen. They may be all right in their own vernacular but they can't speak any universal language at all and culture just doesn't creep in anywhere. There seem to be a number of them in the US forces.

It is being most interesting to me and I'm glad I came. Of course it is always more fun when things go well and it's easier too. I'm beginning to learn a bit about approach to a tricky audience. C.S. helps here. I'm afraid we have all gotten to slightly dreading our US audiences but Alfred has ticked us off and said, rightly, that this is not a very hopeful beginning. I know that if Dick were here he and I could do just the sort of thing they'd love – but not in the programme as it stands because it wouldn't be right or *artistic*! He writes to say he is coming and is going to try and arrange something about our doing stuff with another programme. I don't see how it's to be done but I'm all for it if he can because I *know* we can do the right things and, above all, make 'em sing – which would be out of the picture in our programme.

We have had three or four really super audiences this week. Mostly airmen. They have loved *everything*, including me! (They don't all because monologues scare 'em. I can usually get 'em with my little songs though!)

The company is full of copy but I can't think how to use it! The contralto from Yorkshire who studied in Prague and who retains a European accent except in moments of stress when she becomes a regular Yorkshire pudden'. I almost died when I saw her in her petticoat the other night! It was primrose yellow with a pair of black butterflies embroidered just where you wouldn't put a pair of black butterflies!

She is mad on clothes and plans new gowns all the time. 'A' think A'll get a luvly black vel-vet – just all line with nothing on it except me pearls.' The soprano has ringlets, is near to forty, sings beautifully and is an unbelievable shape. But with quite good legs – her deep pride. She has a husband in Manchester who takes her for granted and she is not the cold type, really. I did some shameless eavesdropping in the bus one night while she told all to the little skinny non-Aryan baritone. He wouldn't play properly and kept failing to return the ball and she was *so* longing to talk about herself and her emotions. He is a neurotic creature with coal-black button-boot eyes and not a glimmer of humour. He thinks he knows about C.S. and talks the most awful rot and takes cough drops and gets a little tight on a couple of Guinnesses and is rather sad. I have *not* admitted my interest in C.S. It's better not in the circumstances – specially as I've had a roaring nose cold since we came! (It's almost gone and I've been able to play every night quite easily.)

Reg writes to say that he hasn't moved yet. But he soon will. Dick says that our HMV record has made a grand start and was broadcast last week, both sides. Everyone is delighted with it and want us to do more. There is talk of our doing a show – revue? – musical comedy? The waltz we wrote for a movie has been thought to be too good for that and ought to go into a show and someone is interested in it. All rather fun. Pa writes that there is nothing to say – he's fire-watched and read and that's all.

Walter Serocold, who used to live in the village, is over here and he invited Gwen Byrne the pianist and me for supper on our night off last week. So we wrapped up against the wind and bus'd over to where we had a wonderful meal by a roaring fire and much enjoyed our four gentlemen friends and the escape from our boarding house repasts.

We've seen some wonderful country and some spectacular views and Gwen and I have enjoyed the idiosyncrasies of the singers together. They are a race apart.

Give my love to Tommy and tell him I just haven't time to write to him separately. He'll see this though, won't he? Love to Lefty too. Tell him I'm enjoying the Irish language enormously. There was a dog fight in the café where I was having my morning coffee last week and when it was over the owner of one dog looked at him and just said: 'Now, conduct yourself'! If it's fine they call it a 'brave day'; when it's not it's 'attacking weather'.

---

*October 18th, 1942*                                     Northern Ireland

Gwen Byrne, our pianist and I walked five miles out to lunch with a nice girl called Christine Burges who lives near where we've been stationed this week. It is Sunday. I read the lesson in bed before breakfast and at 11 we set off. A mild, damp day just *not* raining. It was lovely to get out of the communal atmosphere and we revelled in our escape. Mrs Burges was at school with Wiss and is the same age. I got to know her through some very kind friend of Pauli Feno's[1] who has looked after my welfare all along the line and given me introductions at every stop. This one was a real find. You know, only too well, how lovely and restful it is to be with one's own kind! The house is a large rambling Gothic Victorian number, much too big, full of lovely things and monstrous stained glass and armour just to balance. She had two nice middle aged US officers there by name of Kidd and Parkin. A really delicious lunch – scrambled egg in tomatoes, roast beef with *four* veg! and pineapple soufflé – we were driven back by Parkin and now I'm sitting on my bed in my thick blue dressing gown, even tho' it isn't cold but because it's *so* cosy, writing as much of this letter as I can before our call at 4.15. We are doing two shows tonight and have quite a little drive ahead of us, I think.

    This is a most extraordinary life really. I came out with all sorts of highflown ideas about doing a necessary job as well as I knew how. I'm in danger of falling in with the rest of the company who look on it simply as a job of work and never consider that it's supposed to be a service. I will *not* get sucked in like that. But it needs clear thinking, much getting away by oneself and a continual renewing of motive. You see the musicians in our troupe, while very good really, are none of them first class and the regular money they are getting, together with the applause of uncritical audiences, is going to their heads and they've lost their sense of proportion. Much of the business of living communally as we do is doing me a lot of good. It's not easy and I get moments of acute irritation and long to yell at them in their smug little egocentric worlds. But I'm beginning

---

[1] Pauli, an American friend.

to learn that that does no good and why bother. The singers behave like singers do in books. Specially the soprano and the tenor. They sulk if anyone else gets more applause than they do. And they fuss and fuss and can't see an inch beyond their noses. Both are very provincial and unsure of themselves really. I get on with everyone personally but I keep a bit aloof and I know that's the only way I can maintain a civil tongue! You know how fatal intimacy is. I see a good deal of Gwen Byrne, who is a lady and an RC! She is comfortably remote which I find restful and we find things to laugh at which relieves us both.

The concerts are fairly mixed in reception. This last week's have been less fun really than the week before. We moved to this small agricultural market town last Monday and found a fairly good hotel with rather scrubby little rooms but hot and cold and comfy beds and good food so we can't complain. We did a concert about twelve miles off on Tuesday. (Monday is our night off and we celebrated it by *dining* here instead of our usual high tea! Early to bed.) Tuesday's concert was rather touching: very isolated unit and they seemed to like it well. Wednesday, we drove no less than fifty miles and gave rather a good one and then home another fifty miles. This one was in a vast, old cinema, freezing cold, with hard benches for the audience. The backcloth on the stage was faded yellow with cracks and plumb in the middle was a very small painting of an oriental mosque! The piano was painfully out of tune but it looked lovely, being a grand, and helped to 'dress' the stage very nicely. We had sausages and mash after this in a very dreary officers' mess and then came home through a black wet night. Thursday we did some very touching little far-Western boys in an underground hall built from an old disused mill. The boys were starved for entertainment and while they were quite unfamiliar with the music we gave them they were very appreciative and attentive and one felt they were well worth the effort. My stuff bewildered 'em a bit but they took it kindly and loved my songs.

Our days here have been fairly dull. Breakfast about 9.30 followed by practising for the musicians and endless writing by me. I've done the first of a series of articles on the boys for the *CSM* [*Christian Science Monitor*] but I don't know if it's what they want. I'll hear next week. And of course letters. I've had lots of mail since I was here including a good one from you written at Little Orchard and enclosing such good pictures. How I long to see it all. You don't look fat to me. You look just about right – very nice. Thank you for them all.

We lunch about 1.15 and most afternoons Gwen, and Lillian Warmington, the cellist, and I have gone for an hour and a half's walk. The others have 'nice lay-downs'! Then high tea half an hour before we are due to leave. Not a very exciting life really. Most of these concerts, now I look back on them, have been very worth doing. They've been smaller than the first ones and less spectacular in success but the little audiences have been so grateful and one has been clear that it's a good thing to do. I went out to lunch with Christine Burges, for the first time, on Thursday. Her farm lorry was in with vegetables for market and I drove out in it afterwards beside a completely silent farmer who was obviously terrified by me. She brought me back herself in the trap. This is a pleasing form of locomotion, provided the weather isn't *too* anything.

Friday we gave a concert right here in the town and that went very well. Mrs Burges came to it with the Col's wife and we had a nice and appreciative audience of English Midlanders, well grounded in oratorio work from childhood. Afterwards the officers came down to the hotel with us as their mess was out of action because of repairs and we had drinks in the lounge and talked till 12. One very nice little major, who was somewhat lost among a crowd of 'raound abaout' officers, clung to Gwen and me and yesterday came up to tea with us. He hadn't met anyone for so long who spoke his own language, we gathered.

Last night we drove thirty miles to do a show in a converted cowshed. It was rather a touching little concert. The stage was minute but brave with scarlet curtains. The piano had asthma and the audience was peculiarly simple. They were overcome by my monologues and listened with polite bewilderment! However the tenor caused 'em to whistle and stamp their feet so they got what they wanted.

And that's about all I know really. I'm quite enjoying it all as an experience but you know the funny thing is that I believe I'd be more at home among straight variety people than I am with the rather refined musicians. Gwen and I giggle so at the conversation that goes on every day about what dresses we are all going to wear. Blue is never blue but 'sky' or 'powder'. We hear things like this: 'If I wear my lavender you could wear your wine and Joyce could put on her powder and Gwen her dove', etc, etc.

We move on tomorrow to the city of Belfast. I'm going to stay at a large hotel with Gwen which may well take up all my cash but I just feel I must escape from the school treat for a week in order to be able to remain imperturbable for the next rustic ones we have when we are forced to be all together. It sounds silly to you, I daresay, but somehow I find it vital to get away when I can.

Dick is coming out in November which is a mixed blessing. I'm dying to have him as a companion but there is resentment about his joining us. I must cope with it all somehow. I wish grown-up people could behave as such but it seems a vain wish in artistic circles!

*November 7th, 1942*                                    Northern Ireland

There was a letter from you this week but it took five weeks to come and was written on the first of October!

This week we are in a tiny place called Five Mile Town but it's further than that from the nearest railway. It's just a single street with shops that are ceilinged with heavy boots and floored with grain and, in between, everything else in the world. Gwen and I both had our heads washed in the sweet-shop-cum-coiffeuse and she had to lock the outside door as it was Fair Day and the cows might come in! It's the real Ireland. The first I've seen really. I went for a walk the other day and had a conversation about birds with a farmer – I've made it into a very short little poem and if I remember to I'll put it in at the end of this letter. Our hotel is just big enough to hold our party and no one else – I think there are occasional Commercials but where they sleep I don't know. I've got the best single room with a grand bed – long and soft and warm. There is a picture over the fireplace called 'Love's Whispers' that I'm fond of. And after the really creepy queer RC atmosphere of our last place, the Commercial Travellers' Christian Association Bibles in all our bedrooms here ring a note of pleasing Protestantism. I can think here. And I love the way the country breaks away immediately on either side of the single street. It's pretty country, rolling and unspoilt with tiny little white farms seething in chickens and ducks and *mud*. The people are friendly and always speak to you on the road.

*Next day.* We came on Monday at lunchtime. I had dreaded it a bit. Our rather unattractive manager, who is entirely urban, and a Jew, told us it was going to be an awful week, Nothing To Do, and miles away. I ought to have guessed it would be all right from that because Nothing To Do, being interpreted, means no shops, no movie and no café for morning elevenses. And that is what I like occasionally. Our lady singers, the tenor too, find it very dull but Gwen and Lillian and I have walked miles every afternoon and I've done a lot of writing in the mornings and my bed is good and warm and I like the way we can pop into the kitchen when we want hot water – because although there is a bathroom the water is never warm. You know how I bath? Well I've had *one* in two weeks! Of course I'm far cleaner than if I had had two a day because I have a complete wash, stark naked, every day and the funny thing is that I've gotten almost used to it! However the comforts of the Grand Central in Belfast next week will not be despised!

There's a Col. Parkin from Pennsylvania over here who has been a sort of good godfather to Gwen and me. We met him at Christine Burges's three weeks ago and when he found we were coming here and he had to be in the district he arrived at the hotel within five minutes of our bus. That afternoon he collected us at 2 and took us calling on the nearest (not very, either) camp to meet the officers. All from Minnesota, nice and friendly, not overburdened with brains or external charms but very kind and so glad to see outsiders. They are in a hut encampment and it rains a good deal. We were given hard candies and offered Scotch and then we drove away having invited the Col. and two of his lieuts to sup with us here that night. One of the lieuts – *very* good looking and with a great deal of charm, came from Charleston – is called Frank Smith. From a little place called Somerville, I think he said, just by Charleston. I wonder if the Laws know them? He is about twenty-two, I think and quiet and sweet; and an extremely nice local called Mrs Knox Brown, whom you would adore, has sort of adopted him and writes to his girl-bride and his mother regularly about him.

Mrs Knox Brown is about forty-eight, short, with grey hair that shines and a little, rather thin, straight fringe. She's a Southern Irishwoman and has those wide-apart eyes and the smile and everything else you hope Irishwomen will have after all you've read about them. We met her at a camp concert and at once she invited the whole company to tea. We went. It is a huge hideous Victorian pile full, as usual over here, of good things. Such a mixture of pictures – dim cattle standing in a muddy sunlight looking surprised, bad ancestors and then suddenly a Murillo and some charming engravings. Major Knox Brown's Great Aunt Hannah hangs in the dining room, a dream of elongated elegance in white net with Elizabeth Barrett Browning curls and a lace scarf and such a *Vogue*-like length to the whole thing. Mrs K.B. has all the vitality of a Virginian and might easily be a Langhorne! She told me of her upbringing. 'I was brought up in a smoking room by an eccentric bachelor uncle and three brothers and at the age of ten used to bring out my own cigarettes in the smoking carriage to Dublin and surprise the old gentlemen. When we went to a hotel my uncle would push me into the smoking room there and say he hoped none of the men minded having a girl in there but that I'd sit quiet and smoke and not worry them.' Can't you see her, at ten, about 1892. She told me she smoked

regularly till she was fifteen but then had to break the habit as she
was sent to Cheltenham Ladies' College! Poor child. I do wish you
could have heard her with a very soft voice and a slight brogue and
the bewitching charm. They have no money and live in this colossal
barracks of a house with two or three little maids. One called Liza
looked after us at tea in a pink cotton frock and white apron. Her
kindness, Mrs Knox Brown's I mean, was so warming. We hated to
leave but there was a concert as usual and so we had to go. But before
we went I saw an ivory fan of Great Aunt Hannah's, brought
back from China by a K.B. uncle who owned a fleet of trading
ships.

We did a big concert in a vast barn at Davina's home, now taken
over by the US. Such a mixed company – Mexicans, Harvard law
students, Californian movie men, Apache Indians, etc, etc. Not a
very quiet audience for music but they cared for me! In fact I've had
quite a good week. It's usually a sign of a poor audience, though,
when I go very well and the others only get by. It's not me talent,
in other words, but me dazzling personality and the fact that I am
not shaped like a barrage balloon! Not very complimentary, really.
But on Friday we did an English air force show and it really was a
joy from start to finish. We *all* went well and I went wellest! (Now,
look, all these details are NOT to be read out; they are for your
maternal ear and would bore the pants off anyone else.) That night
I had fans in front and they called out for the things they wanted me
to do, the first time that has happened to me on this tour. Lovely.
And then we had a nice supper with the officers afterwards and a pair
of my fans fêted me and I came away feeling warm as toast. I've told
you that our female singers are mountainous, haven't I? Well, there
was a dear little Belgian pilot at this camp and he was looking after
Gwen. Suddenly she noticed that most of our party had moved out
of the ante-room and said, 'Where are the others?' His answer was:
'The big pieces have gone on in advance.'

I had lunch with a retired general and his wife, daughter and two
granddaughters in *another* Victorian house just nearby. Friends of
Pauli's angelic Lady Stronge[1] who continues to look after me so
kindly. This house had Morris wallpaper, which I have a sneaking
feeling for, and a pair of mid-Victorian portraits of two great uncles
in sailor suits with Lord Fauntleroy haircuts that I would love to
have. There was also a flower table which is a thing I intend having
one day.[2] Just a table covered with all sorts and kinds of vases full

---

[1] Wife of Sir Charles Stronge, MP, Northern Ireland Parliament; became Speaker
in the House of Commons, Northern Ireland.
[2] She did indeed have a flower table and it is still maintained by Reggie Grenfell.

of all sorts and kinds of flowers ending, in the very front, with tiny little pots holding tiny little flowers. It's so old fashioned and gracious, somehow. Indicates a tempo of living that I hanker for and never shall achieve.

Today I am walking three miles to lunch with Sir Basil and Lady Brooke.[1] Gwen comes too. She is, at the moment, practising two doors down at the village music teacher's. I'm up in the proprietors' own sitting room. They have opened it up to us and there is a roaring fire and comfy chairs, and coloured photographs of the owner and his wife and a lampshade with pink fringe and much too much china in a locked cabinet. But it's cosy and very warm and I've got it to myself as the contralto is singing at the camp service this morning. (It's Sunday, I did the lesson through in bed and was late for breakfast at 10.15 in consequence.) The accompanist is with her and the soprano went too, her golden ringlets abob above the ship prow of her unfortunate bosom. Alfred the fiddler's practising in his room, Gwen is down the street, Lillian has just gone to church, our tenor is taking a WAAF for a walk. He met her at breakfast and is a fast worker. A Welshman. Not a very nice piece of work and almost dangerous in his incredible simplicity. But he is a bully and teases where it hurts most (the poor soprano's bosom) and where he knows he'll get nothing back. (She is very kind.) I'm afraid I find it hard to love my neighbours. Suffering fools gladly is one of the chores I've never done well. Yes, I know I don't have to *like* 'em only to love 'em. I do try but there are times . . .

Dick joins us on Tuesday which is heavenly for me. To have someone at last who speaks my own language and has some common tastes – I'm looking forward to seeing him, I can tell you. Gwen is nice and has filled a gap but we have no common tastes really and her funny little RC wall is up between our thinking all the time. Poor Dick is dreading it all! I'm glad in a way because then he'll find it less awful when he comes. And anyway he's got me, whereas I had no one when I started. It's the others. You see they resent us a bit – it's not really personal but our field is different and our popularity wider. However I'm doing a lot of work and I'm sure it's going to be all right. He's a sensitive being and minds things rather. We'll have a good chance of getting things straight slowly this week though, for the others will be in a hostel and he and I are staying at the hotel. Sounds immoral but you know me.

That is all I know for now. There are only two or possibly three weeks left to go and I'm really v. sorry. It's been fun and I like the

[1] Sir Basil Brooke, 1st Viscount Brookeborough, MP, Northern Ireland Parliament since 1929; became Prime Minister of Northern Ireland in 1943.

job. I think I may do more after Christmas. I don't know. I plan to have a week up with R. when I get back.

———◄◉►———

*November 15th, 1942*             Northern Ireland

Back in Belfast but we move south tomorrow for our final week. The news goes on being exciting, doesn't it?[1] We notice how much it affects the general public in our audiences. They are alert and heartened and concentrated instead of restless and disinterested.

Dick crossed from London on Monday night and I met the boat next morning from here. As I wrote you much earlier on I dreaded (and longed for) his coming because of company jealousies and pettiness and because my maternal bosom couldn't bear the idea of people being mean to him. Why? Well, you see he has composed this enormously famous and successful Warsaw Concerto and my little group of second raters can't give it credit as being good because – simply – it is so popular and so successful. Then the thing he and I have been sent here to do is our own stuff – our songs and the way in which we do the better sort of popular numbers – Gershwin, Rodgers and Hart, etc. This was a hell of shock to our party – and was made more awful still by the really grand success we had! I may say that though I'd tried to keep clear about it all I wasn't in the least and my mind was in a fog and I felt horrid. However the whole thing has settled down and I put it all to the credit of God! D. arrived on Tuesday early. We had breakfast and made plans and then got hold of a hotel piano and worked for an hour or so. I invited Alfred (our fiddler and manager) for lunch on diplomatic grounds and it went off all right with all three of us on our guard constantly! After lunch D. went to look at a piano and I took to my bed and slept to make up for my early rise. The concert that night was about eight miles out, a small one in a hut but with a stage and lights. We let the company in easily that night by only doing two of our songs – apart from D.'s concerto – and my monologues. No, I didn't even do a monologue that night. There was a coolness following our pleasant reception but nothing much to worry us. Next night, though, we did a large neurological hospital in a frigid hall and were a very big success indeed and it was tricky coming home in the bus afterwards!

[1] This refers to the Allied landings and advances in North Africa, which started on November 7th. Churchill ordered the church bells – silent since the beginning of the war – to be rung on Sunday, November 15th, to celebrate the event.

The *next* night was the climax. A very nice smallish hall with warmth and we arranged to go on earlier than before. For the first time we really deserved our success for we were good! And because of this – or just plain ugly jealousy – I was attacked by Gwen, and in no uncertain terms, for doing 'unnecessary' stuff in the programme. This, being translated, wasn't really directed against me but was a subtler way of getting at poor D. who comes across her path as a pianist. I felt physically sick and was low indeed. It made him furious, which was a healthier reaction than mine. But the whole thing shook me and I was grateful for it and started to do some real work on the subject of man as a spirit and about there being no lapse from harmony. With the result that the next three concerts have all been big successes for the *whole* company and not just us. Which is perfect. And the atmosphere has un-tensed itself and I'm very grateful indeed.

I'm very well and enjoying it all now. It makes the whole difference having D. here because he is cosy and easy and fun to be with.

R. writes happily. So does Pa.

———◆———

Glenarm,
Northern Ireland[1]

*November 22nd, 1942*

Here I am staying with Peg. It is so cosy and such a blessed change from hotels. I've been living in hotels for eight solid weeks and a private house is strange but good again. I've just had breakfast in bed and done the lesson and now it's nearly 12, Peg is at church and I'm in front of the fire downstairs.

I'll start the week on Monday. Or rather on Sunday after I'd sealed my letter to you. At 2.30 Dick and I went over to the Amer. Red Cross Club in Belfast to sing to the boys. 2.30 is a cruel-ish hour. We found the lounge full of sprawling figures sleeping under newspapers and the atmosphere was heavy with Sunday afternoon coma. However Miss Anderson from Nashville, Tennessee (who is very nice and first rate at her job of programme director), said, 'Just start playing and you'll see what happens.' So with great courage Dick sat down and went into 'I like New York in June' and at once there was a stir and by the end of the tune there was a crowd. A hot, not entirely un-smelly crowd. We sang, they sang, Dick played his concerto and a lovely time was had by all for a full hour. It was

[1] Seat of the Earl of Antrim in Co. Antrim. Peg (the Countess) was Joyce's godmother. The Earl (known as Ducie), was at Eton with Joyce's father.

unbelievably hard work because of the appalling acoustics. Cotton wool. But it was a success and one boy told me afterwards he hadn't had so much fun since he left home a year ago. So that was good. At 3.30 the tea dance started up in the hall so we went to watch. At least Dick watched! I had a whirl, with a sergeant, with a Californian technician who tried to date me up! With a sweetie called Ted who was formerly an Arthur Murray dance teacher and who knew his job to perfection. I was cut in on and made much of and adored it all! Dick was perfectly happy listening to the grand orchestra and watching the jitterbugs. We stayed till 5 and didn't a bit want to leave then but we had to dress for our evening show. This was an RAF one and we were a big hit! Just one of those days. Great fun. We got the most awful giggles coming home and climbing the stairs to our rooms with our arms full of rugs, rubbers and torches. It was really uncontrollable. I had to sit on the stairs and wait for my breath. Dick is the perfect giggler. He gets well away which I love, don't you?

Next day we left Belfast by our horrid old bus for Warrenpoint, down on the border, where 'the Mountains of Mourne sweep down to the sea'. Literally. It was sunny when we got there and we dropped the rest of the party at their ENSA hostel and were grateful to escape to our little Café-cum-baker's-cum-hotel around the corner. We didn't bother to unpack but went straight out to explore. In a tiny little sweet and postcard shop I found a postcard with the words of the 'Yellow Rose of Texas' on it! I'll send you one. Isn't that extraordinary? Where did you first hear it? Do remember, I'd love to know.

After looking at the shops and buying some Guinness for D.'s supper and some cider for mine we went for a walk along the front. It was just like Switzerland. There's a landlocked bay with great mountains on all sides and little villages clustering above the beaches. It was dead still and brilliantly sunny. We saw a postcard sunset and marvelled at the whole scene. Then in to our little hotel where the manageress, thrilled at D.'s presence, arranged for us to have supper in front of the fire in the sitting room. Most of the hotel is now an officers' billets and mess. We had a cosy evening (it was our night off) eating high tea and chops! and reading and talking about God. D. doesn't believe in him, but would like to. He needs to and maybe one day he will. He's not at all hard about it but just can't believe. Oh yes, he believes in goodness and spirit, he supposes; but he doesn't understand it. We sat up far too late and it was 12.30 before I turned the light off up in my very chilly room. Lino on the floor and only a single naked bulb put just where it did no good at all. But the bed was comfy and warm.

Next day. (Breakfast in bed all the week! This semi-invalid

existence is forced on one while touring. You get in *so* late at night and I must admit to feeling mighty tired after it and simply love bed for breakfast.) I wrote letters all the morning and at 12 we walked three and a half miles along the water to Rostrevor for lunch at the railway hotel. Which isn't as awful as it sounds. In fact it's lovely. A perfect *spring* day with hot sun. We sat out in it for an hour after lunch and then took a bus to a small town nearby to see what it was like. It was dreary and we couldn't find a tea shop so, by the time we finally found one, caught our return bus, dressed, drove forty miles in the bus, did a show, we were ready for bed.

*Next day, Wednesday.* Wrote letters and paid bills all the morning and we lunched at the local pub where we had (or rather D. had) drinks in the bar with the world's sweetest sergeant major, Peace, by name, from Walsall near Birmingham. He was short and square and red-headed and oozed charm. He'd done twenty-four years' service and was 'regular browned off now and wants to get home'. He invited us to the Sergeants' Ball on Friday night.

It was cold and grey on Wednesday and we took only a gentle stroll and then went back to our cosy fire where we read and snoozed and I did my nails. We had a good concert that night with a shorter journey, thank goodness.

*Thursday.* I had my hair washed in the morning and we bused over to Rostrevor again for lunch. Then bused back and read and wrote letters by the fire. One or two locals had discovered Dick's existence and copies of the concerto were left at the hotel for him to autograph. We did rather a good concert that night; the audience was rather sticky. But they liked us!

Friday was our last day there and we thought we really ought to cross over the border. All the others had several times. So at 12.30 we took a row-boat and were rowed over the loch. It took ten or fifteen minutes and was cold! We landed and walked up the little Eire village and went into the main pub and grocer's for a pre-lunch drink for D. In the pub was a customs officer and three young American technicians. They at once asked us to join them and I was forced to take a glass of sherry. (It was *delicious!*) After a while the innkeeper's wife and I got talking and she took me into her kitchen. So clean and cosy. Huge china figures on the mantelpiece, white. A painted clock and great china platters hung all around the room. There was a piano with a pink kewpie doll on it! I told her who Dick was and she was thrilled and asked if he'd play the piano. So we all came into her kitchen and I sang and the technicians sang and we had a lovely party and became great friends. Then D. and I went over to the little hotel where we'd ordered lunch and it wasn't too bad.

We crossed back about 3 and the sun had come out. I've never seen such beauty. The glassy water, the low afternoon light on the mountains, the straight line of the houses on the front like a modern Victorian painting, and the beech trees on the hills a real gold.

Our technician friends came over later and we all had tea together at our hotel before they took the train back to Belfast.

That evening was our last concert of the official tour. I'm glad to say that it was a huge success. We were all good and I enjoyed myself like anything and sang nicely too. We had a very gay time in the bus coming home, for everyone had of the drink slightly taken in celebration and there was great singing and giggles. We were rather prim in our front-row seat. Friday night was the Sergeants' Ball D. and I'd been bidden to so when we were dropped at our hotel we just went in to leave all our paraphernalia and then walked the 100 yards or so down the village street to the Town Hall where the ball was in progress. We were greeted with huge enthusiasm by the regimental sergeant major who was thrilled that we'd come and at once asked us to perform. We said we would. He made a big build-up speech and announced who D. was and then D. played Warsaw and I sang our songs and we did 'Jingle Jangle' and 'How About You' and it was all beautiful! Then D. was surrounded by fans and given drinks and I danced with the Brigadier and some sergeants and it was 2 a.m. before we got back to the hotel and there was I with not a single bit of packing done and the bus calling for me at 9.15 next morning! So I packed till 3.30 – it was the only thing to do.

Dick and I breakfasted together and then I left but he went down to Dublin later while I came on up to Belfast with the others. Rather a tiresome morning of luggage and business at the office and then farewells to the others and I gave lunch to Gwen and Lillian at the hotel. Then goodbye to them and then with a very small pageboy to carry my very big suitcase I went to bus terminus to catch a bus here – went to the wrong one first! – and finally got off at 3.15. It took two hours and I caught a flea but still it's lovely to be here.

I'm off to Dublin tomorrow for three days' jaunt! Dick is already there with a friend called Halsey Colchester. I join 'em. Then on Thursday he and I come back to Belfast and do some concerts for the American Red Cross and I then travel home to England on Monday – a week from tomorrow.

I'm very well and the tour was fun. I'm glad it's over though – I've no plans at all. R. rings me tonight and we'll talk a few then maybe.

*December 5th, 1942*          In the train to York from Edinburgh

We got into Belfast for late luncheon and then went to our rooms to rest for a big American Red Cross concert that night at the club. Poor Dick had had a sort of nerve attack the day before. Well, it cleared up completely and he was fine. But *so* apologetic. He minds not being well and does so need C.S.; but doesn't in the least *want* it! The concert hall at the ARC is a dance hall and a basketball gym as well and it holds 1500 without trying. This meant using a mike, which I don't mind, but I do like to get a good rehearsal with it because it's a very tricky thing to use and needs skill. However it went well and they loved us. We did our two songs and 'How About You', 'Jingle Jangle', 'Skylark', 'My Heart Stood Still', 'Love Affair' and 'Harvest Moon'. D. did Warsaw first. Afterwards we listened to Winston on the club library radio and then went home. By this time we were hungry so we sent for sandwiches and cocoa for me and milk for D. and had them in my room where we started talking about performing and whether the sort of entertaining we do is worth it and whether or not I'm wasting my talents. D. says I am. He says I'm big star stuff. (I warn you this is going to be an egocentric letter and for your *ear only* because I'm going to talk freely.) He says that it's a waste for me to toil around with a second-rate programme for musicians, doing hack work and delivering goods too good for the troops. He says I ought either to broaden my monologues for the troops or sing more songs that they like because it's silly to be satisfied if one has pleased six or seven bored officers in the front row when one can please hundreds of men throughout the hall by doing stuff they like. I cannot decide. It's not that I'm modest but I did feel that if one can please the minority who get left out that it was a job worth doing. But now I'm less sure. With Dick's playing we've pleased the whole house every time; but is this enough? I daresay the answer is that it is in wartime. D. was quite ruthless with me and said I was crazy to try to do so much; that I was a creative artist and that it was wicked for me to feel so driven all the time. I do, I know it. I feel I must always be *doing* something. I think it's a war thing maybe. He says that my lyrics and poems are special and that I ought to sit down and work at them. That I ought to work and work to perfect the microphone technique. That I ought to go and be with R. for a while and work by day at writing an operetta! This went on till the early hours and we both felt like rags at the end of it. Lots he said was right; but there is the question of war jobs and I *do* feel I must go on with this entertaining if it is needed. I'm made that way. He says I've done plenty for three years and ought to be still. This is, of course, an un-Scientific argument really. As a matter of fact, and just humanly speaking, I am a bit tired. Not badly so. Just sort of overstretched. But I'm very well, so don't worry. I mean this. I'm going to be sensible I swear because it's right to be.

I talked to R. on the telephone and we planned for me to go to him at York on Saturday. Dick made a proposal and I put it to R. and he said it was a good idea, so we arranged to cross to Glasgow by boat from NI on Wednesday night and stay two days at Edinburgh en route for York, in order to see Noël and Joyce Carey in Noël's new plays.[1] I may say that I shall endeavour to conceal this little jaunt from Aunt N. who could only see harm in it, I'm sure! So accordingly we got our accommodation fixed, packed and finally quit Belfast on Wednesday evening. Tuesday was just a day involving arrangements, a movie and an hour in the gallery of the local dance hall in the evening looking down on the soldiers, sailors and airmen and their girls having fun. I may say that we have been profoundly shocked by all we've seen of the behaviour of your boys on the loose. I suppose it's because they are away from home. Anyhow they drink dreadfully, oh dear, and every doorway, every park bench and even in the public gallery at the dance hall there were couples necking in no uncertain fashion. I'm afraid it was always your boys. It seems to be the accepted thing too. D. and I felt so old and wise and sad about it all. What is the future for those little Irish gals? The boys are well-off and spend freely; they get drunk and have an affair with *any* little girl they happen to find. She is intoxicated by the rush, the liquor and the whirl and quite soon he'll be gone away and she will, like as not, have a baby. Families seem powerless to cope and the churches have little influence. It's a gloomy picture. Is it true that our boys, training with you, are the same? I hope not. From a human point of view some of it is understandable. They came over here to fight and maybe to die. Well, why in the hell not have fun while they can. If it's fun. I do see their limited view. The snag is, though, that they don't die. You know I have grown so hardened to seeing drunk men about, and I mean *really* drunk, not just tipsy, that it no longer surprises me. I'm not even very nauseated by it. That is what seeing the US army and technicians (specially the technicians; and the officers too) in NI has done to me. It's an ugly picture. I wish I knew the cure. Keeping 'em busy is all right for six nights a week but they must get out in between and there seems to be no alternative between drinking and drinking.

Where was I? Oh yes, Wednesday. We embarked at 7.30 and found it was a very small but clean little ship. Slight difficulty on the dock as there wasn't a porter and we had thirteen pieces between us and two of them totally unmovable. I left D. to guard the pile and went

[1] *Present Laughter* and *This Happy Breed*.

in search, as we decided a female supplicant stood a better chance of getting aid. When I returned D. was in helpless giggles because a herd of cattle who were being shipped somewhere had been driven through, over and around him and the luggage. They were all coal black, it was blackout and he said it was only by shining his torch on his face and yelling that he was saved from being trampled to death! I spent the evening in the little lounge, sewing in the lining to my fur coat. It was hanging by a thread all around the edges. The one and only stewardess called me at 7 and I got up brightly. D. joined me in the dining room at 8 and we made a fairly good breakfast. We were, it seemed, at anchor because of fog. It was flat calm. I may say that we were due in at 10 a.m., all immigration papers and customs done. But no. After waiting a while in the dining room we went to my cabin and slumped down on either end of the bed in our fur coats (D.'s is only fur-lined) and just waited. And waited. Then we were told that a tender was coming to take us off to a coast port and we'd be sent in by train to Glasgow. We then took our places on deck, waiting to board the tender. And waited. Finally at 1 we got on and a fine E. wind sprang up. It was freezing hard too. By a miracle I was first off the tender and secured the services of the only porter – a midget, but strong. And by another miracle and the concerted efforts of all three we got all the bags and two seats in a first-class carriage in a train that was just going to leave for Glasgow in five minutes' time. Whew! Thick yellow fog blocked the windows as we crept in. I'll draw a merciful veil over the voyage, with thirteen pieces, from our Glasgow station to another, with the aid of another midget porter – female this time and even stronger than the other. We did ultimately arrive at the Caledonian Hotel, Edinburgh at 5.30 when we'd been due at 1! However Joyce Carey had booked rooms for us and there were seats for the play and it was warm at last, so we began to relax. A hurried boiling bath and my little black suit and a fresh pale blue muslin collar and a pale blue and black turban (scarf; but brilliantly tied by me!) and clean white gloves and we had a piece of fish in a flash and were off to the theatre. We hadn't eaten since 8 except for two buns I cleverly conjured up in Glasgow so the fish was vital if we were to enjoy the evening. As I've told you, Noël is touring with three plays.[1] They do them alternately and that night we struck *Present Laughter* which is a perfect piece of escapist froth, quite beautifully played and with such speed and polish. It is autobiographical really. About Noël and Gladys [Calthrop] and Lorn,[2] his sec., and the whole set up in Gerald Road. It's wildly

---

[1] These were *Present Laughter, This Happy Breed* and *Blithe Spirit*.
[2] Lorn Loraine was Coward's secretary, and effective manager, from 1924 until her death in 1967 aged seventy-three. Coward lived in Gerald Road, S.W.

funny and witty and sometimes wise and always a delight to the eye
for Gladys is good at that sort of thing. And after nine weeks touring
in NI it was a lovely jolt to see first-class work and to see an audience
that knew what it was all about! (They don't always have 'em. Noël
said Hull was entirely lost throughout all three plays.) We adored
every minute of it and so did the huge house. Then around to Noël's
room via Joyce's and back to the hotel in Noël's car. Here he left us
to sup with the Provost and we three had a very cosy table in the
restaurant away from the dancing and noise and talked and talked
and talked. My wig, I was glad to turn off the light that night. It had
been quite a day. The boats and the trains and the fog and then the
excitement of the plays. Grand. I talked to Reg on the telephone next
morning and we made plans about today. I'm longing to see him. I
slept till nearly 11 – having been called at 8 in order to telephone R.;
but I soon fell off again – and didn't get up till lunchtime. Joyce,
Dick and I had it together and talked and talked and talked. I expect
we are bores by now but we hope not. It's so hard not to talk about
the life one has just led.

After lunch Joyce went to rest because of an inoculation she's just
had. D. and I went for a window shopping tour, and while we were
out the fog lifted and it got warmer and we saw a little of Edinburgh
and it looked mighty pretty. Tea in the lounge where a three-piece
orchestra made some curious sounds but we put it down to the war
and tried not to listen. Bath and dressing.

*Blithe Spirit* this time and again so good and charming and Noël
proving his great gifts again. Then round to their rooms and back
in Noël's car with Molly Dalkeith[1]. It's hard to think she's got a
daughter of twenty, I must say. But she isn't my type really. I
suddenly knew I was really theatrical last night! I felt so alien from
strawberry leaves!

After supper in the restaurant we all went up to Noël's sitting
room where he had a lovely piano and his books and photographs
and a fire. He and Joyce have a very good stunt game they play. You
write down the name of a famous person and show it one of them
and then he or she says six or seven words and the other immediately
tells you who the person was. It's a code of course, but impossible
to spot. We tried and tried and were no good at all. Then Noël said,
'Now I want to hear my favourite song, come on you two.' So Dick
went over to the piano and I joined him and we did 'Nothing New'.
I must say Noël couldn't have been nicer about it. He said I was the
most professional thing he'd ever seen. Oh, I did like that. And that
my phrasing and line and the purity of my voice were all perfect.

---

[1] Molly Dalkeith, wife of the 8th Duke of Buccleuch.

That it was the perfect marriage of words and music. 'More', he said. So we did the waltz. 'More', so we did one called 'Drifting', which you will *adore* but it's only half ready really so we're saving it. He said nicer and nicer things and that we must write an operetta and what were we waiting for, etc, etc. It was really very sweet of him. And then I had to do monologues, and it was 2 before we left. He was in raring form and told us some wonderful theatrical anecdotes about the Lunts and we talked about the stage and it was a fair treat. He's a queer fellar, he really is. He made a sharp and beastly attack on Dick for writing film music. Noël hates movies and radio but even so it was unkind and unnecessary and I did so mind for D. He took it well though and tossed it off; but he was hurt, all the same. Noël has a thing like Aunt N. in that he can't resist hurting where he knows it will make the most sting. It's a form of bullying and power. Like some of Aunt N.'s thrusts, it was thinly disguised as a sort of praise. 'You who can do so much, who have such innate musical talent – no one knows a note of your work except Warsaw and it's all wasted on films no one remembers!' He went on and on. I put up a defence but thought it wiser not to interfere really. It was just one of those strange complex things that have some psychological reason. But I couldn't bear to see D. look all hurt inside in spite of his air of not caring. I knew. Oh dear. However this all took place fairly early on so we were able to sublimate it with anecdotes and drink before leaving! But it was cruel of Noël and what's more he knew it. You could see him doing it deliberately. I wonder if he has a heart? C. A. Lejeune[1] in the O said she thought it had at last caught up with him when she saw *In Which We Serve*. He has and he hasn't. What he has got is a colossal and complete ego. But then he has reason to be that way. He is the most talented creature since Michelangelo, I suppose. He can write, act, compose, paint and all well. And now he can make movies, even though he hates them. Well, he could not have been nicer to me. He said he knew where my talent came from too. So take a bow. He said it was the vitality and gaiety of my American side, controlled and disciplined by my English side.

During all this the Duchess sat silent and amazed. I was rather pleased that she should have seen it all somehow, though in a way she spoilt the fun too.

Newcastle and pouring rain. I've just discovered that there is no restaurant car and I have no food! However I've had some rather bitter chocolate and a fruit drop so I shan't starve. I caught the train at 10 a.m. after an early start from the hotel. We had to stand in a long queue at the station before being allowed on to the platform.

---

[1] C. A. (Caroline) Lejeune, film critic of *The Observer* for many years.

But my wily porter caught me a corner seat so I'm very comfy.

Well, all of NI was worth doing; some of it was darned uncomfy and hard and unhappy; but as soon as D. came it was fun and I must say I wouldn't have missed it.

And now back to face life again! I feel like the last days of the hols! There is so much to settle. Mrs P. leaves in about two weeks and what are we going to do with Parr's? And what is my next move? I'll know more when I've seen R. and talked it all over with him this evening. Only an hour and a half more and then we'll be in York. Did I tell you I'd written to Aunt Margaret [Phipps] sounding her about the possibility of P–Ging with her? I haven't had any letters this week so I don't know much.

I'll add to this when I've seen R.

*December 7th. Two days later.* Also in the train, from York to London. It was pouring when the train came into York on Saturday afternoon but there was R. looking so sweet and well and we got a porter and collected all my pieces and eventually landed with them all in Room 80 at the Station Hotel. There was so much to say. I talked and talked and he talked and talked and then I realised I was very hungry indeed so we put on our coats and walked up the town to a tea shop where I tucked into scones and tea cakes and jam and several cups of tea. He likes it up there and is enjoying his practical soldiering. He has a comfy room and it's warm in the mess and altogether it's a lot better than Wiltshire was. After tea we came back to the hotel and had baths and then dined and just sat by the hotel fire and talked some more till time for bed. I really am lucky to have a husband who is, apparently, entirely interested in all my doings, enjoys my career for me and is enthusiastic about all my attempts. You know we've been married for thirteen years next Saturday, December 12th.

As a present R. has had a book, leather bound, made of the poems I've written that he likes best. He has also had those photographs of me at Parr's – like the ones I sent you for last Christmas – put in now and then among me works. It's got 'J.I.G. 1942' on the cover and it's such a lovely present and so full of thought. He had it done by Bumpus.[1] He has included some very early poems that I don't much like but he does and this is really as much a present for him as it is for me. I'm so pleased with it. I brought him some very fine linen hankies from NI and a fountain pen and a Hershey's nut bar in milk chocolate. He likes nuts and milk choc.

Bused into York and out of it again on another one to have tea at

[1] Then one of the best-known London book shops; in Oxford Street.

R.'s mess. He showed me his room and I now know several of the officers and it's clear to see how much they like R. Wise men. We just missed the bus coming back, so sent for a taxi. Then bath and dinner and two large armchairs by the fire in the vast baronial hall of the Station Hotel till 10. So to bed. He left on the 8.15 bus this morning and I am now sitting in the 9.50 train. I've got sandwiches with me as I learned my lesson on Saturday by not bringing any.

We've come to no decision about anything. I talked to Barbara Mallory Burn[1] at Parr's on Saturday night and if they can get a maid they would like to take the house on indefinitely. But it's still vague. Meanwhile R. is due for two weeks' leave and we'd like to be at home for it – or most of it. I'm going to see what my mail brings me in the way of radio news and if there is any further information about the film Anthony Asquith wanted me for and then when I know a bit about plans I'm going to talk to Barbara again and propose that they get out for ten days so that we can enjoy the tail end of Mrs Proctor's stay with us.

---

*December 27th, 1942*                                              Parr's

This is the last Sunday in the Old Home. Gin and Tony are here and Laura [Grenfell]; and of course Reg. We've spent the entire week – or rather R. has – turning out and packing up and now I'll be glad to be done with it all. I hate leaving; but I'm glad to go. You know how it is.

The week began on Monday with a great deal of clearing up. That evening the telephone rang and it was Denham [film studio] telling me I was called for the following day; to be made up at 8 and on the set by 9.[2] So we went early to bed. R. had arranged with the petroleum office for me to use the car so I set off from here at 7 a.m. in pitch darkness. It was rather a long day: a scene in someone's drawing room where the ladies of the village are gathered to discuss what their pageant is to be given in aid of. I play an amiable nitwit, all sweetness and light. I was dressed in a very well-cut wool dress with a very becoming cartwheel hat and rather enjoyed myself. Penelope Dudley Ward[3] saw the rushes next day and said I looked very glamorous and photographed well! It's a tiny little part but may

---

[1] A visiting American.
[2] Joyce's film: *The Lamp Still Burns* from *One Pair of Feet* by Monica Dickens.
[3] Actress, daughter of Mrs Freda Dudley Ward.

be fun to do and will teach me quite a lot, I think. We took the whole morning to do our little scene but got it successfully after two shots. It's the lighting that takes the time; and the sound rehearsals. Puffin could not have been nicer or more friendly to me and he knows his job all right. *So* good with every one and they all like him – the light men and the cameraman and all the electricians.

Next day, Wednesday, we went up to London. I was doing a broadcast and had to rehearse from 3 onwards and R. wanted me to lunch with a business friend at Prunier's. It was cold and foggy and we caught the train ahead of the one we aimed at as it was late. We took up a couple of trunks to put in the boxroom of the flats and while we were there we saw over one like the one I'll be having. R. liked it and thought we'd make it very cosy. Lunch at Prunier was of course fishy. Afterwards R. went down to see over 21 St L.T. [St Leonard's Terrace] and go into the subject of letting it. I went off to rehearse, stopping en route at Dick's to give him a jar of American bacon (a present from the US) and a version of 'White Christmas' I'd written for him, as my Christmas giftys. I couldn't stay as the taxi was ticking. He gave us a jar of tangerines in syrup and I rushed off to rehearse. Which I did endlessly for Stephen's programme called *How?* It's a series and this edition was about how to speak in dialect, how to sing and how to read poetry, with how *not* to for contrast, and I did all the *nots* in the singing and poetry! It was fun to do but very tricky and needed lots of rehearsing to get it right. It came off rather well and was amusing I think. Daddy and R. and Gin and Maria all enjoyed it.

I had to be at Denham by 7.45 next day so arranged for a thermos of tea and some bread and butter and an alarm clock in my room. I was very extravagant and took a car to take me down and, oh boy, it was well worth it too! It fetched me at Gin's at 6.45. This was Christmas Eve. (But gosh, it hasn't felt like it *once*.) We shot till 4.30 then there was a party on the set for the unit and Puffin asked me to stay for it and sing. There was no one to play so I trotted out my only three chords, all in the key of E flat, and we had community singing and I did some songs and it was gay. R. came over and fetched me at 6. Laura arrived soon after we got home. We had supper in the kitchen. (Mrs P. has gone home for Christmas.) We went to bed reasonably early, but slept late on Christmas Day. Aunt N. asked us for tea and supper but couldn't manage us for lunch so we had a very cosy kitchen Christmas dinner with a treat of eggs and bacon and tinned fruit salad! Does it sound sad? It was delicious and a *great* treat.

Laura and R. went to church but I stayed home to cope a bit with domesticity.

We had a quiet afternoon and then went up to C. to tea. Oh, how haunted it is now. Somehow it's worse than not having Christmas at all. Judy Judge there, Alec, Bobbie Shaw and Bill (in bed with concussion from a hunting fall!), Michael and wife, Jakie recuperating from his appendix, Alice and Eliz. and a young ATS girl pilot whose name never reached me. We tea'd quietly and came home to dress for dinner. Aunt N. gave me a *very* pretty gold knot and tassel brooch and two pairs of stockings. All very welcome. I gave her some hand lotion!

*1943*

In the New Year of 1943 Joyce and Reggie left Parr's Cottage, their home for the last six years, and for the first two months of the year led a nomadic life in London. Alice Winn took over the cottage and Joyce stayed with Virginia in Cambridge Square. From there she moved to a flatlet in Knightsbridge, which she referred to as their 'boarding house', and in mid-February she and Reggie moved in to share Aunt Pauline's flat in Ennismore Gardens. However, due to her touring and broadcasting engagements Joyce spent a great deal of time on trains, while Reggie was transferred to the War Office in London, where he worked with David Bowes-Lyon.

The Allies' North Africa campaign came to a successful conclusion in May 1943 and in the same month the RAF made its first thousand-bomber attack on Cologne, followed by the Ruhr, Hamburg and Berlin. In July Allied landings were made in Sicily and Mussolini was deposed. In Russia, German forces suffered repeated onslaughts, and withdrawal and regrouping slowly turned into German retreat.

# *1943*

My Darling Ma,
Haven't heard from you for *ages*. But I soon will I expect. Happy
New Year to you all.

It is a very cold Sunday. Time 1.15. Train just due to leave Euston.
I've had a large, hot lunch in the station dining room and managed
to get a corner seat. There is no heat on and I'm glad of all the clothes
I'm wearing and my little rug. The stations over here all carry slogan
posters saying: 'Is Your Journey Really Necessary?' I know *I* wouldn't
budge an inch unless I had to. It's too darned uncomfortable. I'm
going up to do a broadcast tomorrow night and the reason I'm
travelling today is that I'm coming straight back after it tomorrow
night and I couldn't face the train twice in one day. The reason I've
got to dash from microphone to train tomorrow night is that I'm
wanted on the set at Denham on Tuesday morning by 9! My Bangor
train gets in at 4.15 a.m. And I take the 6.45 down to Denham!!
Pretty thought, isn't it!

We finished our packing at about 6 and sank back to enjoy the fire,
R. with a drink in his hand in order to finish up the bottle before we
left! Aunt N. was having a party for the hosp staff that night to which
we had to go and *how* we wished we didn't. It was so cosy by the
fire and the room looked so tidy and empty (an improvement for it
had become too full) and anyway we were tired. However, we went
and it was fun – except everyone told me I was too thin and it became
boring because, quite *honestly*, I'm not.

R. left next day taking Nan with him. It was a lovely day, hard
and cold and sunny. Two weeks' leave is almost too long because it
really becomes like it used to be and you get so used to it and suddenly
it's over and it's horrid. I didn't have much left to do at home so
after lunch I went over to the hospital and saw some old friends and
visited ward 11 and sat and talked to Edna Leishman and heard all
the local news. And then Aunt N. was having an estate tea party in

the recreation room in order that Uncle W. should tell them all what this new move about the National Trust meant.[1] It was rather sad somehow. Everyone is so *old*! Frank and Ernest and Humphries. And Hopkins and Brooks dead.

R. and I met Emmett in the woods one afternoon and enquired after Mrs Emmett. 'Deaf as a beetle, she is,' he said rather unkindly!

Did I tell you that Diana and Hubert Smith are leaving too? He has got a very good new appointment and it's got something to do with National Trust property all over England. They will be moving at Easter, I believe. Yes, the old days are definitely over. It's quite different and I don't really mind, but it *is* sad.

That evening Sylvia came up to supper with me and I washed my hair and we had a cosy evening by the fire. Aunt N. was so sweet to me about going. She said to remember that it was always my home and that I'd be ever welcome to it and, meanwhile, to treat C. as my home and invite myself there whenever I wanted to. If it wasn't convenient she'd always say so! She was really very sweet and thoughtful and touching and I was sort of pleased.

Next day I left. Mrs P. was to stay on and finally clean up and hand over to Alice on the 1st Jan. We had a touching farewell too, and she was very appreciative and sad at leaving me, and I was sorry to lose her for she's a nice, kindly creature and had done her best all the time. The house was full of sun and looked heavenly when I drove off in the taxi. Oh well, it's not forever, and inside I'm very glad about it all because I really couldn't have gone on coping alone there and I know this move is the right thing. It was just rather sentimental going, that's all. I hope Al. looks after it as we did. We put away *all* our Treasures except my books!!

I had lunch with Clemence Dane and Dick at the Ivy which was very pleasant. She is in the midst of writing a play about Elizabeth and Essex and was full of it and bubbling over when she sailed in at 12.45. (You have to lunch early nowadays or there are no seats and no food left.) She is a nice friendly creature and is always very sweet to me. She brought me a Chanel lipstick and an ashtray from the Christmas Tree we hadn't been able to go to. Very nice, too, it is.

·After lunch I went back to Maria's and read by the fire and in the evening I suddenly got up and took myself off alone to see *Watch on the Rhine*[2] which I'd somehow missed.

(There is a young Amer. officer next to me in here who is *so* restless

---

[1] In December 1942 Waldorf Astor made over Cliveden to the Trust with an endowment sufficient for its upkeep. The Astors continued to live there by arrangement with the Trust. This avoided the destruction of the estate through death duties.
[2] By Lillian Hellman. With Anton Walbrook, Athene Seyler and Diana Wynyard. At the Aldwych.

I'm going to scream in just about five seconds! He waggles his foot, he is chewing gum and he's tapping the book he is reading with his right hand. And now he is stretching. You know, this strange inability to be still seems to be a characteristic of the young men in the US army? Why, it's not just youth. There are two Canadian airmen in deep sleep in corner seats and they are of an age with this 'buddy'. Oh Lor', he's now *slapping* his book! I do understand murder!)

*Watch on the Rhine* is so beautifully acted and produced. In fact it's quite first class and it moved me far too much. Tears shot out of my eyes and fell with *sounds* on to the programme in my lap. I crept out of the theatre quite dazed and went to tell Diana Wynyard how very good I thought she was. She gives a most beautiful performance. It is a treat to see *real* theatre again. Afterwards I had a snack supper with a nice girl I know from broadcasting called Betty Hardy[1] who is also in the play. And so to bed.

I made myself some sandwiches this morning and was scared, rather, of Maria's gas stove but mastered it and then I did the whole lesson as I couldn't make church and then I packed and dressed and came to Euston and took this train which is now rattling along through a wintry afternoon in Midland flatness. And that's all to the present.

I talked to R. on the telephone on Friday and he says Nan has settled down and is loved by all the mess. He hopes his move may be quite soon which will be perfect, won't it? I think London is lonelier than the country so I hope he comes. I've hung about all week waiting to be called to the studio but wasn't wanted till next week. It's every day next week, from Tuesday.

———◈———

At Virginia's
London

*January 10th, 1943*

I've told you that the part I'm playing is that of a sweet silly woman who spreads joy and light, where'er she goes. My little bit in the street scene consisted of riding a bike down a slight hill and seeing Pempi and Larry Olivier and saying 'Hullo –' to her and '*Hullo*. You back?'[2] to Larry. This was only a small piece in the middle of a very

[1] Actress with a long career in London, Stratford and the provinces. Played Anise in *Watch on the Rhine*. Later, became a notable radio actress.
[2] *The Demi-Paradise*, directed by Anthony Asquith with Laurence Olivier and Margaret Rutherford. Pempi is Penelope Dudley Ward.

long and complicated scene introducing all the secondary characters in the movie. We did it thirteen times before Puffin passed it. The business of synchronisation – getting the crowd to move at the right moment; the woman with the dog not to mask me as she crossed the street; the car, to pass at exactly the right moment, etc, etc. We did this scene – it's a wartime sequence on Tuesday. And then the peacetime sequence, which is exactly the same except we're all dressed differently and there are no signs of war, we did on Wednesday.

--- ◈ ---

*January 17th, 1943*        London

Tuesday. I went to see the 'flatlet' – isn't that a revolting word? – and it was very nice and I took it and here I am writing in it now. It's in Beaufort Gardens which is a large cul-de-sac of immense family houses next door to Beauchamp Place, off the Brompton Road. Miss Milne, who runs this one, is a middle-aged spinster, a lady I think, and seems very nice and kind. We've taken what must once have been the drawing room. It's a good big room with two long windows and it's got its own little bathroom and a double bed that lets down out of the wall and vanishes by day behind doors!

Dick rang up to say he'd written a new tune and it was suggested to him by Halsey Colchester who had returned to NI after his leave and had said he wished he could put the clock back. 'Put back the clock,' said Dick, 'a grand title.' And I've made it into *'Turn* back the clock' because 'Turn' is a better word to sing than 'Put'. I arranged to go round to D.'s on Wednesday afternoon to hear the tune so that I could get on with the lyric.

*Later.* R. has arrived and the room looks like an old clothes shop! I may say that the *siren* has just gone and the air appears to be full of planes and gunfire. Having R. here makes the whole difference. He has gone on steadily unpacking and putting away in spite of the noise! I can't say I like it much but I keep thinking of all the Americans who are hearing it for the first time. Poor things. It's a reprisal for Berlin last night, I suppose. Blast the war. Our landlady has just been up to say that there are large cellars here if we want to go down. She is very nice and kind.

I didn't film at all last week but am due to do some this week. I've been asked if I'd like to do a test for *Noël's new film*!![1] I've said yes because it's lovely to be asked but I think the film is to be about a joke C.S. woman and while, as Daddy says, I could obviously do it very well, I don't want to! We shall see.

---

Boarding House
London SW

*January 25th, 1943*

We like our boarding house *so* much. It really does seem to be the answer to our immediate prayers. It is warm, accessible, comfy and quiet. What more? The people are nice and it feels a nice atmosphere. Miss Milne is kind and anxious for our welfare. So we are not making any real efforts to find a flat as yet. With our books and our potted bulbs and lots of photographs and an array of *Lifes* and *New Yorkers* it really looks friendly and welcoming and we are happy in it.

I asked Joyce Carey to lunch with me at the Ivy. She'd been so very nice to me in Edinburgh when I was there with Dick and she and Noël were in London having a week 'out' from their six months' tour. It was quite gay at the Ivy. We talked a lot and I asked her what part it was that I'd been suggested for in Noël's new picture and she said it was her part – the one I told you about of the silly woman who is what Noël thinks a C.S. is like! Isn't it magic? To be offered a very big part in Noël's picture and not to be able to take it from conscience *is* tough!

However I intend to make the test anyway, just to see if I could do it supposing I got the chance.! After lunch I bused down to Westminster to see Veronica Tennant at her big YMCA canteen-hostel there because I felt I couldn't go on just doing nothing (but writing) while I waited days between shootings at the studio. I offered to do some canteening and was leapt on as they are very short-handed and right then and there was poured into an overall and sat at a table to fill bread rolls with cheese-and-celery spread. I did a five-hour shift and R. came and fetched me to go up to Gin's for supper. It was curiously pleasant to feel that kind of tired for a change! You know I'm too used to being full-time busy to really be able to relax with enjoyment for long.

I did a few home chores and wrote to Tommy, and was at the YMCA at 11.45 to prepare lunch and serve it to a big bunch of sailors. Hard work it turned out to be, and when I crept away at 5.14

---

[1] The picture turned out to be *Blithe Spirit*.

I was unbelievably glad to be out of it! But worth doing and they were very sweet sailors. Only one's muscles aren't tuned in to carrying trays and it feels like harder work than it probably really is. I helped put up what are known as 'big suppers' for 150 men and this involved spreading bread for sandwiches and then filling 'em and putting 'em in bags with a sausage roll and a rock cake.

After lunch yesterday, Sunday, we walked around to Chesh. Place and collected Laura and took her off to see the new Astaire film at the Gaumont.[1] Movies now start at 3.30 on Sundays and we walked slowly along in the somewhat misleading spring sunshine (it's deep cold winter again today), and took our places in the already lengthy queue in Jermyn St. (The Gaumont's where the Capitol used to be.) Oh, how I do hate queues. They are the biggest of the petty bores in this war. We got good seats though, and were rewarded in this instance. We were in there about half an hour before the programme was due to start and presently Noël came in with Gladys [Calthrop]. I went over to talk to them and Noël says he very much wants to see my test for his picture as he is sure I could do the part! I hinted that I might not be able to do it and asked him how much of C.S. was mentioned and apparently it isn't mentioned at all in the film script – the whole thing has become the Temple of Spiritual Radiation! So maybe I can do it after all.

This second the telephone had rung and it's Tony Havelock-Allan about the tests.[2] They are starting them next week and any day after Monday I'll be called.

Noël was very nice to me. He always is. He asked after Tommy this time and as usual told me to send you his love.

We thought Fred Astaire divine but took against the aggressive bustness of La Hayworth. Really her built-up bosoms coming into high-lit focus were beyond a joke. Like the nose of a bomber – or rather, like the noses of two bombers!

I lunched with Aunt Pauline who looks well and like a small brown mole or something. She was wearing a black chenille beret with a velvet bow centre front. And a sensible black coat and shoes and was hung about with shopping bags and passes and was well and kind. She has invited R. and me to live with her at the flat! It's the *kindest* thing. It is so tiny though and I wonder how it would work out. There is only one sitting room and the bedrooms really aren't big enough to sit in. I don't know quite what to do about it. It is so thoughtful of her to want us and it would be an economy. I'll talk it over with R. tonight. If one could be quite sure of being able to get

[1] *You'll Never Get Rich*, music by Cole Porter.
[2] Anthony Havelock-Allan was a film producer; first husband of Valerie Hobson.

away or to be able to sit in silence to read of an evening it would be nice. The ideal thing is to be on one's own, but, if not, nothing could be nicer than to be there I must say. I'm rather torn to know what is best. I'll let you know what happens.

I believe our *Lifes* and *New Yorkers* are coming to an end . . .? . . .? So sad about Woolcott.[1]

------◈------

*January 30th, 1943*　　　　　　　　　　　　　　　　London

A letter from you this week. You say my letters are as slow as yours; and you hadn't had one for *three weeks*! Well I write literally every Sunday and mail it on Monday. You can tell by the numbers at the top whether any are missing. So many odd things seem to be happening in my life just now – all fun – that if you miss a week you may miss a full chapter! The photographs T. sent Daddy have come and we've devoured them. How sweet they look together, of course Wilton is *so* like Daddy. Is he in real life? The smile and mouth and line of jaw are identical. I need hardly say that Grandpa is pretty pleased about it. We had quite a difficulty in dividing up the pictures but are both well satisfied with our prizes. Wilton appears to have brains and humour. *You* must have missed him when he left.

R. and I dined in and had our high supper and found it delicious. We discussed the subject of whether or not to acccept Aunt Pauline's very kind offer to go and live in her flat with her and finally decided to say yes. So we are moving there on Feb 13th – which is two weeks from today. So as from then our address is

　　　　c/o Aunt P.
　　　　Flat 8
　　　　70 Ennismore Gardens
　　　　SW7

Aunt P. is very sweet and most pressing, so we have said yes with pleasure. It will be very comfy and a good deal cheaper for us than having a flat on our own. I've written to Aunt P. saying I'll be doing a certain amount of writing and can do it in my room as I feel it's important to be able to get away, from the start!

[1] Alexander Woolcott, American critic who had just died aged fifty-six. He was the original of the character Sheridan Whiteside in *The Man Who Came to Dinner*, by George S. Kaufman and Moss Hart.

Wednesday. By the afternoon post I got the test scenes for Noël's picture, so I tried to learn my part! Rather good little scenes. One lovely one where Sylvia – my part – lets go and says what she's thought about things for a long time. She is a spinster of thirty-five-ish, date 1927, and has a slight accent. This is before she has heard of the Temple of Spiritual Radiation. R. and I dined in that night and I read him my efforts and performed the test scenes to him and he helped with the cues.

Thursday. I went to Fox the costumier to see the dresses for the tests. They have bought an entire wardrobe belonging to a deceased Australian millionairess. There was a wonderful selection of 1927 dresses. The picture is to be in Technicolor and Sylvia is obviously a girl for buffs and beiges, so we finally chose a little georgette number with orange and brown chenille dots in a band slap across the bosom and across the hips where the waistline was kept in 1927. I'm doing my hair in tight plaits over the ears and will look *awful* – but authentic I think.

I still don't know whether to do the part, even supposing I get it. They are testing six or so others so goodness knows. As I told you she is a ridiculous figure who suffers and grumbles all through the first part but who gets hold of Spiritual Radiation (C.S.) and becomes a ray of sunshine and gets better! My latest line on it is that it is perhaps better for me, who knows a little about it, to make the part as inoffensive as possible, rather than let someone else ridicule and make it awful. I don't know. Daddy doesn't know either. I'm going to do my darndest in the test and then let God decide for me! I can't. I don't especially want to do it really. I'll look awful and except that it's an acting part I could do, I think, in my head, I'm not really very interested in it. It would be good money, I expect. I don't know.

Gosh, I don't really know anything about it. It's all very confusing. But I'm going to let it solve itself.

I called on Daddy in his office and we laughed a lot because, what do you suppose now? I've been offered the part of a lady doctor in a serious hospital film!!

It's getting to be funny, I do think. I saw the script of this film and while its subject is to attract girls into the nursing service, my part is too full of blood transfusion and stiff lipped gallantry in raids, and I can't see me doing it. However I don't know . . . Isn't it queer, though? All that remains is for me to be asked to do a phoney life of Mrs E. [Mrs Baker Eddy]! I think it's very odd, I really do.

*February 3rd, 1943*          London

I'm sure you are right about being *still* and leading a normal life. The trouble with the theatre is that it is so abnormal and the life *everyone* leads today isn't particularly normal. It's the day-to-day not knowing about tomorrow atmosphere which, of course, if rightly understood, is as it should be, isn't it.

I know so well that I can of myself do nothing. It is only when I sit back and let things happen – which means, really, letting God do it – only then do things happen rightly.

Don't worry about me, will you? There isn't anything to worry about. I'm fine and I do love being busy – and I'm just beginning to learn that running round in circles isn't necessarily activity!

I do truly try to leave things to God and I know it isn't easy but at the same time I know it's the only way to do.

Ireland taught me quite a lot and I went through the whole lot of inner conflicts, as I wrote you. Daddy says that *the* hardest part of the whole of C.S. is to know what is right. The law of adjustment is a comfort here though, for if one's desires are entirely honest and without motive, even if one *does* take the wrong step, God's law of adjustment won't let you go far and turns you back on to the right way! I mean, one can try quite hard to take the wrong step – innocently! And if one's desires are only for right, all is taken care of.

I've just read this through and I'm sure it reads as if my life was dogged with dark temptations but I promise you it isn't! By the 'wrong step' I mean jobs and one's way of life. Not the 'worse than death' it implies!!!

I'd meant this to be just a note but I see it's only 9.30 a.m. and I can't do the telephone calls I want to do for twenty minutes so I'll write a little more. I rose at 5.45 a.m. on Monday to go down to Denham for the test for Noël's picture. I went by underground and bus and was rather surprised to find that people are still sleeping in the underground stations as they did in the blitz. They looked very squalid and tousled at 6.15 when I got there, poor things.

My Technicolor make-up was interesting but ghastly. Remember I was supposed to be an anaemic spinster of thirty-seven and the year was 1927. My face was a dull grey with no lips and no brows or lashes – I mean no colour on them. In fact, far *too* natural. I looked quite awful but authentic. The scene I did was good to do from a theatrical point of view, ending as it did in an hysterical outburst. I've no idea whether I was frightful or quite good. I just don't know. But I do know that the director made me play it quite differently from the way I'd seen it in my own mind. He may be quite right but it's a little putting off to do things completely opposite. (What a sentence!) So I just don't know anything.

In the afternoon I hurriedly cleaned off the Technicolor face and was made up for some shots in *Demi-Paradise*, where I was dressed as Nell Gwynn in a pageant, a slight contrast to the 1927 dress with its high waistline and my ear-phone hair. This time I wore a huge black velvet picture hat and a list of golden curls and looked ravishing! But I expect I'm as good as invisible in the picture as I was simply atmospheric background.

Pempi Dudley Ward and I came home together by underground. She's a very sweet creature. R. was in when I got back and I told him all about it in detail. He is wonderful and appears to be really interested in it all. Oh dear, I just couldn't be interested in his old City stuff, when he used to come home bubbling with it. However he seems to delight in all my doings and it's such fun having him there to tell it all to.

———◆———

|                                   | Flat 8,                    |
| *February 14th, 1943,*            | 70 Ennismore Gardens,      |
| *St. Valentine's Day*             | SW7                        |

We have moved in here today – a taxi loaded down with bags and bulbs in bowls and loose books, R.'s suits, a mirror, a rug rolled up full of things we couldn't get into cases, etc, etc. Aunt Pauline has been so welcoming and cosy. She has put us into what used to be David and Rachel's room and it is right by itself and has its own bathroom and cupboard space and a sort of bow window that looks very hard but is quite comfy really. And we've got our own radio and our books and photographs out and it couldn't be nicer. It's a very gay room with pale green walls and light chintz like the country. Gertrude, who used to be Barbara's [Bevan] parlour maid in the far off days, is the general here now and she is, I think, fond of us, so that's welcoming too. It is Sunday today and R.'s day off, so he was able to make the move less awful than it would have been alone.

Since we've been in, R. has finished setting his cupboards in order. Aunt Pauline is writing to Rachel at her desk. I'm in the very deep and comfortable sofa writing to you.

We are in for supper.

*Later.* We've just had it and now Aunt P. is playing patience while the news is on. R. is reading this morning's paper and I'm writing to you. We had a delicious dinner of mutton and cauliflower and apple whip. I'll be going to bed quite soon as I've got a very early morning start – called to the studio by 9, which means being called at 6.30, breakfast at 7 and then off by underground to Uxbridge from South Kensington. Then a bus out to Denham. I'm doing another scene as Nell Gwynn in the pageant sequence.

◄●►

*March 22nd, 1943*                                    London

Three letters from you in the past two days. One sent to Pa's and another two to Parr's. I'll answer your questions right away, while I remember. Finance. Our position is good. I'm earning a lot on radio and filming, so please don't *dream* of worrying. I really do mean this. I don't need a thing. Scarves for the head are a lovely refresher to one's wardrobe but I don't need anything. I am NOT sitting up late and I don't really know what I could have said to make you think I was. I should think our average lights out is 10.30 or earlier.

◄●►

*March 28th, 1943*                        70 Ennismore Gardens

We dined at the Normandie with Aunt P., Pa and Nico and Mary.[1] Hadn't seen them for ages until I ran into Nico on a bus a few weeks ago and found out they were back in London. He is very thin now but looks remarkably young and is in high spirits. When he was stationed in the district outside Bournemouth two years ago he made friends with the orchestra at the big hotel and all over the weekends he used to perform with them. And was a riot. However HQ got to hear of it and wouldn't let him go on as he was wearing the uniform of the Brigade of Guards! He says his singing over the mike is exquisite! And his rendering of old numbers like 'Some of These Days' and 'Blue Shoes' just tore 'em up. Mary looks a little older. She's completely happy, leading a dead quiet life of domesticity. She

---

[1] Nico and Mary: Mr and Mrs Nico Llewelyn Davies. He was the fifth and youngest son of Arthur and Sylvia (née du Maurier) Llewelyn Davies, and one of the 'lost boys' whom J. M. Barrie adopted. He and his wife, Mary, had one daughter, Laura.

and Laura, who is now rising fifteen, run an allotment in Campden Hill and she doesn't seem to ask any more of life. However, Nico does; but they continue quite happily with him gadding and she gardening. After all I suppose R. doesn't like life as I do and we get on fine. But I don't go out without him very often. I've always thought that was one of the things that you and Daddy did that widened your gap. If he'd gone out more and learned to like it and you'd stayed in more and ditto . . . Well, I suppose not. All the same I do think continued goings out alone don't do a marriage any good. I go to music alone and there will always be parties that R. won't enjoy which I'll adore. But as a *basic* rule I think separate outgoings are a mistake.

R. and I gave ourselves a long-awaited treat and went to see the new Black show called *Strike a New Note*.[1] The general idea is youth. My golly, there are none of 'em, except the comedian, over eighteen, by the looks of it. Such pep and vitality. Rather frightening in its hardness but refreshing in a way, too. The comedian is Sid Field, a discovery. He's one of the funniest funny men I've ever seen. He's never the same for two minutes and he has the vital attribute of poignancy. He's made one of those overnight hits you read about. Been touring the provincial halls for years too. But now he's discovered and has turned out to be a treasure.[2] Afterwards we dined at the Ivy and it was very quiet and no one to look at!

———◈———

*April 25th, 1943*
*Easter Sunday*                                                    London

The mystery of my film continues. If you remember I wasn't *too* happy about it anyway. Well, the part gets cut and cut and in the end I'll get my money it seems but probably *not* do my guaranteed number of days. I couldn't mind less. But I do rather resent the enforced idleness. Tho' tell the truth, it's not been in the least idle on account of D.'s domestic troubles and I've kept plenty busy doing housework and spring cleaning, which has saved my sanity.

*Monday* of last week: Big start of the week – housework up at

---

[1] George Black, impresario, with a career in variety and a long association with the London Palladium, presented *Strike a New Note* at the Prince of Wales's on March 18th, 1943.
[2] Sid Field, in his first West End appearance, was an immediate hit. His 'feed' was Jerry Desmonde. The show ran for a year. Field's success was brief: he died in 1950.

Mortimer St.[1] – laundry and the start of spring cleaning the spare room. In between we sang a lot. Dick and I went to lunch at the Gargoyle where I'd never been before. In my youth it was always thought to be so giddy, wasn't it? It was decorous as a tomb on Monday, with good food and peaceful surroundings. We did some very blatant eavesdropping on a character in a green turban with ringlets and a forty to forty-five horse face, who told her girl companion her dreams of writing. She was entirely unselfconscious and burbled on about it all – and then went over to education and talked about the 'tots'. I'd forgotten anyone ever did, outside the cynical covers of the *New Yorker*. She had all the language – 'psychological handling of their tiny problems', 'guiding their eager approach to Life', etc. The friend was solemn and rather good looking and a little embarrassed by the gurgles. But she took it well and I'm *afraid* she knew D. and I were enjoying it all – although we tried not to let our interest show.

Thursday, I went up to D. about 4 and we finally finished off the top room. He hoovered while I dusted and the whole place was a prize of gleaming beauty when we left off. I was in the mood for work so I did the stairs and I don't believe Chree can ever have touched them during her administrations! I swept till I choked and then dusted and felt very virtuous at the finish.

---

*May 3rd, 1943* London

The telephone rang and it was Dick, returned from four days in the country. Would I come up? So I did and straightened the flat and made tea and went with him to buy his rations in the next street and then came in again and experimented in cooking asparagus and they were *wonderful*.

He had been far from well while he'd been away. Nerves. But it scared him good and proper and so he is going into a nursing home at the end of this week for a fortnight's observation and treatment. The whole thing is nerves. He's perfectly alright one minute and then completely exhausted and abysmally blue the next. It's no good me talking to him about C.S. He doesn't want it – doesn't know or want to know what it's about. So I never discuss it. But clearly, it's no good him going on like this. He must get right. At the moment he is at Torquay with Victor Stiebel who has a week's leave. They come

[1] Richard Addinsell's flat. Addinsell's housekeeper, Chree, had left.

back on Wednesday and D. and I may do a recording before he goes to his nursing home on Saturday.

*Thursday*: Hunt's Agency rang up to say that they had a German housekeeper who might suit D. so I arranged for her to come to his flat and went up there to help him interview her at 11.30. She was an amiable smiling lump but he took against her eyes – said they were too small. However, we thought it as well to look into her references for you just can't be too snooty nowadays and she wasn't bad. So I wrote off to her, having failed to get an answer from a reference tel. number she'd given Hunt's, and asked her to let me know how to contact her former employer. Since when not a word. So I conclude she took against the whole thing. Which may be as well.

Thursday was the opening of Noël's eight week season. Dick had arranged for R. and me to have seats, for it was very difficult to get in and the agents weren't given any tickets. All allocations came from Noël's management.

Noël's play *Present Laughter* [at the Haymarket] was a riot. I'd loved it when I saw it first up in Edinburgh but I liked it even more this time. It's about wholly immoral people and it's quite without any edifying purpose or moral but it's brilliantly written and played and never lets down for an instant.

Everyone was there as you can imagine. We dined afterwards at the Grill Room and Noël was there with Joyce and his new leading lady Judy Campbell[1] and they had a table for about ten and sat taking congratulations from everyone who passed by. It was very gay and glamorous!

---

*May 9th 1943*                                    In the train to Cambridge

*Thursday*: D. got back from Torquay on Wednesday evening and we talked on the telephone. He had had lots of sun and rest and felt a bit better but had had a couple of bad times down there and was seeing the doctor the next day. Joyce Carey was lunching with me that day and D. asked if he could join us which was lovely, so we all went to the Ivy and had a very pleasing table facing the door so we didn't miss a thing! I got there early and D. had already arrived, having come straight from the doctor's. He is much relieved because he

---

[1] Judy Campbell played Joanna in *Present Laughter* and Ethel in *This Happy Breed*.

really has been what Gert would call 'queer'[1] and has been worrying a lot; it seems it's his blood pressure. He just hasn't got any! It accounts for everything really and the doc says it's easily put right but that he must go to the nursing home and have treatments, etc. So poor old D. is better already just for knowing what it is. We had a very gay lunch and saw a lot of people and sat on talking for a long time. Then we set off together down Shaftesbury Ave and were shop-gazing and talking when Binkie Beaumont[2] caught up with us and we stood gossiping on the corner of Wardour Street for quite ten minutes and caused a crowd to collect for we got into a sort of football huddle and giggled! Binkie *is* Tennent's, the theatrical management that has put on Noël's plays. You can't get a seat for any of them. It's fantastic. Joyce is playing the C.S. part in the film I wrote you about that I tested for. She is a nice person. After our street gossip she and Binkie left us and I accompanied D. to Jacksons [grocers in Piccadilly] to pick up his rations and then went back to Mortimer Street to do a bit of tidying. I don't know how it is that men get places so messy so quick. He'd only been back twelve hours and the place was in fine order when he returned for I saw it before he left. Victor Stiebel had been there for the night and between them it was in a fine state: ashtrays full, magazines in disorder, no washing up. I soon straightened it and then went home and waited for R. to fetch me before we went to have drinks with George Mercer Nairn[3] and wife.

R. and I went with Gin and Tony to see Noël's other play, the family saga called *This Happy Breed*. It's not as good as *Present Laughter* but it has a certain quality. Noël is dead sincere in it and it's full of little touches and observations. Judy Campbell as his wife gives a beautiful performance; Joyce is good as the hysterical spinster who is made better by C.S. and Noël – well, he's Noël and you never quite forget it. He is very moving as the older man and you never lose interest, but somehow it doesn't quite come off. We dined at Quaglino's afterwards and it was packed. No room to dance and the food, though good, took so long to arrive. We got home about 12 and fell into bed.

*Saturday*: I'd arranged to go out to Mortimer St to help get D. off to his nursing home, but I wasn't to go till he'd got rid of Chree. He kept ringing up and saying in desperation: 'She's *still* here and she's been crying again.' However he did get her away at last with all her

---

[1] Gert and Daisy, a Cockney double act performed by Elsie and Doris Waters, sisters of actor Jack Warner.
[2] Director of H. M. Tennent, Ltd, the main theatrical management of the time.
[3] In 1944 succeeded cousin as 8th Marquess of Lansdowne. His father was killed in action in 1914 and his mother, Lady Violet Mary Elliot, married secondly Lord Astor of Hever.

bits and pieces and I got there about 11.30 and there was plenty to be done. He was packed by 12.45 and we'd arranged for the porter from his father's old secretary's London nursing home to come and fetch the stuff later and meet him at Victoria in time for the train, and then we went down to his club and had a lovely cold ham and hot veg. I went to Vic. with him and saw him off and he was very sweet and dazed and sort of helpless and grateful. He looked better merely at the idea of bed and no worries for a fortnight!

---

*May 16th, 1943*                                              London

*Tuesday*: Every day this week I've sent a letter or a postcard or a magazine or something to D. who is in his nursing home in Sussex. He's very easy to write to and I found myself storing up incidents and things I heard to put in the next letter. R. helped with FO stories and my two days at Denham were full of theatrical news so it was rather fun. He is better. Gets low, he says, but is benefiting by the rest and sun. (It's turned wonderful again.)

I was called to the studio on Tuesday and we did a short scene in the first aid room with the lady-doc, giving a blood transfusion to a factory hand who has been in an explosion! We had a real lady-doc down to show me how to do it. She was very nice and capable and quite attractive looking and you'd never guess she was the head of all the transfusing in Southern England. It wasn't a late day so I dined in and went early to bed, for I had an early call next day and that means getting up here at 5.30.

A longer day this time and further shots in the first aid room with me giving out confidence and benevolence in your navy blue Bergdorf jacket with the scarlet line around the yoke. I quite enjoyed it all and found that what you'd said about making people happy by knowing that joy was a true and permanent quality helped me a lot. The day before I'd been irritated by the second rateness around me there!

*Thursday*: D. sent me proofs of 'Someday' to check for words; he'd done the music corrections. He wrote cheerfully. I arranged to meet D.'s father's late secretary's hall porter at Mortimer Street to let me in to do a bit of work on the flat. It was a boiling day, so, when the porter had gone, I took off my skirt and my best blue shoes and borrowed an old pair of D.'s slippers and put on my apron and washed the kitchen floor!

I'd been longing to do it for ages but D. never would let me and this was my chance. The sad thing is that it didn't look much better when I'd finished. Then I dusted everywhere, put away the washing which had arrived and sat in a heap. Then I rested in a very comfy armchair and wrote an account of the afternoon's chores to D. before meeting R. at Swan & Edgars before we went to St John's Wood to dine with Bertie and Joan Farjeon. Heavenly evening, hot and still. We had a good supper cooked by Joan and then just sat and talked very happily till 10.

*Friday*: To the BBC at 12 to see Stephen Potter and discuss a new *How* we are doing together. Then I walked along New Ox. St. to the Ivy where I was lunching with Joyce Carey. I do like her so much. She's a real person and I find her companionable and easy! We talked of this and that and suddenly of God. I told her, under oath of secrecy!, that I was a C.S. and she said she'd long thought it had 'something'! We went into it a little and I was glad.

Here is a sweet story for you to tell anyone who thinks we don't do well among the Indians!

In North Africa the Indian forces were canvassed for volunteers for the parachute troops. They asked what distance they'd have to drop from and were told 600 feet. They went into a corner and discussed it and then representatives came back and said that if the drops could be reduced to 300 feet they'd join the paratroops. It was pointed out to them that the parachute couldn't open nearly so well at 300 as at 600. 'Oh,' said the Indian, 'we didn't know there would be *parachutes*.' Isn't it sweet?

---

*June 5th, 1943*                                          On the train

I lunched with Dick at the Étoile in Charlotte Street and was I glad to see him. He looks much better and *is* better, but he isn't right yet. He's got to go slow for quite a while. Anyway, he is much better mentally and that's the main thing. We talked without ceasing all through lunch and had the most delicious Dover soles, and the sun shone into the restaurant and it was all very nice. Afterwards he and Winifred and Basil Wright[1] and I went to see some Indian Dancers[2] at the Ambassadors Theatre. They weren't very good and the oriental

[1] Basil Wright. Film producer, concerned with John Grierson and others in the development of documentary film.
[2] Indian Dancers: Rafiq Anwar and his Company.

music gave Dick and me those absolutely agonising giggles that you get only in a church or where you know you mustn't. It was torture, and until I got a hankie out and chewed on it hard I really was beyond control. Winifred, on the other hand, was entranced, but Basil on my left covered his face with his hands and just shook in very well governed silence. I couldn't help letting out little snorts, and that quite undid D., who nudged me in a pleading way to shut up. There is nothing so enjoyable, in an awful way, as real giggles. It was the unexpected sounds and scooping half or even quarter tones of the music that killed me.

Afterwards I went back to Dick's and we had tea and I made up the spare bed for Halsey Colchester who was arriving on official leave from Ireland. Then back to dine with R. and mighty early to bed for we were both overcome with sleep.

Next day I worked on the script for a broadcast with Stephen for next week. This time it is 'How to talk to Children' and it should make quite an amusing programme, I think. I'm writing half of it.

I lunched with Anna Millar from the hospital at home. She was up for the day and we had a good old gossip about all the people there. The hosp has closed down completely for the moment and the sisters and doctors are all undergoing a complete field training which leads them to suppose they will be sent overseas after this.

---

Staying with Phyllis & Phil [Nichols].
Lawford Hall,
Manningtree,
Essex.

*June 13th,*
*1943 Whitsun*

Last week. Monday. I went up to the BBC in the morning. Then at 2, I went to D.'s flat and gave it a good dust over and straightening because he was coming back from his family's the next day. Then at 4 I went to the BBC to see Stephen and work on our broadcast, which was also next day.

*Tuesday*: Up to see Stephen again at 12 for a final check on our material before the rehearsal at 2.15. You see I wrote half the script. I lunched with D. at the Étoile. He was in a slight state because his father is supposed to have angina and will die at any time but doesn't know it. He is a very old man. Even so it's not fun really, is it? But it showed me how *much* better D. is, for, in spite of this, he is fundamentally so *much* less nervous, and took it all with philosophy.

I had to hurry away at 2 for the rehearsal. Collaborating with Stephen is fun and we hope to do some more. After all it was my first programme – script, I mean.

*Thursday*: I was a little dazed and remote all morning – not enough sleep. I lunched with Joyce Carey, at the Apéritif and enjoyed it a lot. She is so intelligent and cosy and nice. We talked at length about D. and she said she thought I was good for him which pleased me.

*Friday*: morning, I went down to C. to see Aunt N. and Uncle W. It's the first time they've been back for ages. He's been in Jura and she's been in Devon and I hadn't been down since I left at Christmas. Rather an ordeal I found it. *So* sad. Alice is keeping Parr's very nicely but it isn't the same sameness. Aunt N. was very sweet to me and seemed in good form. Uncle W. looks miles better. It was a hot day and I biked down to the cottage to collect some music while Aunt N., Michael and Alice played tennis.

After tea I had a taxi to take me over to Enid's [Lawson] where I did yet another Wings for Victory.[1]

---

*July 4th, 1943*  In the train to Sheffield

Your gardenia-y letter came a few days ago and filled me with envy. How lovely it all sounds. Once again I repeat the old feeling I've had since the war began – It's a good thing to me to know you are in Tryon and at home. I love knowing you are there. For heaven's sake don't go and join the ARC [American Red Cross] and come over here. You would be entirely wasted. The whole organisation bristles with tough efficiency and quite clearly the main requirements seem to be the constitution of an ox and the ability to do without air or sleep. *Don't* you do it. If anything, there are too many people here.

This train is going to be packed and standing room only. I came up to King's Cross by bus, dragging a case and by skill and good fortune managed to get a seat in a First. But I can see there won't be a space of any sort in a minute. I'm in a slight daze having been up till 2 o'clock at Noël's party. Which was terrific; but more later.

Yesterday was Saturday. After lunch I joined D. at his club and we went back to Mortimer St to really get down to three days' accumulation of unwashed china and general chaos, for he'd had Victor Stiebel staying with him and was having him back and John Bryson too, so three beds to make up as well! It was quite hot and

[1] Special events organised by the National Savings Movement to get people to save more.

we worked hard. D. is *much* better and he admitted it yesterday with such surprise. I left him about 4 and went back to the flat to change, before going to the theatre with him, before going on to Noël's party. Reg was fire-watching so was confined to the War Office from 9 yesterday till 9 today. Noël was giving the party to celebrate the second year of *Blithe Spirit* and the finish of his own present season at the Haymarket. He gave it at the Haymarket and we were bidden to enter through the stage door.

As we walked up Suffolk Street we could see a cluster of fans with autograph books clustered at the door. 'Here's where we are humiliated by non-recognition,' said D. to me and we went on. But far from it! They asked us both for our names by our names so they certainly knew us. Victor was absolutely delighted, because they were all so busy mobbing us that they completely ignored Dame Anna Neagle and Mr Herbert Wilcox[1] who entered the stage door behind us!

*Everyone* in the theatrical world was there. All the old familiar faces – Lilian Braithwaite, Fay Compton, Irene Browne,[2] Leslie Banks[3] etc, etc, and Diana Wynyard and Fanny Day[4] and all the rest! – Lots of the newer ones whom you don't yet know. Managers and movie producers and stars and authors, etc. Ivor Novello came right across the room to tell me how tremendously he loved the songs and how he'd worn out three records of them already! Which was nice. Our eyes were all out on stalks just staring. The party took place in the foyer behind the stalls and there was food and drink and lots of incredible heat. Noël greeted us warmly and he is such a good host. After about an hour and a half of standing and talking, and I must say I enjoyed it all, we sat on the floor and Noël sang his wonderful new song which is called 'Don't let's be Beastly to the Germans' which is very brilliantly witty and full of his very best edge. Then he sang about four or five old songs, and then he suddenly looked over at me and whispered – would I do something? So of course I said yes, and began to tremble like a leaf and didn't dare pass it on to D. who hadn't heard the whisper or seen the look and who might, I felt, leap up and vanish if he had time to reflect on it. Noël sang two more songs and then called on us. We did the waltz first and it went *beautifully* and then 'Nothing New' and they clapped and

---

[1] Anna Neagle and Herbert Wilcox had been inseparable for some time. He would soon produce some of her greatest film successes, including *Spring in Park Lane*. Joyce anticipated her DBE by twenty-six years.
[2] Irene Browne succeeded Fay Compton as Ruth in *Blithe Spirit*.
[3] Distinguished actor (1890–1952), especially between the wars.
[4] Fanny (Frances) Day: American-born actress and vocalist.

clapped and I must say it was very exciting for they were a very sophisticated knowledgeable audience and it was a good test.

—————◆—————

*July 11th, 1943*　　　　　　　　　The Flat [Ennismore Gardens]

I last wrote to you in the train on the way up to Sheffield last Sunday. The concert was a success and there were 2000 people there. I rather enjoyed it. R.'s regimental orchestra and I were the whole programme. It was a 'Holiday at Home' show put on by the civic authorities in the big modern city hall which is lovely for sound. I wore your grey lace again. It's *the* dress in my wardrobe and looks pretty, I'm told. I'm happy in it which is the chief thing *and* it packs. Lace is so practical for my job. One can't get things pressed at hotels nowadays so I'm really forced to stick to your grey until it falls apart.

*Wednesday* three days later!
　Gosh, I'm sorry but there just hasn't been time till now and even now I don't know if I shall have much to get down to this letter in.
　When I got in on Monday morning D. rang up in a small-boy voice and said he was sorry but he had jaundice and no one to cope, and a friend of his called Halsey Colchester, on embarkation leave, staying, so of course it was my high sign to bus up and deal with the situation. Which I've been doing for three days, with Winifred [Clemence Dane] to do the cooking which she does miraculously; and now at last, today, we've got a very nice motherly nurse who is taking over. But you see *why* I haven't had time to write! R. and I had to dine out on Monday with his nice Colonel and I've been coming up to D.'s flat at 10 each day and staying till 7, washing up, dusting and generally housemaiding. Thank goodness I was free and able to do it. I had planned to do another hospital tour but it got postponed so I've had three days free and it *is* a good thing. Winifred has managed meals and I've stood by. The idea is that with jaundice you feel low. But he hasn't and I've been doing my bit about it!

—————◆—————

*July 25th, 1943*　　　　　　　　　70 Ennismore Gardens

The big excitement this week was the safe arrival of your *lovely* parcel. Everything in it is perfect – the skirt, both sweaters (*so* warm for this winter) and all three headscarves. Such a lovely surprise and quite the making of the day. Simply *lovely*. Thank you *so* much.

Nothing very much this week except box-and-coxing with D.'s nurse to let her have time off for he has had a setback and once more is in bed again and been feeling very low and sad and sorry.

*Wednesday*: Pouring day. D.'s in the morning and he was up, rather wobbly, but the doc (a young experimenter, as it since turned out!) urged to him to make the effort and said he should visit him, the doc, that afternoon in Harley St. I went off to lunch with Stephen Potter to discuss the re-broadcast of our 'How to talk to Children' programme next week.

*Thursday*: It seems D.'s specialist was horrified at the treatment ordered by the young doctor, his assistant, and by D.'s lack of progress and put him straight back to bed with lots of pills and diets, etc. As D. only wanted to be allowed to be in bed he was delighted, for he had been feeling like hell. And he had had a bad night. I spent the morning with the ENSA people at Drury Lane planning the tour I'm doing for them next month, starting the 2nd. All hospitals. I'm not much wiser about it all now but undoubtedly I shall be when the time comes.

I spent the afternoon up with D. while the nurse went out. We sat and read in pleasant silence, broken by quotations, from each other's newspapers, or the wonderful bound copies of the *Sketch* D. had bought earlier this year.

*Friday*: Did all the ration shopping for D. and his nurse, and did some of my own chores at the same time Then at 12.30 I went to the Nat. Gal. to hear Myra play two Mozart concerti with the New London Orchestra on the occasion of the *thousandth* concert there! There was an enormous crowd and the Queen came too. They broadcast half of the concert. Darling Myra looked so happy and played like an angel. The artists' room was full of flowers and telegrams and the atmosphere was exciting and proud.

I spent the afternoon at D.'s, reading and setting tea, and I had to go off at 5 to take the chair at the Poetry Society's weekly reading. A great waste of time I thought it but it had a certain collector's-item sort of amusement for me. Very earnest and rather precious. The subject of the day's reading was 'Childhood' and the early part of the programme was very good and well chosen but we deteriorated with A. A. Milne's whimsier works and I was glad I had no one's eye to catch!

We dined in that evening and I did some of my washing. Early to bed.

*Saturday*: I ironed all morning and then had lunch locally before going up to relieve the nurse. Poor D. had had a rotten night and a

poorish morning and was asleep when I took over. So I just sat and
read till he woke up. He was better when I left about 7. We'd had a
peaceful afternoon. I think he just likes having me about and I'm
happy doing the odd jobs. Winifred has retired into a nursing home
for a rest. I've just talked to D. this minute on the telephone and he
sounds much better.

------◆------

*August 1st, 1943*　　　The Flat [Ennismore Gardens]

Tomorrow morning I go up to Manchester to start my week of
ENSA hospitals. I can't say that I want to go one bit. I hate to leave
R. and right now I've been able to do quite a bit for D. who is still
very sick and miserable. But I said I'd give 'em the month of August
so I can't break my word and off I go tomorrow morning. Bank
Holiday too, to Manchester. I'm being reckless and staying in comfort
at the Midland. I just couldn't face a hotel with a lot of unknown
women. I'm going as guest star to a musical unit and they are already
out together. I've no idea what any of them are like. But I soon will!
I've spent all this afternoon washing and pressing and packing and
now I can sit down, knowing my desk is cleared and all the main
part done.

Rather an enjoyable week it's been.

Last Monday I went up to Mortimer St to see D. and had some
lunch with him off a tray. He is still in bed and looks mighty yellow
and thin and doesn't feel a bit good. It's supposed to be a particularly
heavy attack and he isn't strong at all so it's got him down rather.
However he is, literally, entirely different when I'm there, and he
does perk up and I can lift him out of it, I think. True, this is only
temporary and isn't really in the least Science but he does, I think,
feel something solid and safe in me and he does like to know I'm
around.

I read him the bit from your letter last week about wishing he'd
go over to you and recuperate in Little Peach and he was so pleased
at the thought and longed to be able to do so. I am still quite sure
that the moment hasn't come to mention C.S. to him. He is far too
interested in his health to want to deny it! He is, now, at last,
beginning to be a little bored and a little scared about himself and if
ever the time comes that I know is the right time I shall talk to him.
But until it does I know very well that I can do far more good to
him by keeping my own thought clear and not arguing with him.
For it would mean arguments and I couldn't do it. He is madly

opposed to anything in the least like what he believes C.S. to be and
he isn't in the least interested in things metaphysical or spiritual. So
I shall leave it. Someday he may ask me what it is that I've got that
keeps me happy and well and even and then I'll tell him like anything.

———◆———

*August 8th, 1943*                                    In the train to Bristol

I seem to live in trains these days and I wish more people would heed
the official notice up in all the stations: 'Is Your Journey Really
Necessary?' Mine is, but theirs, at the moment, isn't. It's the holiday
season and crowds pour all over the country and are a hell of a
nuisance to people who must travel. I think there should be some
form of priority travel vouchers for us because unless one has the
time to stand in line for one or two hours before the train comes into
the station there isn't a chance of getting a seat. I came down from
Manchester yesterday in order to go down to Bristol today, for the
*day* if you please, to record a broadcast and then take a train back
north to Preston tomorrow morning to rejoin my hospital entertainment unit. I had to miss out last night's concert because it was
otherwise impossible to fit in all the journeys. Then Liverpool, then
finally, Chester. I love it you know.

———◆———

                                                    The Adelphi Hotel,
*[Undated]*                                         Liverpool

Oh. I must tell you what has just happened to me. Two American
sailors called Ralph Anderson, Minneapolis, and Ed Thomas, San
Francisco, liked the look of me and have just tried to date me up!
They are both young and gay and a little fresh but I showed 'em I
was the old-world type and now I'm to be their Momma while
they're in Liverpool and if they get really lonesome and need me they
are coming to find me here! They wanted me to go dancing with
'em this afternoon and I nearly said Yes and then thought better of
it, because I know I couldn't keep up with them and anyway it isn't
quite my style. I've seen a picture of Ed's wife – Dotty from NY –
'You should see the build of her. Whee!' and heard about Ralph's
Polish mother and Swedish father and his six brothers and two sisters.
He is, he tells me, the slow sort – picks the girls slowly and carefully

and then he doesn't get bitten. All this has happened in twenty mins.
They have gone in search of dates.

*August 28th, 1943*                                    Chester

We travel with our own little strip of footlights which plug in anywhere
and immediately transform an ordinary room into something more
exciting. Lighting is *so* important. So, of course, are acoustics and oh
gosh, the piano. On this evening all were good. It's rare. Pianos are
beyond a joke. We had one last week entirely without any Gs in the
bass clef. And often we get permanently operating loud pedals and they
are rarely in tune (pianos, I mean). Friday night was fun from the word
go. The whole show went well and I went *beautifully*! Afterwards there
was a surging round and much autographing and all in all it did the ego
a power of good. I came away in a glow, and found a mouse in my
room which shook me slightly. But I was cheered again by a call from
Dick at 11.30 p.m. just as I got into bed, with some heartening news
about Evelyn Laye[1] singing our new song. He sounds much better at
last though he inadvertently cracked his head on the mantelpiece the
other day, which was a pity. But he says he is up half the day now and
the doctors say he can go away in a week so he is beginning to feel
encouraged. It's been *so* long.

Yesterday was Saturday. Grey and wet. I meandered in the town
all morning doing chores.

*September 7th, 1943*                            Argyllshire,
                                                 Scotland.

I got back from the hospital tour on Sunday and had an awful time
at Euston. R. was working or he'd have met me. But as it was, there
were great crowds and no porters and *no* taxis *and* the train was an
hour and a half late. Very discouraging. I did finally get a taxi, sharing
it with a small naval cadet with white eyelashes who was paralysed
into blushing silence by my company.

---

[1] Evelyn Laye was at this time in the short-lived Hammerstein–Romberg musical,
*Sunny River* (at the Piccadilly), in which she played Marie Sauvinet. At Christmas
she would play the Prince in *Cinderella* at His Majesty's.

*Next day*. I did some washing and ironing and then, about eleven, went up to see D. who is really better. He was up and dressed and was taking me for lunch for his first outing. A big excitement. But there was a lot of work to be discussed before that as I was going to do two big broadcasts on Sunday and we had to plan what I'd sing, and see about orchestration, etc.

*Tuesday*. I lunched with Joyce Carey at the Ivy. She was full of questions about ENSA experiences, for she is off to do six weeks in *Blithe Spirit* for them as from yesterday – And who do you suppose is playing opposite her in Noël's part? Nick [Phipps]. Isn't it lovely for him? You know he's been out in North Africa with Bea and Dorothy and Vivien Leigh, etc, and was a great success.

---

*September 9th, 1943*          In the train to Salisbury

ENSA want me do a nine week tour of garrison theatres with Anna Neagle. *Three* new broadcasts came up. The dates became a little involved and then suddenly Winifred telephoned and I told her I was slightly confused and she said I was mad not to get an agent to cope with all my stuff, that I was a star and needed looking after, etc, etc!!! So I lunched with Pa and told him I had an appointment with the very nice man who handles all the stuff I do with Dick and looks after Celia and Bertie, etc, and asked Pa if he thought I was right? And he said yes.

I saw my agent around 4 and had a long heart-to-heart with him.[1] He said I was mad to go out for nine weeks with ENSA at this time of year but that anyway I couldn't do the whole tour because of my radio dates; so he'd offer me to them for two weeks and if they liked I'd do that to help them out but that I couldn't do more. We talked money and I find I ought to have been paid much more than I am because I write all my own material. So as from Nov 1st he is going to handle me. He talked of a very exclusive, 'special' bit of work on the halls, maybe!

I came away feeling somewhat relieved. I think it is a tidier idea.

Virginia and I Dutch-treated ourselves to lunch at the Apéritif. She has written me a new silly song and possibly a second. We gossiped together and then I went to see Aunt N., who had fully recovered[2]

[1] He was Aubrey Blackburn, who looked after Joyce's bookings till he retired: 'A very happy relationship – no contracts, simply an understanding.'
[2] 'Fully recovered' refers to her involvement in a court case. She had asked a friend in the American Red Cross to bring over some items of clothing; her letter was opened by the censor and she was ordered to appear at Bow Street where she pleaded guilty. She was fined £50 with £10 costs.

and was full of G.B.S., whose hand she's been holding this week since Charlotte died. She says he is wonderful and very spry.

I did some writing that afternoon and then tea'd with Dorothy Toye before meeting R. and Aunt N. and Ronnie at the Playhouse to see *Mr Bolfry*.[1] Very enjoyable play, full of provocative ideas and beautifully acted.

Last Monday I did a hospital for ENSA and as usual, none of the instructions were right and we went to the wrong place first. ENSA is notorious for being third rate, inaccurate and a mess. We all hate it and it's a great pity it's so rotten for it *ought* to be so good. But it's run by *fifth rate* people and their standards are low. It is peopled by little inefficient ex-variety managers who are scared to death they'll be found out so they keep involving things in order to remain busy. It's a wonderful thing really and a great scandal. The mere name of ENSA stinks and deservedly. I'm afraid it's too late to get it sorted out which is sad – it would take years. In fairness I must say that I think the straight plays are handled well; the straight music is OK, but it's just plain entertainment, under which I appear, that is such a mess.

Pause, here, while I had a sleep and read a little.

---

*October 11th, 1943*                                    London

It's Monday and I ought to have written my letter yesterday on my way back from an RAF concert in Wilts, but we all got chatting in the train and I didn't do it. Here it is now. Monday night and if I don't get it off tomorrow I know it won't leave for days, and I do want it to, so I'm going to write as much as I can before I go to bed and if it's a bit measly you'll understand, I know.

*Later.* We have just had a delicious supper in the kitchen, washed up, filled the bottles and set the breakfast and now I've left Aunt P., Phyllis, Phil and R. to listen to the news in the drawing room while I write to you. I hate the radio news and am always glad of a good reason to escape, as Aunt P. likes to hear every word all through and it gets me down.

Last week was rather less busy than I'd anticipated because I had a cold and cancelled three days of concerts in order to get it right. I

[1] Comedy by James Bridie with Alastair Sim as the Minister and Sophie Stewart as his wife. Opened at the Westminster Theatre, August 3rd, 1943. Transferred to the Playhouse.

spent the first day indoors and sewed and read and rested and listened to the radio and it was heaven!

*Next day, Tuesday.* I was much better and at 12 I went up to see Dick who had returned the night before. He is *so* much better. Fatter and quite brown and in wonderful form. We talked and talked and he played some new tunes to me including *the* most lovely special waltz for me. I'm in the throes of writing the lyric and *I think* it is going to be called 'My Heart's as Light as Air'. It's very gay and so lovely to sing. I'm mad about it. We went and had lunch at the Belle Meunière, an old haunt, where we were welcomed back with warmth, and everyone commented on his health. Then we went back to the flat and talked more and I had all the new tunes played over again and again and finally I went home.

That evening I worked on the songs – one is to be a march – and we dined in. Weds. I had a perm on my fringe and it needed it, I can tell you. This took all morning. I then lunched with D. at the club and, after buying his groceries, we went back to 25 and worked over the lyrics I'd written. He made some good suggestions and we got a lot done. At 4 I went to have tea with Miss Glasgow who is head of CEMA – Council for Encouraging Music and Arts[1] – and I'm going to do a week of Land Army Gals' hostels in Sussex during November. We dined in again.

God has provided D. with a treasure called Mrs Henstey who was once a housemaid at the Strathmores, later a second nurse to Princess Eliz. and now is a widow and – so far so – touch wood – she is wonderful. She cooks and cleans and washes his clothes and he expects her to vanish in a dream any day now but she's been there a full week and all is all right so far. Wonderful, it really is.

---◆---

*October 24th, 1943*          In the train to Salisbury

R. borrowed my pen and forgot to put it back in my bag so it's got to be pencil, which is a bore. Sorry. He was filling in the little book he keeps with details about the songs and their finances and I suppose he put it on the desk and I forgot to look for it. Do you ever listen to Gracie Fields' broadcasts? She is said to be mad about our waltz

[1] Mary Glasgow was previously an Inspector of Schools; in 1939 she became Secretary-General of CEMA (actually the Council for the Encouragement of Music and the Arts, the forerunner of the Arts Council), a post she retained until 1951. She later became an educational publisher.

song and sang it all over the ME [Middle East], a week or so ago and has taken it to America, so do let me know if you ever hear her sing it. It is doing very well here and I had a pleasing cheque from the Performing Rights Society last week which gave ample proof of this.

It's a lovely day and I'm going down to Salisbury to give a programme to some ATS [Auxiliary Territorial Service] officers over at Bulford nearby.

———◦———

*November 8th, 1943*           The Flat [Ennismore Gardens],
                               London

Quite a lot to tell you, chief of which is the very thrilling news that I'm going overseas for eight weeks in the New Year to sing in the hospitals! I don't know the details because they are not settled but I do know that I'm going alone with an accompanist and that if – which I'm afraid is unlikely – he is well enough, Dick *might* be it. Anyway it's not with a company which is beautiful, and it's all being done on Noël's recommendation. He is just back from doing the hospitals out there and says there is lots of work to be done there and that it can only be done by solo artists with the personal touch. I went to see him about it last week at Gerald Road and he was *so* nice and helpful and encouraging and said I have just the right qualities for the job and told me it was the most rewarding thing he'd ever done. I'm sure it is. R. doesn't mind me going as it's for so short a time. Originally the ENSA people wanted me to sign on for six months but Noël said that was ridiculous, for one couldn't keep fresh for so long and it was far better to go all out on a condensed tour. I'm all for that too; so is R. Daddy is delighted. Aunt Pauline is thrilled and already going into her trunks and producing quite unwearable garments (Rémonde in 1934) with such kindness and interest! I haven't told Aunt N. yet. Dates aren't settled, nor exactly where I go but probably, Algiers, Egypt, Sicily and I hope Iraq! As I rate stardom I shall be flown, which is an additional luxury and makes it easier.

I know you won't like the idea of this trip at first but you will as you think about it, I'm sure. Lefty will be jealous of me, I bet! Maybe you too?

R. had flu and has been in bed ever since but is loving it and hasn't felt ill once since he took to bed and enjoying the rest, which I think he needed probably. He reads ceaselessly and listens to the radio and eats everything and is very cheerful. In fact having a cosy rest. So, I'm not fussed and the doc who was in this morning says one more day in bed and then he's to get up a bit.

*November 14th, 1943*                                        London

Since writing last week I am not much further advanced in my plans to go overseas in January, but alas it is now sure that D. can't go because the doctor says he really isn't well enough. When I wrote last Sunday I was very doubtful of his going but I saw him on Tuesday and he said that he could and would come, and my heart leapt up, for you see it makes the entire difference to me if he is there – not only because he plays so divinely but because he is cosy and we speak the same language and on a trip like this those things are a big help. He got very excited and we began making plans. He had to go and see his doctor again on Friday and the doctor found his blood pressure was down again and his liver still wrong and he says it would be madness for D. to go. So there it is and I don't know who I'll take. I wish now, of course, there had never been any talk of him going because I had begun to count on it and now feel very let down. However there we are, so it's no good fussing. I want to be back by March 1st because there is a chance we may want to do our musical show in the spring! So far we haven't found the book but D. thinks he's got the right man to write it and I'm to do all the lyrics and D. the music. There is a great deal to do before I set off. Clothes, passports, inoculations (ugh) and a million details so I'm not going to fix up any concerts between December 16th and the time I go as I want a bit of breathing space. I think it will be terrific hard work and I want a rest first. Besides there is Christmas.

*Wednesday.* R. got up in the morning and we went for a gentle little totter up to the park and back. We lunched down in the restaurant and sat by the fire all afternoon.

At 4.30 we tuned in to a programme in praise of D. and his music. It was *so* nice. I was proud. We sat and heard it and were increasingly impressed by his versatility. They played some of *Love on the Dole* film score, and the school hymn from *Goodbye Mr Chips* and his March of the United Nations, and a bit from our MOI short called *Colour* and his men's marching song written for another army picture, *Hold Your Hats On.* They then said he had met me and begun our collaboration and played both sides of our HMV record. To finish the half hour they gave us Warsaw and said just the right things in it. It was a most satisfactory programme and he was as pleased as pie with it. So was I. One thing that pleased him specially was that the factory at the back of his house had the programme relayed throughout the works! (They usually only play the two work-music broadcasts at 10.30 and 3 each day so it was quite a tribute.)

*Friday*. Dentist at 10.45, then some shopping at John Lewis to get some lace to make underwear (no coupons needed) as mine is in rags and I must have some to go away with. Then I lunched with Victor Stiebel to discuss the dress he is going to make for me to go out with. And while I was there (at the United Universities Club) D. telephoned me which was very unexpected somehow and it was to say he'd just seen the doc, and couldn't go. He was very low. So was I. The whole project seemed to lose its lustre somehow. Victor was very sweet and encouraging when I told him. I had to rush afterwards to do two quick concerts and I didn't feel much like it and it was cold and rainy and, which just goes to show something or other!, I was particularly good and the concerts were a big success! I couldn't have felt much less like doing them either but I did a bit of thinking and it was all taken care of in the wonderful way it always is.

*Saturday*. Do you remember me telling you about my radio fan who sends me eggs? Well, for sometime past he has asked me if ever he comes to London one day, would I lunch with him and I said of course I would. He isn't fit for the army it seems but works for the Ministry of Agriculture and is now settled in the heart of Dorset. Well, Saturday was the day, Monseigneur at 12.45 the time. I'd no idea what he was like and couldn't think how we'd meet. When I got there I looked around and couldn't see anyone very likely. Suddenly a little tiny man came up and said: 'It is you, isn't it?' and it was my fan! Oh, he was so sad somehow. *So* small and so shy and so sweet. We had lunch and I kept hard at it or the conversation would have died at birth. We talked about the songs I sing on the air, and the tour I'm going to do and we ate a lot and after coffee he said: 'Er, have you got to – er – dash away – or could you – could you come to the pictures with me before I catch my train back to Dorset?' So we went to the Plaza and saw a piece[1] about two radio script writers with Mary Martin (whom I adore) and then he had to dash for his train back. Just think, he'd *stood* for four hours all the way up and would probably do the same all the way back, all just to

---

[1] *True to Life*, a film comedy in which Mary Martin starred with Dick Powell and Franchot Tone.

give me lunch. Isn't it *awful*! Oh dear. I do hope he had a nice time. I did my best but I felt rather bad at it somehow. Isn't life sad?

*November 18th, 1943*                                        London

By the way, Noël is coming your way fairly soon, en route for South America and West Africa, etc, etc. If he has time and remembers it he *may* telephone you, but you know how it is and he very well may not. I wanted him to tell you about me going overseas and he says he will but I shouldn't count on it.

 *Saturday.* At 10.30 I met a girl called Viola Tunnard[1] at my ma-in-law's in order to see whether she could play the piano adequately and would do as an accompanist for me for the trip. And I very much hope and think she will. I liked her at once. She is quiet and competent and, praise be, speaks the King's English – which does, let's face it, make a difference! She is pretty – dark with a very white skin. Rather shy and rather diffident, which is attractive, and I liked the feeling of her.

Queens Hotel,

*December 5th, 1943*                                        Birmingham

I'm up here with Kay (Tennant) Elliot[2] who is head of the National Council of Girls' Clubs and I did two shows for her yesterday at Redditch, nearby, and we go over to Wolverhampton to do one this evening. I've just had breakfast in bed and I'm wallowing in luxury. I've got an accompanist called Grace Shearer with me and last week we did four days of Land Army Girls' Clubs in West Sussex.

*December 12th, 1943*                                        London

All the letters I'd been awaiting rolled in last week and all were entirely out of sequence but still there they were and it was mighty

---

[1] Joyce and Richard Addinsell heard about this pianist at the Star Studio, where they recorded their songs.
[2] Wife of the Rt Hon. Walter Elliot. In 1948 she was created a life peeress.

nice to get them. Four, there were, and they came in on four successive days! I suppose it's the censoring that holds them up. In reply to your question about warm things that you asked me to cable you about: I can make do for this winter, I truly can. They are getting thin and I darn a good deal but there is wear and warmth in them to last me out. You see, that wonderful blanket dressing gown you sent two years ago is still as lovely as ever and will continue to be for many more to come.

Oh, the hot water bottle! *There* is a welcome item! Gosh, I nearly died when it arrived. *Wonderful*. They are rare as birds of paradise here. I'm saving mine for travel as one can't take a stone one around and yet it does very nicely at home. I'm so thrilled to have a rubber one again! Thank you *so* much. You do spoil me – you really do. I'm what's known as the Envy of My Friends! Thank you.

Last week was by way of being a restful one in which to get organised for the trip to the ME [Middle East] but of course it turned out to be full to the hilt and rushed by in no time at all.

---

*December 22nd, 1943*    London

This is not going to be the letter I'd hoped. There just isn't time. I've been warned by ENSA to be ready any day after December 24th and yet I may be hanging around here for another ten days. No one knows. *Mais c'est la guerre.* But in the meantime I'm madly busy collecting my clothes from the cleaners and Mrs Wollgar – she has altered the corduroy suit and it's a dream. *And* I'm doing a big broadcast tomorrow of which I've written half the script so you see there's plenty to do. I'm going to dash through the doings of last week and then mail this otherwise, if I try to keep it till I've time to do it properly, it will never go. So here you are in brief: Rest of Monday. Work with Stephen Potter on tomorrow's radio script. It's 'How to Give a Party' and we are all doing a collaboration on it – literally. I write one sentence and he writes the next. As it's all in dialogue form, it works out neatly and realistically – so *we* think.

*Wednesday*. Myra and Howard play on two pianos Nat. Gal. lunchtime. To ENSA at 2.15 for second big injection. Came home afterwards. It took rather concentratedly and I had a nasty night. R.'s train was three hours late from York. Arrived here 10.15.

*Thursday*. Recovered rapidly. Tried on dress at Stiebel's and it's lovely. Victor came to see it and gave me lunch at his club afterwards. Rehearsed Viola at 37 Chesham for an hour.

*Friday*. ENSA at 11 to see about passport and get some information if poss. but no one knows anything. Another inoculation at 12.

———◆———

Last letter of 1943               The Flat
December 27th, 1943         [Ennismore Gardens]

We've had a delicious Christmas here in the flat alone and, oh dear, we have enjoyed it so very much more than if we'd been to C.! But never breathe that to a living soul! I had the good excuse of expecting to leave at any moment although as they hadn't sent my passport by Christmas Eve I had a good hunch I wouldn't be off till well afterwards; but I wasn't admitting that, in case I'd have to go down to C. Oh, isn't it awful to feel that way! It's not as if we did anything more glamorous by not going. We just had a cosy time.

*Friday*. Christmas Eve. Spent the morning collecting my travellers' cheques from the bank, buying a glass decanter for Dick as a first performance present for *Alice in Wonderland*[1] due that afternoon, and then had a final inoculation and at 1 met R. at Antoine's on Charlotte Street where we lunched before going to the first performance of *Alice*. T.J. was at the restaurant, lunching with two civil servants and his daughter Eirene who works in Cardiff.

Being a children's play, *Alice* opened at the afternoon performance.

We sat next to Joyce Carey and her mother Lilian Braithwaite. It went off fairly well with a few of those agonising hitches expected and usually endured at such things. D. was in a state – suffering like mad over the delayed entries. It is all a little long and a little pedantic but it has had a good reception and is completely faithful to Lewis Carroll and Sybil Thorndike as both the Queen of Hearts (in Part 1) and the White Queen (in Part 1) is grand. And Zena Dare is very chic as the Red Queen. Little Roma Beaumont, a discovery of Ivor's, and since your day, is perfect as Alice. We went back to D.'s afterwards and he was very down, having felt it had sagged. It had rather, but only because of being too long and not well enough lit. We did our best to encourage him and I think we succeeded. R. and I went up to dine with Gin and Tony and we gave each other our presents.

[1] *Alice in Wonderland* and *Alice Through the Looking-Glass* opened at the Scala on December 24th, 1943; adapted by Clemence Dane; music by Richard Addinsell.

I spent part of Christmas morning telephoning. Aunt N. was so typical! Said she couldn't understand why we weren't at C. It was so odd of us not to want to – she couldn't get over it, etc, etc. I explained about being on a standby call from the plane but she didn't want to be told why. She was alright and only slightly dug at me for being on the stage. But added that she hoped I'd be cured soon. And I said very firmly that I very much hoped I wouldn't. She pretended to be very shocked at this and said wouldn't I rather be a practitioner, and I'm afraid I told the truth when I said no. I also said that we must practice C.S. in the way we best saw it and she did agree there. Oh dear! It no longer gets me down but it does bore me rather. However, she is, I think, fairly fond of me and I'm fond of her when she'll allow me to be.

We had a very cosy lunch and after we'd washed up we listened to the King on the air. Then R. and I walked home where I did up my presents for Winifred, Dick, etc., whom we were going to see that evening, and R. had a doze. About 7 a car came to fetch us to the Churchill Club, where I was going to do an act for the Christmas party. It's a very grand Allied club meant for the intellectuals in the forces and is very well done. Barbie Wallace and little Mrs Randolph Churchill[1] run it and you find people like Margaretta Winchelsea and everyone you can think of waiting on the table. There were about 300 there that night – English, Americans mostly, but lots of Canadians and other Allied forces too. It was nice. Iris Bently came to play for me. Barbie's son then drove R. and me to Winifred's. Her room in the flat over a fruit shop in Covent Garden looked so gay. The grand piano was covered with presents in piles and each pile had a candle on it with one's name on it. Winifred had done most of her parcels up in bright yellow paper. It was so pretty. We had a delicious hot buffet supper, goose again. Dick was there, John Bryson, of Balliol (who is a great friend of his). Gladys Calthrop, Esmé Church[2] who produced *Alice*, Joyce Carey, Victor Stiebel *and* the Lunts![3] Big excitement for me. About five other people. She [Lynne Fontanne] remembered you well. They were so nice to me and, for your motherly ear, Alfred Lunt was very impressed with my stuff, for I need hardly say that I performed. D. and I did all our songs and several others and I did monologues. And it was all very cosy and intimate and we had a grand time. R. enjoyed it too.

[1] Pamela, daughter of Lord Digby. Later wife of Leland Hayward and, after his death, of Averell Harriman.
[2] Actress and director (1899–1972)
[3] Alfred Lunt and Lynne Fontanne. They were appearing in London in Robert E. Sherwood's *There Shall Be No Night*, which opened at the Aldwych on December 13th, 1943.

D. gave me a perfectly lovely little enamelled eighteenth-century box for my dressing table – or bag. I'll fill it with cold cream, I think – perfect for travelling for it's just the right size for my bag. Winifred gave me a book, some 'Peggy Sage' pale pink polish! *Gosh* and a couple of little dressing table dishes! We left about midnight and Joyce, Gladys, R. and I *walked* home. Not a sign of a taxi and the buses and underground had stopped. I can't see you being much of a night bird in London these days! It wasn't too bad, for we'd all known we'd probably have to and put on the right sort of shoes. It was a delightful party and so was all of Christmas.

*Boxing Day*. We had another slow idle morning, with R. taking hours over Vim-ing the bath and doing the shoes to the perfection he demands! I wrote some letters and darned some vital holes. Then we lunched at the Apéritif and sat next to Elsie and Doris Waters – 'Gert and Daisy' – and we talked together. They are *so* nice. Then R. and I went to see the new Terence Rattigan play[1] for which I'd booked seats three weeks ago in a good piece of thinking-aheadishness

---

[1] *While the Sun Shines*, directed by Anthony Asquith. It opened at the Globe on December 24th, 1943.

*1944*

The first days of the New Year found Joyce waiting impatiently for her departure to the Middle East. As she and Viola Tunnard were ranked only as second lieutenants they had no priority rating for a flight to North Africa. They would have to travel by sea. Joyce could make no plans and ENSA, frustratingly, had no news for her. Finally, on January 13th, she and Viola took the train at Euston and left for an 'unnamed western seaport' (Liverpool), where they boarded a former P & O liner, SS *Strathmore*, and set sail for Algiers.

# 1944

*January 2nd, 1944* London

Darling Ma,
Did I tell you – I *think* I did – that Dick's *Alice* has had a wonderful
press, is doing huge business and is a big success. Isn't it lovely? I
feel so happy about it for him.

*Tuesday.* Had lunch with the matron and nurses of the Elizabeth
Garrett Anderson hospital – then Christmas dinner and then did a
show for them afterwards. It's an all-women hospital – doctors,
surgeons, anaesthetists – all women. And *so* nice. Viola Tunnard
played for me for the first time. It was OK. Afterwards I went to tea
with Dick at 25 and we just chatted. It's been *so* long since he's had
time to be idle and I must say I've missed him. He is so cosy. In a
funny way I'm not sure whether you'd like him. He's very difficult
to understand, moody and incalculable. But I do know him as well
as anyone and I like him and he trusts me. I find him gentle and
sweet and easy. But he has a funny butting-off front. And a dozen
complexes. If anyone had ever told me I could have been fond of
someone with all his different facets I'd have said it wouldn't be
possible. But we speak the same language. R. has got to know him
much more lately and they like each other.

*Wednesday.* To ENSA to enquire. No information but I got the
extra coupons allowed me for the necessary bits of clothing for the
trip. I had lunch with Winifred and Esmé Church – she produced
*Alice* – up at the Belle Meunière in Charlotte St. Then I went
shopping in search of stays. There are of course no pull-on belts and
in despair I finally bought the least cumbersome and least distorting
pair I could find at John Lewis. I always used to wear heavenly things
called Vassarettes, which were particularly good because they were
very long and had a special band at the top which prevented a roll.
And of course no bones. I also bought a pair of tailored trousers
because they told me at ENSA I'd need them for flying. I look like

Annie said you did – 'a little ole bear' in trousers and hate the idea
but they are warm and practical & I expect it's best. I went to church
with Pa at 6.30. In for supper here later.

R. is about to become a major and will go to a new job quite soon.
Still in London we hope. He hopes it will be an active one,
later, going once overseas. I hope it isn't. It will be a staff job anyway.

Much love
Joyce

————◆————

*January 9th, 1944*                                        London

*Saturday*. It really looked for a moment as if I might be off yesterday
but the excitement simmered down again and I'm still here. I met D.
at the recording studios yesterday morning to make some more discs.
These were so good that we were overcome by their beauty and very
moved by their emotion! We walked slowly down Bond St in a sort
of daze after we'd done them and it was only 12.30. Went into the
Ritz where D. had a drink. Then we lunched at his club and dreamed
dreams of the sort of show we'd try and write and put on. Lovely
fanciful stuff and very enjoyable. After which we went to see *Sweet
and Low*,[1] a revue we'd seen before. It was only fairly good the
second time so we didn't quite stay to the end but went back to 25
and made tea and talked a great deal and played our beautiful records
and got a bit homesick about me going and then it was 6.30 and time
I came back here. All in all, a very cosy day. I find D. the perfect
companion.

R. and I dined in with Aunt P. and did the crossword and were
cosy and we went to bed early. Today is Sunday. Very long lie and
then a lovely leisurely getting up. R. washes his hair on the Sabbath
and we read the papers slowly. Then I went to church with Pa and
afterwards he joined R. and me at Queen's for lunch. Then we went
up to see Gin and Tony and we all decided to go and see a new
British picture called *San Demetrio*,[2] about an oil tanker, that had
had 'rave' notices in all the papers this morning. Deservedly too.
Wonderful picture and so exciting. And now we've had supper, heard

[1] Revue at the Ambassadors with Hermione Gingold. It enjoyed a long run.
[2] *San Demetrio, London*, in which the survivors of a crippled tanker bring it back
home. An Ealing film, with Walter Fitzgerald, Robert Beatty, and Mervyn Johns,
directed by Charles Frend.

the news and it's bedtime. I sort of hope I write my next letter from somewhere else on the map.

⋯◦❖◦⋯

*January 1944 [undated]*
For security reasons I can't tell you anything! Which will make for a very dull letter, I'm afraid. No dates allowed, no addresses, no mention of weather – nothing.

In the end, after waiting for weeks and weeks we have finally come by sea and I write this en route. Viola is very nice and speaks my language – good sense of humour and quiet, intelligent, and *nice*. We had two very busy days before we came and I'm a bad leaver and I hated that but, like you, I recuperate quickly and was glad to be off at last. There is an officer from R.'s regiment with us and he has been most solicitous and kind and he has several friends here so we've been squired all along. We are not the only females on board. All of us are going to do a job with the exception of some diplomatic wives and I suppose even they have a sort of a job. We have been very lucky in getting single cabins and that makes the whole difference. The food is good and in spite of some really quite tough going we haven't missed a meal and we are *very* proud. There is a library and we use it. We walk for miles and sleep a lot and there is a piano which Viola has played several times and played really beautifully. She has a true gift and has a lot of sensitivity which isn't always the case with players. She is very shy and almost too humble but when she does finally play it is heavenly and everyone loves it. We have only done one concert so far, last night in the second and third class lounge to which the crew were invited too. Very nice it was. There are only two other ENSAs on board, mercifully, and they are a fairly well known music-hall team called the Two Leslies.[1] They do songs and stories and are fairly coarse but I'm afraid the troops *do* seem to like it. Our femininity is a good contrast I think! Anyway we went well too.

The movie apparatus has blown up which is a pity and means we have organised pastimes instead. V. plays each afternoon for eightsome reels, run by an earnest young Scot who calls the figures and sees that it's all done properly. I adore it because the bright young things are so ungraceful and galumping and their rhythm is nil but they glow and glisten and a fine time is had by all; specially me on

---

[1] Leslie Sarony and Leslie Holmes, variety artistes. They composed many of their own songs.

the sidelines. There are to be 'games' tonight. And V. and I are to run a sing-song. This is a very slow method of travelling and I'm furious at the waste of time involved. It's maddening.

A group of nurses have a very decrepit portable gramophone and a collection of my worst sort of records – Humoresque, bits from the *Tales of Hoffmann*, etc, *sort* of classics worn to a thread – and they play it in the lounge in the mornings to the fury of those who want to read! The handle squeaks and there is something wrong with the whole thing for it runs down halfway through each record and has to be squeakily rewound. I believe a signed protest is being sent in!

*Later*. There is literally nothing to tell you. It's a soul-destroying existence, for we kill time from dawn to dusk and one gets lazier and lazier. I read a bit and write a little and wash me smalls and play tennis and walk and talk and talk. We sing too and I have even danced a reel and felt better for it. I'm afraid this letter will take ages to get to you. We had church today and songs and hymns with great force. Viola played.

I'm so sorry this is so dull. I can't say *any* more. Wish I could. All is OK.

Much love, J.

On Tuesday, January 25th, 1944, Joyce Grenfell and Viola Tunnard arrived in North Africa for the beginning of their first overseas ENSA tour. On each of these tours, while continuing to write regularly to her mother, to Reggie, and Virginia Thesiger, Joyce also kept a detailed journal . . .

# Acknowledgements

If Maureen Lipman had not asked me to write an entertainment for her, *Re: Joyce!*, based on the life and work of Joyce Grenfell, these letters might have lain dormant in their faded folders for many more years.

This edition is dedicated to Reggie Grenfell and Frances Campbell-Preston who from the very start made me so welcome, providing me with lunches, before starting work in Joyce's study, and then with plastic carrier bags with which to carry away load after load of letters, manuscripts, and diaries. I would like to thank Catherine Treasure who devoted some months to typing out all the letters, and the Joyce Grenfell Trust which made this possible. To Wendy Trewin I am indebted for her patient tracking down of clues and writing of footnotes, short biographies, and the family tree. All my life I have been indebted to J. C. Trewin and now, from the sidelines, he has thrown light upon one query after another. Thanks, too, to Mrs Alice Winn (a first cousin of Joyce) for her help in identifying many names in the text. To Stephanie Darnill, the copy editor at Hodder and Stoughton, I would like to express gratitude and appreciation for her discernment, accuracy, and diligence; and to Wendy Hall for her generous help in checking the proofs.

From the start I was excited by these letters but there were those who tried to discourage me from getting involved and so I want to pay especial thanks to Gerald Isaaman who, over lunch one day at the Garrick Club, said to me, 'Have you shown these letters to Ion Trewin at Hodder and Stoughton? I think he might be interested.' Ion Trewin read the entire collection of letters and reacted at once with enthusiasm. His support and encouragement throughout, as also that of Joyce Grenfell's agent, Richard Simon, has enabled me to tackle what, at times, seemed a hugely daunting task.

JAMES ROOSE-EVANS

# Index

Names and places marked with an asterisk * are included in the
biographical and residential notes, pp. xiii–xvi.

'n' after a page number indicates a footnote reference.

Crichton, Viscount 151n
Cripps (butler) 41
Crisham, Walter 140, 176n, 178, 179, 199n, 250
Criterion Theatre 100, 173–4, 176, 188n, 256
Cromer, 2nd Earl of 159n
Cromer, Lady Ruby 159
Culford Gardens 188
Cumberland Hotel 249
Cunard, Lady 186n
Cunningham, Elly 134, 186
*Curtain Goes Up, The* (radio programme) 201
Curtis, Lionel 16
Curtis, Pat 16, 19
Curzon of Kedleston, Marquess 11n
Czechoslovakia 32, 52n, 58, 68

*Daily Express* 13, 249
*Daily Mail* xx
*Daily Sketch* 10
*Daily Telegraph* 186, 263
Daisy (dresser) 86, 138
Dalkeith, Molly, Duchess of Buccleuch 293, 294
Dall, Evelyn 47
Dane, Clemence (Winifred Ashton)* xx, 138, 139, 179n, 253, 258, 269, 302, 321, 323, 326, 335, 336, 339
Daniels, Bebe 141, 183
D'Aranyi, Jelli 12
Dare, Phyllis 211n
Dare, Zena 211, 334
Darewski, Jean 147
Darrieux, Danielle 56
Davies, Betty-Ann 84n, 86, 88, 138, 263
Davies family (Wiltshire) 193
Davies, Gwen 59, 63
Davies, Lady Margaret 57
Davies, Margaret 59, 63
Davies, Sir Walford 57, 59n, 63, 75
Davis, Bette 224
Davis, Norman 11
Day, Frances (Fanny) 320
De la Mare, Colin 200
De la Mare, Walter 123–4
Dean, Basil 233n, 250n
Delysia, Alice 211
*Demi-Paradise, The* 303n, 310

Denham film studio 50, 296, 297, 301, 309, 311, 316
Desborough, Lady 48, 115n
Desborough, Lord 46n, 115n, 332
Desmonde, Jerry 312n
Dewar, John Arthur 209n
Dewar, Kathleen 209, 210, 211
Dickens, Monica 296n
Dickson, Dorothy xx, 92, 95, 138n, 176n, 178, 179, 183, 190, 191, 195, 199n, 206, 216, 217, 218, 326
Dionne quins 224n
Ditchley* 186n, 217
*Diversion* xx, 176, 178, 184, 186, 189, 199, 206, 212, 214, 250
*Diversion No. 2* 199, 201
Donat, Robert 136, 138, 141, 142
Dorchester Hotel 211
Douglas, Patty 13
Douglas-Pennant, Sheila 84n
Draper, Ruth 12, xix–xx, 33, 63, 77, 79, 85n, 95, 199n, 201, 235
Dreyfus, Louis 267
'Drifting' (song) 294
Dropmoor 206
Drury Lane, Theatre Royal 267, 268, 271, 322
Dublin 289
Dudley Ward, Freda 60n, 159, 296n
Dudley Ward, Penelope (Pempi) 60n, 296, 303n, 310
Dudley Ward, William 60n
Dugdale, Blanche (Baffy) 11
Dugdale, Edgar 11n
Dunkirk 130, 149n, 152, 216
Dunn, Lady Marcia Anastasia 13
Dunn, Sir James (Hamet) 13n
Durbin, Deanna 24n, 125
Dutton Homestall 209

Eames, Clare 236
Easden, Mrs 253
Easden, Rene* 8, 79, 105, 106, 112, 113, 115, 132, 135, 149, 163, 171, 173, 177, 183, 184, 189, 203, 208, 216, 219, 230, 231, 232, 233, 234, 236, 241, 253
East End (of London) 165, 167, 184, 214
East Grinstead 209, 210
'Easy to Love' (song) 23
Eaton Square 97, 98

Pooh (Ferguson's housekeeper) 142
Porter, Cole 306n
Portland, Duke of 47n
*Postscripts* 165n
Potter, Gillie 233
Potter, Stephen* 74, 201, 227, 228,
    235n, 269, 297, 317, 318, 319, 322,
    333
Powell, Dick 331n
Powell, William 13
Power, Tyrone 168n
*Present Laughter* 291n, 292, 314, 315
Preston 324
Priestley, J. B. 59, 165
'Princess Margaret Rose' (sketch) 74
Pritch (pianist) 88, 182
Proctor, Mrs Ivy 232, 233, 233–6, 237,
    239–42, 244, 251, 254, 263, 264,
    266, 268, 271, 295, 296, 297, 302
Proctor, Shirley 234, 237
Proctor, Truda 234, 237
Prowse, Keith 267
Prunier (restaurant) 297
Pump Room, Tunbridge Wells 105n
*Punch* 8, 173
Pytchley Hunt 34n, 49n

Quaglino (restaurant) 315
Quayle, Anthony 138n
*Queen Mary* (liner) 54, 90
Queen's Hall 40, 134, 135, 164, 211
Queensberry, Lord 13
*Quiet Weekend!* 230

*Rage of Paris* 56
Rainer, Luise 86
Ramage, Cecil 200
Rattigan, Terence 336
Raven (hospital patient) 254
Raven, Mrs 254–5
Ravensdale, Baroness Irene 11, 190
Rawson, Mrs Mildred* xxi, 84, 87, 91,
    117, 126, 150, 178, 190, 255
Reading 110, 231
Red Cross 40, 137, 154, 156, 255, 260
Redditch 332
Reed, Carol 258
Rees, Dilys 176n, 199n
Reeve, Edward 103
Reeve, Elizabeth *see* Phipps, Elizabeth
Reynolds, Alfred 263n

Ribbentrop, Joachim von 11n
Ridgeway, Mr 145
*Rise Above It* 250
Ritchard, Cyril 83n, 84n, 86, 89, 92,
    116, 122, 138, 139, 141, 176
Ritz, The 340
Robey, George 138, 141
Rochester 107
Rockefeller Institute 209
Rolfe (butler) 116n
Rollo, Bill 168
Rollo, Lady Kathleen 168
Rollo, Prim *see* Niven, Prim
Romberg, Sigmund 325n
Rommel, Erwin 248
Roosevelt, Franklin D. 55, 157
Roosevelt, Theodore, Jr. 11
Rose Cottage 80
Rose (servant) 70, 93, 153
Rostrevor 288
Rothschild family 126
Rowe family 164–5
Royal Academy of Dramatic Art xvii
Royal Air Force 127, 131, 160–61, 287,
    300, 327
Royal Artillery (RA) 224
Royal Command charity matinée 137–8
Royal Court Hotel 261
*Royal Divorce, A* 50n
Royal Navy 112n, 118n
*Royal Oak*, HMS 118
Ruhr 300
Russia 144, 198, 216n, 248, 265, 300
Rutherford, Margaret 51n, 303n
Rutland, 8th Duke of 74n

St George's, Hanover Square 79n
St Helier, Ivy 123
St James's Square, No. 4* 10, 39, 43, 44,
    52, 59, 60, 63, 93, 110, 153
St James's Theatre xx
St John's, Smith Square 61
St John's Wood 74, 75, 77, 122, 159, 317
St Just, Edward Grenfell, 1st Baron
    225n
St Just, Florrie 225
St Leonard's Terrace, Chelsea, No. 21*
    xvii, xviii, 2, 297
St Leonard's Terrace, Chelsea, No. 28*
    xviii, 188, 207
St Martin-in-the-Fields 63

April : 23 : 1939

Darling Ma.

well ———

It seems as if the inherited talent isn't too bad! I just can't believe any of it. I seem to be a hit —— and yet I'm not much good really. However they seem deluded and I'll not let down the illusion unless I can help it. Here are the chief cuttings — Alice has sent you the best one I believe — Agate in the Sunday Times. He who is always such a sour old puss. Just another proof that it wasn't me at all; just "Mind disguised in a grey chiffon frock and your coral red coat."

I'll try to tell you all.

Last Sunday I left here with my suitcase for Aunt Pauline's flat in Simnecon Gardens. I was low. Why did I ever consider doing such a rediculous thing? Be on the stage? Pooh. Church with Daddy in the morning, then lunch with Aunt Margaret. Rehearsal at three till midnight! Back to the flat —— by far the nicest in London. My room had peach walls and chintz — a wide window onto a blossoming garden and perfect quiet. Also its own bathroom.

April 23rd, 1939